T0332639

Design, Applications, and Maintenance of Cyber–Physical Systems

Pierluigi Rea
University of Cagliari, Italy

Erika Ottaviano
University of Cassino and Southern Lazio, Italy

José Machado
University of Minho, Portugal

Katarzyna Antosz
Rzeszow University of Technology, Poland

A volume in the Advances in
Systems Analysis, Software
Engineering, and High Performance
Computing (ASASEHPC) Book Series

Published in the United States of America by
    IGI Global
    Engineering Science Reference (an imprint of IGI Global)
    701 E. Chocolate Avenue
    Hershey PA, USA 17033
    Tel: 717-533-8845
    Fax: 717-533-8661
    E-mail: cust@igi-global.com
    Web site: http://www.igi-global.com

Library of Congress Cataloging-in-Publication Data

Names: Rea, Pierluigi, 1975- editor.
Title: Design, applications, and maintenance of cyber-physical systems /
  Pierluigi Rea, Erika Ottaviano, José Machado, and Katarzyna Antosz,
  editors.
Description: Hershey, PA : Engineering Science Reference, [2021] | Includes
  bibliographical references and index. | Summary: "The objective of this
  book is to give an insight about cyber-physical systems (CPS) as tools
  for integrating the dynamics of physical processes with those of the
  software and networking, providing abstractions and modelling, design,
  and analysis techniques for their smart manufacturing interoperation"--
  Provided by publisher.
Identifiers: LCCN 2020052946 (print) | LCCN 2020052947 (ebook) | ISBN
  9781799867210 (hardcover) | ISBN 9781799867227 (paperback) | ISBN
  9781799867234 (ebook)
Subjects: LCSH: Cooperating objects (Computer systems)
Classification: LCC TK5105.8857 .D484 2021 (print) | LCC TK5105.8857
  (ebook) | DDC 006.2/2--dc23
LC record available at https://lccn.loc.gov/2020052946
LC ebook record available at https://lccn.loc.gov/2020052947

This book is published in the IGI Global book series Advances in Systems Analysis, Software Engineering, and High Performance Computing (ASASEHPC) (ISSN: 2327-3453; eISSN: 2327-3461)

British Cataloguing in Publication Data
A Cataloguing in Publication record for this book is available from the British Library.

All work contributed to this book is new, previously-unpublished material.
The views expressed in this book are those of the authors, but not necessarily of the publisher.

For electronic access to this publication, please contact: eresources@igi-global.com.

Advances in Systems Analysis, Software Engineering, and High Performance Computing (ASASEHPC) Book Series

ISSN:2327-3453
EISSN:2327-3461

Editor-in-Chief: Vijayan Sugumaran, Oakland University, USA

MISSION

The theory and practice of computing applications and distributed systems has emerged as one of the key areas of research driving innovations in business, engineering, and science. The fields of software engineering, systems analysis, and high performance computing offer a wide range of applications and solutions in solving computational problems for any modern organization.

The **Advances in Systems Analysis, Software Engineering, and High Performance Computing (ASASEHPC) Book Series** brings together research in the areas of distributed computing, systems and software engineering, high performance computing, and service science. This collection of publications is useful for academics, researchers, and practitioners seeking the latest practices and knowledge in this field.

COVERAGE

- Metadata and Semantic Web
- Computer Networking
- Storage Systems
- Human-Computer Interaction
- Performance Modelling
- Distributed Cloud Computing
- Computer Graphics
- Software Engineering
- Network Management
- Computer System Analysis

IGI Global is currently accepting manuscripts for publication within this series. To submit a proposal for a volume in this series, please contact our Acquisition Editors at Acquisitions@igi-global.com or visit: http://www.igi-global.com/publish/.

Titles in this Series

For a list of additional titles in this series, please visit:
http://www.igi-global.com/book-series/advances-systems-analysis-software-engineering/73689

Handbook of Research on Software Quality Innovation in Interactive Systems
Francisco Vicente Cipolla-Ficarra (Latin Association of Human-Computer Interaction, Spain & International Association of Interactive Communication, Italy)
Engineering Science Reference • © 2021 • 501pp • H/C (ISBN: 9781799870104) • US $295.00

Handbook of Research on Methodologies and Applications of Supercomputing
Veljko Milutinović (Indiana University, Bloomington, USA) and Miloš Kotlar (University of Belgrade, Serbia)
Engineering Science Reference • © 2021 • 393pp • H/C (ISBN: 9781799871569) • US $345.00

MATLAB® With Applications in Mechanics and Tribology
Leonid Burstein (Independent Researcher, Israel)
Engineering Science Reference • © 2021 • 368pp • H/C (ISBN: 9781799870784) • US $195.00

Advancements in Fuzzy Reliability Theory
Akshay Kumar (Graphic Era Hill University, India) Mangey Ram (Department of Mathematics, Graphic Era (Deemed to be University), India) and Om Prakash Yadav (North Dakota State University, USA)
Engineering Science Reference • © 2021 • 322pp • H/C (ISBN: 9781799875642) • US $245.00

Impacts and Challenges of Cloud Business Intelligence
Shadi Aljawarneh (Jordan University of Science and Technology, Jordan) and Manisha Malhotra (Chandigarh University, India)
Business Science Reference • © 2021 • 263pp • H/C (ISBN: 9781799850403) • US $195.00

For an entire list of titles in this series, please visit:
http://www.igi-global.com/book-series/advances-systems-analysis-software-engineering/73689

701 East Chocolate Avenue, Hershey, PA 17033, USA
Tel: 717-533-8845 x100 • Fax: 717-533-8661
E-Mail: cust@igi-global.com • www.igi-global.com

Table of Contents

Preface... xiv

Chapter 1
Challenges and Applications of Cyber Physical Systems....................................1
    Rachna Jain, JSS Academy of Technical Education, Noida, India

Chapter 2
From the Digital-Twin to the Cyber Physical System Using Integrated
Multidisciplinary Simulation: Virtualization of Complex Systems.....................18
    Daniele Catelani, MSC Software, Italy

Chapter 3
Development of Tangible Interfaces for Cognitive Development: MOBEYBOU40
    Hugo Lopes, 2Ai-EST, Polytechnic Institute of Cávado and Ave,
        Portugal
    Vítor Carvalho, 2Ai-EST, Polytechnic Institute of Cávado and Ave,
        Portugal & Algoritmi Research Center, University of Minho,
        Portugal
    Cristina Sylla, University of Minho, Portugal

Chapter 4
Graphical-Based Authentication System and Its Applications...........................63
    Priti Golar, Department of Computer Science & Engineering, Amity
        University, Raipur, India
    Brijesh Khandelwal, Department of Computer Science & Engineering,
        Amity University, Raipur, India

Chapter 5

An Effectiveness Modelling Approach for IoT-Based Smart Grids.....................92
Dongming Fan, Beihang University, China
Yi Ren, Beihang University, China
Qiang Feng, Beihang University, China

Chapter 6

Health Index Development for Fault Diagnosis of Rolling Element Bearing ...112
Kumar H. S., NMAM Institute of Technology, Udupi, India &
Visvesvaraya Technological University, Belagavi, India
Srinivasa P. Pai, NMAM Institute of Technology, Udupi, India &
Visvesvaraya Technological University, Belagavi, India
Sriram N. S., Vidya Vikas Institute of Engineering and Technology,
Mysore, India & Visvesvaraya Technological University, Belagavi,
India

Chapter 7

Integration of Cutting-Edge Interoperability Approaches in Cyber-Physical
Production Systems and Industry 4.0..144
Luis Alberto Estrada-Jimenez, CTS UNINOVA, Faculdade de Ciências e
Tecnologia, Universidade Nova de Lisboa, Portugal
Terrin Pulikottil, CTS UNINOVA, Faculdade de Ciências e Tecnologia,
Universidade Nova de Lisboa, Portugal
Nguyen Ngoc Hien, Mondragon Unibertsitatea, Spain
Agajan Torayev, Institute for Advanced Manufacturing, University of
Nottingham, UK
Hamood Ur Rehman, University of Nottingham, UK & TQC Ltd., UK
Fan Mo, Institute for Advanced Manufacturing, University of
Nottingham, UK
Sanaz Nikghadam Hojjati, CTS UNINOVA, Faculdade de Ciências e
Tecnologia, Universidade Nova de Lisboa, Portugal
José Barata, CTS UNINOVA, Faculdade de Ciências e Tecnologia,
Universidade Nova de Lisboa, Portugal

Chapter 8

Intelligent Traffic Signal Monitoring System Using Image Processing.............173
SureshKumar M., Sri SaiRam Engineering College, India
Anu Valliammai R., Sri SaiRam Engineering College, India

Chapter 9

A General Overview of E-Maintenance and Possible Applications 196
    Pierluigi Rea, University of Cagliari, Italy
    Erika Ottaviano, University of Cassino and Southern Lazio, Italy
    José Machado, University of Minho, Portugal
    Katarzyna Antosz, Rzeszow University of Technology, Poland

Chapter 10

Network Intrusion Detection System in Latest DFA Compression Methods
for Deep Packet Scruting 219
    Vinoth Kumar K, New Horizon College of Engineering, India

Chapter 11

The Contribution of Obeya for Business Intelligence 244
    Gonçalo Sousa, School of Engineering, Polytechnic of Porto, Portugal
    José Carlos Sá, School of Engineering, Polytechnic of Porto, Portugal
    Gilberto Santos, Design School, Polytechnic Institute of Cavado and
        Ave, Portugal
    Francisco J. G. Silva, School of Engineering, Polytechnic of Porto,
        Portugal
    Luís Pinto Ferreira, School of Engineering, Polytechnic of Porto,
        Portugal

Compilation of References 270

About the Contributors 305

Index 312

Detailed Table of Contents

Preface... xiv

Chapter 1

Challenges and Applications of Cyber Physical Systems.......................................1
Rachna Jain, JSS Academy of Technical Education, Noida, India

Cyber physical systems integrate actuators or sensors with networking technologies. Latest innovations in the area lead to cyber social systems or cyber physical social systems. Industry 4.0 amalgamates all major technologies including internet of things, big data, cloud computing, and smart systems under CPS. Cyber physical systems comprise of physical layer devices connected to the internet. It has vast applications in the areas like manufacturing, healthcare, energy, automation, robotics, smart building, meteorology, and transportation. Cyber and physical components interaction, training and adaptation ability, interoperability using IoT devices, information security using firewalls and cryptosystems, system robustness, and intervention of human inside and out of the loop are the major focusing areas in any CPS. In this chapter, application areas and challenges faced by cyber physical systems are discussed in detail.

Chapter 2

From the Digital-Twin to the Cyber Physical System Using Integrated
Multidisciplinary Simulation: Virtualization of Complex Systems....................18
Daniele Catelani, MSC Software, Italy

Simulation has been a competitive differentiator for engineering-driven businesses, available at all stages of the development process and lifecycle, used by the various domains within an organization, not necessarily simulation experts. It requires discipline integration, scalability, reduced-order model, and democratization. The concept of digital transformation involves new approaches for data and lifecycle management, the understanding of the digital thread, digital twin, predictive and cognitive capabilities, including improvement of model complexity, integration of physics, increase of knowledge. These trends require bringing the physical and virtual worlds closer together and also the adoption of cyber-physical model at all stages of design, production, and operation. To overcome the drawback of simulation and the need to balance the computational effort with accuracy and efficiency, new modelization strategies are adopted with ML and AI, which use a combination of virtual and physical data for training ROM, with an order of magnitude faster than the multiphysics one.

Chapter 3

Development of Tangible Interfaces for Cognitive Development: MOBEYBOU40

Hugo Lopes, 2Ai-EST, Polytechnic Institute of Cávado and Ave, Portugal

Vítor Carvalho, 2Ai-EST, Polytechnic Institute of Cávado and Ave, Portugal & Algoritmi Research Center, University of Minho, Portugal

Cristina Sylla, University of Minho, Portugal

This chapter presents the development of a low-cost tangible interface to enhance children's learning through collaborative storytelling, using a set of movable blocks, with a high degree of autonomy and the ability to exchange information with each other. Taking into account the context of the existing game model and on the basis of which this study was developed, the function of these removable blocks is to allow children to create and recreate their own narratives in permanent interaction by manipulating the physical blocks, which trigger the associated virtual representations (characters, e.g., animals, objects, locations, or others). It is expected that children will be able to project these representations on a screen through the activation and manipulation of the physical blocks by adding, removing, moving the blocks while interacting with each other and creating narratives. The authors have attempted to apply a method that could present a new approach to the educational gaming industry.

Chapter 4

Graphical-Based Authentication System and Its Applications 63

Priti Golar, Department of Computer Science & Engineering, Amity University, Raipur, India

Brijesh Khandelwal, Department of Computer Science & Engineering, Amity University, Raipur, India

Authentication systems are the protective barrier of any software. They make sure that the right people enter the system and access the right information. As per available literature, there are basically three authentication techniques. This research study is based on the knowledge-based authentication, since it is the most widely accepted technique for securing resources from unauthorized access. As an initial step, the existing knowledge-based authentication system has been studied for its highlights, comparative facts, advantages, and disadvantages. For acceptance of any secure system, the usability aspect is the first step in the authentication process. The various usability evaluation parameters of the existing systems and an approach towards developing a modified usable authentication system have been briefly discussed. An initial lab study for the proposed system was conducted to analyze the comparative results. The future scope of other dimensions, namely randomness and security, as well as a thorough investigation, has been highlighted as the research work's concluding remark.

Chapter 5

An Effectiveness Modelling Approach for IoT-Based Smart Grids....................92
    Dongming Fan, Beihang University, China
    Yi Ren, Beihang University, China
    Qiang Feng, Beihang University, China

The smart grid is a new paradigm that enables highly efficient energy production, transport, and consumption along the whole chain from the source to the user. The smart grid is the combination of classical power grid with emerging communication and information technologies. IoT-based smart grid will be one of the largest instantiations of the IoT in the future. The effectiveness of IoT-based smart grid is mainly reflected in observability, real-time analysis, decision-making, and self-healing. A proper effectiveness modeling approach should maintain the reliability and maintainability of IoT-based smart grids. In this chapter, a multi-agent-based approach is proposed to model the architecture of IoT-based smart grids. Based on the agent framework, certain common types of agents are provided to describe the operation and restoration process of smart grids. A case study is demonstrated to model an IoT-based smart grid with restoration, and the interactive process with agents is proposed simultaneously.

Chapter 6

Health Index Development for Fault Diagnosis of Rolling Element Bearing ...112
    Kumar H. S., NMAM Institute of Technology, Udupi, India &
        Visvesvaraya Technological University, Belagavi, India
    Srinivasa P. Pai, NMAM Institute of Technology, Udupi, India &
        Visvesvaraya Technological University, Belagavi, India
    Sriram N. S., Vidya Vikas Institute of Engineering and Technology,
        Mysore, India & Visvesvaraya Technological University, Belagavi,
        India

Condition monitoring (CM) is the process that assesses the health of equipment/ systems at regular intervals or continuously and exposes incipient faults if any. Bearing failure is one of the foremost causes of breakdown in rotating machine, resulting in costly systems downtime. This chapter presents an application of health index (HI) for fault diagnosis of rolling element bearing (REB) which has been successfully used in diverse fields such as image processing, prognostic health management (PHM), and involves integration of mathematical and statistical concepts. There is hardly any effort done in developing HIs using different aspects of wavelet transform (WT) for fault diagnosis of REB. A comparison of the performances of the identified approaches has been made to choose the best one for REB fault diagnosis.

Chapter 7

Integration of Cutting-Edge Interoperability Approaches in Cyber-Physical Production Systems and Industry 4.0..144

Luis Alberto Estrada-Jimenez, CTS UNINOVA, Faculdade de Ciências e Tecnologia, Universidade Nova de Lisboa, Portugal

Terrin Pulikottil, CTS UNINOVA, Faculdade de Ciências e Tecnologia, Universidade Nova de Lisboa, Portugal

Nguyen Ngoc Hien, Mondragon Unibertsitatea, Spain

Agajan Torayev, Institute for Advanced Manufacturing, University of Nottingham, UK

Hamood Ur Rehman, University of Nottingham, UK & TQC Ltd., UK

Fan Mo, Institute for Advanced Manufacturing, University of Nottingham, UK

Sanaz Nikghadam Hojjati, CTS UNINOVA, Faculdade de Ciências e Tecnologia, Universidade Nova de Lisboa, Portugal

José Barata, CTS UNINOVA, Faculdade de Ciências e Tecnologia, Universidade Nova de Lisboa, Portugal

Interoperability in smart manufacturing refers to how interconnected cyber-physical components exchange information and interact. This is still an exploratory topic, and despite the increasing number of applications, many challenges remain open. This chapter presents an integrative framework to understand common practices, concepts, and technologies used in trending research to achieve interoperability in production systems. The chapter starts with the question of what interoperability is and provides an alternative answer based on influential works in the field, followed by the presentation of important reference models and their relation to smart manufacturing. It continues by discussing different types of interoperability, data formats, and common ontologies necessary for the integration of heterogeneous systems and the contribution of emerging technologies in achieving interoperability. This chapter ends with a discussion of a recent use case and final remarks.

Chapter 8

Intelligent Traffic Signal Monitoring System Using Image Processing.............173
    SureshKumar M., Sri SaiRam Engineering College, India
    Anu Valliammai R., Sri SaiRam Engineering College, India

This project aims at making an intelligent traffic signal monitoring system that makes decisions based on real-time traffic situations. The choices will be such that the traditional red, green, or amber lighting scheme is focused on the actual number of cars on the road and the arrival of emergency services rather than using pure timing circuits to control car traffic by using what the traffic appears like via smart cameras to capture real-time traffic movement pictures of each direction. The control system will modify the traffic light control parameters dynamically in various directions due to changes in traffic flow, thus increasing the traffic intersection efficiency and ensuring improved traffic management. This work involves performing a traffic management study of the city.

Chapter 9

A General Overview of E-Maintenance and Possible Applications..................196
    Pierluigi Rea, University of Cagliari, Italy
    Erika Ottaviano, University of Cassino and Southern Lazio, Italy
    José Machado, University of Minho, Portugal
    Katarzyna Antosz, Rzeszow University of Technology, Poland

I4.0 concepts allow a very important approach concerning improving competitiveness of modern industry and services in several domains of economic activity. Maintenance of cyber-physical systems is an important issue that can be crucial for the availability of those systems for developing their activities in a standard way, with respective desired behavior. With the most recent evolution of methodologies and available tools, e-maintenance is a concept that has been evolved in last years, and the use of this approach is of the utmost importance for the competitiveness of companies at several levels. In this chapter, the authors highlight the benefits of using an e-maintenance approach for the success of maintenance of cyber-physical systems, mainly when, on those systems, it is critical to keep and assure the reliability of respective behavior. For this purpose, a robot, as an illustration example, is used, and some conclusions are obtained concerning this global overview and proposed approach.

Chapter 10

Network Intrusion Detection System in Latest DFA Compression Methods
for Deep Packet Scruting 219
    Vinoth Kumar K, New Horizon College of Engineering, India

The vast majority of the system security applications in today's systems depend on deep packet inspection. In recent years, regular expression matching was used as an important operator. It examines whether or not the packet's payload can be matched with a group of predefined regular expressions. Regular expressions are parsed using the deterministic finite automata representations. Conversely, to represent regular expression sets as DFA, the system needs a large amount of memory, an excessive amount of time, and an excessive amount of per flow state, limiting their practical applications. This chapter explores network intrusion detection systems.

Chapter 11

The Contribution of Obeya for Business Intelligence..244
Gonçalo Sousa, School of Engineering, Polytechnic of Porto, Portugal
José Carlos Sá, School of Engineering, Polytechnic of Porto, Portugal
Gilberto Santos, Design School, Polytechnic Institute of Cavado and Ave, Portugal
Francisco J. G. Silva, School of Engineering, Polytechnic of Porto, Portugal
Luís Pinto Ferreira, School of Engineering, Polytechnic of Porto, Portugal

The main objective of the study is to minimize interdepartmental communication, potentiation of fast and efficient decision making, and computerization of data. Using software such as MS Excel® and MS Power BI®, a Power BI® tool was conceived to be capable of incorporating, for the entire company, the dashboards that collect the main KPIs of each department. After the tool was implemented, the company's paradigm shift was noticeable. Quickly, the weekly meeting of the planning team began to take place using the MS Power BI® dashboard. In this way, processes were automated and the important data for the normal functioning of the company became accessible to all departments, thus minimizing interdepartmental communication. The chapter shows an Obeya Digital that was implemented in a company in which all the performance indicators of each department are incorporated. In this way, information becomes accessible to all employees and manual data update processes are minimized.

Compilation of References 270

About the Contributors 305

Index 312

Preface

Cyber-Physical Systems (CPS) can be defined as those in which physical objects are represented in digital world and integrated with computation, storage, and communication capabilities, being connected to each other in a network. CPS therefore involve computation, networking, and physical processes, merging theory of cybernetics, mechatronics, design, and process science. Examples of CPS include smart grid, autonomous mobile systems, medical monitoring, industrial control systems, robotics, Internet of Things (IoT), smart anything (e.g., Cars, Manufacturing, Appliances, Maintenance), just to list some of them.

The objective of the book is to give an insight about CPS as a tool for integrating the dynamics of the physical processes with those of the software and networking, providing abstractions and modelling, design, and analysis techniques for their smart manufacturing interoperation. Therefore, the book has an impact to the research on robotics, mechatronics, integrated intelligent multibody systems, industry 4.0, production systems management and maintenance, decision support systems, Maintenance 4.0.

The goal in the use of the CPS is integrating the dynamics of the physical processes with those of the software and networking, providing abstractions and modelling, design, and analysis techniques for the integrated whole. The notion of CPS is linked to concepts of robotics and sensor networks with intelligent systems proper of computational intelligence leading the pathway. Recent advances in science and engineering improve the link between computational and physical elements by means of intelligent systems, increasing the adaptability, autonomy, efficiency, functionality, reliability, safety, and usability of cyber-physical systems. The potential of CPS will spread to several directions, including but not limited to: intervention (e.g., path planning and collision avoidance); precision manufacturing (e.g. monitoring systems); operation in dangerous or inaccessible environment (e.g., search and rescue, firefighting, and deep-sea-exploration); coordination (e.g. urban and air-traffic control, war fighting); efficiency (e.g. energy buildings); and augmentation of human capabilities (e.g. in health monitoring and delivery, augmented reality).

Cyber-physical systems, due to the possibility of collecting and recording data, are also used in Maintenance 4.0 technologies. This is especially important for many sectors, e.g. cognitive maintenance (CM). Solutions for cognitive maintenance (CM) are largely based CPS and advanced techniques of artificial intelligence. These systems combine an intelligent approach to deep learning and intelligent decision making techniques that can be used by maintenance engineers working with modern equipment. These systems provide technical solutions for online maintenance tasks in real time, eliminating downtime caused by equipment failures and ensuring continuous and proper operation of equipment and production resources. Furthermore, the use of CPS in maintenance can improve resource management strategies to the new level, providing resources with self-preservation and predictive capabilities.

Target users of the book are scientists working in Academia and engineers employed in companies who want have an insight and more deep understanding of Cyber-Physical Systems (CPS), their design, application and maintenance, with an eye on modern technologies on one of the natural relapses of Industry 4.0 and Maintenance 4.0.

THE CHALLENGES

Topics and challenges covering the design, utilization, applications and maintenance of the CPS are related to:

- Smart grid,
- Autonomous systems and interfaces,
- Industrial systems,
- Robotics and mechatronics, multibody systems,
- Internet of Things (IoT),
- Smart anything (e.g., Cars, Manufacturing, Sensors, Appliances, Maintenance),
- Technologies of maintenance 4.0,
- Intelligent maintenance/Maintenance strategies

ORGANIZATION OF THE BOOK

The book is organized into 11 chapters. A brief description of each of the chapters follows:

Chapter 1 identifies challenges and applications of Cyber Physical Systems. The chapter reports the latest innovations in the area leading to cyber social systems or cyber physical social systems. Industry 4.0 amalgamates all major technologies including internet of things, big data, and cloud computing, and smart systems under CPS. Applications in the areas of manufacturing, health care, energy, automation, robotics, smart building, meteorology and transportation are listed. Cyber and physical components interaction, training and adaptation ability, interoperability using IoT devices, information security using firewalls and cryptosystems, system robustness and intervention of human inside and out of the loop are the major focusing areas in any CPS.

Chapter 2 reports new trends on the creation of the Digital Twin, which is related to an integrated multidisciplinary simulation approach. The use of multi-disciplinary CAE simulation is most effective in the design phase and the author shown how the CAE tools can be used in an integrated, collaborative environment, in which co-simulation techniques are fundamental. The chapter described how the adoption of physical sensors transform a mathematical model into a Digital twin before, and into a Cyber-Physical model later. The Digital Twin concept is effective for the design, the production, the monitoring, the life-cycle prediction, the maintenance of products.

Chapter 3 presents the development of a low-cost tangible interface to enhance children's learning through collaborative storytelling, using a set of movable blocks, having the main goal of a high degree of autonomy and the ability to exchange information. Taking into account the context of the existing game model and on the basis of which the reported study was developed, the chapter describes useful models to allow children to create and modify their own narratives in permanent interaction by manipulating the physical blocks. The chapter proposes a new approach to the educational games' industry.

Chapter 4 covers basic concepts on authentication systems, which are the protective barrier of any software ensuring that selected people are allowed entering a system and get access the information. This chapter describes the three main authentication techniques, and focuses on the Knowledge Based Authentication, since it is the most widely accepted technique for securing resources from unauthorized access. The existing knowledge-based authentication system is described, and then the usability evaluation parameters of the existing systems and approach towards developing a modified usable authentication system are discussed, together with an initial laboratory set-up.

Chapter 5 reports a modelling approach for IoT based smart grid, which is the combination of classical power grid with emerging communication and information technologies. The effectiveness of IoT-based smart grid is mainly reflected in observability, real-time analysis, decision-making, and self-healing. A proper effectiveness modelling approach should maintain the reliability and maintainability of IoT-based smart grids. In this chapter, a multi-agent-based approach is proposed to model the architecture of IoT-based smart grids. A case study is reported to model an IoT-based smart grid with restoration.

Chapter 6 presents an application of Health Index (HI) for fault diagnosis of Rolling Element Bearing (REB), which has been successfully used in several fields, such as Image processing, Prognostic Health Management (PHM) and involves integration of mathematical and statistical concepts. Condition monitoring (CM) is the process that assesses the health of an equipment / system at regular intervals or continuously and exposes incipient faults if any. Bearing failure is one of the foremost causes of breakdown in rotating machine, resulting in costly systems downtime. In the chapter, a comparison of the performances of the identified approaches is made for choosing the best one for REB fault diagnosis.

Chapter 7 addresses an integrative framework to understand common practices, concepts, and technologies used in trending research to achieve interoperability in production systems. Interoperability in smart manufacturing refers to the way of how interconnected cyber-physical components exchange information and interact. This is still an exploratory topic and despite the increasing number of applications, many challenges remain open. The chapter revises the concept of interoperability and discusses different types of interoperability, data formats, and common ontologies necessary for the integration of heterogeneous systems and the contribution of emerging technologies.

Chapter 8 proposes an intelligent traffic signal monitoring system. The model is developed on the actual number of cars on the road, the arrival of emergency services, rather than using pure timing circuits to control car traffic, making use of smart cameras to detect real-time traffic movement in each direction. The control system is designed to modify the traffic light control parameters dynamically due to changes in traffic flow, thus increasing the traffic intersection efficiency and ensuring improved traffic management.

Chapter 9 reports a general overview of e-Maintenance considering an application to Robotics. Maintenance of CPS is an important issue that can be crucial for the availability of those systems for developing their activities in a standard way, with respective desired behaviour. In this chapter, the authors intend to highlight the benefits of using an e-Maintenance approach for the success tasks of maintenance of CPS, mainly when, for those systems, it is critical keeping and assuring reliability of respective behaviour. For this purpose, a robot is used, highlighting the global overview of the proposed approach.

Chapter 10 presents and analyse system security applications in today's systems, based on Deep packet inspection. In recent years, regular expression matching are used as an important operator. Regular expressions are parsed using the Deterministic Finite Automata representations. Conversely, to represent regular expression sets as DFA the system needs large amount of memory, an excessive amount of time, or an excessive amount of per flow state limiting their practical applications. There are several compression techniques available, which provide memory efficient finite automata. This Chapter presents the analysis of several compression techniques, and Intelligent Optimization Grouping Algorithms (IOGA).

Chapter 11 reports an overview and application of Obeya Digital for business, with the main objective of minimizing interdepartmental communication, optimizing decision-making, and computerization of data. A tool is developed in MS Power BI® being capable of aggregating all the dashboards of the different departments. Thanks to the preponderance of the tool, training sessions were held for the Quality department, Project and Commercial Managers, demonstrating the utility of the application for the execution of the daily work of each employee. The main goal of the proposed approach in the Chapter is to enhance the skilful decision-making of the company and increase business performance.

Pierluigi Rea
University of Cagliari, Italy

Erika Ottaviano
University of Cassino and Southern Lazio, Italy

José Machado
University of Minho, Portugal

Katarzyna Antosz
Rzeszow University of Technology, Poland

Chapter 1
Challenges and Applications of Cyber Physical Systems

Rachna Jain
ⓘ https://orcid.org/0000-0001-9794-614X
JSS Academy of Technical Education, Noida, India

ABSTRACT

Cyber physical systems integrate actuators or sensors with networking technologies. Latest innovations in the area lead to cyber social systems or cyber physical social systems. Industry 4.0 amalgamates all major technologies including internet of things, big data, cloud computing, and smart systems under CPS. Cyber physical systems comprise of physical layer devices connected to the internet. It has vast applications in the areas like manufacturing, healthcare, energy, automation, robotics, smart building, meteorology, and transportation. Cyber and physical components interaction, training and adaptation ability, interoperability using IoT devices, information security using firewalls and cryptosystems, system robustness, and intervention of human inside and out of the loop are the major focusing areas in any CPS. In this chapter, application areas and challenges faced by cyber physical systems are discussed in detail.

I. INTRODUCTION

Cyber Physical Systems interact computing and communication devices with constant interaction at the physical layer (Xu, Z et al., 2008). Sensors and actuators work in the feedback loop using human intervention so that their behavior could be changed as per user's requirement (Ashibani and Mahmoud, 2017). Technical requirements of CPS system require large memory to store data generated from embedded systems.

DOI: 10.4018/978-1-7998-6721-0.ch001

System dynamics and control algorithm governing functioning of any CPS system must consider computing complexity of the system. Quality control of any system may be governed using feedback loop in any system.

Other challenges of any CPS system include excessive information overflow in a collaborative network. This abundance of data result in increase of noise in any system which is present in form of pop up windows, spam folder, contextual advertising related to any information. Growth of IoT paradigm has led to energy enhanced communication between cyber and physical entities. Critical aspect is interaction of humans with the machines. Awareness of threats must be there while realizing any cyber physical system (Bhattacharya, R., 2013). Multiple level security check must be there at all the levels of stakeholders. Data transportation among different systems demand for better communication among devices. Tampering of physical devices for example mishandling of wearable body sensors may result in huge loss like losing information about critically ill patient. Figure 1 demonstrates the importance of digital transformation in industry 4.0.

Figure 1. Digital Transformation in industry 4.0 (Source: Maskuriy et al., 2019)

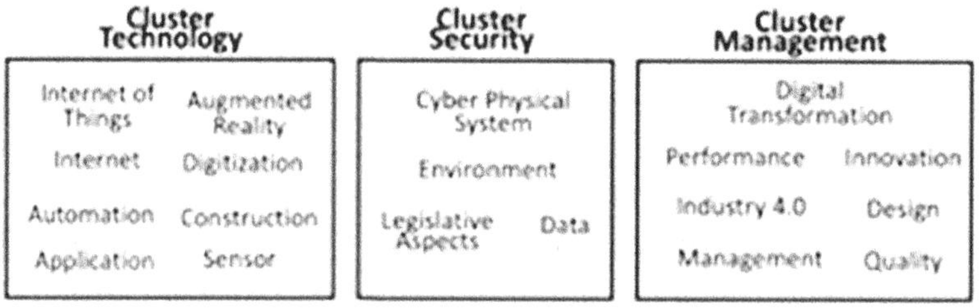

II. LAYERED ARCHITECTURE OF CPS

Different layers such as physical layer, interface layer and business layer of CPS systems are explained as:

i) Physical Layer/Perception layer:-

Sensors and actuators help in sensing the data at the physical layer. These modern sensors gather information from the surroundings. Hardcore infrastructure is provided by the sensors, actuators and the computer servers.

ii) Integration Layer/Network layer:-

Sensors and actuators connect to wireless networks through 2G, 3G, 4G, Bluetooth or Zigbee networks. 6LoWPAN allows IPv6 packets to be sent over low power personal area networks. IPv6 is even helpful in smart grid which allows formation of mesh network to send the data for billing system.

iii) Application Layer/Business layer:-

This layer provides services according to context awareness (Sethi and Sarangi, 2017). There can be opportunistic connection among devices as per the user's requirements (Guo, B, 2013).

Figure 2 exemplifies the layout of the industrial cyber physical system. Internet of things technology has revolutionized industrial applications also. Earlier whenever connectivity is required there is limited architecture with controlled firewalls etc. However, emergence of cyber physical systems and IoT devices has completely accentuated the growth of Industrial IoT (IIoT). IIoT conceptualizes the control by Programmable Logic Controller (PLC) and Intelligent Electronic Devices (IED); thus minimizing the role of human intervention. Supervision layer ensures the complete control using Advanced Process Control (APC).

This paper discusses practical applications which show its impact on construction industry revolution through IIoT. Stankovic, 2014 has identified key research areas in IoT domain. The author has highlighted key areas as massive scaling where trillion objects will connect to the internet, existing standards for regulating, architecture and dependencies, for example two different automatic systems could cancel each other's operations, creating vast amount of data, robustness to ensure run time certification, openness specially for Industrial IoT (IIoT), security, privacy and humans in the loop which is most difficult aspect being different physiological and behavior changes in the human beings.

In this paper, section I discusses introduction, section II elaborates layers of CPS system, section III explains state of art, section IV highlights challenges of deploying CPS, section V illustrates uses of CPS in industry 4.0, section VI exemplifies real case scenario of construction industry in IIoT and last section VII shows future road by involving human emotions in the loop.

III. STATE OF ART

Cryptography and Steganography are commonly used techniques for maintaining data security (Vegh, L., and Miclea, L., 2014). Privacy enhancing technologies (PET)

Figure 2. Layered architecture of industrial CPS (Source: Huang, Zhou and Yang, 2015)

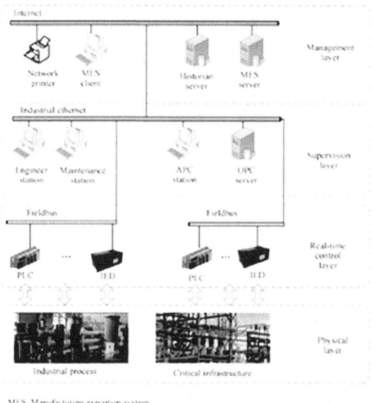

MES Manufacturing execution system
APC Advanced process control
OPC OLE (Object linking and embedding) for process control

PLC Programmable logic controller
IED Intelligent electronic device

help to up keep the anonymity of the users (Lu, T et al., 2015). Different objective functions for maintaining Quality of Service (QoS) requirements of the network must be taken care while maintaining security of the data. Peng et al. have suggested harmony search algorithm for proposing low energy, low latency routing in Wireless Sensor Networks (WSN) (Peng, Z, 2015). Hackmann et al., 2013 have proposed cyber physical system that flexibility based localization technique in distributed WSN for healthcare system. The authors have propounded the distribution function for Damage Location Assurance Criterion (DLAC). The author has amalgamated defects in structural engineering (physical components) with WSN using cyber components. The proposed scheme has resulted in better energy saving scheme.

Wan et al., 2013 have elucidated application of CPS as energy management framework (EMF) towards autonomous electric vehicle (AEV). (Chen, C et al.,

2015) have signified the importance of CPS systems in industrial automation. Real time data of industrial automation such as temperature, humidity, viscosity etc. have been sensed and associated with CPS. There exists a gap between this huge data collected with distributed systems and application of CPS. (Wan et al., 2013) have emphasized on Machine to Machine (M2M) communications as special case of Human Cyber Physical Systems (HCPS).

Maheshwari, P., 2016 has highlighted security issues on CPS systems. (Lyn, K. G., 2015) has proposed Trustworthy Automatic Interface Guardian Architecture (TAIGA) for supervising communication between embedded systems and physical devices. (Munir, S., Stankovic, J. A., Liang, C. J. M., & Lin, S. 2013) have demonstrated key challenges while employing human in the feedback loop. It has been emphasized that real time embedded aspects of human computing must be tackled. (Pu, 2011) has emphasized on the importance of distributed event based CPS/ IoT systems and QoS parameters such as privacy, availability, reliability and security has been discussed for distributed systems. (Calvaresi and Calbimonte, 2020) have implemented distributed artificial intelligence for computing real time behavior in critical applications such as healthcare system using Multi Agent Systems (MAS). (Nakagawa et al., 2020) have designed MAS for finding solutions for farm monitoring system in real world. Source model has been constructed to design components and labeled for relationship between these components. (Ziegler et al, 2020) have proposed a unique method Advanced Network Agents for security and trust assessment in CPS/IoT architectures (ANASTACIA).

(Kirkpatrick et al., 2009) have introduced unique Physical Unclonable Function (PUF) that creates unique value based on hardware used. (Ashibani and Mahmoud, 2017) have suggested that cryptographic technique should be lightweight such that resource constrained devices should be able to afford it. There is a need of lightweight robust authentication scheme that should prevent unauthorized access in the system. (He et al., 2016) have proposed lightweight parity Concurrent Error Detection (CED) for resource constrained devices used in CPS. Experimental results have shown the protection in block ciphers to enhance the system security. (Chen et al.,2016) has proposed unique identity based scheme for Machine to Machine (M2M) communication involving both wired and wireless systems to exchange the information regarding environment etc. without involving direct human intervention. The authors have suggested Authenticated identity based cryptography without key escrow (AIBCwKE). The proposed scheme helps in transmitting authenticated message from the transmitter. In the proposed scheme only partial information is stored in M2M Service Provider (MSP) instead of saving full secrets. In this paper examples of M2M communication such as hospital ward management and air pollution monitoring has been elaborated. The proposed scheme has proved effective against Man in middle attacks, impersonation attacks, DoS attacks and compromised attacks etc. (Alappatt and Prathap, 2020) have proposed Diffie Hellman method hybridized with elliptic curve cryptography (HDHECC) to ensure more secure and robust key exchange among nodes. The simulation results have proved better end to end delay and Packet Delivery Ratio (PDR).

Bhasin and Mukhopadhyay, 2016 have elucidated protection against fault attacks on omnipresent embedded systems used in IoT devices. (Saha et al., 2009) have explored diagonal fault attack by examining multiple byte faults in the state matrix. The attacks does not confine to single diagonal elements rather all other possible attacks on multiple diagonal elements have been thoroughly analyzed. (Lee, 2008) has elucidated design challenges while making a cyber physical system. The author has emphasized that physical component are qualitatively different from software components; so threads do not work in this scenario. The author has also emphasized on the fact that to fully explore the importance of CPS systems, physical dynamics and networking abstractions have to be re- build. (Baheti and Gill, 2011) have advocated that there is a need to design and analyze components at different levels of abstraction. The author has taken the case study of vehicle management system which considers the interaction among different components of the vehicle such as engine, brakes, steering and suspension to ensure different performance parameters as reliability, stability while optimizing the cost of the vehicle. The authors have further highlighted that while adopting component level approach there is a need of robust system to ensure overall safety of the design. The authors have exemplified the opportunities of CPS in the domain of next gen transportation systems, renewable energy and smart grid, widely used distributed computing in healthcare systems. Control engineer can play an important role for deciding reliability of CPS systems.

(Lee, Bagheri and Kao, 2015) have propounded a unique 5 layer architecture for implementing CPS systems. 5C architecture consists of smart connection involving plug and play at lowest layer of abstraction. Second level consists of data to information conversion level comprising of multi dimensional data correlation and smart analytics for overall health of the machine. Third level is cyber level, fourth level is cognition level and highest level is configuration level for resilient system in industry 4.0. (Rajkumar et al., 2010) have proffered research challenges while designing CPS as composition, robustness, safety and security of time based and tag based systems. There is a need of mixed calculus which can hybrid time based system with event based system to control feedback loop. Verification and Validation (V&V) gaps must be bridged for testing of heterogeneous models. (Sha et al., 2008) have emphasized on zero energy green buildings by using CPS. There must be a system which can address QoS dimension of CPS systems. The authors have highlighted that safety critical services should be able to handle errors and security breaches of the system.

Gisin et al., 2002 have introduced the concept of cryptography at quantum level. Naor et al., 1994 have elucidated a scheme based on visual method to decode image without the help of any cryptographic computation. The authors have claimed the scheme to be very secure and easy to implement. (Menezes et al., 2018) have enlisted all the major techniques of cryptography. The authors have demarcated ciphers as encryption techniques applied to words and characters. Digital signatures have been popular application of public key cryptography.

IV. CHALLENNGES OF DEPLOYING CPS

Security of CPS systems can be classified into two categories:

i)   Security of information which focuses on encryption and data security
ii) Security of dynamics governing physical systems

ISO/IEC 27001:2013 standards reveal that information security deals with authenticity and integrity of data in a network. Major factor governing performance of CPS systems is:-

i)   **Safety Factors**: - Safety is the foremost criteria through which infrastructure safety can be ensured in case of equipment failure or faulty operations of the system. (Koopman et al., 2014) have emphasized on safe transportation systems; where even a single fault could result in loss of many critical hours. Autonomous technologies must have hundred percent sureties of safety features. (Medawar et al., 2017) have elucidated Safe Co-operating CPS using wireless systems (SafeCOP). Multiple stakeholders using co-operating CPS (CO-CPS) are major users of SafeCOP systems. (Choley et al., 2016) have amalgamated functional topologies and components topologies of the system to ensure reliable behavior of CPS systems. The authors emphasized on the need of design modifications to remove redundancies in any CPS systems. (Romanosky and Goldman, 2016) have emphasized on collateral damage in CPS systems which is damage to civilian accidently in a military regimen. The authors have undertaken the connection among cyber and CPS systems and highlighted that it is much difficult to predict collateral damage.

ii) **Confidentiality:** - Any unauthorized person should not be able to access the information in a network. (An and Yang, 2019) have proposed new opacity framework while proposing CPS as linear time invariant system. Interference attenuation capacity (IAC) of any CPS system is called secret. Opaqueness of the system infers that intruder should not be able to access IAC of the system.

Opacity of the algorithm is preserved using Q-learning based algorithm. The advantage of proposed approach is those people need not to know dynamics of the system for applying algorithm. (Huang & Dong, 2020) have proposed a unique watermark based fault detector in a CPS system. The authors have classified the faults as detectable and undetectable. Data driven switching controller is suggested to propose any fault tolerant system. The proposed approach has been validated using an illustrious example.

V. USES OF CPS

CPS comprises of heterogeneous units amalgamated between physical and cyber units. These systems are used to control the physical world through many application areas like smart grid, automation, industrial control, automation as shown in figure 3. Despite of its vast applications devices at physical layer are prone to attacks. Opacity is the property of any system through which any outsider can infer secret of any system based on system structure and behavior. Computer science programmer has apprehensions about opacity in a Discrete Event Systems (DES). Distinguishing features of any CPS system include usage of cross domain sensors and data flow.

i)   Industrial control system (ICS):-

Skare, P. M. (2013) has patented an idea using Supervisory Control And Data Acquisition (SCADA) system for controlling and monitoring the industrial system. In industrial system different units collaborate to achieve any target. Wired or wireless communication can be integrated to accomplish the task.

ii)   **Smart Grid System**:-

Smart grid is digitized communication between utilities and its customers (H. Farhangi, 2010). Electric grid comprising of substations has been replaced with internet, automation and new technology. Smart grid can predict the power outage and prevent complete shutdown (Köhlke, J. 2019). To supply continuous power with minimum wastage is the key challenge in the upcoming decade. These smart grids must be able to supply reliable and sustainable energy to the consumers (Liu, J, 2011).

iii)   Transport:-

In today's world automation of vehicles is an important milestone to achieve (Yongfu et al., 2012). CPS can play a major role in achieving the targets. Public

Figure 3. Application areas of cyber physical space
(Source: Alguliyev, Imamverdiyev and Sukhostat, 2018)

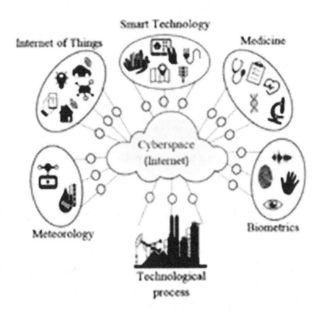

transport system should be efficient enough to predict jams and to provide better routes to the buses etc. and to ensure safety of pedestrians as well (Sun, Y., & Song, H. (Eds.), 2017).

iv)   Agriculture:-

This is another important application since we have to provide enough food for the growing population with minimum disruption with the environment (Rad, C. R., Hancu, O., Takacs, I. A., & Olteanu, G., 2015). Distributed sensors to employ automatic watering of the farmlands, intelligent software can yield maximum production with minimum environment deterioration.

v)   Smart Buildings:-

Future smart building should be able to predict real time customer's requirements, to minimize destruction caused by weather. Buildings must be built in such a way that these minimize carbon footprint in the environment (Shih, C. S, 2016).

vi)   Healthcare:-

Wearable sensors can help in monitoring and improving health conditions of the critical patients. Vital body parameters of senior citizens who are living alone can be monitored by the government agencies to provide timely help to the patients (Zhang, Y, 2015).

vii)   Urban water metering:-

(Boyle, T, 2013) have proposed smart metering system in urban areas to deploy water requirements by the user. The author emphasizes on the concept of sustainability for any particular generation. The author has demarcated between use and end use of water such as in toilets and gardens along with data management, security and skills of workforce.

VI.   Practical application of CPS systems in construction industry 4.0

Figure 4 displays the application of IIoT in construction industry by modernizing renovation, conceptual design, construction and fabrication while emplifying Building Information Modelling (BIM) as core of cyber physical space. Figure 5 strengthens bidirectional domain with BIM at its core between physical space and cyber space.

Figure 4. Building Information Modelling (BIM) as core of CPS (Source: Maskuriy et al., 2019)

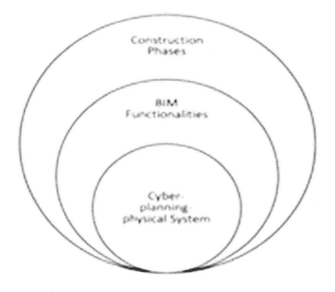

Figure 5. Bidirectional domain between physical space and cyber space (Maskuriy et al., 2019)

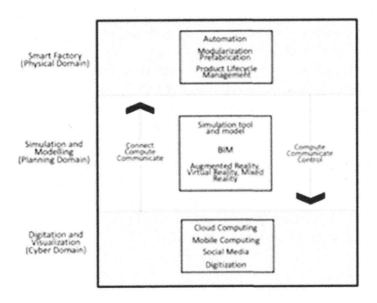

Liu, B., Zhang, Y., Lv, J., Majeed, A., Chen, C. H., & Zhang, D. (2021) have conceptualized deep learning based feature extraction methods for automating shop floor instead of using shallow techniques by human beings as shown in figure 7. Gunes, B., Kayisoglu, G., & Bolat, P. (2021) have exemplified the automation of sea port containers. Many connected devices in any industry leads to device threatening. This issue has been resolved by device fingerprinting (Babun, L., Aksu, H., & Uluagac, A. S., 2021). Qi, R., Ji, S., Shen, J., Vijayakumar, P., & Kumar, N. (2021) have suggested Artificial Intelligence (AI) based techniques to prevent unauthorized access to patient's data in industrial medical CPS. Although researches have elucidated many techniques to prevent unauthorized access in IIoT yet there is a need of strong quantam sensing or bio sensing techniques to make the system more robust.

VII. FUTURE SCOPE

There is a need to enhance clustering and data mining techniques to involve human behavior in the loop. There is also need of Component Models of Emotions (CME) for analyzing emotional behavior of human being. Large scale of devices and their interconnections to cyber and physical world need more focus on security and openness issues. Other factors involve large number of wireless devices are susceptible to DDOS attacks. Designing fault tolerant CPS systems is the need of the hour. New technologies including quantum sensing and bio sensing should be developed to meet security standards for CPS systems. In the future run cyber physical systems will dribble to students of engineering stream and schools also so that they can face the challenges of real world while realizing any physical system. In large automation systems physical world and computer control are actually dispersed. Physical systems are different from computing environment run with the help of software. In the future, microprocessor based subjects may be even replaced by real time physical systems. Another important area to be pondered upon is to prevent cyber espionage. These activities are very crucial as these activities provide decoupling with the digital era. Future CPS systems will include integration of hardware, software and human behavior in the loop also there is only partial information of the constituting systems then model should be able to place complete behavior of system. Fault tolerant and secure end product results in successful model.

REFERENCES

Alappatt, V., & Prathap, P. J. (2020). Hybrid cryptographic algorithm based key management scheme in MANET. *Materials Today: Proceedings*.

Alguliyev, R., Imamverdiyev, Y., & Sukhostat, L. (2018). Cyber-physical systems and their security issues. *Computers in Industry*, *100*, 212–223.

An, L., & Yang, G. H. (2019). Opacity enforcement for confidential robust control in linear cyber-physical systems. *IEEE Transactions on Automatic Control*, *65*(3), 1234–1241.

Ashibani, Y., & Mahmoud, Q. H. (2017). Cyber physical systems security: Analysis, challenges and solutions. *Computers & Security*, *68*, 81–97. doi:10.1016/j.cose.2017.04.005

Babun, L., Aksu, H., & Uluagac, A. S. (2021). CPS Device-Class Identification via Behavioral Fingerprinting: From Theory to Practice. *IEEE Transactions on Information Forensics and Security*, *16*, 2413–2428.

Baheti, R., & Gill, H. (2011). Cyber-physical systems. *The Impact of Control Technology*, *12*(1), 161-166.

Bhasin, S., & Mukhopadhyay, D. (2016, December). Fault injection attacks: Attack methodologies, injection techniques and protection mechanisms. In *International Conference on Security, Privacy, and Applied Cryptography Engineering* (pp. 415-418). Springer.

Bhattacharya, R. (2013). A comparative study of physical attacks on wireless sensor networks. *International Journal of Research in Engineering and Technology*, 2(1), 72–74. doi:10.15623/ijret.2013.0201014

Boyle, T., Giurco, D., Mukheibir, P., Liu, A., Moy, C., White, S., & Stewart, R. (2013). Intelligent metering for urban water: A review. *Water (Basel)*, 5(3), 1052–1081.

Calvaresi, D., & Calbimonte, J. P. (2020). Real-time compliant stream processing agents for physical rehabilitation. *Sensors (Basel)*, 20(3), 746.

Chen, C., Yan, J., Lu, N., Wang, Y., Yang, X., & Guan, X. (2015). Ubiquitous monitoring for industrial cyber-physical systems over relay-assisted wireless sensor networks. *IEEE Transactions on Emerging Topics in Computing*, 3(3), 352–362. doi:10.1109/TETC.2014.2386615

Chen, S., Ma, M., & Luo, Z. (2016). An authentication scheme with identity-based cryptography for M2M security in cyber-physical systems. *Security and Communication Networks*, 9(10), 1146–1157.

Choley, J. Y., Mhenni, F., Nguyen, N., & Baklouti, A. (2016). Topology-based safety analysis for safety critical CPS. *Procedia Computer Science*, 95, 32–39.

Farhangi, H. (2010). The path of the smart grid. *IEEE Power & Energy Magazine*, 8(1), 18–28.

Gisin, N., Ribordy, G., Tittel, W., & Zbinden, H. (2002). Quantum cryptography. *Reviews of Modern Physics*, 74(1), 145.

Gunes, B., Kayisoglu, G., & Bolat, P. (2021). Cyber security risk assessment for seaports: A case study of a container port. *Computers & Security*, 103, 102196.

Guo, B., Zhang, D., Wang, Z., Yu, Z., & Zhou, X. (2013). Opportunistic IoT: Exploring the harmonious interaction between human and the internet of things. *Journal of Network and Computer Applications*, 36(6), 1531–1539. doi:10.1016/j.jnca.2012.12.028

Hackmann, G., Guo, W., Yan, G., Sun, Z., Lu, C., & Dyke, S. (2013). Cyber-physical codesign of distributed structural health monitoring with wireless sensor networks. *IEEE Transactions on Parallel and Distributed Systems*, 25(1), 63–72. doi:10.1109/TPDS.2013.30

He, W., Breier, J., Bhasin, S., & Chattopadhyay, A. (2016, May). Bypassing parity protected cryptography using laser fault injection in cyber-physical system. In *Proceedings of the 2nd ACM International Workshop on Cyber-Physical System Security* (pp. 15-21). ACM.

Huang, S., Zhou, C. J., Yang, S. H., & Qin, Y.-Q. (2015). Cyber-physical system security for networked industrial processes. *Int. J. Autom. Comput.*, *12*(6), 567–578. doi:10.100711633-015-0923-9

Huang, X., & Dong, J. (2020). Learning-based switched reliable control of cyber-physical systems with intermittent communication faults. *IEEE/CAA Journal of Automatica Sinica, 7*(3), 711-724.

Kirkpatrick, M., Bertino, E., & Sheldon, F. T. (2009, January). Restricted authentication and encryption for cyber-physical systems. DHS CPS Workshop Restricted Authentication and Encryption for Cyber-physical Systems.

Köhlke, J. (2019). *Relevance and boundaries of innovation cooperation in the Smart Grid and its influence on energy transition*. Academic Press.

Koopman, P., & Wagner, M. (2014). *Transportation CPS safety challenges*. Carnegie Mellon University.

Lee, E. A. (2008, May). Cyber physical systems: Design challenges. In *2008 11th IEEE international symposium on object and component-oriented real-time distributed computing (ISORC)* (pp. 363-369). IEEE.

Lee, J., Bagheri, B., & Kao, H. A. (2015). A cyber-physical systems architecture for industry 4.0-based manufacturing systems. *Manufacturing Letters*, *3*, 18–23.

Liu, B., Zhang, Y., Lv, J., Majeed, A., Chen, C. H., & Zhang, D. (2021). A cost-effective manufacturing process recognition approach based on deep transfer learning for CPS enabled shop-floor. *Robotics and Computer-integrated Manufacturing*, *70*, 102128.

Liu, J., Li, X., Chen, X., Zhen, Y., & Zeng, L. (2011, February). Applications of internet of things on smart grid in China. In *13th International Conference on Advanced Communication Technology (ICACT2011)* (pp. 13-17). IEEE.

Lu, T., Du, S., Li, Y., Dong, P., & Zhang, X. (2015). A framework for analyzing anonymous network topology. *International Journal of Future Generation Communication and Networking*, *8*(4), 1–16. doi:10.14257/ijfgcn.2015.8.4.01

Lyn, K. G. (2015). *Classification of and resilience to cyber-attacks on cyber-physical systems* (Doctoral dissertation). Georgia Institute of Technology.

Maheshwari, P. (2016). Security issues of cyber physical system: A review. *International Journal of Computers and Applications*, (1), 7–11.

Maskuriy, R., Selamat, A., Ali, K. N., Maresova, P., & Krejcar, O. (2019). Industry 4.0 for the construction industry—How ready is the industry? *Applied Sciences (Basel, Switzerland)*, *9*(14), 2819.

Medawar, S., Scholle, D., & Šljivo, I. (2017, June). Cooperative safety critical CPS platooning in SafeCOP. In *2017 6th Mediterranean Conference on Embedded Computing (MECO)* (pp. 1-5). IEEE.

Menezes, A. J., Van Oorschot, P. C., & Vanstone, S. A. (2018). *Handbook of applied cryptography*. CRC Press.

Munir, S., Stankovic, J. A., Liang, C. J. M., & Lin, S. (2013). Cyber physical system challenges for human-in-the-loop control. *8th International Workshop on Feedback Computing (Feedback Computing 13)*.

Nakagawa, H., Ogata, S., Aoki, Y., & Kobayashi, K. (2020, March). A model transformation approach to constructing agent-oriented design models for CPS/IoT systems. In *Proceedings of the 35th Annual ACM Symposium on Applied Computing* (pp. 815-822). ACM.

Naor, M., & Shamir, A. (1994, May). Visual cryptography. In *Workshop on the Theory and Application of of Cryptographic Techniques* (pp. 1-12). Springer.

Peng, Z. R., Yin, H., Dong, H. T., Li, H., & Pan, A. (2015). A harmony search based low-delay and low-energy wireless sensor network. *Int. J. Future Gener. Commun. Netw*, *8*(2), 21–32. doi:10.14257/ijfgcn.2015.8.2.03

Pu, C. (2011, July). A world of opportunities: CPS, IOT, and beyond. In *Proceedings of the 5th ACM international conference on Distributed event-based system* (pp. 229-230). ACM.

Qi, R., Ji, S., Shen, J., Vijayakumar, P., & Kumar, N. (2021). Security preservation in industrial medical CPS using Chebyshev map: An AI approach. *Future Generation Computer Systems*.

Rad, C. R., Hancu, O., Takacs, I. A., & Olteanu, G. (2015). Smart monitoring of potato crop: A cyber-physical system architecture model in the field of precision agriculture. *Agriculture and Agricultural Science Procedia*, *6*, 73–79.

Rajkumar, R., Lee, I., Sha, L., & Stankovic, J. (2010, June). Cyber-physical systems: the next computing revolution. In *Design automation conference* (pp. 731–736). IEEE.

Romanosky, S., & Goldman, Z. (2016). Cyber collateral damage. *Procedia Computer Science, 95,* 10–17.

Saha, D., Mukhopadhyay, D., & Chowdhury, D. R. (2009). A Diagonal Fault Attack on the Advanced Encryption Standard. *IACR Cryptol. ePrint Arch., 2009*(581).

Sethi, P., & Sarangi, S. R. (2017). Internet of things: Architectures, protocols, and applications. *Journal of Electrical and Computer Engineering, 2017,* 2017. doi:10.1155/2017/9324035

Sha, L., Gopalakrishnan, S., Liu, X., & Wang, Q. (2008, June). Cyber-physical systems: A new frontier. In *2008 IEEE International Conference on Sensor Networks, Ubiquitous, and Trustworthy Computing (sutc 2008)* (pp. 1-9). IEEE.

Shih, C. S., Chou, J. J., Reijers, N., & Kuo, T. W. (2016). Designing CPS/IoT applications for smart buildings and cities. *IET Cyber-Physical Systems: Theory & Applications, 1*(1), 3–12.

Skare, P. M. (2013). *Method and system for cyber security management of industrial control systems.* U.S. Patent No. 8,595,831.

Stankovic, J. A. (2014). Research directions for the internet of things. *IEEE Internet of Things Journal, 1*(1), 3–9. doi:10.1109/JIOT.2014.2312291

Sun, Y., & Song, H. (Eds.). (2017). *Secure and trustworthy transportation cyber-physical systems.* Springer Singapore.

Vegh, L., & Miclea, L. (2014, May). Enhancing security in cyber-physical systems through cryptographic and steganographic techniques. In *2014 IEEE International Conference on Automation, Quality and Testing, Robotics* (pp. 1-6). IEEE. 10.1109/AQTR.2014.6857845

Wan, J., Yan, H., Li, D., Zhou, K., & Zeng, L. (2013). Cyber-physical systems for optimal energy management scheme of autonomous electric vehicle. *The Computer Journal, 56*(8), 947–956. doi:10.1093/comjnl/bxt043

Wan, J., Yan, H., Liu, Q., Zhou, K., Lu, R., & Li, D. (2013). Enabling cyber–physical systems with machine–to–machine technologies. *International Journal of Ad Hoc and Ubiquitous Computing, 13*(3-4), 187–196. doi:10.1504/IJAHUC.2013.055454

Xu, Z., Liu, X., Zhang, G., He, W., Dai, G., & Shu, W. (2008, June). A certificateless signature scheme for mobile wireless cyber-physical systems. In *2008 The 28th International Conference on Distributed Computing Systems Workshops* (pp. 489-494). IEEE. 10.1109/ICDCS.Workshops.2008.84

Yongfu, L., Dihua, S., Weining, L., & Xuebo, Z. (2012, July). A service-oriented architecture for the transportation cyber-physical systems. In *Proceedings of the 31st Chinese Control Conference* (pp. 7674-7678). IEEE.

Zhang, Y., Qiu, M., Tsai, C. W., Hassan, M. M., & Alamri, A. (2015). Health-CPS: Healthcare cyber-physical system assisted by cloud and big data. *IEEE Systems Journal*, *11*(1), 88–95.

Ziegler, S., Skarmeta, A., Bernal, J., Kim, E. E., & Bianchi, S. (2017, June). ANASTACIA: Advanced networked agents for security and trust assessment in CPS IoT architectures. In 2017 Global Internet of Things Summit (GIoTS) (pp. 1-6). IEEE.

Chapter 2

From the Digital-Twin to the Cyber Physical System Using Integrated Multidisciplinary Simulation:
Virtualization of Complex Systems

Daniele Catelani
MSC Software, Italy

ABSTRACT

Simulation has been a competitive differentiator for engineering-driven businesses, available at all stages of the development process and lifecycle, used by the various domains within an organization, not necessarily simulation experts. It requires discipline integration, scalability, reduced-order model, and democratization. The concept of digital transformation involves new approaches for data and lifecycle management, the understanding of the digital thread, digital twin, predictive and cognitive capabilities, including improvement of model complexity, integration of physics, increase of knowledge. These trends require bringing the physical and virtual worlds closer together and also the adoption of cyber-physical model at all stages of design, production, and operation. To overcome the drawback of simulation and the need to balance the computational effort with accuracy and efficiency, new modelization strategies are adopted with ML and AI, which use a combination of virtual and physical data for training ROM, with an order of magnitude faster than the multiphysics one.

DOI: 10.4018/978-1-7998-6721-0.ch002

INTRODUCTION

The pillars of multibody simulation, namely real behavior prediction, time-to-market and cost reduction, innovation, risk avoidance related to physical test have received an endorsement from recent digitalization developments and continuous increasing worldwide competitiveness. This has boosted the utilization of virtual simulation tools and increased collaboration between the virtual world and the physical world, with the goal to improve the quality and productivity, without neglecting efficiency and accuracy.

For achieving and maintaining competitive advantages, technology needs innovation: it implies the adoption of a digital process in the design cycle of product to investigate virtually its development, feasibility, performance, durability, cost, and manufacturing. This ambitious goal requires multidiscipline integration, *co-simulation* technology, optimization, data and process management, improvement of the correlation between physical and virtual tests. This means the adoption of the so-called Digital Twin, for integrating different simulation disciplines, tools and methodologies to better estimate system performances with respect single feature tools and including smart features like cyber-physical systems, data acquisition and management, human-machine interfaces. The Digital Twin, properly developed, adopted and installed, allows a full and direct control of the simulated process through its monitoring and, combined with simulation model estimation, improves and optimizes the full process, modifying its parameters, anticipating and predicting loss of efficiency and performances during production and operating life, optimizing maintenance actions. The accuracy of a virtual model is related to the collection, identification, and prediction of working conditions, but requires the right and acceptable compromise between accuracy and efficiency.

Other aspect to consider, to optimize, to simulate, to predict in a design, is the energy consumption and simulation tools can help to evaluate energy efficiency, through a right combination of empirical data/information and mathematical model, and – again - this is becoming relevant especially for real-time models for monitoring application.

Same importance has the estimation and prediction of end of life of components, generically evaluated using rough calculations, which could be too conservative or inaccurate.

A model-based approach has the ability to incorporate physical understanding of the monitored system, but it sometimes requires a very complex, difficult modelling activity, and it can be difficult, if not impossible, to catch the system's behavior: many users could be skeptical about estimation using this method. Instead, nurturing the model using real data from sensors increases the capability of understanding and predict degradation's behavior. Since they are based on real monitored data, current component degradation condition can be estimated. On the other side, some difficulties related to the lack of efficient procedures to collect and use data could require need to be managed efficiently.

The Digital Twin

In a competitive sector like high-technology industry (aerospace, automotive, general machinery, and so on) is needed not only to maintain but to increase value, skills, competence, efficiency (Armendia et al., 2019).

This objective can be achieved addressing current trends, initiatives like Industry 4.0 topics, which includes development towards cyber-physical systems (CPS), Internet of things (IoT) and cloud computing, allowing the generation of new machines, systems, products, generally defined as digital-twin or cyber-twin.; (Rajkumar et al, 2010; Dervojeda et al, 2015; Kagermann, & Wahlster, 2013, Liu and Xu, 2017;. Benveniste et al., 2012).

The convergence of cyber-physical technologies, with advances in data management, artificial intelligence (AI), machine-learning (ML), and communications via the Internet of Things (IoT) is already challenging traditional industrial product manufacturing processes. There is an acceleration of digital transformation happening across all industry sectors (Abdul-Kadir et al., 2011; Hoffmann & Maksoud, 2010; Lee et al., 2015). Manufacturers today are starting to implement detailed systems-design processes that accommodate the complexities of developing multi-disciplinary systems, with high-fidelity virtual prototypes, or 'digital twins', at the core of their development process. Tools exist today to overcome these new challenges and connect digital threads with feed-forwards and feed-backwards loops between design and computer-aided engineering simulations and measured manufactured and lifetime product data that provide cost savings, higher quality products, high levels of productivity and innovation, retaining simulation accuracy.

The digital twin, which includes devices for data acquisition and advanced human–machine interfaces, is a full digitalization of the physical system, for sure not a new concept, but nowadays partially adopted or implemented. Incomplete versions of the virtual representation of systems have been developed with the contribution of software vendors, through computer-aided design (CAD), computer aided manufacturing (CAM), computer-aided engineering (CAE) tools, which have allowed the optimization of designs, reducing time, costs, risks, opening minds to new solutions and, as main goal, reducing the need of physical prototypes, (Fig. 1).

Simulation tools play an important role in industry expertise to increase competitiveness: however, most available software tools deal with point-solution features of systems and processes, allowing partially the management of increasing complexity, because they suffer for a lack of integration of the different key features.

It is required, instead, the adoption of multidiscipline and co-simulation technology (Hanna, 2019; Brecher & Witt, 2006; Zehn, 2021). It is also fundamental to increase the knowledge of the process interacting with the real representation of the machine, combining the real data with the simulation models, monitoring the process allowing control, maintenance, optimization: it is the digital twin concept (Magargle et al., 2017). The right and balanced combination of models and process monitoring is useful not only in the development and design stages, but effectively during the production stage to check that everything is running in the right way, detecting defects and problems without the need to halt the production and, disruptively, predict component failures. Moreover, recently new application of the digital twin is becoming predominant, particularly the virtual commissioning, where a virtual representation of the system is used to design, program and validate the controller.

This new approach affects all the different stages of the life cycle of the system and process, accelerating the design development with a general time reduction, optimizing the process set-up and then productivity, improving the maintenance strategy, which is driven by the analysis of root cause, with the prediction and avoidance of quality problems, and increasing the production system life-time with better management of components and systems.

Figure 1. Merging the real and virtual world

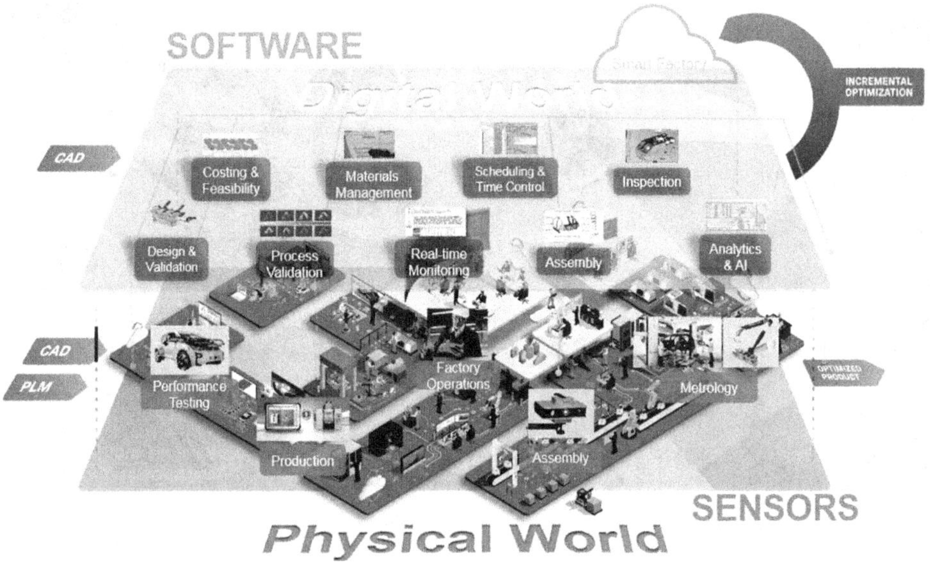

Evolution of CAE: Multidiscipline and Co-Simulation

The state of the art in virtual prototyping of complex systems (aircraft, vehicle, machine tools, robot) shows great capabilities on prediction of trajectory, force, torque, power, deformation, stress, noise, fatigue life, stability, vibrations, and so on.

Some available software packages are able to analyze single feature only (kinematics, dynamics, structure, noise), are model-based or data-driven, are not open to new challenges like introduction of new material for lightweight modern system, or higher dynamics requirements, require prohibitive computational resources (computer hardware, software, engineer and computer time), and/or are not enough easy-to-use, for a wide audience of users, (Fig. 2).

Figure 2. Example for CAE in industry as point solution

The main current limitation is that there is not one tool capable to afford all the different problems using one unique mathematical model, and probably this is not the goal to achieve.

Instead, it is evident that the main effort (with excellent outcome) is in the integration of all the solutions proposed and in the possibility to calibrate and scale the models in order to increase/reduce mathematical and numerical complexity on demand, on purposes, if/when/where needed, (Fig. 3).

Multibody analysis could be the core of an integrated simulation environment in which FEA provides flexible description of components, control code provides actuators and control logic, CFD, hydraulics, electric tools provide forces, and so on. As alternative, multibody analysis could be a block of a chained and interconnected simulation environment, in which data and output are transferred forth and back between different codes, and integrated sensors improve the quality of the results, and help the system monitoring and diagnostic. With this approach different but glued models can be developed on different tools which must collaborate among them, working together and exchanging data during analysis (co-simulation), or feeding each other with their results for subsequent analysis (chained simulation). The model can be improved or simplified removing or replacing components; the tools must expand their features with open architecture; the users must have full control and knowledge about methodology, numerical parameters and algorithm embedded in the code. The tools must be more easy-to-use without losing value, accuracy, and quality. The so-called CAE democratization does not mean "black-box" tool, but implementation of automatic or semi-automatic routine, methodology and procedure for allowing the access to the technology and for facilitating integration across different physics. For example, the design of the mechanical system for extraction and retraction of high-lift device, as the flap of an aircraft, requires, as preliminary design, the definition of a pure kinematic model, neglecting at the beginning the compliance and friction effects, aerodynamic loads, hydraulic circuit or electric motor issues. The designer is fully focused on the evaluation of the best mechanical system able to provide full extraction and retraction satisfying fundamental requirements: achievement of at least 3 flight configurations of the flap, cruise, take-off and landing. The requirements are provided by aerodynamic departments: every configuration is associated to aerodynamic force able to provide the right lift to the aircraft; by wing design department: the flap region is assigned and limited, during the movement it must be taken into account the presence of wing, of fairing, of other mobile surfaces, and collision and interference must be avoided; by flight control system department: size, weight, power of the actuators to apply movement to the flap; and so on, (Fig. 4).-

Once the mechanical system has been modelled, tested, verified from kinematic point of view, the model representation must include flexibility of the structure, deformation, stress, and fatigue evaluation. In addition size, location, power of hydraulic or electric circuit should be included to provide the control of the movement of the flap; aerodynamic distribution on the flexible surface for considering

Figure 3. Unified portfolio for cosimulation

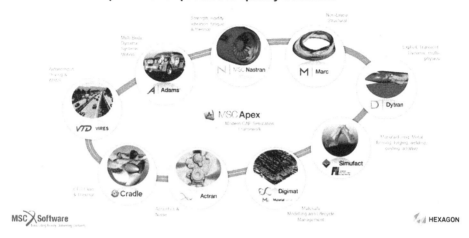

Figure 4. Multidiscipline tools for flap design

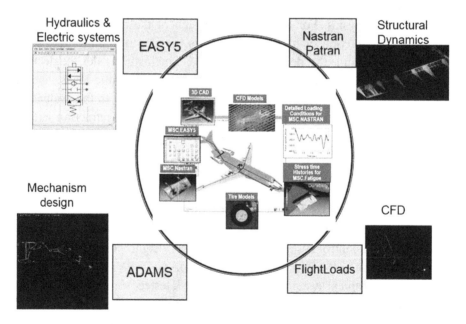

Figure 5. Multidiscipline flow for flap design

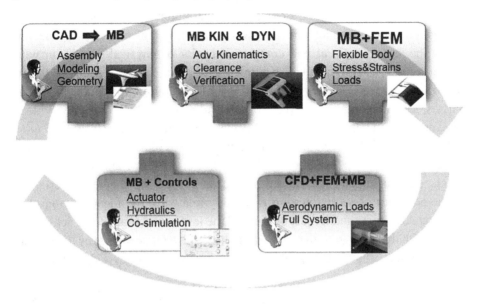

aeroelastic effect; noise and vibration, which could affect performances and comfort; manufacturing process for evaluating risk of presence of defects and assembling errors; ergonomic feature, for allowing maintenance and repair; safety, allowing simulation of every kind of failures; and that's not enough, (Fig. 5).

Figure 6. Example of Multibody -CFD co-simulation

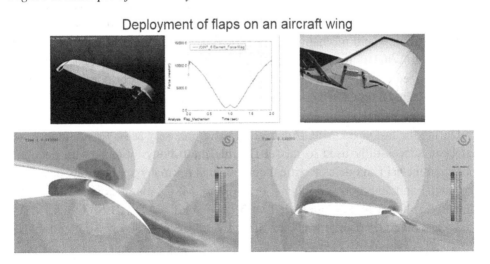

The process and model must deliver realistic certainty, and to achieve this goal every aspect, which includes different disciplines and physics, must be considered in conjunction, requiring integration and co-simulation. The numerical model must predict the same nonlinear and complex behavior of physical system, in which structure, control, aerodynamics, dynamics, hydraulics, avionics, acoustic, thermal act and interact together, where there is no space for brutal simplification, for isolated analysis, for limited and incomplete model and results, which do not provide the full overview and comprehension of the phenomena to be analyzed.

This advanced approach implies more and intense collaboration and integration among departments, people, competence, knowledge, OEM and suppliers, tools, models, data, and opens new challenging scenario for design and engineering.

The accuracy of virtual system is directly related to the identification of the operating conditions and it must be defined the level of accuracy to be achieved, in parallel with the efficiency, the simulation time which is acceptable by the industry. Great effort has been always spent to improve both the accuracy and computational efficiency.

Considering this, and based on the peculiarity of different disciplines (FEM, CFD, control), it is evident that there is no a predominant technology or an all-in-one tool, but, especially for mechanism design, multibody analysis can be identified as a good, if not the best, candidate to be positioned at the core of a multidiscipline, integrated environment where many players contributes to achieve the goal of prediction of system's behavior, the digital twin. (Moi et al., 2020).

For the coupling of dynamics, structure and control, there are two main approaches: replacing models, where simplified models (highly nonlinear rigid mechanism including linear flexibility or approximated stiffness and damping matrices) are combined with the control loop model; and co-simulation, where two or more simulation environments are coupled via interfaces (Multibody, FEM, Control): mechatronic models of systems can be achieved. The same for simulating aerodynamics loads on structure and mechanism: it is possible to evaluate separately from CFD code or from Wind tunnel test maps of pressure distribution on surfaces at different but discretized configuration and using interpolated routine for considering their variation during a time-variant analysis; using advanced CFD-FEM and CFD-MB co-simulating models, (Fig. 6).

During the last years, MSC Adams and more precisely MSC Cosim glue code has been successfully used to model flexible multi-body systems with detailed local nonlinear FE models of critical components for many applications in space, aeronautic and automotive domains. In addition, MSC Adams is a powerful and validated solution for the interfaced with codes like MATLAB Simulink, MSC Easy5 and all codes using FMU paradigm. Even if there is no one single tool, the wide portfolio and the excellent integrated solution allows detailed, precise, accurate, superior modelization of complex systems.

The developed tools are now capable of managing Multiphysics simulation, but there are three evident drawbacks: increase of requirement about competence on different physics and CAE technologies; huge increase of amount of data to collect and management of results; higher complexity of modelization and computational effort.

In addition, we cannot neglect the fundamental industry requirements: quality, reliability, durability and efficiency of design and product, perfectly balanced with time and cost.

For sure, management of model, management of files, management of data must be tuned case by case and system by system: nothing is for free, requires effort, but with the wide portfolio of tools in your hands and with the right training and competence about their use, you can afford every problem, introducing acceptable simplification when possible, requiring complexity when needed, balancing modelization with computational time, accuracy with efficiency, and optimizing management of huge volume of results

In every design process, it is possible to start using the rigid-body kinematics of the system, adding step-by-step, after validation and verification, compliances, lumped or distributed, nonlinearity of structures, distributed and time variant or space variant loads, time- or frequency-dependent loads and conditions. In addition, it is possible of simulating events and sequence of maneuvers, taking decisions, improving model, expanding when needed the embedded solution through open architecture, open solver and programming features. Definitively, with the right competence, skill, approach to the problem interactions among physics and execute coupled simulation can be simulated without neglecting accuracy or reducing efficiency. In the contrary, it is always the user to decide the level of complexity of model and analysis, while important is from the software vendor to provide the architecture to synchronize concurrent simulations performed in different environments ad to allow easier access to different tools, GUI, models, data.

From Cosimulation to AI and ML: CAE and Digital Twin

As underlined previously, it is mandatory for innovation to increase product complexity: as immediate consequence, the design challenges become more and more complex and every decision has a dramatic impact on the full design process, difficult to be completely understood and managed. Without embracing the right simulation methodology, the risk is to invest more time in the engineering phase, increasing cost or to take trade-off decisions, which could reduce quality product, with bad consequences on brand product perception from customers. To be competitive, smart and advanced CAE simulation adoption and usage must be increased in the design process to optimize design, to drive engineers to the right product development: smart and advanced means that simulation tools must offer, first of all, accurate and reliable results, but also that results must be provided immediately, quickly, in real-time (Bouchiba et al., 2020).

Consequently, the CAE industry is evolving for addressing new engineers expectations and to overcome the traditional bottlenecks like the long time to get results in some instances, the lack of availability of valuable model data, the cost and effort of a good modelization, the complexity of analysis when many physics are involved, the difficulties for taking decision searching the best solution among terabytes of output. There is an evident trend toward predictive adaptive CAE model and tools, to allow the exploration of new design variants without affecting the product quality. And in parallel, to reduce the discrepancies between the digital and real worlds, the digitalization process, the fusion of the two worlds, is strategic and opens new scenario and new challenges: Big Data Analytics, Cyber-Physical Systems, Cloud Computing and the Internet of Things, pillars of Industry 4.0, are providing intelligent machines, equipment and products which independently must exchange information, initiate actions, and individually control or influence each other.

The goal is to improve industrial processes along the entire product lifecycle and manage the increasing complexity of manufactured products, handling the development of data driven systems for knowledge capture and industrial good judgement.

The main aspect is that CAE design tools should be integrated into the real world of production facility quality process of the product through a full or end-to-end digital representation of data, the digital twin. The new approach of CAE tools adoption goes from the traditional and widely consolidated conceptualization, prototyping, testing and design optimization phases, to the operation phase with the target to use them throughout the whole product life cycle and beyond, till to retirement or recycling, as required by modern circular economy.

From pioneering period of Spatial mission, in the '60s, through the fast and disruptive diffusion during the last 50 years, the importance of numerical CAE simulation tools in combination or replacement of tests and experiments in all the phases of research and development have been proven with no any doubts: nowadays, the potential for real-time availability of accurate CAE data in the operational phase opens up inevitably new scenarios for monitoring and improving operations throughout the life cycle of a product, with huge cost saving and quality implications for any product.

The digital representation to simulate virtually a real-life object, process or system requires the physical object in the real world, the virtual object in the digital world and the capability to connect them through data and information, (Fig. 7).

Digital twins include laws of physics, material properties, virtualized sensors, causality. Engineers can build digital twins of complex systems using design, test, manufacturing, but also inspection, sensor and operational data.

With respect to traditional usage of CAE, not more used when production starts, a digital twin is extensively used throughout production and into post-productions phase.

It is evident that a digital twin can be used for the maintenance of a product, but also for predictive CAE analysis since it also contains measurement of data provided from internal sensors due to feedback loops. Moreover, data becomes more and more valuable and understandable because are derived from real context, and are evaluated with clear intent: consequently, the accuracy of the digital twin increases as more data are used to refine the mathematical model.

Figure 7. Digital twin concept

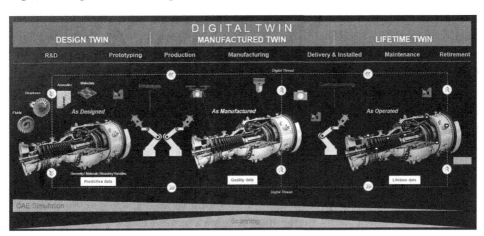

With this approach, digital twin technology includes simulation, testing and operation of products. To be effective, a digital twin must account for every change or variant and must have representations for taking into account historical data and tests: we have to consider the fundamental role (for completeness and cost perspective) of physics-based CAE simulation to manage models with existing data but also that there is often deficiency of them throughout a product lifecycle. Modern techniques as Machine Learning and Artificial Intelligence could help to correlate and automate these data sources, and the digital twin, built on physics-based simulation data, increases itself adding, through machine learning, physical measurements.

Industries, in manufacturing sector, are deploying high-fidelity virtual prototypes, the digital twins, as the core of a product development process, with the main benefit to produce great amount of simulated data. If we consider the Automotive industry, it is well known that the physical system for designing new cars usually requires millions of testing miles: adoption of the digital twin of the car allows to cover billions of virtual miles, enhancing robustness through radar and image recognition, and vehicle-to-vehicle communication capabilities; this is possible because a virtual testing environment can go potentially through an infinite number of repetitions and scenarios. As first consequence the simulated produced data can then be used to train the AI model, teaching potential real-world conditions, also dangerous, rare or never exploited before in the testing phase.

Looking to innovation and beyond the actuality, a digital twin can be used not only to represent reality but also to plan and test new features. Engineers can use virtual models to virtually create scenarios and cases of tomorrow, repeating and performing analysis all the needed times until an optimal solution has found and the best decision could be taken. The evident improvement in design and engineering simulation with the adoption of digital twin, to feed great and valuable source of data to AI models, has its drawbacks and challenges; first of all, data security, quality, availability and reliability: from design perspective, to be reliable the data are available only a posteriori, and a virtual representation of the physical world based on real time data from measurements can be effective allowing us to anticipate and predict behavior and problem before they occur. It means that in any moment things can change, predictions can change. Related to this, real time data means real time solvers, with the needed evolution of the technology, both on modelling and solver side. Predictive models must be based on realistic description of physics, so cross-integration of disciplines is mandatory.

The evolution of simulation technology requires for sure the improvement of physics-based modeling, based on observation of a physical phenomenon of interest, development of its mathematical representation (with different level of accuracy, precision, details) and its numerical solution: emphasis and effort are on co-simulation techniques, real-time solvers, GUI development, automatization of process, democratization of procedures and methodologies, increase of collaboration among users and specialists.

They are fundamental in the design phase and to start implementing the digital twin, (Fig 8).

But, on the other side, to overcome the bottleneck of the computational effort required by high-fidelity models, there is a great impulse to development of Reduced Order Models (ROM) (Kayvantash et al., 2015; Kayvantash et al., 2019), which requires very small amount of time and reduced level of competence to explore the design space, to provide results, to efficiently establish a predictive digital twin; it is a different paradigm for simulation, based on data-driven modeling: increasing feeding of data, even from unknown physics, in a digital twin context, with the tuned

Figure 8. Evolution of CAE, Digital twin and AI

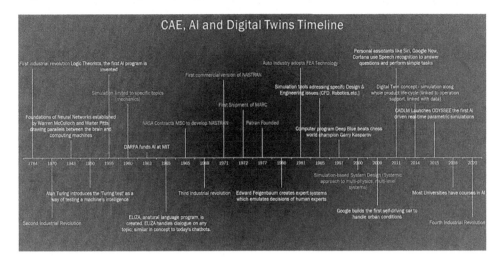

computational infrastructure (CPU or GPU) and high quality training resources, using smart data analysis (ML and AI) make the process more intelligent by getting more accurate data and predictions.

The data-driven models continue improving while more and more data (and experiences) become available. The core is the training part of the data-driven model: a poor or misleading training might drive to instability of the solution. If correctly trained, the model is stable and good for predictions. By adding machine learning into a CAE workflow, it is possible to search and find previously unthinkable combinations of data, (Fig. 9).

Machine learning can be used to simplify a high-fidelity dynamic model into a ROM that preserves the main behavior and the more important effects reducing the solution time or storage capacity required. ML can be applied to multiple range of physics, included highly non-linear with tremendous advantage over traditional surface responses because it has the ability to deliver time-dependent responses in the same way a Multibody or Crash analysis would.

This approach combines physics-based modeling (CAE mathematical laws to represent and understand with accuracy the reality) and data-driven modeling (efficiency and capabilities to identify multiple patterns thank to ML and AI algorithms).

Physics-based CAE simulation supply data to AI, essential to reduce time and effort to solve complex engineering problems and to realize a digital twin throughout a full product's lifecycle. As already said, manufacturers have recognized that it is mandatory to improve the old CAE-based design approach based on single-point

Figure 9. AI/ML for a predictive digital twin

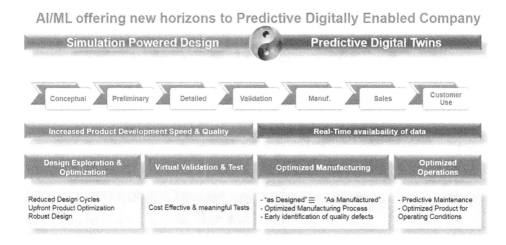

features tools and many of them have already implemented multi-disciplinary design processes to afford the complexities of simulating reality.

From CAE vendors' point of view, there is the need to evolve for addressing user expectations and facilitate usage, management, scalability, judgement of multi-disciplinary complex model: CAE simulation cannot be too expensive, or take too long, or too difficult to manage.

As already underlined, AI in CAE implies new challenges: we need to know what we are doing, we need to be conscious and aware about the AI process, we need to understand the value, the technology, the solution, (Fig. 10). AI can be used only if the CAE simulation provided satisfactory and validated result. (Fig 11) This means to understand if, when, where and how to combine it with physics-based

Figure 10. Values and challenges of Digital twin

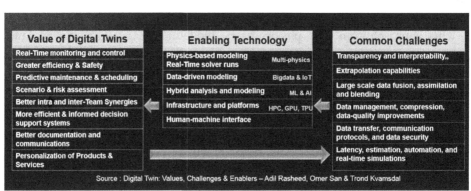

Figure 11. Benefits of AI

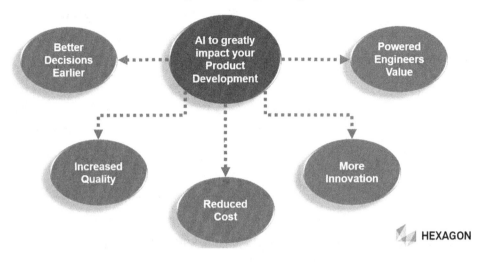

simulation. An engineer must have basic knowledge about AI algorithm and how it works; otherwise, he cannot trust a data-driven model (Huguenin et al, 2019). This is in contrast with the current trend to use machine learning algorithms as black boxes, but evidently we need someone involved in the engineering workflow able to understand the process, in order to verify and validate that the right problem is solved in the right way. When the AI model is properly trained, it is very useful for

Figure 12. How ML works

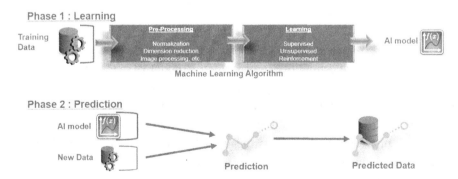

Figure 13. Industrial case of study

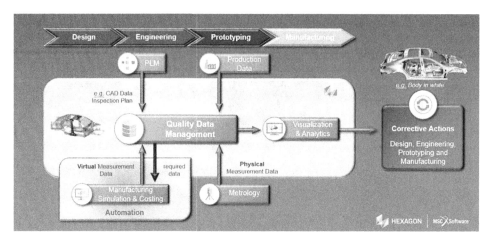

making predictions, but if it is used badly, that is blindly by a designer, results can be accepted only in limited context, too dependent on the provided data, in a limited time or period: in a few words, without monitoring of the process predictions can be partial or misleading, a AI model only know what you teach it, (Fig 12).

Going back to automotive industry, another pillar of Industry 4.0 is the development of solution for autonomous vehicles: it is evident that trust on drivers based on AI technology are great example of the issues shown previously. In addition, in any case, if there are lack of data or confusion of data, our models will be less predictive, not able to anticipate critical conditions. Everything can affect mechanism performance, like environmental conditions, and every time we want to automate a process based in predictive model we cannot skip to provide data and to use validated physical-based model and to feed our digital twin using measured data (from sensors or other tools): it is a continuous model refinement and validation.

The Cyber-Physical Model

The importance of co-simulation, as CAE drives design, as the design is evolving to Digital Twin model and how the right usage of modern CAE techniques like AI and ML helps the industry to be competitive and the engineers to expand their competence, capability, having possibility to explore new solutions.

This can be, as already anticipated, improved merging the virtual world and the physical world, providing with sensors the model, to measure, monitor, predict, anticipate, control behavior of complex system, in terms of performances, features, energy demand, end-of-life estimations, (Fig.13).

Cyber-physical system (CPS) can be defined as physical and engineered systems whose operations are monitored, coordinated, controlled and integrated by a computing and communication core and are considered as one of the main enablers for flexibility and productivity in industry manufacturing processes.

CPSs are observed as smart device that interacts with the machine (through sensors and actuators) to increase its performance. For example, an intelligent gripper of a robot which controls and regulates the clamping force based on sensor data and an intelligent actuator which control trajectory of end effector with vibration compensation and adaptive control system.

Consider also COBOT, working in a collaborative human-machine environment, fully equipped with many different sensors able to guarantee efficiency in production and safety of workers; or automatic movement of actuators for moving flaps, rudders, and stabilizers to avoid risk of stall, to compensate a failure in an engine, to quickly response to gust and wind shear phenomena, (Fig. 14).

Figure 14. Cyber Physical model applied to COBOT

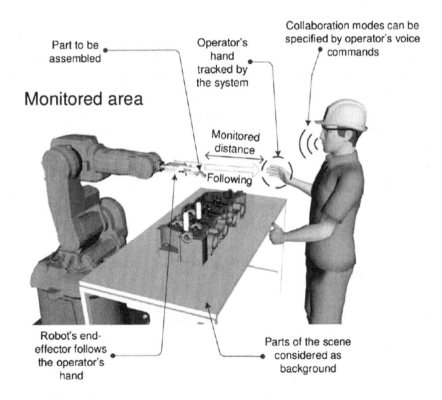

Another fundamental field of usage of CPS is the end-of-life estimation of the components: with numerical analysis, from multibody we can extract history of variable loads applied to structure of the mechanism, from FE code we can evaluate the stress conditions, from material code we can investigate material influence, from Fatigue code the engineers can use all of previous data (for instance, crack by fatigue wear and corrosion) to estimate component life,: but the full process could be affected by some ignorance and simplification, by lack of reliable data: this drives to very conservative or inaccurate estimations of component and system life.

A new methodology based on data-driven prognostics is becoming predominant: it is based on transformation of the data provided by the sensors into relevant models (which can be parametric or nonparametric) of the degradation's behavior. Since they are based on real monitored data, current component degradation condition can be estimated. To monitor a system, data acquisition and data processing must be considered.

The selection of the sensors for data acquisition is dependent on the type of system, mounting options, process influences, signal amplitudes and process disturbances: internal and external sensors, to evaluate position, force, torque, power, acceleration, condition, requiring hardware; virtual sensor, for measure/estimate some feature through other measurements, like component life and wear, requiring simulation. In order to access and collect the data, it is needed connected hardware and integration of some intelligence in the system, the implementation of communication protocol, the adoption of a structured and secured network infrastructure: data flow and encryption, sensor signals, history data, certification, signature, authentication.

We have also to consider the management of Big Data, when volume, velocity, variety of data are high: in industry, in the full life cycle of a product, we encounter high rate production of data from many different types of measurements and with high daily volume. Traditional software is not designed to handle this massive amount of data but new technologies based on distributed computing are spreading providing scalability, extending storage and computation capabilities implementing HPC resources, allowing rapid deployment of cloud-oriented architecture.

CONCLUSION

In the chapter, it has been endorsed the importance of CAE simulation for prediction, time-to-market and cost reduction, innovation, risk avoidance related to physical test and the new trend to digitalization developments which allows to maintain and increase industry competitiveness. The use of multi-disciplinary CAE simulation has been most effective in the design phase and it has been shown how the CAE tools are used in an integrated, collaborative environment, in which co-simulation technique are fundamental and the adoption of physical sensors for transforming a mathematical model into a Digital twin before, a Cyber-Physical model later. The application of machine learning enables digital twins to enhance the full end-to-end product development process improving robustness and reducing computational time, but the CAE analyst maintains the fundamental role to judge results: he has the responsibility about the implementation of AI technology to create, manage and supervise automated AI workflows. The CAE engineer needs to improve his knowledge about machine learning algorithms: in this way, it will be effectively possible to merge the digital and the physical worlds, making the Digital Twin concept real for the design, the production, the monitoring, the life-cycle prediction, the maintenance of products: in a few words, to the innovation.

REFERENCES

Abdul-Kadir, A., Xu, X., & Hämmerle, E. (2011). Virtual machine tools and virtual machining—A technological review. *Robotics and Computer-integrated Manufacturing, 27*(3), 494–508. doi:10.1016/j.rcim.2010.10.003

Armendia, M., Alzaga, A., Peysson, F., Fuertjes, T., Cugnon, F., Ozturk, E., & Flumm, D. (2019) Machine Tool: From the Digital Twin to the Cyber-Physical Systems. In Twin-Control. Springer.

Benveniste, A., Bourke, T., Caillaud, B., & Pouzet, M. (2012). *Hybrid Systems Modeling Challenges Caused by Cyber-Physical Systems?* Available at: http://people.rennes.inria.fr/Albert.Benveniste/pub/NIST2012.pdf

Bouchiba, K., Kayvantash, K., & Hanna, K. (2020). *The Emergence of Artificial Intelligence & Machine Learning in CAE Simulation Executive summary*. White paper. https://www.researchgate.net/publication/346420781_The_Emergence_of_Artificial_Intelligence_Machine_Learning_in_CAE_Simulation_Executive_summary

Brecher, C., & Witt, S. (2006). Simulation of machine process interaction with flexible mulit-body simulation. *Proceedings of the 9th CIRP International Workshop on Modeling of Machining Operations*.

Dervojeda, K., Rouwmaat, E., Probst, L. & Frideres, L. (2015). *Internet of Things: Smart machines and tools*. Report of the Business Innovation Observatory for the European Commission.

Hanna, K. (2019). *Co-Simulation - Breaking the Back of Multiphysics CAE Simulation, MSC Software, IDC: Artificial Intelligence Global Adoption Trends and Strategies.* IDC Report 2019. https://www.idc.com/getdoc.jsp?containerId=US45120919

Hoffmann, P., & Maksoud, T. M. A. (2010). Virtual commissioning of manufacturing systems: a review and new approaches for simplification. *Proceedings of 24th European Conference on Modelling and Simulation.* 10.7148/2010-0175-0181

Huguenin, M., Archour, G., Commun, D., Pinonand, O. J., & Mavris, D. N. (2019). *3D Cloud Modeling using Data Fusion and Machine Learning Techniques.* In AIAA Aerospace Sciences Meeting, AIAA SciTech Forum, San Diego, CA.

Kagermann, H., & Wahlster, W. (2013). Recommendations for Implementing the strategic initiative INDUSTRIE 4.0. In *Final Report of the Industrie 4.0 Working Group.* Forschungsunion Press.

Kayvantash, K., Kolera-Gokula, H., Scannavino, F., Chene, M., & Spote, R. (2019). *Enabling Accurate Design Decisions while Compressing Engineering Timelines with CADLM Technology.* Hexagon MSC Software. https://www.mscsoftware.com/sites/default/files/enabling-accurate-design-decisions-while-compressingengineering-timelines-with-cadlm-technology.pdf

Kayvantash, K., Thiam, A.-T., Ryckelynck, D., Ben Chaabane, S., Touzeau, J., & Ravie, P. (2015). *Model Reduction Techniques for LS-DYNA ALE and Crash Applications.* In 10th European LS-DYNA Conference 2015, Würzburg, Germany.

Lee, J., Bagheri, B., & Kao, H.-A. (2015). A cyber-physical systems architecture for industry 4.0-based manufacturing systems. *Manufacturing Letters*, *3*(3), 18–23. doi:10.1016/j.mfglet.2014.12.001

Liu, C., & Xu, X. (2017). Cyber-physical machine tool—the Era of Machine Tool 4.0. In *Proceeding of The 50th CIRP Conference on Manufacturing Systems* (vol. 63, pp. 70-75). Elsevier. 10.1016/j.procir.2017.03.078

Magargle, R., Johnson, L., Mandloi, P., Davoudabadi, P., Kesarkar, O., Krishnaswamy, S., Batteh, J., & Pitchaikani, A. (2017). A simulation-based digital twin for model-driven health monitoring and predictive maintenance of an automotive braking system. In *Proceedings of the 12th International Modelica Conference* (Issue No. 132, pp. 35–46). 10.3384/ecp1713235

Moi, T., Cibicik, A., & Rølvåg, T. (2020). Digital twin based condition monitoring of a knuckle boom crane: An experimental study. *Engineering Failure Analysis.* doi:10.1016/j.engfailanal.2020.104517

Rajkumar, R., Lee, I., Sha, L., & Stankovic, J. (2010). Cyber-physical systems: the next computing revolution. In *Proceedings of 47th ACM/IEEE, Design Automation Conference* (pp. 731-736). Association for Computing Machinery Press.

Zehn, M. (2021). *Benchmark-January-2021-Future-of-Simulation-Setting-a-Realistic-Agenda*. https://www.nafems.org/

Chapter 3
Development of Tangible Interfaces for Cognitive Development:
MOBEYBOU

Hugo Lopes
2Ai-EST, Polytechnic Institute of Cávado and Ave, Portugal

Vítor Carvalho
ⓘ https://orcid.org/0000-0003-4658-5844
2Ai-EST, Polytechnic Institute of Cávado and Ave, Portugal & Algoritmi Research Center, University of Minho, Portugal

Cristina Sylla
University of Minho, Portugal

ABSTRACT

This chapter presents the development of a low-cost tangible interface to enhance children's learning through collaborative storytelling, using a set of movable blocks, with a high degree of autonomy and the ability to exchange information with each other. Taking into account the context of the existing game model and on the basis of which this study was developed, the function of these removable blocks is to allow children to create and recreate their own narratives in permanent interaction by manipulating the physical blocks, which trigger the associated virtual representations (characters, e.g., animals, objects, locations, or others). It is expected that children will be able to project these representations on a screen through the activation and manipulation of the physical blocks by adding, removing, moving the blocks while interacting with each other and creating narratives. The authors have attempted to apply a method that could present a new approach to the educational gaming industry.

DOI: 10.4018/978-1-7998-6721-0.ch003

INTRODUCTION

Describe the general perspective of the chapter. End by specifically stating the objectives of the chapter. Make-believe play in early childhood, which involves the use of fantasy and symbolism, is important for children's overall cognitive development. According to (Fein, G.,1987) play is a symbolic behaviour in which one thing is treated as if it were another. He also underlined the importance of the sensations related to play and considered that affection linked to the game itself is a natural form of promoting creativity (Fein, G.,1987). Research has also highlighted that play is important in the development of creativity as many of the cognitive and affective processes involved in creativity occur when playing (Fein, G.,1987; Russ, S.,1993,1996). The model of affection and creativity identifies the main cognitive and affective processes involved in creativity and their relationship (Russ, S.,1993).

Playing also facilitates divergent thinking because, in play, children exercise the capacities of divergent thinking using objects that represent different things and imagining various scenarios throughout the process (Singer, D. L., & Singer, J.,1990). (Liebennan, J. N., 1977) identified a relationship between play, containing affective components of joy and spontaneity, and divergent thinking in preschool children. Some studies point to a relationship between affective processes during play and creativity as well as recognizing more easily danger (Christie, J., & Johnson, E.,1983; Singer, J. L., & Singer, D. L.,1981).

Creative narratives may be the most appropriate context to stimulate language development in young children, as well as narrative competences (Morais, J., 1994). Storytelling is a social activity, based on shared experiences that can introduce new vocabulary and may also include elements that help to develop phonological awareness, as are often found in repeated patterns, rhymes or funny stories (Sylla, C. et al., 2016). The narratives that occur naturally in children's play is particularly important to stimulate their imagination, to acquire and practice different linguistic styles and to explore their social roles (Meltz B.F., 1999). All kinds of narratives are the basis for understanding and creating our experiences and the world around us. At the individual level, the narratives that we listen to throughout life allow us to build our "role" in the world. At the family level, narratives are often involuntarily used to socialize children to teach them values and principles. When exposed to these stories' children develop their own narrative skills. At the cultural level the narrative gives cohesion to the transmission of principles and values (Cassell, J., & Ryokai, K., 2001). It has been argued that children can use more elaborated language in their narratives than in their everyday conversations (Peterson C, McCabe A.,1983). Knowing how to read and write remains the basis of education and a prerequisite in other scientific fields, such as science, mathematics and technology. Through participation in language games, narratives, children's interaction with peers contributes to the development of these skills. In this context, of strong interaction, in order to be sure that their messages are clearly perceived children surpass themselves and stimulate each other (Goncu, A., 1993), thereby developing their capacity to build and tell stories (Cassell, J., 2004). The same process occurs through storytelling between tutors and children. Children who show greater interest and involvement in activities related to narratives also demonstrate greater activation in the association areas on the right side of the cerebellum during the task and greater functional connectivity between this activation cluster and the areas of language and executive functions (Hutton, J. S. et al., 2017). Recent studies suggest a potential cerebellar response mechanism at the level of child involvement that can contribute to the development of emerging literacy during childhood and synergy between guardian and child during story sharing (Hutton, J. S. et al., 2017).

Collaboration is an important competence that can have very beneficial effects on children's learning and development, particularly in the early years and in primary education (Rogoff, T., 1990; Topping, K., 1992; Wood, D. & O'Malley, C.,1996).

Technology offers opportunities to support and facilitate collaborative learning in many ways (Barfurth, M.A., 1995; O'Malley, C 1992), for instance, computers can provide a common frame of reference and be used to support the development of ideas among children. However, neither learning nor collaboration will take place simply because two children share the same computer. Learning and collaboration only occurs if the technology is designed according to the contexts of use and the purpose for which it is intended. Otherwise, the interface can become a barrier to learning (O'Malley, C., 1992).

The difference between a graphical user interface (GUI) and a tangible user interface (TUI) is that the latter combines the technology of a virtual interface with the physical world. Traditional GUIs are characterized by virtual elements such as windows, icons, menus, and the user's interaction with the computer is done using devices such as mouse and keyboard. By contrast, the manipulation of a physical (tangible) interface is done through objects that combine the physical with the virtual world.

TUIs were initially explored with the "Bricks" prototype by (Cottam, M., & Wray, K., 2009). TUIs have great potential to support "hands-on" learning (Marshall, P., 2007). However, it would be necessary to prove its usefulness concretely.

By combining the physical with the virtual world, TUIs can play a very important role in literacy development as well as in other educational areas. The development of technology and the widespread access to increasingly small electronic components makes it possible to develop learning materials, which could translate into an improvement in children's cognitive development. The creation of tangible interfaces endowed with autonomy, capable of recognizing each other and interacting with a graphic environment can be an important step to support and facilitate collaborative learning.

Examples such as mobile phones, tablets, or specific gaming platforms as Nintendo Wii, demonstrate the ability to apply technology to objects as a way of interacting with the virtual world in a non-traditional way. This bring out a reduction in the cost of developing new devices and their use is becoming more and more common. Transposing these types of characteristics to educational materials and tools may translate into an improvement in cognitive development in children. The widespread access of these components allows and increasingly facilitates the creation of new prototypes of TUI interfaces (Cottam, M., & Wray, K., 2009).

This chapter presents the design of a tangible, technologically advanced object, framed in the project Mobeybou project, which currently uses the TOK platform hardware (Sylla, C. et al., 2016). In order to optimize the already developed hardware here we describe the development of a hardware solution that acts as a complement that can be integrated into the existing graphic environment. To this end, we took into account the previous developed hardware and the main features of the system. Regarding Cyber-physical Systems (CPS) the presented solution will evolve to an Internet-of-Things (IoT) approach as all system users' actions will be monitored and stored in the cloud allowing further studies on user interaction.

This chapter is organized in 6 sections. Section 2 describes the motivation, state-of-the-art and the previous developed platform. Section 3 describes the main concepts associated with the communication and filtering methods used in the developed solution. Section 4 describes the implemented hardware and software solution. Section 5 describes the testes carried out with two groups of children and finally, section 6, presents the main conclusions and proposes some further work approaches.

BACKGROUND

This section describes the background research, motivation, state-of-the-art and previous work.

State-of-the-art

Over the recent years, several types of TUIs, with different purposes, have been developed and studied. FlyStick, PrimBox (Kumar, P. et al., 2009), i.e., aims to teach geometry in high school. A virtual world was built to help students comprehend different geometric concepts and with it has got two types of tangible interfaces in which the first controls a virtual object with six degrees of freedom and the second changes the object attributes, like position, size, rotation and colour.; Others are based on AR (Augmented Reality) like T4T (Xiao, J. et al., 2013), a 3D interface that allows object manipulation in different AR scenarios, Finger Trips (Altini, M., 2010), recreates a 3D tangible map projected into a table so that students could easily build those with different materials like clay, or ARPB (Liu, H. et al., 2007) that allows some type of immersive experience between the virtual world and the real by recreating 2D images from books and transposing those into 3D objects and animations providing an attractive and fun way to learn; but the closest developed TUI to what we propose in this paper is Siftables (Yang, Z. et al., 2013). These are little block computers, with a small display, movement reaction and with interaction between them depending on position. Each block has a rechargeable battery that enables three game hours between charges. The commercial use of this TUI faces several issues, including limited scalability, loosing blocks, tiredness provoked by extensive long usage.

Previous Work

The original tangible interface includes a graphical component and two main tangible objects, the pieces / blocks, and a board. Each block has a capacitive sensor at its base that contains information about its identity (ID). Each block is associated with a graphic element. When placing a block on the board, it is recognized by the sensors of the electronic board and its identification is communicated to the graphical environment which in turn triggers a virtual graphical representation of the respective element that is displayed on the computer / tablet screen. The application allows users to mix all the narrative elements, and this depends on the choice of blocks placed on the platform, and this potential way to engage children in exploring different narratives. TOK has enormous potential in terms of the ease of creating different blocks. The total number of different blocks that can be created is quite high but limiting the number of blocks that can be read by the board is a disadvantage in the case where the pieces identify objects and not characters. Taking into account that the aim of this work is to continue the Mobeybou project, it proved essential to look for an innovative alternative in relation to the existing solutions, through a TUI prototype with a significant degree of autonomy - which the state of the art does not reveal to have been achieved until now - verifying, on the other hand, that the identification of this object requires a study of the different types of approach using technology currently on the market.

Autonomy, as both energetic as functional, is the key issue in any technological object and this kind of object is no exception, insofar as an object that is restricted to a physical connection (by cables, for example) and powered by the power grid has "infinite" autonomy, while an object that it is movable has a limited energetic autonomy, although it can be recharged / powered by renewable energy resources, for example. On the other hand, the way that an object identification is generated requires a study of the different types of possible approach using technology currently on the market. It is also important to use cross-cutting and unified technology.

What we propose is to make the game scalable, mouldable, customizable, modellable and flexible, making use of most of the elements of the work done up to that point. The use of currently available technology, namely computers, graphics and interfaces environments offer an opportunity to support and facilitate collaborative learning. In order to reinforce the importance that tangible objects bring to children's cognitive development, it is proposed to elaborate an object that can be integrated in a graphic environment already created, but with an advantage over the solutions tested so far.

Motivation

Knowing how to read and write remains the basis of education and a prerequisite in other scientific fields, such as science, mathematics and technology. Through participation in language games, narratives, children's interaction with peers contributes to the development of these skills. In this context, of strong interaction, children outdo themselves and stimulate each other to make sure that their messages are clearly perceived (Cottam, M., & Wray, K., 2009), thereby developing their ability to elaborate and tell stories (Marshall, P., 2007). For children, the theory suggests that supporting physical actions on computational objects, therefore virtual, makes it difficult to perform hard mental tasks. However, recently there have been experiments in which traditional teaching methods are compared to the manipulation of physical objects in which any aspect of their shape represents abstract concepts. Tangible interfaces can play a very important role in literacy and other fields in education. With the development of technology and electronic components increasingly smaller, the application of these in everyday objects facilitates the interaction between the user and the virtual world.

THEORETICAL CONCEPTS

This section presents the main theoretical concepts associated with the Bluetooth technology, Received Signal Strength Indicator (RSSI) and Extended Kalman Filter necessary to better understand the project solution implemented.

Bluetooth Technology

Bluetooth® 5 technology has significant advantages over other solutions, when, as is the case, the aim is to locate and exchange information between TUI objects, namely in indoor environments (Bluetooth SIG., 2019). Bluetooth®, in addition to low power consumption, omnipresence, low cost and easy use, is immune to electromagnetic noise and it is easily scalable for scenarios with multiple agents. Other solutions, such as Wi-Fi, GPS (Global Positioning System), RFID (Radio Frequency Identification) etc., are not suitable for locating devices for the following reasons: GPS requires a line of sight with at least four satellites, so it is not suitable for indoor environments; RFID is not capable of communication; although Wi-Fi has a higher data rate and high power consumption is inadequate; other technologies, such as Zigbee, are not widespread and are not available on laptops, smartphones, desktops, among others (Raghavan, A. N. et al., 2010). Bluetooth® 5 brings vast advances to this technology and as the potential to become an alternative (Simon, H. & Robert, H., 2009; Anastasi G., 2003; Bargh, M. & Groote, R., 2008; Jevring, M. et al., 2008; Huang, A., 2005; Bruno, R. & Delmastro, F., 2003, Hallberg, J. et al., 2003; Pandya, D. et al., 2003). Using an approach based on the Received Signal Strength Indicator (RSSI) (Bahl, P. & Padmanabhan, V. N., 2000), one of the simplest and most widely used for indoor location, we tried to use Machine Learning and Deep Learning algorithms, most used in Artificial Intelligence, analysis of large collections of data and image processing, that can make RSSI-based localization more accurate. In addition, Kalman filters were applied to the RSSI values, aiming to improve the accuracy of the readings. All the technology was applied to the TUIs, the blocks, to make them "smart" in some way.

Bluetooth® devices can play different profiles as part of a communication, differently from a communication between a server and a TCP (Transmission Control Protocol) client. The most usual connection can be described by a master and a slave, in which the slave periodically sends his identity and some characteristics about himself allowing the master to discover him and proceed with the connection. This connection can be originated by any device and ends when the master disconnects. This condition is called pairing between Bluetooth® devices. However, this requires greater energy expenditure as it relies on a constant exchange of information. Instead, a much simpler method can be resolved by exchanging information through observer and advertiser, since a device advertises a packet with information and other collects this packet, thus reducing greatly energy consumption.

RSSI - Received Signal Strength Indicator

RSSI is a unit signal of power measurement. Unlike dBm (decibel-milliwatts), which also represents a signal strength measurement unit but in absolute value, the RSSI is used to measure the relative quality of the signal strength between devices. The scale is set by the manufacturer and varies between 0 and -255, but in all cases, it can be inferred that the closer to 0 the better the signal. Therefore, not being a scale that allows to quantify exactly the distance between two devices, it has been studied to obtain an approximation of an indoor location in substitution of other technologies that do not allow it, as the case of GPS.

The approach based on RSSI is one of the simplest and widely used for indoor location (Yang, Z. et al., 2013; Ladd, A. M., 2005). Using the RSSI and a simple model of signal propagation loss over space (Kumar, P. et al., 2009), the distance d between the transmitter (TX) and receiver (RX) can be estimated by:

$$RSSI = -10n \log 10 (d) + A \qquad (1)$$

where n is the exponent of propagation loss (varies between 2 in open line and 4 with many obstacles) and A is the reference transmission value. Finding a device using RSSI can be done in different ways. In the case of trilateration or trilateration by N-points, used for example in the GPS signal, RSSI is used to estimate the absolute distance between the device to be located and at least three reference points, usually referred to as anchors. This method applies basic geometry and trigonometry. Although this approach is simple and easy to implement, it suffers from little precision due to the characteristics of the RSSI signal, especially in conditions where there is no line of sight, in which the signal attenuation results from obstacles and walls causing large fluctuations in the RSSI ((Yang, Z. et al., 2013; Xiao, J.,2013). However, different types of filters can be applied to mitigate these effects. Nevertheless, it is unlikely to obtain location with high precision without the use of complex algorithms.

One approach that has been studied is the use of Machine Learning and Deep Learning algorithms, most used in Artificial Intelligence, analysis of large data collections and image processing, but which can make the location based on RSSI more accurate, as previously referred.

In the case of neural networks, ANN (Artificial Neural Networks), the location is obtained through classifiers and forecasting scenarios. The neuronal network is trained with the different RSSI values corresponding to a given location in an offline process (Altini, M., 2010). Once trained, it can be used to obtain the location of any other device that obviously has the same characteristics as RSSI. The MLP (Multi-Layer Perceptron) network with a hidden layer is one of the most used and common networks in this type of approach (Liu, H., 2007). As an input, a vector with RSSI values is multiplied by weights and added to an input layer bias, as long as the bias is selected. The result obtained is then placed in the transfer function of the hidden layer. The output product of the transfer function and the trained weights of the hidden layer are added to the hidden layer bias. The network's output is the device's intended estimated location.

On the other hand, the application of clustering algorithms can also help in obtaining more accurate results for the location of devices. This is the case with the kNN (k-Nearest Neighbours) algorithm. The algorithm depends on RSSI online to obtain the closest matches, based on the measured RSSI values, previously stored in a database in the offline process, from known locations using the Root Mean Square Error – RMSE (Liu, H., 2007; Zafari, F., 2019).

Extended Kalman Filter

Kalman filters have been applied in navigation situations. This method, developed by Rudolf Emil Kalman in 1960, was originally designed and developed to solve the navigation problem in the Apollo project (Grewal, M. S. and Andrews, A. P., 2010).

Although it can be described by a single equation, the Kalman filter is usually divided into two distinct phases: Prediction and Update and its purpose is to use measurements of quantities performed over time, with a high degree of noise and other associated uncertainties to obtain results that are close to the actual values. It performs efficiently, accurate inferences about a dynamic system. It is computationally lightweight and relatively easy to implement on systems with few input variables.

Prediction uses the previous state estimate to obtain an estimate of the current state in time, which is called an a priori estimate. The Update is called a posteriori, as it combines the current observation to improve the estimate. Prediction is given by:

$$x_k = x_{k-1} \tag{2}$$

$$P_k = P_{k-1} + Q \tag{3}$$

where xk and xk-1 are the estimate of the state and the a priori state, Pk and Pk-1 are the estimate of the covariance error and the a priori state and Q covariance of the system noise. And, the update by:

$$K_k = P_k \left(P_k + R \right)^{-1} \tag{4}$$

$$x_k = x_k + K_k \left(z_k - x_k \right) \tag{5}$$

$$P_k = \left(1 - K_k \right) P_k \tag{6}$$

where R is the covariance of a posteriori noise, therefore the observation, Kk is the Kalman gain and zk the measured value. To use the Kalman filter model, it is only necessary to provide the state matrices, the initial parameters and the covariance matrices Q and R. In order to form a well-structured opinion on the characteristics of the RSSIs in these devices, some samples were collected between two devices that showed a rapid change of positions. In fact, RSSI values change quite sharply when they are in a fixed position and often overlap. Since the values are integers, it is difficult to obtain a resolution that allows accurate distances to be inferred. After applying the Kalman filter and adjusting the parameters: Q - Covariance of the system noise; R - Covariance of the observation noise; P - Estimate of the covariance error; we can see an improvement of the signal values.

SYSTEM DEVELOPMENT

This section describes the solution developed considering its requirements and approach implemented (Lopes, H. et al., 2021).

Requirements

The objective of this work is to design and develop a tangible, low-cost interface, with the ability to be integrated into a virtual platform. In order to make the game competitive in terms of the market, it is important to choose the technology that allows to obtain validation of the proposal and that has the minimum associated cost.

In order to make the game scalable and flexible, we thought of a solution that keeps up with the existing model. To this end, the idea would be to transform each block into a device that is autonomous and that collects information from other blocks in the vicinity.

Due to the RSSI characteristics, different from manufacturer to manufacturer, we chose to use only the RSSI values between devices and not considered the RSSI between computer - devices.

Every physical object, block, must meet the following parameters: transmitting information of their identification; recognize adjacent parts for interaction between them; switching status (on/off); be autonomous and have reduced price; allow easy integration in a graphic environment; and, meet the physical size appropriate to the game.

Approach

In order to design physical objects, a prototype was developed at an early stage using nRF52840 Chip/SoC, not only due to its reduced price, but also due to the characteristics in terms of development.

Different tests were carried out to measure the RSSI values in order to be able to draw conclusions about the methodology to be followed. After registering the RSSI values of these components, based on the Chip/SoC nRF52840, it was developed a functional prototype of the blocks, Figure 1.

Figure 1. Block Case

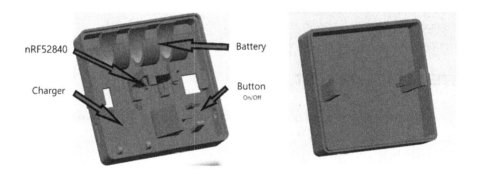

The case consists of a printed circuit board, a 2700mAh battery, a TP4056 based Chip/SoC board, with charge protection diode, to charge the battery and a button.

Each BLE Chip/SoC was programmed so that it would perform the role of observer and advertiser at the same time with appropriate intervals. For the sake of autonomy, it is intended that both the observer and advertiser profiles consume as little energy as possible without changing the game dynamics.

A block that finds another one in the vicinity is able to determine the RSSI value, filter it and transmit the value in the advertisement package to the API.

Due to the size of the advertisement package, 31 bytes were attempted to find a solution that would allow to collect and transmit as much information about the respective object and others in the vicinity. The advertisement package was configured to transmit the information of the game name, "MBBou", the object identification and the identification of the objects in the vicinity, together with their RSSI value. Each block manages the IDs between the blocks and the RSSI values that pass through a Kalman filter before they are included in the package. All information happens dynamically, that is, if a block meets another block, it adds the identification of the second block and the filtered RSSI to the package, when the second disappears, the package undergoes the corresponding change.

Thus, the processing shifts, Figure 2, are to be done in the graphical environment itself and not in each block. In this case, the UWP application must be able to collect all the information of the blocks and all that is around them and make conclusions about these data and be able to transmit them to the game engine.

Figure 2. Firmware Flowchart Block

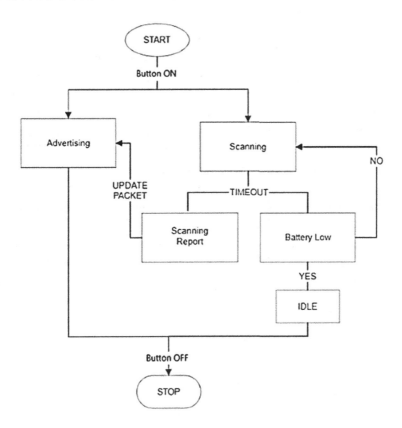

In Figure 2 when the button ON is pressed, the block switches to both the Advertising and Scanning profiles. At the end of the Scan time, the Chip/SoC reports the data to a variable that contains the information of the other blocks found, if applicable. The instant the data reported by the scan is received, the information is organized to allow it to be included in the advertisement package. The block is switched off when the button is pressed again. Thus, the operation of the blocks is almost independent of the rest of the application so it can create different ways of reading the information transmitted by them.

RSSI Values at Different Distances

In order to automate the system to the maximum and achieve the best possible performance, a test was carried out in which devices separated by distance intervals were placed at different signal strengths. The BLE Chip/SoC allows you to change the TX transmission power, which in turn can result in a reduction of energy consumption.

It is therefore important to establish a comparison between the power of the TX signal and the different positions. Initially, the test was carried out with nRF52840 - dongle. 100 samples of the RSSI were extracted at different transmission powers for eight positions approximately 10 cm apart. The readings include the Kalman filter. Between 40 and 60 cm there is a signal distortion, and it can be seen that RSSI values overlap. On the other hand, if the block undergoes a rotation, the RSSI's behaviour also changes. We can see that the values at different emission intensities have almost the same behaviour, so choosing a lower intensity allows a lower energy consumption taking into account the variation of the RSSI values at given distances. One of the characteristics that is also important to mention is that along an axis and at different distances, if the block undergoes rotation there is a discrepancy in the values read. This becomes relevant when the block is positioned in different ways. Since it will display a sticker with the object's representation, it is important to know if a rotation in the block position influences the RSSI values.

Tests were carried out on the RSSIs values from some blocks to others. The values differ between blocks and, therefore, the readings present some differences. The values between the blocks with identification 1, 2 and 3 were measured. The Kalman filter was adjusted to obtain a better performance. For each position, 100 samples of the measured RSSI values were taken. The values measured between blocks 1 and 2 are different from those measured between 2 and 1.

In general, the Kalman filter greatly attenuates the error associated with the RSSI values but depending on the blocks (in this case different Chip/SoCs), even after filtering, there are quite relevant differences between the values. It will be necessary to infer about the value after filtering and the theoretical value, being able to affirm that at the beginning a triangulation by geometric shape will have errors too large to be considered in anyway an accurate measurement.

Therefore, inference of the positions of blocks will have to be determined by an application which will allow to obtain satisfactory results and thus will reduce to maximum propagated errors of real positions.

The relationship between the different RSSI values shows that it is possible to infer at least two things: whether a block is near or far from another. In this sense, the approach contemplates a solution whereby, after reading the values by any device that is able to read the information of the blocks and worked on these data, it reports the state of the blocks to the game engine so that it subsequently reacts accordingly. For this, the API was developed in UWP, not only to allow access to Bluetooth® in the Windows operating system, but also to allow visualization of the data in a graphical environment to be later integrated in the Unity platform.

Following a Graph Theory model, in which the relationships between objects of a given set are described, each block represents a vertex (node) and an RSSI value between nodes represents an edge with a weight that is the RSSI's own value. The data can be visualized in a simple way by representing an adjacency matrix.

When the application is started, Figure 3, it checks whether the Bluetooth® module on the device is running, whether it is compatible with Bluetooth® Low Energy or if any other error has occurred. After successful confirmation from the BLE module, the application goes into scanning mode and, in parallel, starts a timer to communicate the status of the devices to the game platform. The scanner reads the information transmitted by the devices, these readings being almost random in the sense that it does not have a predetermined time (a block can be read 4 times in one second and 9 times in the other). This allows the scanner of the devices to work in parallel with the gaming platform so any changes to the way the data is organized, and the information read does not influence the way the scanner works. On the other hand, you can configure the time when the platform accesses the device information and the time for a block to be considered off. In the game platform it is only necessary to create a function to register the event.

After performing tests of the hardware components, it was realized that it would be extremely difficult to build a neuronal network that contemplated all possible variations to determine the distances between blocks with the smallest possible error because, due to the characteristics of the devices, all classifications would depend on the number and the position of the blocks. For example, for a set of 10 blocks with a 10-position matrix, the neuronal network would have to be classified with several different values, since the RSSI value between block 1 and block 2 differs from block 2 and block 1, Figure 4.

Although some tests were carried out with a multilabel classifier, the results proved to be inconclusive for the reasons described. From all the previously studied papers on indoor location with neural networks using RSSI values, it was concluded that, although it is possible to obtain better results than other approaches, training with a Bluetooth® Low Energy Chip/SoC gives different results that of from training with another Bluetooth® Low Energy Chip/SoC. In all cases, there is no specific

Figure 3. Application Flowchart

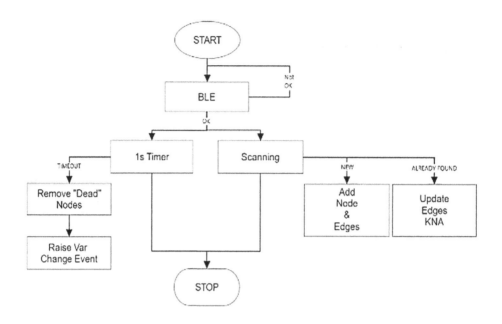

description of this type of detail, so it is not shown to work on any device without having to undergo prior training.

Field Test

The game developed consists of blocks with different representations in the form of stickers with correspondence in the graphic environment. To start playing, simply requires switching the different blocks on or off, which will then appear or disappear in the graphical environment, allowing the player to observe this behaviour and interactions between characters and consequently develop a story from these elements.

Tests were carried out with children from two different age groups, 10 years and 5 years, from two classes with different educators, Figure 5. Although the graphic environment was not completed in order to achieve the expected, since the interactions between the characters occurs in a random way when the blocks are connected and not when there is an approximation between them, it was possible to demonstrate that there is a good reaction on the part of the children. Each child took a block at will and, almost as if taking possession of it, switched them on and off in order to understand what the game provided. Supposedly (this was the intention behind the experimentation) they should have had to switch on the block, place it on the table and move it closer or further away from the others.

Figure 4. RSSI = -10n log10(d) + A; A = -4 dBm; n = 4; (a1) (a2) from block 1 to 2; (b1) (b2) from block 2 to1

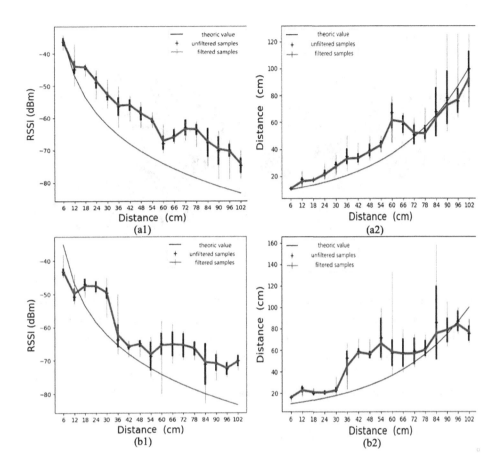

To the 10-year-old children was asked, after handling the game, to write a group story with the theme "Christmas in India" in which the game characters would be included and the 5-year-old children to draw individually, with the same theme, a representation of what they had played. The 5-year-olds understood the intention better, perhaps because the 10-year-olds were already familiar with TOK, and were able, despite not seeing the characters in order to copy them, to draw all the elements included in the game, one of them represented even in its design, the flute notes. One of the problems they mentioned, in both groups, was the time it took the character to disappear when they disconnected the block. Among the 5-year-olds it was a child with special needs, who had a hard time figuring out how to connect the block so he/she needed help at first; however, although he had this kind of difficulties, he/

she realized that the representation of the character in the block was the same that appeared in the graphic environment, which brought visible satisfaction.

Figure 5. Field Experiment

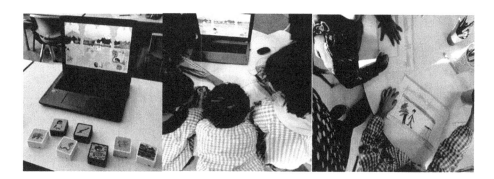

In general, the game was very well accepted by both children and educators. The report in both groups on the way they played and how they observed / interpreted the interactions between the characters was revealing that bonds were created between the children, which, in the long run, may even improve their social behaviours. Note that family and school environments determine children's narrative discourse. One of the children reported family experiences around the characters in the game. According to this, the snake represented a member of the family and, the interaction of the snake with the elephant, led her to say, in a group, that ... she was going to prison for having made the elephant pass out.

CONCLUSION AND FUTURE WORK

Creating interactive solutions using technologies for the development of tangible interfaces is an asset for cognitive development in children of different age groups. The development of the narrative supported by these supports allows children to enhance communication, discourse and the emotional and affective relationship between them. For this project, an attempt was made to create a physical interaction that could be represented graphically in order to engage social and cognitive development. The use of features and details of some existing technologies which allows, with some creativity, to develop applications for which they were not foreseen or which for that purpose have not been developed.

In this project, an attempt was made to create an alternative to a method previously developed, in order to make it flexible and scalable, and simultaneously compatible with the reduced cost for which it is intended. For this, a widely disseminated technology, Bluetooth®, was used, so that it could be applied to a game engine without the need to introduce "adapters" and other types of readers. An experiment was made to adopt a method that could somehow allow a new approach to the educational games industry, namely, to create a triangulation to determine the position of Bluetooth® devices. Although, no results were obtained that would allow to obtain a precise location. This gave way to a more simplified form, in which interaction in a graphic environment is achieved only by the proximity of physical objects, fulfilling the purpose of the study. Due to the characteristics of the new Bluetooth® devices, some difficulties were found in the integration between the operating systems, namely Windows 10, and the Unity game engine. The use of a system such as the Universal Windows Platform is very reductive in the sense that one does not understand why one has to use a single platform and different from other systems to access the peripherals of a computer, such as Bluetooth®. Since Unity allows to create games for different operating systems, we would expect that there would be no difficulties to use a game engine for Windows 10. On the other hand, the characteristics of RSSI of Bluetooth® Low Energy do not allow the location of devices in a small space, although it is possible to infer about the relative proximity between two devices. This raises some doubts in studies on indoor location even when other types of distances are involved and other types of sensors may be associated, such as accelerometers and gyroscopes, which for this case were not considered due to the associated cost. Some other methods, beside Kalman filtering, should be tested, namely MARS, CMARS and/or RCMARS, to improve the readings of Bluetooth® RSSI values.

The prototype met some limitations; therefore, some limitations were found in the way the block casing was built, namely in the way the on and off button was developed. The children experienced some difficulties in the connection phase of the blocks. This was evident by the child with special needs during the field test performed. In developing the prototype on a 3D printer, it was possible to quickly create a working prototype. Due to the size of the battery, the prototype was slightly larger than what was expected, compared to the blocks of the previous TOK project.

Considering future developments, there are some improvements and modifications that can be made to the blocks, namely in the way they connect and disconnect. One of the proposals would be the integration of a capacitive sensor that would allow to connect the block through touch. Regarding the size of the block, it could be improved by choosing a battery of different capacity, which in turn changes to a different size. From these first tests it was possible to prove the functioning of this prototype, even if the graphic environment is not prepared for these blocks. In this sense, it would be necessary to adapt the game for the use of these blocks and to elaborate the exploratory tests again to draw conclusions. The same is true with the number of characters, that is, the number of blocks should be greater because one of the children's remarks was exactly the reduced number of characters in relation to the other game, TOK.

Moreover, conclusive results on the use of neural networks for the location of the blocks were not obtained, the prototype allows to compare a group of a certain age to another group of players with another age. By recording the proximity between the blocks and the relationships in which children use them, one can, in some way, create relationships between groups of children with and without special needs, for example. This method can help to understand the level of narrative development between classes with identical or diversified characteristics and even among children of different ages. As indicated in the Introduction sections and in connection with the Cyber-physical Systems the presented solution will consider an IoT approach recording all users' actions in a cloud environment allowing further studies on user interaction.

REFERENCES

Altini, M., Brunelli, D., Farella, E., & Benini, L. (2010). Bluetooth indoor localization with multiple neural networks. *Wireless Pervasive Computing (ISWPC), 2010 5th IEEE International Symposium on*, 295–300. 10.1109/ISWPC.2010.5483748

Anastasi, G., Bandelloni, R., Conti, M., Delmastro, F., Gregori, E., & Mainetto, G. (2003). Experimenting an indoor Bluetooth-based positioning service. *Proceedings of the 23rd International Conference on Distributed Computing Systems Workshops*, 480–483.

Bahl, P., & Padmanabhan, V. N. (2000). RADAR: An In-Building RF-Based User Location and Tracking System. Proceedings of IEEE Infocom 2000, 775–784.

Barfurth, M. A. (1995). Understanding the Collaborative learning process in a technology rich environment: The case of children's disagreements. *Proc CSCL 1995*. 10.3115/222020.222042

Bargh, M., & Groote, R. (2008). Indoor localization based on response rate of bluetooth inquiries. *Proceedings of the first ACM international workshop on Mobile entity localization and tracking in GPS-less environments.*

Bluetooth® SIG. (2019). *Bluetooth® 5 Core Specification*. https://www.bluetooth.com/specifications/bluetooth-core-specification

Bruno, R., & Delmastro, F. (2003). *Design and analysis of a Bluetooth-based indoor localization system*. Personal Wireless Communications. doi:10.1007/978-3-540-39867-7_66

Cannavò, A., Cermelli, F., Chiaramida, V., Ciccone, G., Lamberti, F., Montuschi, P., & Paravati, G. (2017). T4T: Tangible interface for tuning 3D object manipulation tools. *2017 IEEE Symposium on 3D User Interfaces, 3DUI 2017 - Proceedings*, 266–267. 10.1109/3DUI.2017.7893374

Cassell, J. (2004). Towards a model of technology and literacy development: Story listening systems. *Journal of Applied Developmental Psychology, 25*(1), 75–105. doi:10.1016/j.appdev.2003.11.003

Cassell, J., & Ryokai, K. (2001). Making space for voice: Technologies to support children's fantasy and storytelling. *Personal and Ubiquitous Computing, 5*(3), 169–190. doi:10.1007/PL00000018

Christie, J., & Johnson, E. (1983). The role of play in social-intellectual development. *Review of Educational Research, 53*, 93-115.

Cottam, M., & Wray, K. (2009). Sketching tangible interfaces: Creating an electronic palette for the design community. *IEEE Computer Graphics and Applications, 29*(3), 90–95. doi:10.1109/MCG.2009.51 PMID:19642619

Fein, G. (1987). Pretend play: Creativity and consciousness. In P. Gorlitz & J. Wohlwill (Eds.), *Curiosity, imagination, and play* (pp. 281–304). Lawrence Erlbaum Associates, Inc.

Garber, L. (2012). Tangible user interfaces: Technology you can touch. *Computer, 45*(6), 15–18. doi:10.1109/MC.2012.218

Goncu, A. (1993). Development of intersubjectivity in the dyadic play of preschoolers. *Early Childhood Research Quarterly, 8*(1), 99–116. doi:10.1016/S0885-2006(05)80100-0

Grewal, M. S., & Andrews, A. P. (2010). Applications of Kalman filtering in aerospace 1960 to the present [historical perspectives]. *IEEE Control Systems Magazine, 30*(3), 69–78. doi:10.1109/MCS.2010.936465

Guerrero, G., Ayala, A., Mateu, J., Casades, L., & Alamán, X. (2016). Integrating Virtual Worlds with Tangible User Interfaces for Teaching Mathematics: A Pilot Study. *Sensors (Basel), 16*(11), 1775. doi:10.339016111775 PMID:27792132

Hallberg, J., Nilsson, M., & Synnes, K. (2003). Positioning with Bluetooth. *Proceedings of the 10th International Conference on Telecommunications*, 2(23), 954–958.

Huang, A. (2005). *The use of Bluetooth in Linux and location aware computing*. Master of Science dissertation.

Hutton, J. S., Phelan, K., Horowitz-Kraus, T., Dudley, J., Altaye, M., DeWitt, T., & Holland, S. K. (2017). Story time turbocharger? Child engagement during shared reading and cerebellar activation and connectivity in preschool-age children listening to stories. *PLoS One*, *12*(5), 1–20. doi:10.1371/journal.pone.0177398 PMID:28562619

Jevring, M., Groote, R., & Hesselman, C. (2008). Dynamic optimization of Bluetooth networks for indoor localization. *First International Workshop on Automated and Autonomous Sensor Networks*. 10.1145/1456223.1456357

Kumar, P., Reddy, L., & Varma, S. (2009). Distance measurement and error estimation scheme for RSSI based localization in Wireless Sensor Networks. *Wireless Communication and Sensor Networks (WCSN), 2009 Fifth IEEE Conference on*, 1–4. 10.1109/WCSN.2009.5434802

Ladd, A. M., Bekris, K. E., Rudys, A., Kavraki, L. E., & Wallach, D. S. (2005). Robotics-based location sensing using wireless ethernet. *Wireless Networks*, *11*(1-2), 189–204. doi:10.100711276-004-4755-8

Liebennan, J. N. (1977). *Playfulness: Its relationship to imagination and creativity*. Academic.

Liu, H., Darabi, H., Banerjee, P., & Liu, J. (2007). Survey of wireless indoor positioning techniques and systems. *IEEE Transactions on Systems, Man and Cybernetics. Part C, Applications and Reviews*, *37*(6), 1067–1080. doi:10.1109/TSMCC.2007.905750

Lopes, H., Carvalho, V., & Sylla, C. (2021). Mobeybou-Tangible Interfaces for Cognitive Development. *International Conference on Innovation in Engineering*.

Marshall, P. (2007). Do tangible interfaces enhance learning? *Proceedings of TEI'07*, 163–170. 10.1145/1226969.1227004

Meltz, B. F. (1999). Pretend play enriches development. *Boston Globe*, p. C1.

Morais, J. (1994). *L'Art de Lire*. Odile Jacob.

O'Malley, C. (1992). Designing Computer Systems to support peer learning. *European Journal of Psychology of Education*, *7*(4), 339–352. doi:10.1007/BF03172898

Palaigeorgiou, G., Karakostas, A., & Skenderidou, K. (2017). Finger Trips: Learning Geography through Tangible Finger Trips into 3D Augmented Maps. *Proceedings - IEEE 17th International Conference on Advanced Learning Technologies, ICALT 2017*, 170–172. 10.1109/ICALT.2017.118

Pandya, D., Jain, R., & Lupu, E. (2003). Indoor location estimation using multiple wireless technologies. *14th IEEE Proceedings on Personal, Indoor and Mobile Radio Communications, 3*, 2208–2212.

Peterson, C., & McCabe, A. (1983). *Developmental psycholinguistics: three ways of looking at a child's narrative*. Plenum. doi:10.1007/978-1-4757-0608-6

Raghavan, A. N., Ananthapadmanaban, H., Sivamurugan, M. S., & Ravindran, B. (2010). Accurate mobile robot localization in indoor environments using Bluetooth®. *Proceedings - IEEE International Conference on Robotics and Automation*, 4391–4396. 10.1109/ROBOT.2010.5509232

Rogoff, T. (1990). *Apprenticeship in Thinking: Cognitive development in social context*. Oxford University Press.

Russ, S. (1993). *Affect and creativity: The role of affect and play in the creative process*. Lawrence Erlbaum Associates, Inc.

Russ, S. (1996). Development of creative processes in children. In M. Runco (Ed.), Creativity from childhood through adulthood: The developmental issues (vol. 72, pp. 3 1-42). San Francisco: Jossey-Bass. doi:10.1002/cd.23219967204

Simon, H., & Robert, H. (2009). Bluetooth Tracking without Discoverability. *LoCA 2009: The 4th International Symposium on Location and Context Awareness*.

Singer, D. L., & Singer, J. (1990). *The house of make-believe*. Harvard University Press.

Singer, J. L., & Singer, D. L. (1981). *Television, imagination, and aggression*. Lawrence Erlbaum Associates, Inc.

Sylla, C., Pereira, I. S. P., Coutinho, C. P., & Branco, P. (2016). Digital Manipulatives as Scaffolds for Preschoolers 2019; Language Development. *IEEE Transactions on Emerging Topics in Computing, 4*(3), 439–449. doi:10.1109/TETC.2015.2500099

Topping, K. (1992). Cooperative learning and peer tutoring: An overview. *The Psychologist, 5*(4), 151–157.

Wood, D., & O'Malley, C. (1996). Collaborative learning between peers: An overview. *Educational Psychology in Practice, 11*(4), 4–9. doi:10.1080/0266736960110402

Xiao, J., Wu, K., Yi, Y., Wang, L., & Ni, L. M. (2013). Pilot: Passive device free indoor localization using channel state information. *Distributed computing systems (ICDCS), 2013 IEEE 33rd international conference on*, 236–245. 10.1109/ICDCS.2013.49

Yang, Z., Zhou, Z., & Liu, Y. (2013). From RSSI to CSI: Indoor localization via channel response. *ACM Computing Surveys*, *46*(2), 25. doi:10.1145/2543581.2543592

Yilmaz, R. M., Kucuk, S., & Goktas, Y. (2017). Are augmented reality picture books magic or real for preschool children aged five to six? *British Journal of Educational Technology*, *48*(3), 824–841. doi:10.1111/bjet.12452

Zafari, F., Gkelias, A., & Leung, K. K. (2019). A Survey of Indoor Localization Systems and Technologies. *IEEE Communications Surveys and Tutorials*, *21*(3), 2568–2599. doi:10.1109/COMST.2019.2911558

Chapter 4
Graphical–Based Authentication System and Its Applications

Priti Golar
Department of Computer Science & Engineering, Amity University, Raipur, India

Brijesh Khandelwal
Department of Computer Science & Engineering, Amity University, Raipur, India

ABSTRACT

Authentication systems are the protective barrier of any software. They make sure that the right people enter the system and access the right information. As per available literature, there are basically three authentication techniques. This research study is based on the knowledge-based authentication, since it is the most widely accepted technique for securing resources from unauthorized access. As an initial step, the existing knowledge-based authentication system has been studied for its highlights, comparative facts, advantages, and disadvantages. For acceptance of any secure system, the usability aspect is the first step in the authentication process. The various usability evaluation parameters of the existing systems and an approach towards developing a modified usable authentication system have been briefly discussed. An initial lab study for the proposed system was conducted to analyze the comparative results. The future scope of other dimensions, namely randomness and security, as well as a thorough investigation, has been highlighted as the research work's concluding remark.

DOI: 10.4018/978-1-7998-6721-0.ch004

INTRODUCTION

Authentication is the first step in securing data. A critical objective of the authentication scheme is to assist users in creating stronger passwords. A graphical password is a type of authentication that requires the user to choose from a set of images displayed in a graphical user interface in a specific order. Graphical passwords are more secure than text-based passwords because many people use familiar terms to memorize the passwords of text-based. A lexi conquest always returns a password, allowing a hacker to quickly gain access to a device. However, if successive screen pages contain a set of selectable images, and if each page contains numerous images, a hacker attempts any probable combination at random.

Authentication is the process of information security. As shown in Figure 1, authentication methods can be classified into three main categories.

Figure 1. Authentication Methods

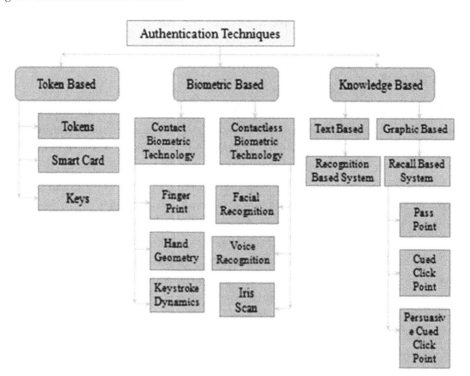

The details of the above figure can be understood by the following-

1.   Token-based-systems—Token-based systems are usually used for key cards and smart cards. Numerous token-based systems incorporate knowledge-based security techniques as well. For instance, the PIN for DEBIT/CREDIT cards. It is based on a possession that you possess (Patra et al., 2016).

2.   Biometric based - Fingerprints, iris scans etc., biometric-based authentication methods have yet to achieve worldwide adoption. The primary disadvantage of this approach is the high cost of such systems, as well as the slow and frequently unreliable identification process (Patra et al., 2016). The process of establishing a user's identity by physical or behavioral characteristics is recognized as biometric authentication. It is based on a short story called Something You Are. It uses physiological or behavioral features such as fingerprint or facial scans, iris or voice recognition to authenticate individuals.

3.   Knowledge based-The most critical authentication techniques are knowledge-based ones, which include both text-based and image-based passwords. KBA is a form of authentication that requires the user to answer at least one "secret" question. Knowledge-based authentication is the most common method of authentication, which includes both text-based and image-based passwords. KBA is based on a piece of information that the user has. Alphanumeric and Graphical Password are the two types of knowledge-based authentication. The primary disadvantage of Token-Based and Biometric-Based Authentication is their high cost and requirement of specialized hardware. Graphical-based password techniques have been proposed as a possible alternative to text-based password techniques, based in part on the fact that humans recall images better than text.

Recognition-based graphical systems and recall-based graphical systems are two types of picture-based techniques(Biddle et al., 2012). In recognition-based techniques, a user is given a selection of images to choose from, and then the images are recognized and identified during the registration process. Passfaces, for example, is a graphical password scheme based on human face recognition. Users are given a broad selection of photos to choose from when creating a password. Users must identify the pre-selected image from many images provided to them in order to log in (Boonkrong, 2019).

A user can reproduce something he or she created or selected earlier during the registration process using recall-based techniques. For example, in the Passpoint system, a user can click any point in an image to generate the password and a tolerance around each pixel is determined.To login, the user must select the points inside the tolerance in the correct order during authentication (Biddle et al., 2012).

The fact that the humans can remember pictures better than text, has triggered the invention of graphical password schemes.

Comparison of Different Password Authentication Systems

Comparative study of password authentications systems with respect to various parameters such as Security, Cost, Usability and User Friendly as shown in Table 1.

Table 1. Comparative Analysis

Password Authentication System	Cost	Security	User Friendly	Usability
Token Based	Less	Less	Yes	Easy
Biometric-Based	High	High	No	Complex
Knowledge Based	Less	Very High	Yes	Easy

The four parameters seem to be best for Knowledge Based as compared to the others. Hence Knowledge based password authentication systems are more preferred as compared to the other two authentication systems.

Organization of the Various Sections

Following a brief introduction, it becomes necessary to organize the various sections of this research study in order to justify the chapter's flow.

The following section summarizes a brief review of the available literature on existing 2D systems. This section is further divided into two sub sections, the first of which discusses the advantages and disadvantages of existing knowledge-based authentication systems. The findings can be summarized in order to complete the Research Methodology section of this study. The subsequent section discusses real-time applications that can be used to design the proposed system.

The Research Methodology section discusses the objectives, problem statement, mapping challenges, and a justification for the sample size and variation included in the proposed system. Additionally, this section discusses the scope of this research study in terms of its approach to usability. Any system's success is contingent upon the users' adaptability and satisfaction. Thus, the various dimensions of the proposed system's usability parameters are identified.

The flow of information within various modules of the usability parameter is detailed in section of proposed systems. Each module is thoroughly described in terms of flow charts that can aid in the proposed system's successful implementation.

The proposed system is evaluated in terms of the initial laboratory study, which serves as a model for the actual web-based application. The samples collected in this initial lab study are analyzed to determine the various dimensions of usability. The proposed system's comparative facts and figures with existing systems aims to provide a superior option in the domain of knowledge-based authentication systems.

Finally, the research study's concluding remarks and future scope are discussed. The future scope includes additional features such as randomness and, most importantly, security against various attacks. The authentication system's scalability, image collection storage, and overall system security against various venerable attacks all contribute to the scope of this research study's future development.

LITERATURE REVIEW

This section summarizes the existing literature on knowledge-based authentication systems. The comparative analysis aides in identifying existing flaws that can be used to define the proposed problem statement. These references bolster the case for developing a novel system with a focus on usability. Additionally, this section discusses real-time applications of graphical password authentication systems.

Survey Study of Existing Knowledge-Based Authentication Systems

Patra K, Nemade B, and Mishra P (2016) include persuasion on Cued Click Point, a technique that makes use of circular tolerance. CCP with circular tolerance is found to be superior to CCP with rectangular tolerance. The display of the second image is dependent on the display of the first image, which adds to the login time due to CCP. Usability and security parameters are evaluated and implemented. The research also provides a comprehensive analysis of the Persuasive Cued Click Points Graphical Passwords scheme. The image is divided into rectangular grids using CCP, which explains why the radius of tolerance area, r, is not evenly distributed. If the image is divided into circular grids, however, r is evenly distributed, and this small error is avoided (Patra et al., 2016).

According to Boonkrong (2019), grid-based systems (Grid Cell-30,60,90,120,150&180). The user must select eight cells. Each cell is randomly assigned a number between 0 and 9 and The grid's size can be adjusted to meet specific requirements, and there is some debate over grid size and memorability. It performs a security analysis on such a system. The way users specify cell positions in various grid sizes has an influence on the system's overall security (Boonkrong, 2019).

The Jumbled PassSteps method was proposed by Jerome P. and Ariel M. (2019). Even if attackers observe the log-in session, attackers are unable to easily guess the user's original pass-image by transforming the PassMatrix method's single discretized image into many separate images and using a random grid traversal method. Since the one-time grid traversal steps are acquired via earphones, the attacker cannot decide the path or number of traversals performed during a specific session, even though the session is camera captured. Experimental findings show that Jumbled PassSteps effectively defeats hotspot guessing attacks and offers superior resistance to shoulder-surfing attacks (Jerome & Ariel, 2019).

Zujevs (2019) contains the array concept is comprised of color, shape, and number, with the password being stored as images. The proposed scheme defends passwords from shoulder surfing, removes the need for external devices, makes passwords easier to remember, and can be enforced on mobile and ATM devices, to name a few advantages. Icons make up the user's graphical password. Any picture, with or without meaning, can be used as a symbol say animal, color, etc., or various unnamed points or lines. Each symbol is distinct and belongs to a single array with a particular feature (animal, color, or digit). This code is in charge of storing passwords in a database and generating graphical password images. In this case, arrays have the properties "color," "number," and "geometric shapes."

Figure 2. A single picture with just a single combination

Each array's combination is one symbol that is shown as a single image, as shown in Figure 2. It is made up of the number one, the form square, and the color blue. Each picture must have at least one combination.

Figure 3. Three different combinations in one image

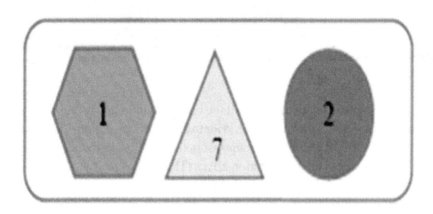

Figure 3 illustrates an image of three different combinations: numbers 1, 7, 2, hexagonal, triangle, and circle forms, and colors green, yellow, and blue. During the authentication method, only one form of image can be used – no mixing of images is permitted (Figure 2 and Figure 3). The dictionary refers to the set of arrays. The dictionary, for example, includes color, shape, and number arrays (Zujevs, 2019).

Nida and Quasim (2019) focused mainly on four stages of Picture Selection, Picture Division, Pattern Generation and Grid Shuffling as shown in Figure 4. In authentication, the image will be displayed to the user with same grids, but in shuffled form shown in Figure 5. By introducing the idea of shuffling of pictures into an image, there is a reduction in shoulder surfing attack (Nida & Quasim, 2019).

Charles, Zhen Yu, Hesanmi Olade, Hai-Ning Liang (2016). In a 3D virtual world, users are encouraged to interact with 3D objects.Only cubes are used as 3D objects, and each one is simply labelled with a letter.

It's important to keep track of the order in which the cubes are touched (Zhen & Hesanmi, 2016).

Thorpe and MacRae (2014) includes an image presentation style that draws a curtain around the image, and memorability is high due to only one password reset occurring. The Presentation Effect is straightforward and palatable. The "presentation

Figure 4. Picture selection and Grid no. selection

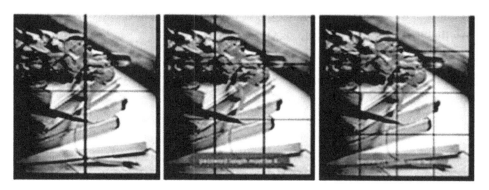

effect" in this interface refers to how well the background image is presented to the user during the password creation phase.Prior to password formation, a comparative user study was conducted with two groups using the same background image in two different ways to assess the presentation effect (Thorpe & MacRae, 2014).

S. Chiasson et al. (2012) had conducted a cohesive evaluation of the PCCP Graphical Passwords schemes, which includes the evaluation and implementation of usability and security parameters. A password authentication scheme can encourage users to use strong passwords that are also easy to remember. Authentication schemes in this framework offer users a choice while encouraging them to use stronger passwords. Furthermore, choosing weak passwords (which are easily guessed by attackers) becomes more time consuming, preventing users from doing so.In essence, this method forces you to choose a safer password since it is the path of least resistance. It's better to follow the system's instructions for a safe password—a function that most schemes lack—rather than adding to the user's burden. As a result of this approach, the world's first persuading click-based graphical password system was developed (Chiasson et al., 2012).

Saeed and Sarosh Umar (2015) proposed a novel graphical authentication system that combines both recognition-based and dynamic graphics. This new study established the new scheme's robustness, security, and usability. The scheme focuses on shoulder surfing resistance without compromising usability, as well as guessing attack resistance. The proposed work employs a novel dynamic graphics concept in which colored objects are linked to individual password portfolio images and their colors change rapidly on the screen (Biddle et al., 2012).

R. Biddle et al. (2012) emphasized novel characteristics of existing approaches. The research study addresses issues like usability and stability, as well as device evaluation. The research study starts by listing current methods, highlighting novel features of selected schemes, and highlighting key usability and security benefits.

Figure 5. Shuffled picture

It goes through the criteria for usability in knowledge-based authentication as they relate to graphical passwords. Determine the security risks that these systems would counter, as well as previous attacks. It goes through the methodological problems surrounding empirical evaluation and points out areas where more study and better methods are required (Saeed & SaroshUmar, 2015).

Andrea B, Ian O, and Hyoungshick K. (2016) examined PassBYOP's usability, security, and reliability in three feasibility studies. The study shows the feasibility of image-based passwords and suggests acceptable device thresholds—password items should have a minimum of seven features, with 40% of them having to geometrically match originals stored on an authentication server to be considered equivalent. Task completion times and error rates are 7.5 seconds and 9%, respectively, according to the usability report. These figures are in line with previous graphical password schemes that relied on static digital images. The security study highlights PassBYOP's resistance to observation attacks: three attackers were unable to compromise a password through shoulder surfing, camera-based observation, or malware (Andrea et al., 2016).

A. Bellam (2013), research study aims to persuade users to use more safe passwords. When using click-based graphical passwords, this paper explores how to convince users to select more random and difficult-to-guess passwords. The process of click points is used on five images in this paper to improve protection. It also allows users to use less predictable passwords, thus assisting them in choosing more stable passwords (Bellam, 2013).

Khalifa H. and colleagues (2013) proposed and evaluated Edge Pass, a novel algorithm for extracting the edges of pass images for use in graphical systems. The results of the experiments show that the proposed system is more reliable. This proposed scheme will serve as the foundation for our graphical password system's growth. Edge detection, image fusion, and component extraction with a high spatial frequency are all part of the device framework. The aim of the proposed algorithm is to figure out if the process pixel I(x,y) is dark or light. If the target pixel I(x,y) is bright, it represents an edge; if it is dark, it represents a background. The findings of the experiment proved the effectiveness of the proposed procedure (Khalifa & Siong, 2013).

Radha A. (2013) discusses a technique for increasing the security level through persuasion using dynamic user blocks. The user is persuaded to construct a more stable password by this system. The PCCP approach, which uses dynamic user blocks, makes it easier to change the protection level in response to the user's needs. Although the proposed system assists the user in selecting click points, it also allows the user to choose the level of protection they desire. Audio support can also be given to help the user remember the password. As a result, the device persuades the user to construct a more random click-based graphical password, which hackers would find more difficult to guess (Radha, 2013).

Kumar Sarohi H and Ullah Khan F (2013) discussed a variety of usability and security issues. Authentication tends to be slower than with a text-based method, according to their findings. The recall parameter, on the other hand, is advantageous, and attacks like dictionary and brute force attacks can be mitigated with a graphical-based authentication scheme. The current state of graphical authentication systems is examined in detail in this article. They've classified these techniques into three different categories: Recognition-based, pure recall-based, and cued recall-based recall schemes are the three forms of recall schemes. Include their protection and usability issues, since these two aspects decide the efficacy of a picture password (KumarSarohi & UllahKhan, 2013).

S. Ansari, J. Rokade, I. Khan, and A. Shaikh (2018) proposed a Cued Click Points and Multiple Image Persuasion in a Graphical Password Scheme. Persuasion is used in the proposed framework to give users some control while allowing them to use better, less insecure passwords. The proposed framework makes the job of choosing less safe (and thus hackable) passwords more tedious, preventing users from doing so. In fact, this method relieves clients of the pressure of choosing a more reliable secret key, as well as making it easier to follow the framework's guidelines for a safe password—a function that many systems lack. Traditional authentication methods such as text-based passwords and other types of traditional authentication are feasible alternatives to CCP (Ansari et al., 2018).

Zhi, S. Qubin, and L. Yong, 2005, emphasized on the zero-knowledge proof principle, a proposed design was included to defeat the shoulder-surfing attack. The image is divided into a number of small areas, each of which is called a locus. As opposed to conventional text-based password authentication, this article takes advantage of the human cognitive capacity of association-based memorization to make authentication more user-friendly. To solve the shoulder-surfing attack problem without adding any additional complexity to the authentication protocol, improve the primary architecture based on the zero-knowledge proof principle. Their recommendations are backed up by research and comparisons of device results (Zhi & Qubin, 2005).

A. Manaf, F. Towhidi (2011), discussed the attacks on textual and graphical passwords according to the CAPEC standard, as well as their effects on both traditional and image passwords. The effects of common knowledge-based authentication attacks on textual and graphical passwords are discussed in this article. The failure of the human memory to remember strong and stable textual passwords, on the other hand, has resulted in a greater focus on the protection of graphical passwords (Towhidi & Manaf, 2011).

S. Alhrbi and H. Alhakami (2020) stressed that memorability is the main barrier to KBA because users try to use basic passwords or combine passwords across different services, which leads to issues and non-compliance with security policies. Furthermore, due to recall-based authentication, the technique of merging username and password is regarded as a significant challenge for KBA. It also provides a comparison of KBA's strategies, as well as decision-making guidelines based on trade-offs. The results of this study will help organizations create recommendations for a KBA technique that is appropriate for them (Alhakami & Alhrbi, 2020).

G. Agrawal, S. Singh (2018)emphasized the aim of usability in authentication systems as assisting users in choosing better passwords, thus increasing protection by extending the effective password space. The research also looks into the protection of knowledge-based graphical passwords and the methods used to create them. The findings of an initial user study are presented in this report, which includes a statistical analysis of information technique (Agrawal & Singh, 2018).

P. Golar (2016) performed the initial lab analysis consists of two sets of photographs: public domain images used in previous research studies and private domain images chosen by users. For the two sets, the success rate, password entry time, and hotspot coverage are determined. Furthermore, the randomness, password space, and password entropy are examined. The first goal is to determine the internal consistency of the two sets of images in terms of the aforementioned factors. Second, these two sets can be compared to the most recent graphical password scheme (s). The comparison results show that there is room for a new graphical password scheme to be created (Golar & Adane, 2016).

Real Time Applications of the Graphical Password Authentication Systems

This section discusses several real-world applications in the field of graphical password authentication.

Real Time Applications Used by- FASTag

To meet the electronic tolling needs of the Indian sector, the National Payments Corporation of India (NPCI) developed the National Electronic Toll Collection (NETC) programme. It provides a statewide toll payment solution that is interoperable. FASTag is a toll-paying system that uses radio frequency identification (RFID) technology to enable drivers to pay tolls while on the road.

FASTag (RFID Tag) is attached to the vehicle's windscreen and enables customers to pay tolls directly from the account associated with FASTag. Since the consumer is not expected to wait at a toll plaza, FASTag blends the ease of cashless payment with additional benefits such as fuel and time savings.

Real time applications developed by Confident Technologies

- Confident Technologies, headquartered in San Diego, California, United States. A specialises in online account, identity, and transaction verification and strong authentication protection solutions. For the business, ecommerce, financial, healthcare, social networks, and online gaming, their security solutions protect confidential information and transactions.
- Confident Technologies offers enterprise-level verification and strong authentication protection solutions that protect confidential data and transactions.
- Confident Technologies provides image-based authentication solutions for websites and mobile applications.

Some of the product developed by Confident Technologies are-

- Confident ImageShield is a medium for image-based authentication. Users look for images that fit into the categories they've selected previously. Confident ImageShield can be easily integrated into websites, web apps, and other security solutions by organisations and developers.
- Confident Captcha- With Confident CAPTCHA, users can protect your site while still improving the user experience. Confident CAPTCHA is an image-based human verification technology that protects the users while preventing bot traffic.
- Confident Multifactor Authentication - Confident Multi-Factor Authentication creates one-time passwords by asking users to complete an image-based challenge on their phone. Multi-Factor Authentication (MFA) is a secure, out-of-band (OOB) authentication mechanism for you and an easy-to-use extra layer of protection for your users.

Real Time Applications Developed by PixelPin's

PixelPins Headquarters and Location are in London, England and United Kingdom. PixelPin's mission is to safely remove the need for passwords log in and become the authentication solution of choice for all businesses and users around the world. PixelPin offers a one-of-a-kind solution that allows customers to use creative picture-based authentication to log into any website or mobile app with ease. PixelPin replaces passwords with pictures to make logging into any mobile app or web application easier, more personal, and more secure.

By selecting four points in a series, users will create an infinite number of variations, making ones customer's account safer than it has ever been. Customer uploads a favorite picture, selects four secret points, and creates a secret log in a simple story.

RESEARCH METHODOLOGY

This section begins with an analysis of existing systems, followed by objective and problem statements, a map of the challenges, and justification for sample size and image set selection. The approach to the usability parameter serves as a guide for both the implementation requirements of the proposed study and the analytical analysis of this research work.

Analysis of the Existing Systems

The following section discusses some of the paper's shortcomings and findings in order to develop a novel authentication system.

Since the login time is greater than the maximum available authentication system, the usability parameter can be effected. To address this issue, the proposed system can be designed in such a way that it takes less time to log in than these systems. This can be accomplished by providing a proper orientation and user manual to the proposed authentication system's end users.

Existing systems store passwords in the database as image sequences, which consumes a large amount of memory. The proposed system can be thought of as storing the password in the form of a coordinate system that can be accessed quickly.

The existing systems do not provide adequate support for user satisfaction analysis. In terms of user satisfaction, the proposed system can collect data from both homogeneous and heterogeneous groups of users, thereby providing versatility and flexibility.

The following section discusses how to approach the usability aspect of developing a superior authentication system in terms of various usability evaluation parameters.

Objectives

The above advantages and disadvantages of current structures contribute to a detailed analysis of the following objectives:

1.   Create a novel authentication method based on the key phases.
2.   To create the evaluation criteria for the usability aspect.
3.   To design the various modules for the implementation of a web-based application.
4.   To conduct an initial lab study for the analytical study as to identify the comparative facts and figures.
5.   Analyzed the proposed work using various metrics related to usability.

Problem Statement

"The major goal of this research work is to create an innovative Graphical Based Authentication System and to study its Usability aspect to extend the adaptability of the system".

Mapping of Challenges

Following are the identified challenges for the development of the proposed system.

1.   Implementing and testing the proposed authentication system.
2.   To provide training to the end users.(Sample)
3.   To analyze Short term and long-term success rate.
4.   To increase the performance of Usability Parameters.
5.   Adaptability of the system.

Rationale for Sample Size and Image Sets

A homogeneous group of 50 undergraduate students was chosen for the analytical study. Prior to conducting the initial lab study, these selected students received adequate training and awareness of the system. The proposed system includes two variants based on the Public image set and the Private image set. The public set is the system's predefined set, whereas the private set allows the user to enter their own image set. The public image collection contains the majority of the images used in previous studies of the existing system. The Public set is limited to 20 images, which are provided by the system. The Private set of images was limited to 25 images depicting various events, campus infrastructure with multiple objects, and so on. In this variation mode, users are given the option of entering and storing their preferred images. The variation between these two modes reflects the unbiased selection of images from the Public set, which is unrelated to the students. The private set of images prejudges the selection of an image set for password protection, as students are already familiar with some or all of the images and are in the habit of recalling them easily.

Approach Towards Usability Parameter

On the basis of the available research papers and their detailed analysis, the prominent approach toward usability can be proposed for the study of problem definition. The various usability parameters can be combined to create an entirely new graphical password system. The usability parameter, as it defines the system's acceptance by end users in a variety of domains and complex environments, requires in-depth analysis. The various dimensions in which the usability parameter can be evaluated are mentioned in Table 2.

Table 2. Details of Usability Evaluation Parameters

Usability Evaluation Parameter	Description
Authentication Process	Defines the complete Authentication Process along with recognizing a user's identity. The credential often takes the form of a password, which is a secret and known only to the individual and the system.
Image Selection	Appearance and Presentation of an image. What type of an image should provide to the users like black and white or colorful image.
Login Time	Calculated from start to end process of Authentication. Password entry time report is for total time taken to complete a phase from the time the first image was displayed to the time that they pressed the login button which included time spent thinking about their password.
Memorability	Indicates that how much time is required to recall the password.
Success Rate	Success rate is the ratio of the number of successful trails to a number of trials. Success Rate can be calculated on short term and long term basis.
Users	Homogeneous or Heterogeneous group of people
User Satisfaction	Can be conducted through Questionnaire
Storage	Password stores in the form of images or coordinates.
External Devices	For compatibility of the system.

The existing and the requirement towards building a novel graphical knowledge-based system is discuss below.

1. **Authentication Process:** Authentication process is based on displaying the sequence of images. In some authentication process images are present in the Grid Cells. Image present in the form of array. So, in proposed system images can be displayed randomly.

2. **Image Selection:** According to the existing theories the user selects the most likely images depending on the favorite or peripheral events. The existing systems reflects combining several images in one picture or one click per image. One or more clicks on multiple images with multiple objects may be compared to the proposed scheme.

3. **Login Time:** It is one of the concern areas where the user can enter the secure system in a minimum login time. Since various images and the correct location of the password can require more login time. The proposed system should design in such a way that it requires less login time and should have an easy authentication process. The proposed system can contain a 2-tier/ 3-tier authentication process as to provide a more secure environment.

4. **Memorability:** Provided with the predefine set of images, many of the existing systems had used the concept of hotspot, tolerance area and prominent objects as to recall the correct password coordinate or pixels. The proposed system can be in line with the existing system with an addition of multiple object concepts and a circular tolerance area.

5. **Success Rate:** Success rate can be calculated without errors. For simplicity the set of images with more objects can be provided in initial stage. This would help the end user to recall their password which would ultimately increase the success rate. The success rate of the proposed method must be measured on a daily, weekly, and monthly basis.

6. **Users:** In most of the existing systems homogeneous group of people were used. In proposed system heterogeneous group of people can be considered to avoid any kind of prejudice.

7. **User Satisfaction:** After providing the proper training and implementation of the secure system the review from the end users is a necessary step. The threshold values provided in the feedback will define the degree of user satisfaction towards the proposed system. Many of the existing research work had shown the identical approach for finding the user satisfaction towards the respective authentication system.

8. **Password storage in the database:** In most of the existing systems password stored in the form of images. To save memory space in the proposed scheme, passwords may be stored as co-ordinates.

9. **External Devices:** External devices such as scanners, web cameras, and fingerprint readers have been incorporated into existing systems. The primary disadvantage is that these external devices are prone to damage or malfunction, and even the additional cost associated with these devices is a major concern. Thus, the proposed system eliminates the need for any external device other than a choice between code generation and OTP generation.

The initial laboratory study analyzes the login time and success rate for the comparative study. Additionally, a Password space has been included to allow for system adaptability based on security concerns. The remaining parameters related to usability can be expanded for future research.

PROPOSED SYSTEM

What will be the final system configuration in the proposed solution, so that we can split the entire system into different modules? These phases are represented in terms of flowchart for Training Module, Registration Module, Login Module, and Design Module.

Training Module

Provide instruction to users by demonstrating on a sample password during the training process. Create a password and store raw data in the database during training, and then verify the training as shown in Figure 6.

Registration Module

The user should fill out the registration form with demographic details as well as an authenticated Email-Id/Mb. No./ 4 digit secret code. Before capturing the graphical password, the Email-Id/Mb. No./4digit secret code is used for two-way authentication.

The aim of two-way authentication is to improve the system's performance and, as a result, reduce the risk of a security attack. After that, provide images with multiple objects and tolerance. After selecting the first image with the first click, information is stored in the database, and the registration process is finally completed, as shown in Figure 7.

Figure 6. Training Module

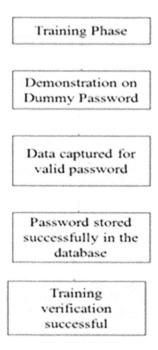

Login Module

During the login process, the user must enter his or her registered user name, as well as the option of creating an OTP or entering his or her four-digit secret code. After that, the user must create a password. After clicking in the correct tolerance area of an image, the user is authenticated. In the case of a password mismatch, the system allows for five trials to match the password before completing the login process, as shown in Figure 8.

Design Module

Design module of proposed system is given in Figure 9. To begin, there are 20 images with multiple objects from which to generate a password. Instead of being shown in order, the images would be displayed at random. The system will allow for a single or multiple click on multiple images.

During the password generation process, the system allows for a shuffled viewport repositioning. The highlighted area is known as the viewport. The user will have the option of selecting several images from the system. Lab study can be conducted on a sample of heterogeneous group of people to avoid any kind of biasness.

Based on the maximum permutation of the graphical password, this can result in a number of image selections. To save memory space, the password is stored as the coordinates of the corresponding image. There are no external devices in the framework that is being proposed.

Figure 7. Registration Module

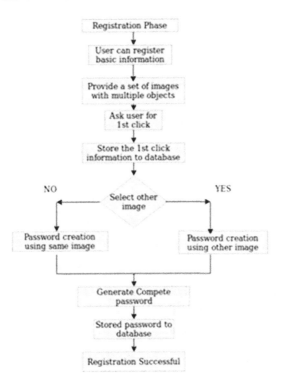

1. Mobile App with touch screen facility: The miniature device can be supposed to be use as to provide the compatibility to this system. This will exclude any possibility of unavailability of device as to operate this system.
2. Web application for resource access authentication. The platform for the implementation can be the Web application for providing the gateway to this system. The web application can also be designed with the security dimension which can provide a safe authentication to access the concern resources.

Figure 8. Login Module

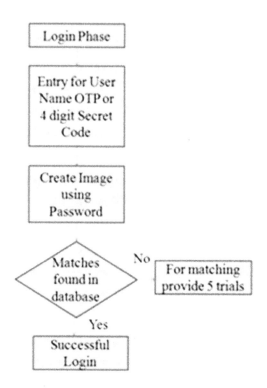

3. Folder Locking: On an individual basis, this system can be used for folder locking in a system. Hence in this case, the confidentiality and authentication can be achieved by this system.

INITIAL LAB STUDY AND COMPARATIVE RESULT ANALYSIS

This section confirms the attempt for end results obtained by conducting an initial lab study. This could be a first step of a pilot survey, where the analytical results can provide a better option in form of the proposed system, as compared to the facts and figures of the existing systems.

Initial Lab Study

The proposed framework is the result of a review of current knowledge-based systems' shortcomings. The foundation for this innovative approach can be planned and tested

Figure 9. Design Module

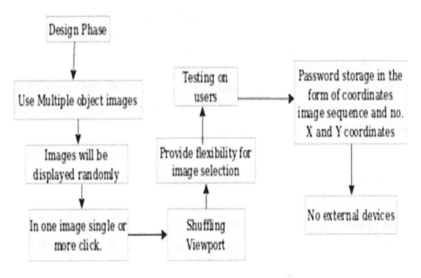

by adding modifications and variations in the constraints defined in these systems. As an initial step, a small pilot study based on 50 under graduate students has been conducted for the adoptability of this system. The training session and weekly/monthly periodic schedule can be studied for the remembrance (memorability) parameter. In view of the registration module, an additional variation in the analytical study includes two sets of images, namely the private set and the public set. The login module should be optimized in such a way that the worst type of attack, such as the shoulder suffering attack, is minimized.

The login process has two tiers, the first of which is two-way authentication, in which the user is asked to send their name and a 4-digit secret code, or generate an OTP to their registered mobile number.

When the match is found in the database, the 2nd tier is carried out. The user is provided with the registered collection of images in order to evaluate the click points stored in the database. The click points in the images chosen by the user are obtained and the coordinates are stored in the database.

The click points in the images are used to generate the password and the generated password is represented as a curve showing the lines joining the chosen click points. When an appropriate match is found, the login phase is marked as successful; otherwise, the user is given three attempts to enter a forgotten password.

During password creation, the user is first registered by entering the name and then can proceed by pressing the shuffle button. The user can select the image that is displayed randomly. Users can click anywhere on the images they want. Figure 10 depicts the user interface of a private domain image.

Users must choose a maximum of five click points on a single image or multiple images in this method. If a user clicks a maximum of five clickable points on multiple images, the security would be high. Users make an unmoving choice, but they are not constrained in their choice. By pressing the save button, the password is generated, which can be seen in a statement box. Thus, the user gets a successful registration for using the created graphical password. In the event of an incorrect password submission, the user is given the opportunity to try again. The user is valid when login is successful.

Figure 10. Design Module

The viewport is placed at random. The viewport and shuffle button appear only during the password creation phase; images are shown normally after that, as shown in Figure 11. The user must choose five click points on a single or multiple images in this case. Users can use the shuffle button to show the image randomly during password creation, and they can click anywhere on the images. It will increase security if a user clicks five clickable points on multiple images.

Figure 11. Password Creation using viewport

Comparative Result Analysis

The various evaluation parameters of the usability aspect have been mentioned in the following 4 tables. The first two parameters are reflected in the implementation of the proposed system and the conduction of the initial lab study. The memorability in terms of time taken to recall the correct image sequence for password along with the last four evaluation parameters can be extended for further study. The three evaluation parameters, viz.- The Password Space, Password Entry Time and Success Rate, represent the facts and figures used to conduct the comparison study and are discussed further down.

Success Rate

The number of successful trials for a given number of trials is known as the success rate. The number of trails completed without failures or restarts is used to measure the success rates. On the first attempt, as well as after four attempts, success rates are registered. When the password is entered correctly on the first trail without any errors, it is considered a success on the first attempt. There are less mistakes if you get it right the second time. From the first week to the fourth week, success rates are highest in all studies. After the first attempt, the success rate steadily declined until the fourth attempt. The weekly analysis shown in Table 3 and Table 4, After the first attempt, the success rate steadily decreased again.

Table 4. Login Success Rates for Public image set

Login Attempt ↓	Duration (in week)			
1st	100%	70%	52%	88%
2nd		43%	22%	12%
3rd		27%	10%	4%
4th		13%	3%	2%

From the above two tables, it can be seen that the public domain image collection has a higher login success rate than the private domain image set. Also, as per the available literature, the login success rates of PCCP, CCP and PP are low as compared to the two versions of the proposed system (Chiasson et al., 2012). As a result, the proposed system offers a better alternative in terms of Login success rate, which would undoubtedly improve the adaptability of the system.

Table 3. Login Success Rates for Private image set

Login Attempt ↓	Duration (in week)			
1st	100%	58%	62%	83%
2nd		33%	25%	10%
3rd		17%	10%	5%
4th		15%	5%	1%

Password Entry Time

The actual time from the first click point to the last click point was registered as the password entry time in seconds. Table 5 shows the average time between these two points for password entry. The proposed system's internal consistency is reflected in the first two columns. The comparative figures of the previous systems are in the last three columns.

Table 5. Password entry time

System Type	Private Image Set	Public Image Set	PCCP	CCP	PP
Average Time Required for password Entry(in seconds)	30-68	26-19	11-89	7	9-25

Table 5 shows that the password entry time is the best only for CCP. The user has the option of choosing an object in a private domain image scheme, which takes more time. As a result, this scheme keeps track of more time. Users in the public domain image framework have fewer options when it comes to selecting objects. As a result, it takes less time than a private domain image scheme. The results of the lab study show that image selection has a huge effect on usability in all areas.

Password Space

Password strength directly depends on the password space i.e. maximum possible number of passwords generated by the system. In the mention scheme the total number of images says N in private domain and public domain are 20 and 25 respectively. Any authentication's password space will be

$$R_1 = \sum\nolimits_{i=1}^{p} N^i \tag{1}$$

Where p denotes the maximum number of images that can be used to create the password. If the size of each image is M x N (400x300 pixels) and the number of clickable points is q (maximum 5) with a tolerance area of n x n (19x19). After that, the password space is provided by

$$R_2 = \sum\nolimits_{j=2}^{q} \left[j! \times \left(\frac{M \times N}{n^2} \right)^j \right] \tag{2}$$

We can get the available password space of our scheme by combining (1) and (2). The password space is

$$P = R_1 \times R_2 \tag{3}$$

Table 6. Analysis of Password Space

Domain Set	No. of Images	Password Space
PCCP	17	$4.0460 \times 10^{18} = 2^{63}$
Private Domain	20	$1.6414 * 10^{21} = 2^{70}$
Public Domain	25	$4.9571 * 10^{21} = 2^{70}$

The partial increment in the images, proportionately increases the password space and is found to be consistent in the two variations of the proposed system. As seen in Table 6, the Two-Tier Authentication scheme is capable of providing a very large password space as compared to the most recent analysis of a current PCCP method. The enormous increase in the password space suggests that a brute force attack (or dictionary attack) against this proposed scheme will take a considerable amount of effort. As a result, this could be beneficial to the proposed system's adaptability in terms of security.

CONCLUSION

This research work is an attempt to develop an innovative, robust, secure authentication system which covers the scope of knowledge-based Graphical Authentication System. In terms of a homogeneous set of users, the scope of this research study revolves around the usability aspect. This study initially focused on the identification of nine evaluation parameters under the usability aspect for developing a novel authentication system. Some of the highlights of this study are given below-

1. The available literature supports identifying the problem statement as to developing the proposed system having the two variations of modes based on Public and Private image set.
2. The design and implementation of the web-based application is analyzed for the usability aspect by performing the initial lab study including the homogeneous group of students.
3. The performance parameter of success rate in the case of a public domain image set is higher than the private domain image set. Thus, the unbiasedness of the images provided in the public images set rules out the deviation towards the set of concerned images of the private domain.
4. The performance parameter of password entry time is adequate for the usability aspect. The modification in the proposed system leads to an increase in the

password entry time, which has a significant impact on the choice of images to create the password.

5. The increment in password space provides the adaptability of the proposed system in terms of security aspects. A brute force (or dictionary) attack against this proposed scheme would take a tremendous amount of time and effort.

Thus, the comparative facts of this research study provide a better option for defining a novel and usable knowledge-based authentication system.

FUTURE RESEARCH DIRECTION

The proposed system can be analyzed on the usability parameter for homogenous groups as well as heterogeneous groups. The evaluation parameters of user satisfaction can be analyzed by taking the user feedback. The private set is being studied for its scalability issue in relation to the storage of a set of images. A potential goal of this research is to conduct a thorough investigation and analysis of the different usability evaluation parameters on a wider group of users. In addition, developing a secure system based on randomness and various attacks equally matters. Concerning societal benefits, the following applications have been identified that can be supported by the proposed system of this research study.

1. Secure System Login
2. A mobile app with a touch screen.
3. Web application for resource access authentication.
4. ATM Card application.
5. Hard disk locking
6. Folder locking

ACKNOWLEDGMENT

There was no particular grant for this research from any funding agency in the public, private, or non-profit sectors.

REFERENCES

Agrawal, G., & Singh, S. (2018). Analysis of knowledge based graphical password authentication. *Computer Science & Education (ICCSE 2011).*

Alhakami, H., & Alhrbi, S. (2020). Knowledge based Authentication Techniques and Challenges. *International Journal of Advanced Computer Science and Applications, 11*(2). doi:10.14569/IJACSA.2020.0110291

Andrea, B., Ian, O., & Hyoungshick, K. (2016). PassBYOP: Bring Your Own Picture for Securing Graphical Passwords. *IEEE Transactions on Human-Machine Systems, 46*(3).

Ansari, S., Rokade, J., Khan, I., & Shaikh, A. (2018). Graphical Password Scheme Using Cued Click Point and Persuasion with Multiple Images. *International Journal on Recent and Innovation Trends in Computing and Communication, 6*(4), 2321–8169.

Bellam, A. (2013). An Effective User Authentication Method Using Persuasive Cued Click Points. *International Journal of Computational Engineering Science.*

Biddle, R., Chiasson, S., Stobert, E., Paul, C., Oorschot, V., & Forget, A. (2012). Graphical Passwords: Learning from the First Twelve Years. *ACM Computing Surveys, 44*(4), 1–41. doi:10.1145/2333112.2333114

Boonkrong, S. (2019). *An Analysis of Numerical Grid-Based Authentication.* School of Information Technology Suranaree University of Technology Thailand ACM Association for Computing Machinery. doi:10.1145/3357419.3357434

Chiasson, S., Stobert, E., Paul, C., Oorschot, V., & Forget, A. (2012). Persuasive Cued Click- Points: Design, Implementation and Evaluation of a Knowledge-Based Authentication Mechanism. *IEEE Transactions on Dependable and Secure Computing, 9*(2).

Golar, P., & Adane, D. (2016). Critical Analysis of 2-Dimensional Graphical Authentication Systems. In *International Conference on Computing, Analytics and Security Trends (CAST).* IEEE. 10.1109/CAST.2016.7914957

Jerome, P., & Ariel, M. (2019). *Jumbled PassSteps: A Hotspot Guessing Attack Resistant Graphical Password Authentication Scheme Basedon the Modified Pass Matrix Method ICCSP.* Malaysia ACM Association for Computing Machinery.

Khalifa, H., & Siong, L. (2013). Graphical Password: Pass-Images Edge Detection. IEEE.

KumarSarohi, H., & UllahKhan, F. (2013). Graphical Password Authentication Schemes: Current Status and Key issues. *IJCSI, 10*(2).

Nida, A., & Quasim, A. (2019). Conundrum-Pass: A New Graphical Password Approach. *IEEE, International Conference on Communication, Computing and Digital Systems.*

Patra, K., Nemade, B., Mishra, P., & Satapathy, P. P. (2016). Cued-Click Point Graphical Password Using Circular Tolerance to Increase Password Space and Persuasive Features. *Procedia Computer Science, 79,* 877–0509. doi:10.1016/j.procs.2016.03.071

Radha, A. (2013). *A Persuasive Cued Click-point based Authentication Mechanism with Dynamic User Blocks. International Journal of Research in Engineering & Advanced Technology.*

Saeed, S., & SaroshUmar, M. (2015). A Hybrid Graphical User Authentication Scheme. In *International conference on Communication, Control and Intelligent Systems.* IEEE.

Thorpe, J., & MacRae, B. (2014). The Presentation Effect on Graphical Passwords. ACM.

Towhidi, F., & Manaf, F. (2011). *The Knowledge Based Authentication Attacks.* Academic Press.

Zhen, Y., & Hesanmi, O. (2016). Usable Authentication Mechanisms for Mobile Devices: An, Exploration of 3D Graphical Passwords. Xi'an Jiaotong-Liverpool University.

Zhi, L., & Qubin, L. (2005). *An Association Based Graphical Password Design Resistant to Shoulder Surfing Attack.* IEEE. doi:10.1109/ICME.2005.1521406

Zujevs, N. (2019). *Authentication by Graphical Passwords Method 'Hope'.* IEEE.

Chapter 5
An Effectiveness Modelling Approach for IoT–Based Smart Grids

Dongming Fan
Beihang University, China

Yi Ren
Beihang University, China

Qiang Feng
Beihang University, China

ABSTRACT

The smart grid is a new paradigm that enables highly efficient energy production, transport, and consumption along the whole chain from the source to the user. The smart grid is the combination of classical power grid with emerging communication and information technologies. IoT-based smart grid will be one of the largest instantiations of the IoT in the future. The effectiveness of IoT-based smart grid is mainly reflected in observability, real-time analysis, decision-making, and self-healing. A proper effectiveness modeling approach should maintain the reliability and maintainability of IoT-based smart grids. In this chapter, a multi-agent-based approach is proposed to model the architecture of IoT-based smart grids. Based on the agent framework, certain common types of agents are provided to describe the operation and restoration process of smart grids. A case study is demonstrated to model an IoT-based smart grid with restoration, and the interactive process with agents is proposed simultaneously.

DOI: 10.4018/978-1-7998-6721-0.ch005

1 INTRODUCTION

During the past decade, high-capacity and long-transmission power networks have been widely used to meet the growing demand for electricity in the past few decades (Sylla C, 2016; Dranka GG, 2020). There is a mentionable transformation in all segments of the power industry worldwide, from generation to supply. A power system that is more reliable, scalable, secure, interoperable, and manageable while being cost-effective (Bari, 2014) is required by modern society. In the vision of Horizon Europe 2021–2027 (Guo, 2016; Horizon Europe, 2019), the next-generation electric power system will be a "smart grid" (American Public Power Association, 2018), referring to a self-healing-capable grid (Massoud, 2014) that can provide reliable, energy-efficient, and quality power. The configuration of smart grids continues to evolve, as shown in Figure 1 (Fan, 2021).

Figure 1. Evolution of smart grid (Elsevier, 2021)
Source: Elsevier, 2021

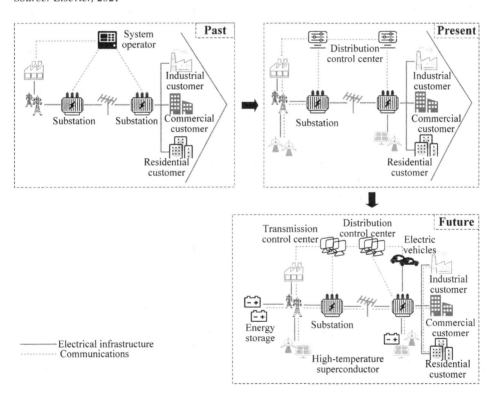

A smart grid can enhance the current grid system by renewable energy resources, such as wind, solar, etc. (Espe, 2018; Tuballa, 2016). These new power generating systems can be smaller, more environmentally, and can be distributed around the load centres, to maintain the reliability of grids. More specifically, the benefits associated with the smart-grid include (but not limited):

- More efficient transmission of electricity;
- Quicker restoration of electricity after power disturbances;
- Reduced operations and management costs for utilities, and ultimately lower power costs for consumers;
- Reduced peak demand, which will also help lower electricity rates;
- Increased integration of large-scale renewable energy systems;
- Better integration of customer-owner power generation systems, including renewable energy systems;
- Improved security.

These advantages benefit from the two-way flows of energy and real-time information, which offers tremendous benefits and flexibility to both users and energy providers. These characteristics are inline to the Internet of Things (IoT) domain. IoT is the communications paradigm that can provide the potential of ultimate communication. Its paradigm describes communication not only human to human but also machine to machine without the need of human interference. IoT-based smart grid will be one of the largest instantiations of the IoT in the next future. The effectiveness of IoT-based smart grid is mainly reflected in observability, controllability, real-time analysis, decision-making, and self-healing. A proper effectiveness modelling approach should be implemented to maintain the reliability and maintainability of IoT-based smart grid.

2 IOT-BASED SMART GRID ARCHITECTURE

Compared to classical power grid, the smart grid highly integrates information and communications technology on the whole energy chain (from producers to end-consumers), through the large-scale deployment of different kind of sensing, actuating and other embedded devices, in addition to the use of smart meters, smart appliances and e-cars, all of them sharing the capacities of computing and communication.

Generally, IoT-based smart grid is usually considered as a three-layer architecture (sensor layer, communication layer and application layer), as shown in Figure 2. The coupled three layers achieve the established functions, and maintain the reliability and maintainability of IoT-based smart grid. In this section, we firstly describe the architecture of IoT-based smart grid, and then discuss the advantages that IoT enabling technologies make the smart grid more powerful and intelligent.

2.1 Sensor Layer

Figure 2. IoT-based smart grid architecture (Springer, 2018)
Source: Springer, 2018

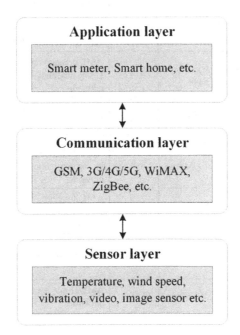

The instrumentation and measurement play vital role in IoT-based smart grid systems. The sensing devices and other instrumentation components comprise the data acquisition interface of IoT in a smart grid application. The sensors, actuators, and smart components acquire the required data from related things and transmit to the database or cloud interfaces. Although wireline transmission has been a legacy for a long while, wireless networks and meshes are now widespread.

2.2 Communication Layer

There are several types of communication technologies available for smart grid such as power line communication (PLC), ZigBee, WiMAX, third/four-generation (3G/4G) cellular networks, global system for mobile communication (GSM), general packet radio service (GPRS), etc. However, each type has its own advantages and disadvantages, as shown in Table 1.

Table 1. Available communication technologies for smart grids

Technology	Spectrum	Data rate	Range	Applications	Limitations
GSM	900-1800 MHz	Up to 14.4 Kpbs	1-10km	Advanced Metering Infrastructure (AMI), demand response, Home automation networks	Low data rates
GPRS	900-1800 MHz	Up to 170 Kpbs	1-10km	AMI, demand response, Home automation networks	Low data rates
3G	1.92-1.98 GHz	384 Kbps-2 Mbps	1-10km	AMI, demand response, Home automation networks	Costly spectrum fees
4G	0.7-2.6GHz	100Mbps	1-10km	AMI, demand response, Home automation networks	Bad signal during zone switching
WiMAX	2.5 GHz 3.5 GHz 5.8 GHz	Up to 75 Mbps	10-50km	AMI, demand response, Home automation networks	Not widespread
PLC	1-30 MHz	2-3 Mbps	1-3km	AMI, Fraud detection	Harsh, noisy channel environment
ZigBee	2.4 GHz, 868-915 MHz	250 Kbps	30-50m	AMI, Home automation networks	Low data rate, short range

ZigBee is ideal for energy monitoring, home automation and automatic meter reading. Besides, ZigBee equipment has low deployment costs and has the best performance in terms of demand response, real-time pricing schemes, real-time system monitoring, and advanced metering support (Wheeler, 2007; Ashok, 2012). However, ZigBee has a short distance and cannot meet the requirements of the smart grid to cover a larger distance.

Wireless mesh is a flexible network composed of a group of nodes (Akyildiz, 2005; Akyildiz, 2005). Data is transmitted through the nodes of the network, and each node acts as a repeater. This makes the network self-healing. If a node exits the network, the information can be rerouted through other nodes. Smart grids use this method for self-healing and situational awareness within the grid.

Cellular networks such as GSM (Reed, 2003), 3G (Dahlman, 2009), 4G cellular networks (Basagni, 2004) and WiMAX (Gray, 2006) can also be used for smart grids. The use of existing communication infrastructure can save costs. In addition, the data transmission speed of cellular networks is much faster than other technologies. However, existing cellular networks also share data streams with customer markets, which may have a negative impact on network performance.

PLC utilizes existing power lines to transmit data at high speeds (Yoon, 2017). Since this method uses existing power lines, deployment costs are significantly reduced in many countries. PLCs are the primary choice for electrical grids because they already exist and connected to meters. Also, the security of PLC is stronger than other technologies. However, the transmission medium of the power lines is very noisy and harsh. In addition, the more devices that are connected to the power line in a neighbourhood affect the overall quality of the data transmitted as well. In short, PLCs are sensitive to disturbances and are poorly suited for data transmission.

2.3 Application Layer

The ubiquitous structure of IoT requires a services-oriented architecture (SOA) to meet the requirements of smart grid applications. A huge number of IoT applications have been improved for any aim ranging from residential usage to industrial areas. The applications need services to optimize the operation, integration, and interoperability along smart grid devices and services.

2.3.1 Smart Meter

Before the advent of automatic meters, humans would manually record household usage, and customers were often overcharged. In the 1990s, utility companies began to introduce automatic meter reading, which can measure household electricity, natural gas or water consumption (Ejaz, 2017). As a result, billing costs are significantly reduced and measurements are more accurate. A smart meter is a highly accurate electronic device with various applications for two-way communication with power companies and consumers. Smart meter applications include anti-theft, remote connection/disconnection, real-time pricing, power quality measurement, load management, power outage notification, etc. Smart meters maintain a continuous flow of information from homes to utilities, allowing real-time system analysis and upload energy usage feedback to smart meters. Therefore, users can monitor their usage in real time and better manage energy (Hai, 2020).

2.3.2 Smart Home

Smart home appliances (lighting, heating, air conditioning, computers, etc.) and systems are often found in newer homes. In contrast, most traditional homes do not have these appliances and systems built in (Hai, 2020; Oliveira, 2020). However, an affordable approach for homeowners is to retrofit them into their households. Smart appliances can be found from many smart home companies such as Notion, Canary, Iris, HomeSeer, Control4, Vera, Savant, Wink, SmartThings, etc (Su, 2011).

3 RELIABILITY CHALLENGES ON IOT-BASED SMART GRID

Each of these layers in IoT-based smart grid architecture has its specific technologies, and they do bring reliability issues and challenges at the same time. In this section, some challenges on reliability modelling and evaluation that IoT technologies may bring to the smart grid (sensor, communication and application layer) are analyzed.

3.1 Sensor Layer

Sensor layer is the lowest layer of the IoT-based architecture of smart grid. The main task of this layer is to sense the data. At first the object must be identified and then collect the data from the objects for example sensors. According to the McKinsey survey in 2017, 75 percent of experts consider the heterogeneity of data to be a top priority. And until 2020, more than 30 billion IoT-based devices are likely already connected in smart cities (Su, 2011), including electric vehicles (EVs), devices in smart homes, and industrial applications (Moore, 2020). Generally, various types of sensors will be attached on these devices. These sensors provide large amounts of heterogeneous data, adding complexity to grids and making their reliability more difficult to evaluate and manage.

3.2 Communication Layer

The expansion of distributed network automation, distributed energy access, and bidirectional real-time consumer communication means there is a need for high-precision data and accurate information on network status. This need has not been satisfied, and there is a huge gap in data collection and control.

Regarding to future communication technologies of smart grids, 5G is a promising research avenue. The maturity of 5G networks will help solve the bottlenecks and remove the obstacles in the restoration of smart grids. The combination of low latency, large bandwidth, and wide connection between services can enhance the restoration technology of smart grids. Typically, the application of 5G in smart grids is divided into two main categories: control and collection.

- Control: 5G provides more timely and accurate data to power system operators and has the potential to enhance system observability and controllability. If smart grids break down, the failed node and data can be sensed and transmitted with low latency, and each unit around the failed node will be available to play the role of decision maker. This can shorten the time for fault isolation and reconfiguration and improve the reliability of smart grids.

- Collection: 5G provides a higher data acquisition frequency with low-cost connections between devices and can collect the finer information on customer consumption. Importantly, it will help balance the load of smart cities to reduce electricity peaks and take full advantage of distributed generators, such as EVs (Mohammadi, 2016; Cuadra, 2015) and energy storage system (ESS), thus improving the reliability and availability of smart grids.

The real-time situational awareness brought by 5G technology brings more possibilities for the rapid restoration of the power grid. A new era of the Internet of Everything with 5G has the potential to reshape smart grids and our lives.

3.3 Application Layer

Decision-making algorithms mainly rely on mathematical analysis or heuristic algorithms. With the increased interoperability and complexity, the real-time decision-making of smart grids is becoming an urgent problem. A large number of customers, distributed energy sources, electric vehicles, and other devices are all connected to smart grids, challenging the existing algorithms.

Moreover, the cascading failures models especially in interdependent networks should be further considered in the modelling of smart grids (Cuadra, 2015; Peng, 2018). Targeted attacks may cause the interdependent power networks to collapse on a larger scale due to the complex dependencies.

Fortunately, the integration of edge computing and industrial artificial intelligence (IAI) is a promising direction in interdisciplinary research (Davis, 2020). By using distributed servers, even mobile terminals, edge computing can realize calculation, decision-making, and optimization at the edge of devices, providing more efficient and accurate strategic support for the restoration of smart grids while reducing the computing pressure in the central cloud. Meanwhile, the powerful computing could enhance the ability of situation awareness, and thus help the operators to make better decision when a disturbance occurs on the system. However, how to build an edge computing framework for smart grids and embed the appropriate intelligent algorithm of IAI into the framework remains a topic for future research.

Table 2. Challenges and opportunities for IoT-based smart grids

Challenges	Opportunities
1. Human factors in digital twin applications on restoration 2. Modelling of interdependent networks 3. Fault propagation model in interdependent networks 4. Modelling framework with IoT 5. Build the framework of edge computing for the restoration of smart grids 6. Edge computing for large amounts of heterogeneous data (distributed generations, load, EVs, ESS) in the process of reconfiguration 7. Reconstruct the topology and connection relationship in interdependent networks under cyber-attack 8. Data transmission latency 9. Rapid decision-making and optimization algorithm 10. Lack of appropriate IAI algorithm embedded 11. Mitigate and optimize the cascading failure propagation in interdependent networks	**Digital twins:** 1. Exact cyber copy of a physical system that truly represents all of the functionalities 2. Knowledge- and data-driven 3. Prognosis of complex dynamic behavior and the restoration process of smart grids **5G technology:** 1. Timely and accurate data with higher data acquisition frequency 2. Distributed decision to shorten the time for fault isolation, reconfiguration 3. Distributed energy regulation **IAI/edge computing:** 1. More efficient and accurate strategic support for the restoration of smart grids 2. Improve the reliability of cyber-physical system systems under different edge repairing strategies

4 MODELLING APPROACH FOR IOT-BASED SMART GRID

To master the high complexities of future IoT-based smart grids, where intelligence is distributed over autonomously acting and interacting components, it is necessary to explore techniques based on distributed artificial intelligence (AI). One of the most relevant technologies seems to be the Multi-agent system (MAS) approach (Davis, 2020; Nguyen, 2012). A MAS is a collection of autonomous computational entities (agents), which can be effective in broad applications to perform tasks based on goals in an environment that can be difficult to define analytically (Meskina, 2016; Zheng, 2018). The agents interact via messages to coordinate their behaviours to achieve equilibrium between local and global goals. Compared with the traditional approach of centralized control, the framework based on the MAS is developed to solve the restoration problem owing to the following advantages of the decentralized architecture.

1) Since each agent is autonomous, each agent has its own process, which is often asynchronously performed according to its own operation mode without requiring the entire information of the system.

2) The MAS could avoid a single point of failure effectively owing to the distributed control at the component level.

3) Because of the interaction between various agents, some distributed complex problems would be solved effectively.

4.1 Agent Framework for Smart Grid

Compared with the traditional grid, the nodes in the smart grid are connected to each other, so as to obtain a two-way communication network. Embedded with the intelligence software, the original hardware has expanded the capability of calculation, so as to implement the demands of perceiving, analysing, deciding and executing. Therefore, the physical entities, composed of hardware and software, are abstracted as agents, and a decentralized and self-organizing framework addressing the reliability and load balancing in a distributed scenario is proposed in Figure 3 (Ren, 2019). The framework deploys a communication network of cooperative agents solving the trade-off problem between reliability and load balancing and has a decentralized paradigm.

Figure 3. Agent framework for smart grid (Elsevier, 2019)
Source: Elsevier, 2019

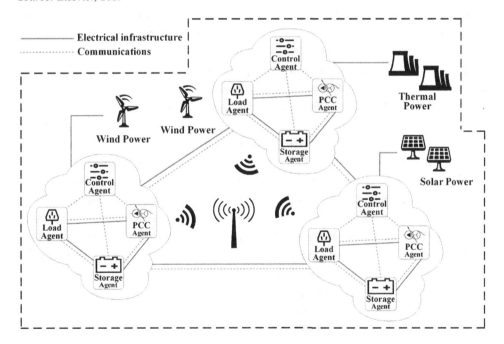

In Fig. 3, the framework provides two networks, namely, the communication network and electrical network. The purple full lines represent the electrical infrastructure and transfer electricity from the generators (thermal, wind and solar power) or ESSs to the customers by the points of common couplings (PCCs). Additionally, the blue dotted lines denote the communications for each agent to transfer information and develop an optimal strategy for the grid. Meanwhile, the communication network $G = (V, E)$ between agents is a directed graph, where $V = (v_1, v_2, ..., v_n)$ denotes the agent set and E is the edge set (Habib, 2017). Regarding the modern smart grid, ESSs, as vital facilities, are established in the grid system. Because of the uncertainty and instability of renewable energy resources, ESSs could enhance the supplements of electricity to industrial, commercial and residential customers.

Moreover, the control systems are discretely located to collect local information and evaluate the status of the grid system. By means of communication among the control systems, the data and statuses of the nodes can be obtained, and the restoration algorithm can be accomplished under the architecture of the MAS (Habib, 2017).

4.2 Agent Description in IoT-Based Smart Grid

The agents in the IoT-based smart grid are heterogeneous and cooperative. Heterogeneity arises from the various agents' capabilities: sensing widely differing things, activating diverse controllers, negotiating the completing of varied tasks, and finding acceptable solutions to alternative models. They are cooperative in that they all contribute to a larger overall objective, even if they have their own localized goals to achieve. Some common types of agent include: sensor agent, device agent, distributed resource agent, consumer agent, switch agent, energy storage agent, control agent.

Sensor agents: which are responsible for sensing the health status of device. Generally, each sensor agent can only perceive part of the environmental information, and its state can be divided into normal working state and failure state. They have the largest quantity of agents in IoT-based smart grid, including temperature sensor, wind speed sensor, vibration sensor, video sensor, image sensor etc.

Device agents: which represent all the entities in IoT-based smart grid, including cable, transformer, voltage regulator, energy storage device, relays etc. Each device agent has its own functions, and the interaction with other device agents. The operation mechanisms (operating frequency and voltage, generator synchronization status, quality of power level, and devices not operating properly etc.) are embedded into the device agent, to ensure the agents have the similar function with the real physical entities. Meanwhile, the failure state and maintenance behavior are also required into device agents. With the data transmitted by sensor agent, device agent can monitor and evaluate the status and predict the remaining useful life by embedded algorithm. The maintenance requirement will be transferred to high-level agents simultaneously.

Distributed resource agents: which are employed within microgrids. If the power available from a main distribution circuit is not sufficient for the critical load of the users of that local area, then the Consumer agents carry out a negotiation process with the distributed resource agents to purchase power from those distributed resource agents.

Consumer agents: which provide interfaces with power consumers, monitoring, modelling, and estimating power consumption demand at end-user sites and initiating negotiation with distributed resource agents as needed to obtain power from a source (such as a distributed resource agent) that is adequate to meet demand.

Switch agents: which are responsible for the connection and disconnection of cables, to realize reconfiguration and self-healing of IoT-based smart grid.

Energy storage agents: which are utilized to store the extra electricity. The energy storage agent communicates with the device agent. If the electricity of the distributed resource agent is greater than the demand of the consumer agent, the electricity would be saved in the energy storage agent. Additionally, when a fault occurs, the energy storage agent would receive a rescue message. If the energy storage agent meets the demand, the agent sends a request for support; otherwise, a "load shedding" request is sent to the consumer agent.

Control agents: which analyze state data that can reveal that malfunctions have occurred in the grid, and demand a response to maintain high-performance system operation. These agents report their conclusions to their supervisor agents that determine and implement optimal strategies. The presence of these agents fits with the view of the smart grid as a "sense and respond" adaptive control system.

5 CASE STUDY

In this case study, we will model an IoT-based smart grid utilizing agent system. Five types of agents that described in section 4.2 are illustrated to model an IoT-based smart grid. Because of the distribution and renewable resources being integrated, the smart grid contains multiple subsystems and has significant multidisciplinary features (Zhao, 2018; Coelho, 2017). Generally, a smart grid can be simply structured into an electricity distribution network, distributed renewable energy system (e.g., wind power and solar power) and ESS. We consider that one fault has occurred on one device; then, the conjoint downstream un-faulted area will also black out. On the one hand, with the help of a storage system, the faulted bus can be rescued by its corresponding storage system. The topological structure of the system remains constant. On the other hand, the faulted bus will send a "rescue" message to the other buses when its corresponding storage system does not have the ability to continue the aid. Thus, the topological structure of the system has to be changed. Owing to the restoration strategy, the underpowered load will be redistributed to other buses, which leads to a change in the system topological structure and a load imbalance.

5.1 Restoration Modes

With the development of information and communication technologies, the physical entities in the smart grid are designed to have interaction and communication capabilities. Furthermore, this approach facilitates a trend of applying MAS technology on the modelling, calculation and evaluation of smart grids. With the characteristics of communication and interaction between the agents, the entities are abstracted as the various kinds of agents, and the communication and interaction among the agents are also designed as practical processes to accomplish the normal operation of the smart grid and the handling of abnormal conditions (Li, 2015).

In this chapter, we mainly focus on the restoration of the smart grid after failure occurs so that the system can achieve a high-level reliability. Three types of rescues for the PCCs are proposed: self-rescue, load shedding and rescue with other PCCs, respectively.

Self-rescue: If one PCC is under fault, the point is rescued by its corresponding storage system immediately, and there is no need to send rescue messages to the other PCCs.

Load shedding: When the total surplus electricity from the other buses is still not sufficient to rescue the faulted PCC, the broken-down bus will reduce its load by the energy saving factor.

Rescue with other PCCs: This approach is the main algorithm that the chapter focuses on. If other PCCs can provide electricity to the faulted PCC, the load will be redistributed to the PCCs that are involved in the rescue. The goal of the algorithm is to make the reliability of the system the highest with the highest equilibrium state of the loads.

5.2 IoT-Based Smart Grid Modelling Based on Multi-Agent System

With the characteristics of communication and interaction between the agents, an illustration of the modelling of the communication between agents for the restoration of the smart grid, as well as the physical entities, are shown in Figure 4. In the activity diagram of Agent-UML, each partition represents one type of agent, and each rectangle represents an activity of the various agents. Through the transmission of messages, the agents can accomplish the functions and decisions according to the pre-design, and the three modes (self-rescue, load shedding and rescue with other PCCs) of restoration can be accomplished simultaneously.

Corresponding to the three types of restoration modes above, if the electricity of the energy storage agent is enough for the rescue, the "Self-rescue" restoration mode starts, which is denoted by the green line. If the electricity of the energy storage agent is enough for self-rescue, the restoration mode "rescue with other PCCs" starts. The control agent sends a message to the other PCC agents in the grid system to ask for rescue, and the rescuable PCC agent will provide electricity to the consumer agent, which is denoted by the red line. In addition, if all of the PCC agents could not accomplish the rescue, the control agent would send the "load-shedding" message to the consumer agent, which is denoted by the blue line. Moreover, the agent-based

Figure 4. Modelling communication between the agents for the restoration of the electric power system (Elsevier, 2019)
Source: Elsevier, 2019

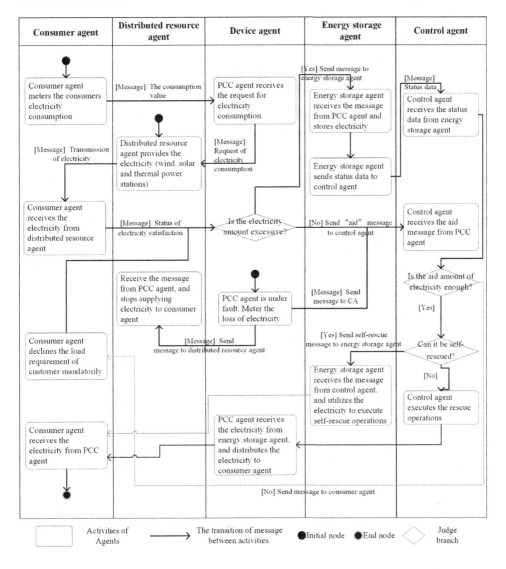

wolf pack reinforcement learning algorithm is proposed in this chapter. Embedded into the control agent as an algorithm, the capabilities of computing and decision making of the agents are enhanced by the heuristic algorithm, and the algorithm depends on the communication between the agents to explore the solution space more thoroughly.

CONCLUSION

Smart grids have become a necessity that addresses the challenges due to rapid urbanization. This chapter firstly proposed an architecture of IoT-based smart grid, and described the corresponding three layers of smart grid (sensor layer, communication layer and application layer). Then, some reliability challenges on three layers are concluded, respectively. In section 4, we utilized multi-agent system to model the IoT-based smart grid. Some types of agent are proposed in this chapter, and a solution highlighted in this chapter demonstrate the model of smart grid with restoration. In the future, the decision-making and controllability of smart infrastructure enabled with IoT have great potential for further development.

REFERENCES

Akyildiz, I. F., & Wang, X. (2005). A survey on wireless mesh networks. *IEEE Communications Magazine, 43*(9), 23–30. doi:10.1109/MCOM.2005.1509968

Akyildiz, I. F., Wang, X., & Wang, W. (2005). Wireless mesh networks: A survey. *Computer Networks, 47*(4), 445–487. doi:10.1016/j.comnet.2004.12.001

American Public Power Association. (2018). *Creating a smart city roadmap for public power utilities.* https://www.publicpower.org/system/files/documents/APPA-Smart-City-Roadmap-FINAL.pdf

Ashok, S. N. (2012). ZigBee: A low power wireless technology for industrial applications. *International Journal of Control Theory & Computer Modeling, 2*(3), 27–33. doi:10.5121/ijctcm.2012.2303

Bari, A., Jiang, J., Saad, W., & Jaekel, A. (2014). Challenges in the smart grid applications: An overview. *International Journal of Distributed Sensor Networks, 4*(2), 1–11. doi:10.1155/2014/974682

Basagni, S., Conti, M., Giordano, S., & Stojmenovic, I. (2004). *Mobile Ad Hoc networking with a view of 4G wireless: imperatives and challenges.* Wiley-IEEE Press.

Coelho, V. N., Cohen, M. W., Coelho, I. M., Liu, N. A., & Guimaraes, F. G. (2017). Multi-agent systems applied for energy systems integration: State-of-the-art applications and trends in microgrids. *Applied Energy, 187*, 820–832. doi:10.1016/j. apenergy.2016.10.056

Cuadra, L., Salcedo, S. S., Ser, J. D., Fernández, S. J., & Geem, Z. W. (2015). A critical review of robustness in power grids using complex networks concepts. *Energies, 8*(9), 9211–9265. doi:10.3390/en8099211

Dahlman, E., Jading, Y., Parkvall, S., & Murai, H. (2009). 3G radio access evolution—HSPA and LTE for mobile broadband. *IEICE Transactions on Communications, 92*(5), 1432–1440. doi:10.1587/transcom.E92.B.1432

Davis, R., Vochozka, M., Vrbka, J., & Neguri, O. (2020). Industrial artificial intelligence, smart connected sensors, and big data-driven decision-making processes in Internet of Things-based real-time production logistics. *Economics. Management and Financial Markets, 15*, 1–16.

Dranka, G. G., & Ferreira, P. (2020). Towards a smart grid power system in Brazil: Challenges and opportunities. *Energy Policy, 136*, 1–16. doi:10.1016/j. enpol.2019.111033

Ejaz, W., Naeem, M., Shahid, A., Anpalagan, A., & Jo, M. (2017). Efficient energy management for the Internet of Things in smart cities. *IEEE Communications Magazine, 55*(1), 84–91. doi:10.1109/MCOM.2017.1600218CM

Espe, E., Potdar, V., & Chang, E. (2018). Prosumer communities and relationships in smart grids: A literature review, evolution and future directions. *Energies, 11*(10), 1–24. doi:10.3390/en11102528

Fan, D. M., Ren, Y., Feng, Q., Liu, Y. L., Wang, Z. L., & Lin, J. (2021). (20201). Restoration of smart grids: Current status, challenges, and opportunities. *Renewable & Sustainable Energy Reviews, 143*, 1–17. doi:10.1016/j.rser.2021.110909

Gray, D. (2006). *Mobile WiMAX-Part I: a technical overview and performance evaluation*. Mobile Wimax White Papers.

Guo, M. J., Liu, Y. H., Yu, H. B., Hu, B. Y., & Sang, Z. Q. (2016). An overview of smart city in China. *China Communications, 13*(5), 203–211. doi:10.1109/CC.2016.7489987

Habib, H. F., Youssef, T., Cintuglu, M. H., & Mohammed, O. A. (2017). Multi-agent-based technique for fault location, isolation, and service restoration. *IEEE Transactions on Industry Applications, 53*(3), 1841–1851. doi:10.1109/TIA.2017.2671427

Hai, F. Z., & Wei, H. S. (2020). *Design of Multiple Protection Mechanism for Smart Meter Data Transmission Communication*. Value Engineering.

Horizon Europe. (2019). *The next EU research & innovation investment programme (2021-2027)*. https://ec.europa.eu/info/sites/info/files/research_and_innovation/strategy_on_research_and_innovation/presentations/horizon_europe_en_investing_to_shape_our_future.pdf

Lan, T., Kang, Q., An, J., Yan, W., & Wang, L. (2011). Sitting and sizing of aggregator controlled park for plug-in hybrid electric vehicle based on particle swarm optimization. *Neural Computing & Applications*, *22*(2), 249–257. doi:10.100700521-011-0687-2

Li, G. F., Bie, Z. H., Kou, Y., Jiang, J. F., & Bettinelli, M. (2015). Reliability evaluation of integrated energy systems based on smart agent communication. *Applied Energy*, *167*, 397–406. doi:10.1016/j.apenergy.2015.11.033

Massoud, A. (2014). A smart self-healing grid: In pursuit of a more reliable and resilient system. *IEEE Power & Energy Magazine*, *12*(1), 112–110. doi:10.1109/MPE.2013.2284646

Meskina, S. B., Doggaz, N., Khalgui, M., & Li, Z. W. (2016). Multiagent framework for smart grids recovery. *IEEE Transactions on Systems, Man, and Cybernetics. Systems*, *47*(99), 1284–1300.

Mohammadi, H. S. M., Fereidunian, A., Shahsavari, A., & Lesani, H. (2016). A healer reinforcement approach to self-healing in smart grid by PHEVs parking lot allocation. *IEEE Transactions on Industrial Informatics*, *2*(6), 2020–2030. doi:10.1109/TII.2016.2587773

Moore, S. J., Nugent, C. D., Zhang, S., & Cleland, I. (2020). IoT reliability: A review leading to 5 key research directions. *CCF Transactions on Pervasive Computing and Interaction*, *2*(3), 147–163. doi:10.100742486-020-00037-z

Nguyen, C. P., & Flueck, A. J. (2012). Agent based restoration with distributed energy storage support in smart grids. *IEEE Transactions on Smart Grid*, *3*(2), 1029–1038. doi:10.1109/TSG.2012.2186833

Oliveira, L., Mitchell, V., & May, A. (2020). Smart home technology—Comparing householder expectations at the point of installation with experiences 1year later. *Personal and Ubiquitous Computing*, *24*(5), 613–626. doi:10.100700779-019-01302-4

Peng, H., Kan, Z., Zhao, D. D., Han, J. M., Lu, J. F., & Lu, Z. L. (2018). Reliability analysis in interdependent smart grid systems. *Physica A*, *500*, 50–59. doi:10.1016/j.physa.2018.02.028

Reed, J. L., Vo, T. D., Schilling, C. H., & Palsson, B. O. (2003). An expanded genome-scale model of Escherichia coli K-12 (iJR904 GSM/GPR). *Genome Biology*, *4*(54).

Ren, Y., Fan, D. M., Feng, Q., Wang, Z. L., Sun, B., & Yang, D. Z. (2019). Agent-based restoration approach for reliability with load balancing on smart grids. *Applied Energy*, *2019*, 46–57.

Su, K., Li, J., & Fu, H. (2011). Smart city and the applications. *International Conference on Electronics, Communications and Control (ICECC)*.

Sylla, C., Pereira, I. S. P., Coutinho, C. P., & Branco, P. (2016). Digital manipulatives as scaffolds for preschoolers language development. *IEEE Transactions on Emerging Topics in Computing*, *4*(3), 439–449. doi:10.1109/TETC.2015.2500099

Tuballa, M. L., & Abundo, M. L. (2016). A review of the development of smart grid technologies. *Renewable & Sustainable Energy Reviews*, *59*(Jun), 710–725. doi:10.1016/j.rser.2016.01.011

Wheeler, A. (2007). Commercial applications of wireless sensor networks using ZigBee. *IEEE Communications Magazine*, *45*(4), 70–77. doi:10.1109/MCOM.2007.343615

Yoon, S. G., Kang, S. G., Jeong, S., & Nam, C. (2017). Priority inversion prevention scheme for PLC vehicle-to-grid communications under the hidden station problem. *IEEE Transactions on Smart Grid*, *9*(6), 5887–5896.

Zhao, T., & Ding, Z. (2018). Distributed finite-time optimal resource management for microgrids based on multi-agent framework. *IEEE Transactions on Industrial Electronics*, *65*(8), 6571–6580.

Zheng, J. S., Ma, J. Y., & Wang, L. (2018). Consensus of hybrid multi-agent systems. *IEEE Transactions on Neural Networks and Learning Systems*, *29*(4), 1359–1365.

ADDITIONAL READING

Ali, A. R. A., & Aburukba, R. (2015). Role of Internet of Things in the smart grid technology. *Journal of Computer and Communications*, *3*(5), 229–233. doi:10.4236/jcc.2015.35029

Catalao, J. P. S. (2017). *Smart and sustainable power systems: Operations, planning, and economics of insular electricity grids.* Taylor & Francis Group Press. doi:10.1201/b18605

Ejza, W., & Anpalagan, A. (2018). *Internet of Things for smart cities: Technologies, big data and security.* Springer Press.

Kabalci, E., & Kabalci, Y. (2019). *From smart grid to Internet of Energy.* Elsevier Press.

Patel, G. S., Rai, A., Das, N. N., & Singh, R. P. (2021). *Smart agriculture: Emerging pedagogies of deep learning, machine learning and Internet of Things.* Taylor & Francis Group Press. doi:10.1201/b22627

Pathan, A. S. K., Guerroumi, M., & Fadlullah, Z. M. (2018). *Smart grid and Internet of Things.* Springer Press.

Tomar, P., & Kaur, G. (2019). *Green and smart technologies for smart cities.* Taylor & Francis Group Press. doi:10.1201/9780429454837

Turjman, F. A. (2020). *Smart grid in IoT-enabled spaces: The road to intelligence in power.* Taylor & Francis Group Press. doi:10.1201/9781003055235

KEY TERMS AND DEFINITIONS

Digital Twins: A digital twin is a virtual representation that serves as the real-time digital counterpart of a physical object or process.

Edge Computing: Which is a distributed computing paradigm that brings computation and data storage closer to the location where it is needed to improve response times and save bandwidth.

Industrial Artificial Intelligence: Usually refers to the application of artificial intelligence to industry. It is more concerned with the application of such technologies to address industrial pain-points for customer value creation, productivity improvement, cost reduction, site optimization, predictive analysis, and insight discovery.

Internet of Things: The internet of things (IoT) describes the network of physical objects-"things" or objects, which are embedded with sensors, software, and other technologies for the purpose of connecting and exchanging data with other devices and systems over the internet.

Multi-Agent System: A multi-agent system is a computerized system composed of multiple interacting intelligent agents. Multi-agent systems can solve problems that are difficult or impossible for an individual agent or a monolithic system to solve. Intelligence may include methodic, functional, procedural approaches, algorithmic search, or reinforcement learning.

Reliability Engineering: Which concerned with the ability of a system or component to perform its required functions under stated conditions for a specified time.

Smart Grid: A smart grid is an electrical grid which includes a variety of operation and energy measures, including advanced metering infrastructure, renewable energy resources and so on.

Chapter 6

Health Index Development for Fault Diagnosis of Rolling Element Bearing

Kumar H. S.

ⓘD https://orcid.org/0000-0002-3238-0250

NMAM Institute of Technology, Udupi, India & Visvesvaraya Technological University, Belagavi, India

Srinivasa P. Pai

ⓘD https://orcid.org/0000-0002-3858-6014

NMAM Institute of Technology, Udupi, India & Visvesvaraya Technological University, Belagavi, India

Sriram N. S.

Vidya Vikas Institute of Engineering and Technology, Mysore, India & Visvesvaraya Technological University, Belagavi, India

ABSTRACT

Condition monitoring (CM) is the process that assesses the health of equipment/ systems at regular intervals or continuously and exposes incipient faults if any. Bearing failure is one of the foremost causes of breakdown in rotating machine, resulting in costly systems downtime. This chapter presents an application of health index (HI) for fault diagnosis of rolling element bearing (REB) which has been successfully used in diverse fields such as image processing, prognostic health management (PHM), and involves integration of mathematical and statistical concepts. There is hardly any effort done in developing HIs using different aspects of wavelet transform (WT) for fault diagnosis of REB. A comparison of the performances of the identified approaches has been made to choose the best one for REB fault diagnosis.

DOI: 10.4018/978-1-7998-6721-0.ch006

INTRODUCTION

Condition monitoring (CM) consists of extraction of information about particular parameters from machines and analysis of data to predict the health of the machines, without disturbing their operation (Jardine et al., 2006). Rolling Element Bearing (REB) are critical components widely used in rotary machines, which will perpetually produce a range of faults due to harsh working environment and complex operating conditions, disturbing the safe and stable operation of the machine. Industries spend millions of dollars for plant maintenance operations and it has been reported that maintenance costs may account for as much as $1/3^{rd}$ of the manufacturing costs of the product (Abdusslam, 2012). The components of a typical REB are "outer ring, rolling elements, cage and inner ring". REB defects are classified as localized defects and distributed defects. Localized defects most commonly occur and include cracks, pits and spalls caused by fracture on the rolling surfaces. Distributed defects include surface roughness, waviness, misaligned races and off-sized rolling elements (Lin et. al., 2017, Pirra, 2012, Tandon, & Choudhury, 1999). Different methods are used for revealing and identification of REB faults (Alguindigue et. al., 1999, Tandon & Nakara, 1992). They are wear analysis, temperature, acoustic and vibration measurements. Among these, vibration signature analysis is widely used as reported in (Patil, M. S. et. al., 2008). A major share of the research work on REB fault diagnosis is based on signal processing techniques which primarily include Time, Frequency and Time-Frequency domain techniques. The details and use of time and frequency domain technique can be found in (Abdusslam, 2012, Lin et. al., 2017, Pirra, 2012, Tandon & Nakara 1992, Patil, M. S. et. al., 2008, Tyagi, 2008). Fast Fourier Transform (FFT) is not appropriate for transient vibration signal analysis, as it is unable to reveal transient / non-stationary information contained in it. These transient components contain vital information about bearing defects. Hence, Wavelet Transform (WT) is commonly used to analyze them as reported in (Randall & Anthony, 2011, Smith & Randall, 2015, Castro et. al., 2008, Peng & Chu, 2004) and use of Time Frequency Analysis (TFA) technique can be found in (Tyagi, 2008, Castro et. al., 2008, Smith & Randall, 2015). The WT is a preferred TFA technique, when compared to other techniques, as it provides flexibility in the window and, analyzes high frequency signal with a short duration function waveform (Randall & Anthony, 2011, Smith & Randall, 2015). An extensive review on WT and its applications is available in (Peng & Chu, 2004, Yan et. al., 2014). Based on the signal decomposition paradigms, WT can be classified as "Continuous Wavelet Transform (CWT), Discrete Wavelet Transform (DWT) and Wavelet Packet Transform (WPT)". Researchers have used them individually or have combined them suitably (for e.g. CWT and WPT) for fault diagnosis (Peng & Chu, 2004, Yan et. al., 2014, Vijay, 2013).

Raw vibration signals contain useful information along with the noise. Several denoising methods have been used by researchers and industries for reducing noise in the acquired or measured raw bearing vibration signals. The Adaptive Noise Cancellation (ANC) and High Frequency Resonance Technique (HFRT) generally termed as envelope detection have been used for denoising bearing vibration signals (Pirra, 2012, Tandon & Nakara, 1992). Generally, denoising is superior when Signal-to-Noise Ratio (SNR) and Kurtosis are higher and Root Mean Square Error (RMSE) is lower (Lin et. al., 2017, Peng & Chu, 2004, Smith & Randall, 2015, Yan et. al., 2014). Denoising is used in different areas, for example image processing, bearing signal investigation, Electrocardiogram (ECG) signal investigation etc. (Abdusslam, 2012, Vijay, 2013, Mamun et. al., 2013, Sumithra & Thanuskodi, 2009, Üstündağ et. al., 2013 Shinde, et. al., 2012). Bearing signals are transient in nature generated by localized defects. Thus, the acquired signal free of background noise will enhance the performance of the fault diagnosis method (Pirra, 2012, Randall & Anthony, 2011, Vijay, 2013). Most of the conventional denoising methods generally require the resonant frequency of the system to be known and practically it is difficult to find out the same (Peng & Chu, 2004, Abboud, D, et. al., 2019). Therefore Wavelet Based Denoising (WBD) methods are widely used due to its merits such as simplicity, effectiveness and being independent of resonant frequency of the REB system (Randall & Anthony, 2011, Vijay, 2013). The conventional soft thresholding methods of wavelet based denoising and other modified soft thresholding techniques discussed by several researchers (Vijay, 2012, Abboud, D, et. al., 2019, Mallat, 1999, GS, 2012) fail to capture the impulsive characteristics. This is because, they tend to smooth out the impulses in the signals under investigation. This has led to the use of customized WBD techniques, which retain the impulsive characteristics in the denoised signals and lead to higher kurtosis values. Thus, the denoised REB vibration signals always have higher kurtosis value. (Smith & Randall, 2015, Rafiee et. al., 2010, Khanam et.al., 2014, Donoho, 1999, Vijay 2013).Wavelet based denoising schemes are effectively used in REB fault diagnosis (Sreejith et. al., 2010, Zen et.al., 2008).

The WT of vibration signals is said to be effective only when proper mother wavelet (MW) is used. This is due to the fact that improperly selected MW applied on the same vibration signals will give varying results. This necessitates the need for selection of a proper MW, for extracting fault characteristic information from the vibration signals (Zaeri et. al., 2011). A review on MW selection can be found in (Yan, 2007, Kankar et. al., 2011). Various methods are available to choose the best MW for fault diagnosis (Rafiee et. al., 2010, Khanam et. al., 2014, Kankar et.al., 2011). Features are the parameters derived from the vibration signals that robustly pin point the REB defects. Time-frequency domain features are superior (Randall & Anthony, 2011), as it is capable of identifying frequency (scale) components, simultaneously with their locations in scale and hence they are widely used in REB fault diagnosis (Randall & Anthony, 2011, Peng & Chu, 2004). Feature extraction using WT/ DWT improves the fault diagnosis performance as established (Tyagi, 2008, Javed et. al., 2013, Wang et. al., 2009, GS et. al., 2012). Generally, feature extraction leads to large data size, with lot of redundant and irrelevant features. Using all these features might reduce the performance of the classifiers like Artificial Neural Network (ANN), Support Vector Machine (SVM), Convolution neural network, etc. Thus, to separate the differentiating features from the vibration signal, Dimensionality Reduction Techniques (DRTs) are very much essential. Also, huge data set increases the computation time of classifiers, thus DRT provides a solution to this problem (GS et. al., 2012, Rao et. al., 2012, Guo et. al., 2020). DRTs like Singular Value Decomposition (SVD), Fisher Discriminant Analysis (FDA), Kernel FDA (KFDA), Separation Index (SI) etc. are commonly used(Vijay, 2013, GS et. al., 2012, Rao et. al., 2012. These reduced features are used for REB fault diagnosis (Ramani, 2008, Javed et. al., 2014, Pinheiro et.al., 2019).

This chapter focuses on the use of all important aspects of WT to develop HI for effective REB fault diagnosis. Researchers have used some aspects of WT individually in detail to develop their own HI for REB fault diagnosis i.e. different types of WTs, signal denoising, statistical features, DRTs. Also, there is hardly any effort on using more aspects of WT and different domain concepts (such as Image processing, Prognostic Health Management (PHM) etc. in developing HI for REB fault diagnosis. So, an effort has been made to bridge this gap by using different aspects of WT and using concepts from different domain areas in the development of HI. Finally, this work provides a platform for the integration of aforementioned concepts to devise HI construction approaches. An assessment of the stated approaches has been made to identify the best HI for REB fault diagnosis in this work.

The chapter is organized as follows Section I provides introduction to bearing CM, section II contains the background of the work, experimental setup and data acquisition is explained in section III, health index construction approaches are discussed in section IV, section V compares the developed approaches to identify the best approach for REB fault diagnosis followed by conclusions.

BACKGROUND

Wavelet Transform

WT is used in analyzing signals from different physical phenomena, from climate change to financial indices, heart signal analysis to condition monitoring, from seismic signal denoising to image denoising etc. WT analysis uses wave like functions termed as wavelets (Mojsilovic et. al., 2000). The purpose of WT is to extract relevant information associated with the signal. Mathematically this can be stated as

$$C_n = \int\limits_{-\infty}^{\infty} x(t)\,\psi_n^{*}(t)\,dt \tag{1}$$

where $(.)^{*}$ indicates the complex conjugate of the function, $(\bullet)$. Defining the inner product between the two functions $x\,(t)$ and $\psi_n(t)$ as (Zaeri et. al., 2011, Kankar et. al., 2011, Gao et. al., 2010)

$$\langle x, \psi_n \rangle = \int x(t)\psi_n^{*}(t)\,dt, \quad \|x\|^{2} = \langle x, \psi_n \rangle \tag{2}$$

Equation (1) can be written as $C_n = \langle x, \psi_n \rangle$ (3)

Using the notation of inner product, the WT of a signal $x\,(t)$ can be written as (Gao et. al., 2010)

$$wt(s,\tau) = \langle x, \psi_{s,\tau} \rangle = \frac{1}{\sqrt{s}} \int\limits_{-\infty}^{\infty} x(t)\psi^{*}\left(\frac{t-\tau}{s}\right)dt \tag{4}$$

where s and τ represents scale and shifting parameters respectively. WT can be represented in continuous i.e. CWT as well as in discrete form as DWT. Information related to CWT and DWT are described below:

The CWT of a signal $x\,(t)$ can be obtained using a convolution operation between the signal $x\,(t)$ and the complex conjugate of the wavelet families, which is given by (Gao et. al., 2010)

$$cwt(s,\tau) = \frac{1}{\sqrt{s}} \int\limits_{-\infty}^{\infty} x(t)\psi^{*}\left(\frac{t-\tau}{s}\right)dt \tag{5}$$

where $\psi^{*}(\bullet)$ is the complex conjugate of the scaled and shifted wavelet function $\psi^{*}(\bullet)$ (Al-Badour et. al., 2011, Gao & Yan 2010, Kankar et. al., 2011).

CWT performed on the entire signal, will provide repetitive information, as s and τ are altered continuously. Redundant data is useful in signal denoising and feature extraction, but the computation time will be high. Also, it requires more memory space. But some applications like image processing and numerical computation stress more on reduced computation time and data size. This has led to the development of DWT. It not only reduces redundancy of the data, but also provides quality information contained in the original signal. Dyadic scales (s=2, $\tau = k\,2^j$) is used to achieve this (Yan & Ruqiang, 2007).

DWT is expressed as

$$DWT(j,k)=\left\langle x(t),\psi_{j,k}(t)\right\rangle=\frac{1}{\sqrt{2^j}}\int_{-\infty}^{\infty}x(t)\psi^*\left(\frac{t-k2^j}{2^j}\right)dt \tag{6}$$

where the symbol $\langle\,''\,\rangle$ denotes inner product operation. the basic step of decomposition is shown in fig. 1.

Figure 1. Basic Decomposition step

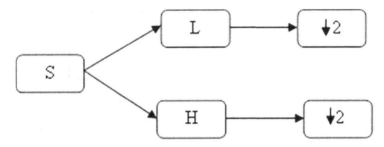

The details of DWT & its implementation are effectively demonstrated by Mallat in (Mallat, 1989). L is a low pass filter, H is high pass filter and the symbol 2 indicates the down sampling. Thus, single level DWT can be written as (Kumar et. al., 2013)

$$x(t)=CA_1+CD_1 \tag{7}$$

Low and high-frequency components as given in equation 8 (GS et. al., 2012, Yan & Ruqiang, 2007, Ramani & Akarsha, 2008, Kankar et. al., 2011)

$$a_{j,k}=\sum_m h(m-2k)a_j \quad j=1,\ldots m$$
$$d_{j,k}=\sum_m g(m-2k)a_j \quad j=1,\ldots m \tag{8}$$

In the equation (8), $a_{j,k}$ are the approximation and $d_{j,k}$ are detailed coefficients, which corresponds to signal's high-frequency components (Yan & Ruqiang, 2007,

Kankar et. al., 2011). The limitation of the DWT is that it has low resolution in high frequency region. This draw back hinders DWT to analyze high frequency transient components. To address this problem, WPT was developed, which decomposes approximation coefficients of the signal in high frequency region, thus providing a solution to this problem. Fig. 2 shows a 3- level WPT decomposition resulting in 8 sub-bands (Mamun et. al., 2013, Javed et. al., 2013). More details related regarding WPT can be found in (Sreejith et. al., 2010, Saravanan & Ramachandran, 2011, Kankar et. al., 2011, Tarighat, 2016).

Figure 2. A 3- Level Wavelet Packet Decomposition (Zhang et. al., 2005)

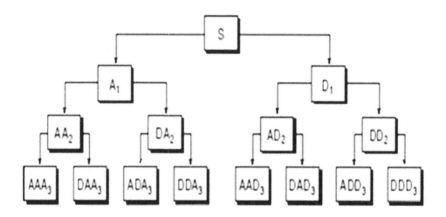

Fault diagnosis can be carried out using soft computing techniques like ANN, SVM etc. and using Health indices (HIs). Literature reveals use of ANN & machine learning techniques for REB fault diagnosis. The limitations of ANN and other techniques are that: it is necessary to randomize the patterns so that the classifier differentiates all types of patterns in the input data. Also, there are no strategies to set the number of hidden layers and number of neurons in the hidden layers, which have an influence on the results. ANN has a complex structure, which needs to be defined based on the problem (input and output data). In addition to these, it requires more computation time compared to the HIs (Akhbardeh et. al., 2007, Wang et. al., 2009). HI development approach involves the use of mathematical equations for condition classification. Fault diagnosis using HI primarily comprises of three steps namely: feature extraction, feature selection and fault categorization. Feature extraction is a fundamental step, which involves statistical parameters derived from the original signal to showcase the existence of defects as described in (Ramani,

2008, Javed et. al., 2014, Akhbardeh et. al., 2007, Wang et. al., 2009, Chen et. al., 2018). The bearing condition classification using HIs has certain merits over the use of soft computing techniques which includes: simplicity and less computation time. The limitation of this approach is: expert knowledge is essential as the individual needs to take decisions regarding the fault conditions. The expert should be clear with the mathematical concepts behind the HI as reported in (Wang et. al., 2009, Tao et. al., 2013, Jin et. al., 2012, Soylemezoglu et. al., 2010, Caesarendra et. al., 2013, Vishwash et. al., 2014, Duong et. al., 2018, Brusa et. al., 2020).

EXPERIMENTAL SET UP AND DATA ACQUISITION

The vibration signals acquired from a 'live' rotating machine having REBs are complex with signal being acquired from several sources. Correlation of vibration signal features with the bearing defects is a tough task. Hence, there is a need to design and develop a test rig, where REBs with artificially seeded defects can be tested and the generated vibration signals analyzed and its features can be used to develop health indices for REB fault diagnosis using different approaches. In (Vijay, 2013), the author conducted literature review to propose the preliminary design of the bearing test rig used in this research work. The findings of the review were as follows: The bearing test rigs used by various researchers consisted of a horizontal shaft supported on bearings. Cylindrical roller, taper roller and spherical rolling element bearings have been tested. Load has been applied either radially or both radially and axially. The means of load application has been mechanical, hydraulic or pneumatic and in one case it has been applied using an electrical dynamometer. The speed of the shaft ranged from 600 to 3000 rpm. The radial load applied varied from 0.1 to 8.86 kN. The defect dimensions varied as follows: lateral or diametrical 0.1178 to 1 mm and depth 0.1 to 0.981 mm. The data acquisition sampling rate varied between 2.5 to 49.152 kHz (Patil, M. S. et. al., 2008,Tyagi, 2008,Randall & Anthony, 2011, Smith & Randall, 2015, Castro et. al., 2008, Peng & Chu, 2004, Vijay, 2013). In most of the test rigs, the motor shaft has been directly coupled to the test bearing shaft and in other cases it has been through a belt drive. By considering the aforementioned points, he designed and fabricated a customized bearing test rig to acquire the vibration data. The maximum motor speed of the experimental test rig is 1400 rpm, with a speed reduction ratio of 1: 2.25. Hence, the maximum speed attained at the shaft is 622 rpm.

Four conditions of REB were analyzed using vibration signals. He used soft computing techniques to analyze the vibration signals for defect characterization. Fig.3 shows the photographic view of the test set-up used in this work. The test bearing is located on the left side and the support bearing is mounted on the right side as shown in the figure. The shaft is driven by an induction motor with variable speed controller. Drive to the shaft from the motor is achieved through timer belt drive in order to avoid transmission of motor vibration to the shaft and also to ensure positive drive for maintaining constant rotation speed. Two accelerometers of Integrated Circuit Piezoelectric (ICP) make with side connector (MMF Germany) piezo design (compression ceramic), with magnetic base were used for data acquisition and the detailed specifications about the accelerometers can be found in and also methodology in acquiring vibration signals can e found in (Vijay, 2013). The sampling rate used in this work for data acquisition is 48 ksamples per second and the shaft speed is 622 rpm (10.36 rotations per second). Hence, the number of samples in two shaft revolutions is $(48000 \div 10.33) * 2 = 9293$, which is approximated to 10000 samples). Based on the methodology adopted in acquiring vibration signal (samples and creating bins) to classify REB conditions (Sreejith et. al., 2008), in this work, sample size of each bin is taken as 10000 samples with total number of sample 250000. The X direction (vertical) vibration signals are more sensitive to REB conditions, since accelerometer axis is parallel to the loading direction. Defects have been seeded on the contact surfaces of the inner race (IR), outer race (OR) and on ball element (B) of the REB, by mechanical indentation, to emulate the localized defects (Vijay, 2013, Kumar et. al., 2017). Acceleration signals at 48k sampling rate are gathered for 5 seconds. Signals are gathered for four types of bearing (one normal and three defective) - under two radial loads viz., low (0) and high (1.7 kN) and speed of 622 rpm. A total of eight data vectors are acquired. In this work vibration signals acquired at 1.7 kN load and 622 rpm shaft speed have been considered for further analysis.

Test Rig Modification for Generation of Validation Data

In this study, a need has been felt to increase the shaft speed available from the test rig. Accordingly the shaft pulley has been modified to obtain higher shaft speeds. The dimensions of original shaft pulley and the modified shaft pulley have been given in table 1.The reduction of outer diameter in modified pulley compared to original pulley and teeth on modified pulley has been reduced to 36. This has led to an increase in the shaft speed up to 922 rpm. The data collected at this shaft speed with 1.7 kN load has been used for validation of the results obtained in investigating different aspects of WT for analysis carried out in this work.

HEALTH INDEX CONSTRUCTION APPROACHES

The word 'index' has several meanings. For example, in mathematics (2^3, index of the base 2 is 3). In finance, an index is a statistical indicator providing a representation of

Figure 3. Photographic view of the Rolling Element Bearing test setup (Vijay, 2013)

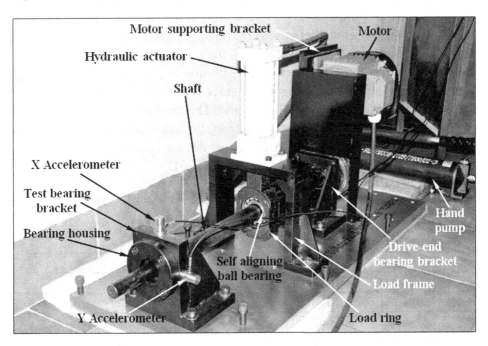

the value of the securities which constitute it. In this, it is a numerical value calculated from a set of variables based on the vibration signals and is compared with some reference value. Majority of the research in developing HIs uses statistical features extracted from the vibration signals. The index, in contrast to other fault diagnosis schemes, serves a natural way to define the health condition (Miao et. al., 2007, Wang et. al., 2017). Thus use of HIs for fault diagnosis is better when compared to use of soft computing technique like ANN, as it is simple and consumes less time for computation (Huang et. al., 2005). The various aspects of WT used in the development of various HI approaches have been discussed in subsequent sections.

Table 1. Shaft pulley dimension specifications

Shaft pulleydetails	Outer diameter(mm)	Inner diameter (mm)	Teeth on pulley
Original	145	22	55
Modified	96	22	36

Selection of MW

The choice of the proper mother wavelet (MW) plays a vital role in the efficiency of WT. This is because different MWs used on the vibration signals will give diverse results. This necessitates the need for the selection of proper MW for extracting fault characteristic details from the REB signals. If the MW is similar to the signal under study, then WT analysis will be effective. This can be observed in the wavelet coefficients i.e. bigger the wavelet coefficients, the more similar the MW and the signal under study (Kankar et. al.,, 2011). Generally, wavelets are grouped as: Real-valued and complex-valued wavelet (Zaeri et. al., 2011). Table 2 lists some of the real and complex – valued wavelet families.

Table 2. Types of wavelets

Sl. No	Types of wavelet	
	Real valued	Complex-valued
1	Daubechies wavelet family (Db1, Db2, ..)	Complex morlet
2	Symlet family (sym1, Sym2, ...)	Complex Gaussian
3	Coiflet family (Coif1, Coif2, ...)	Complex Shannon

Energy (E)

The energy content of the signal uniquely characterizes the signal. The amount of energy in the signal can be computed by

$$E_{x(t)} = \int |x(t)|^2 dt \tag{9}$$

$$E_{energy} = \iint |W(s,\tau)|^2 ds d\tau \tag{10}$$

Eqn.10 indicates the energy computation using wavelet coefficients of a signal (Yan & Ruqiang, 2007). WT is said to effective only when more energy is extracted from the defect induced vibration signal. Hence, energy is taken as a criterion for selecting the MW (Zaeri et. al., 2011, Vishwash et. al., 2014).

Entropy

The amplitude of the defect induced vibration signal is different for different conditions. Hence, the frequency distribution of the signal needs to be considered for effective feature extraction from the defect induced vibration signals. More information about entropy is available in (Sreejith et. al., 2010, Saravanan & Ramachandran, 2011, Yan & Ruqiang, 2007, Vishwash et. al., 2014).

$$E_{entropy}(s) = -\sum_{i=1}^{N} p_i \log_2 p_i \qquad (11)$$

where p_i is the energy probability distribution of the wavelet coefficients.

Energy-to-Shannon Entropy Ratio

As reported in literature (Sreejith et. al., 2010, Yan & Ruqiang, 2007), some wavelet selection criteria aims at maximization (energy, correlation coefficient) while minimizing others (Shannon entropy, joint entropy), which are in general conflicting with each other. In order to balance these selection criteria two new criteria's were developed namely: (a) Energy–to-Shannon entropy ratio ($R(s)$)& (b) MinMax Information measure (Sreejith et. al., 2010, Saravanan & Ramachandran, 2011, Yan & Ruqiang, 2007, Vishwash et. al., 2014, Zaeri et. al., 2011). In this work, $R(s)$ is used and is given in eqn. (12):

$$R(s) = \frac{E_{energy}(s)}{E_{entropy}(s)} \qquad (12)$$

More the $R(s)$ value, better the MW for vibration signal analysis (Kankar et. al., 2011).

The three real-valued wavelet families listed in table 2 are available in the MATLAB library and these MWs have been used in this investigation. The vibration signals from the bearing with four conditions (N, B, IR and OR) have been considered for the analysis. WPT has been used to decompose the vibration signals into 3 levels using a customized programme written using MATLAB 2012 (Misiti et. al., 2012). Further the energy and entropy values have been calculated. As the bearing with OR defect has the highest energy compared to IR, B and N conditions, hence, plots pertaining to OR condition has been included.

Sixteen MWs are pre-selected from four wavelet families listed in table 2. The energy and entropy values extracted from the vibration signals by these MWs are tabulated in table 3. As per maximum energy criterion, '*db44*' can be chosen as the most appropriate MW as it has highest energy, when compared to other base wavelets. It is evident from table 3 that energy value increases in ascending order in each wavelet family (Kankar et. al. 2011). As reported in (Yan & Ruqiang, 2007), higher order MW within a wavelet family has high degree of regularity, leading to better energy extraction from the vibration signal than lower order(Yan & Ruqiang, 2007). Based on the minimum Shannon entropy criterion (MSEC), '*dmey*' wavelet is considered as the most appropriate MW. This decision is not consistent with '*db44*' wavelet selected using maximum energy criterion. To overcome this problem, the $R(s)$ value is computed and the results are tabulated in table 3. Based on $R(s)$ criteria, '*dmey*' wavelet possesses the highest value and thus it is considered as the appropriate MW to analyze OR vibration signals (Kankar et. al. 2011).

Table 3. Energy, Minimum Shannon entropy &Energy–to-Shannon entropy ratio values for Outer race vibration signals

Sl. No.	Mother wavelet	Energy	Minimum Shannon entropy criteria	Energy–to-Shannon entropy ratio	Sl. No.	Mother wavelet	Energy	Minimum Shannon entropy criteria	Energy-to-Shannon entropy ratio
1	db1	41	138.5	1.825	9	*db44*	*54.8*	46.3	3.8682
2	db2	42.3	111.2	2.068	10	coif1	41.9	107.2	2.0923
3	db3	44.1	93.5	2.303	11	coif3	48.4	67.1	2.8763
4	db4	45.4	80.7	2.535	12	sym2	42.3	111.2	2.0701
5	db6	47.9	68.1	2.860	13	sym3	44.1	93.6	2.2980
6	db8	49.4	62.3	3.056	14	sym4	45.8	81.3	2.5313
7	db10	50	56.4	3.280	15	sym8	49.2	60.9	3.1067
8	db20	52.9	51.2	3.537	16	*dmey*	*54.3*	45.9	**3.8867**

Further $R(s)$ have been tabulated for vibration signals corresponding to N, B, IR and OR bearing conditions and the results have been tabulated in table 4. The results reveal that 'dmey' is the best possible MW to analyse vibration signals for REB fault diagnosis.

Wavelet Denoising

Similarity between the MW and the signal under study plays a very important role as it is one of the factor which decides the denoising efficiency (Kankar et. al., 2011).The WBD schemes have been used by researchers for capturing the defect

Table 4. Energy–to-Shannon entropy ratio values for Normal,Ball and Inner race vibration signal

Sl.No.	Mother Wavelet	Energy–to-Shannon entropy ratio values		
		Normal	*Ball*	*Inner race*
1	db1	0.835897	1.146643	1.730667
2	db2	0.904348	1.235294	1.847926
3	db3	0.969259	1.386161	1.963576
4	db4	1.090416	1.377778	2.045918
5	db6	1.0625	1.513064	2.194545
6	db8	1.077505	1.560096	2.278293
7	db10	1.085227	1.553659	2.330189
8	db20	1.10687	1.63038	2.342803
9	db44	1.10566	1.633166	2.384321
10	coif1	0.914186	1.249501	1.822727
11	coif3	1.078394	1.530516	2.189531
12	sym2	0.895652	0.9108	1.854071
13	sym3	0.969259	1.339583	1.995017
14	sym4	0.985663	1.359914	2.037225
15	sym8	1.071563	1.62	2.269517
16	*dmey*	*1.116635*	*1.684211*	*2.470588*

characteristic information from the REB vibration signals, as it is independent of the resonant frequencies. In this work, five denoising schemes from different domains are used and are shown in table 5. More details and the mathematical background can be found in (Vijay, 2013, Mamun et. al., 2013, Sumithra & Thanuskodi, 2009, Üstündağ et. al., 2013 Shinde, et. al., 2012).

For denoising performance evaluation a single bin with 10000 samples of vibration data has been considered for OR condition. Table 5 provides kurtosis and RMSE values of unprocessed vibration signals from OR defective conditions and denoised using the five identified schemes. MATLAB codes are used to execute the following schemes p_1, p_3, p_4 and p_5. p_2 scheme is implemented using graphical user interface (GUI) of MATLAB 2012 (Misiti et. al., 2012).

Table 5. Results of wavelet based denoising of vibration signals from bearing with Outer race

Sl. No.	Denoising schemes	Kurtosis	RMSE
	Raw signal	40.3	
1	*Scheme 1(p_1)*	9.4	0.10
2	*Scheme 2(p_2)*	14.4	0.058
3	*Scheme 3(p_3)*	57	0.05
4	*Scheme 4(p_4)*	100	0.02
5	*Scheme 5(p_5)*	142	0.019

Comparison of Denoising Techniques

The denoising performance is assessed using Kurtosis and RMSE. p_3 is simple, but the noise is calculated based on the largest amplitude of the wavelet coefficients, which is not there in conventional soft and hard thersholding rules. It is better than frequency selective filtering and stationary wavelet transform (SWT) technique. p_1 is selected from speech signal analysis domain. The thresholding scheme is better than hard and soft. p_1 has given good results even with strong Gaussian noise. Though p_1 and p_3 are good, they tend to remove or smooth out impulsive characteristics in the denoised signal, thereby making it unsuitable for analysis. Hence, p_4 is selected, which resulted in higher kurtosis value compared to p_1 and p_3. p_2 has been considered because, usually PCA is used for data reduction and rarely used for denoising. The Principle Components (PC) is related to denoising effect and the loss of information in the signal to each wavelet level. WT display vital information of the signal in high frequency region than low frequency region. Thus, reduced number of PCs is able to provide better denoised signal. As it is evident from the table 5, *Scheme 5(p_5)* is the superior scheme as it possesses highest kurtosis (K) value and lowest RMSE value. Therefore p_5 scheme is competent in retaining impulsive characteristics in the denoised vibration signal.

In p_5, threshold value is calculated at each wavelet level as the CA and CDs have varying amplitude. This aspect is not found in the earlier thresholding schemes. It takes least time for computation and performs calculation of threshold and interval selection automatically and provides the results instantly. Thus p_5 scheme i.e. interval-dependent denoising scheme is the best WBD scheme investigated in this work (Kumar et. al., 2016).

The real-time bearing vibration signals obtained from the test rig for four conditions namely, N, B, IR and OR, at 1.7 kN load with shaft speed of 622 rpm has been subjected to the Interval-dependent denoising scheme *(p_5)*. The **discrete**

meyer (dmey) MW has been used for the decomposition of the signals. As the sampling frequency for acquiring the real-time vibration signals is 48k samples/s, as per Nyquist criterion, the maximum frequency of the signal is expected to be f_{max} =24 kHz (Vijay, 2013). The plots of raw and Interval-dependent denoised signals are shown in fig. 4 (a) and (b) respectively, for 622 rpm speed and 1.7 kN load. By comparing the plots and the kurtosis values in the figure 4, the effectiveness of the Interval-dependent denoising method is evident.

Figure 4. (a) raw and (b) Interval-dependent denoised vibration signal

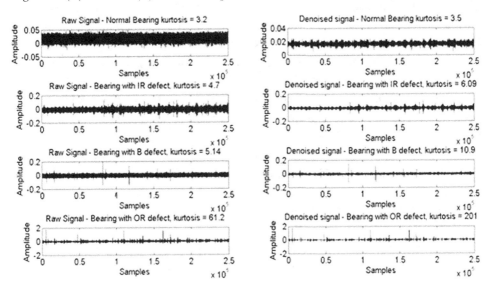

Statistical Feature Extraction and Feature Selection

REB malfunction leads to rise in down time and financial losses to the industries. This necessitates the need for improving the fault diagnostic approaches. Features play a vital role in classifying machine defects. The bearing vibration signals obtained from the REB experimental setup has a vector size of 250 k samples. Different features are required to be extracted from the non-overlapping bins of the bearing vibration signals, such that each bin corresponds to one shaft rotation. A non-overlapping bin of size 10000 samples has been considered in this work, for 4 bearing conditions (N, B, IR and OR), two loads (0 and 1.7kN) and one shaft speed (622 rpm), eight vibration signal vectors are available resulting in $8 \times 25 = 200$ bins. Of these, 100 bins corresponds to 1.7 kN load and the remaining 100 bins corresponds to 0 kN load. The first, second, third and fourth segments corresponds to N, B, IR and OR conditions of the REB i.e. 25 segments for each condition. The same is true for 0 kN load condition. These features have been normalized so that each feature value varies between 0 and 1.

Kumar et al. (2013) showed that statistical features obtained from 2nd level detailed wavelet coefficients (CD2) using DWT resulted in improved ANN performance. Hence, in this work, statistical features are extracted from the CD2 and are used in developing HIs. The details of seventeen statistical features used in this work can be found in (Vijay, 2013, Kumar et. al., 2017). Generally, large data is derived from various defective conditions. This results in poor fault diagnosis which may lead to reduction in classification accuracy and increased computation time of the classifiers (Jardine et. al., 2006, Patil et. al., 2008, Tao et. al., 2013). Literature reveals various DRTs namely Singular Value Decomposition (SVD), Separation Index (SI), Principal component analysis (PCA) Fischer discriminant analysis (FDA) etc. PCA and FDA are linear DRTs, as they consider linear correlation among the variables and they are not suitable for non-linear / non-stationary features (Zang et. al., 2005). Thus non-linear DRTs namely Kernel PCA (KPCA) and Kernel FDA (KFDA) have been developed to handle non-linear features (Tao et. al., 2013, Jin et. al., 2012, Chakraborty et. al., 2010). In this study, feature selection has been performed using SVD and KFDA. The details of DRTs i.e. SVD and KFDA can be found in (Rao et. al., 2012, Zhang et. al., 2005, Chakraborty et. al., 2010).

Singular Value Decomposition

SVD is used in modeling, prediction and compression of data sequences. In SVD, singular values are uniquely related to eigen values. The SVD is simple when compared to PCA as it requires least time for computation. SVD is extremely robust, and the singular values in SVD can be computed with greater computational accuracy than eigen values, since it compresses the data by taking the square root of the eigen value (Chakraborty et. al., 2010, Kumar et. al., 2017).

Generally SVD is applied to the entire data set to obtain singular values and then used for further processing. Since the focus of this work is to develop an index, SVD is applied on each statistical feature to know its values under different operating conditions, which then can be used to classify different bearing conditions. Considering the shaft speed of 622 rpm and load of 1.7 kN, data set for normal condition is 17×25. On applying SVD for the N condition, we get 17×1. Similar procedure is applied to the remaining three conditions and the final feature set (one normal & three defective conditions) has been reduced from 17×100 to 17×4. SVD approach selects three statistical features, namely Root mean square (*RMS*), standard deviation (*SD*) and peak (P_k) among the seventeen statistical features considered in this investigation. Table 6 shows singular values of the statistical features for different conditions of the bearing at varying load and constant speed. The singular values corresponding to *RMS, SD* and P_k shows different values and hence can be used for REB fault diagnosis. The remaining features fail to demonstrate this trend and hence are not indicated in table 6 (Chakraborty et. al., 2010). The use of statistical features in bearing fault diagnosis can be found in (Caesarendra et. al., 2013).

Kernel Fischer Discriminant Analysis

As bearing vibration signals are non-stationary in nature, linear DRTs fail to capture vital information in non-linear / non-stationary signals (Zheng et. al., 2013). Also, the use of KFDA in dimensionality reduction can be found in (Chakraborty et. al., 2010, Kumar et. al., 2017). A brief overview, methodology and mathematical details about KFDA can be found in (Rao et. al., 2012, Zhang et. al., 2005, Chakraborty et. al., 2010, Kumar et. al., 2017). Vijay et al. (2015) compared linear (PCA, FDA) and non-linear DRTs (KFDA) based on ANN performance. KFDA has been applied to seventeen statistical features. KFDA resulted in highest classification accuracy on test data with a dimensionality reduction of 1/3rd of the feature size for different loads and speeds considered. Kernel Fisher Discriminant Powers (KFDP) are arranged in descending order and by trial and error, the following number of features were selected namely 4, 5, 6, 7, and 8. These selected features were given as inputs to ANN and it was found that for six features the classification accuracy on test data was the highest, when compared to the other features. Applying this approach to the seventeen statistical features, resultedin six features selected by KFDA namely: Mean, Skewness, Crest factor, Impulse factor, Log-log ratio, Weibull Negative Log Likelihood at 0 & 1.7 kN load and shaft speed of 622 rpm.

HI APPROACHES

Singular Value (SV) Based HI

In this approach singular value obtained from SVD (as shown in table 6) is used to develop HI. SVD has considerable stability and changes negligibly when matrix elements change (Kankar et. al., 2011, Wang et. al., 2009). The singular values are computed for varying load (0 and 1.7 kN) and at constant shaft speed (622 rpm). Table 6 reveals a constant value, which is independent of the operating conditions (Chakraborty et. al., 2010, Kumar et. al., 2017). The *RMS* and *SD* values are almost same and exhibit same trend. Therefore, only *RMS* and P_k are considered in developing HI approach. *RMS* and P_k are showing an ascending trend in singular values for different conditions of the bearing (Chakraborty et. al., 2010). Hence, singular values represent a characteristic number, which can be used as an index. The index values are always positive and greater than zero for different conditions of the REB. The developed HI is proportional to the singular value of these statistical features i.e.

$$HI_I = \text{Singular value of the statistical feature } (S_c) \tag{13}$$

where '*c*' indicates bearing condition.

Table 6. Singular values of the features for 0, 1.7 kN load and 622 rpm shaft speed

Sl. No	Feature	0 kN				1.7 kN			
		Normal	Ball	Inner race	Outer race	Normal	Ball	Inner race	Outer race
1	RMS	0.206	0.244	0.630	1.680	0.005	0.176	0.320	3.155
2	SD	0.207	0.244	0.630	1.680	0.006	0.176	0.320	3.155
3	Pk	0.025	0.206	0.589	1.619	0.008	0.148	0.345	2.411

Average Value of the Cumulative Feature Based (AVCF) HI

Features with monotonic trend indicate failure progression, where as non-monotonic features fail to show this trend. Cumulative feature is a time series indicator which transforms the ordinary feature into its cumulative form, which attains monotonic trend and can be used for predicting remaining useful life (RUL). The mathematical details about cumulative feature and the procedure to transform ordinary features into its cumulative form can be found in (Javed et. al., 2013). In this method, the features selected using KFDA are transformed into its cumulative form. Consider, Wnl feature for normal condition of size 17 × 25. After transforming it into its cumulative form, the data set for normal condition will be 17 × 25. Hence, Wnl feature for normal condition comprises of two matrices of size 17 × 25 for ordinary as well as for cumulative transformed one. Therefore final feature set i.e. N, B, IR and OR will have 17 × 200 data. Figure 5 shows the plot of ordinary and cumulative transformed Weibull Negative Log Likelihood (Wnl) feature.

The cumulative feature display a descending trend in categorizing different conditions of the bearing. This is due to the monotonic character exhibited by it. However at the initial stage, cumulative transformed features are converged which is a limitation of this approach. To overcome this, Average Value of the Cumulative transformed Feature (AVCF) has been computed and used in proposed HI approach (Kumar et. al., 2017). Thus AVCF provides a distinctive value for each condition

Figure 5. Variation of cumulative transformed and ordinary Weibull Negative Log Likelihood feature

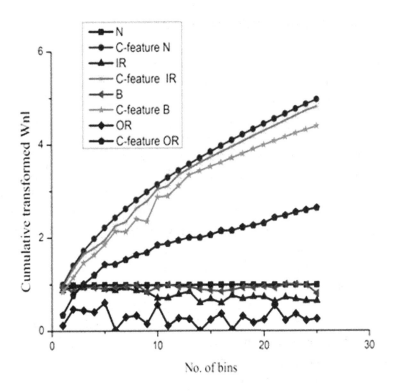

which is shown in table 7. The same procedure is repeated for the remaining five features as they failed to classify the different conditions.

Table 7. HI variation based on Average value of the cumulative feature

Sl. No.	Feature	Normal	Inner race	Ball	Outer race
1	Weibull Negative Log Likelihood	3.39	3.25	3.01	1.86

Thus, health index is given by

$$HI_{II} = Average\ Value\ of\ the\ Cumulative\ Feature \tag{14}$$

This establishes its possibility to be used as an index. In this approach, HI value is indicated by a single number.

Mahalanobis Distance (MD) Based HI

Mahalanobis distance (MD) method was proposed by Mahalanobis P.C. (Soylemezoglu et. al., 2010). In this work, MD values are computed from features selected using KFDA. A normal data set is formed from the features of healthy condition of REB, and their MD values constitute a reference space termed as Mahalanobis Space (MS). The mathematical procedure involved in computing Mahalanobis Space (MS), validation of MS and decision making is given in(Tao et. al., 2013, Jin et.al., 2012, Soylemezoglu et. al., 2010). An inbuilt MATLAB function with the syntax $d = mahal$ (Y, X) is used to compute the MD using MATLAB R2012, where Y is the observations from the defective conditions and X is observations from normal condition of the bearing (Tao et. al., 2013, Jin et.al., 2012, Soylemezoglu et. al., 2010, Kumar et. al., 2017). As per MD method, decision is made based on the following condition. MD values > 1, are attributed to the signals related to the defective conditions and indicates need for corrective actions to be taken (Soylemezoglu et. al., 2010).

Considering 622 rpm shaft speed and load of 1.7 kN for normal condition, the Wnl feature data set is of dimension 17×25. The remaining dimension of 17×75 corresponds to B, IR and OR conditions. Figure 6 shows the variation of MD for Wnl feature for four bearing conditions.

Fig 6 clearly demonstrates the ascending trend of MD values for defective conditions in the following sequence IR, B and OR (Kumar et. al., 2017). Among the six KFDA selected features only Wnl feature properly classified the different conditions of the REB and thus HI developed in this approach is given by

$$\text{HI}_{\text{III}} = \text{Mahalanobis Distance for Weibull Negative log likelihood feature}$$

$$(15)$$

This research work's main focus is to use different aspects of WT and integrating these aspects in developing three HI construction approaches for REB fault diagnosis using vibration signals at loads and constant shaft speed. Accordingly, three approaches have been devised and presented. Finally, a comparison of these approaches are presented in the following section leading to the selection of the best HI construction approach for REB fault diagnosis.

Figure 6. Variation of Mahalanobis Distance for Weibull Negative Log Likelihood feature

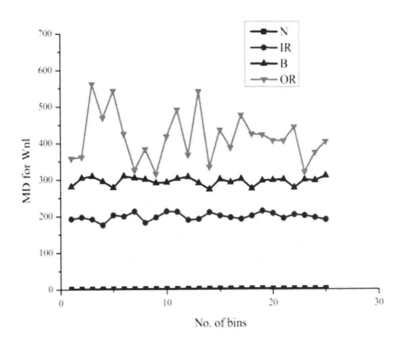

Comparison of the Proposed Approaches

This section presents the comparison of the approaches considered in this work. Since the SV based HI is applied to individual feature array (i.e. m-by-1 or 1-by-m) of a signal, it gives a unique singular value, which is insufficient to classify different conditions of the bearing (Akhbardeh et. al., 2007). Table 6 indicates no much difference in singular values between N, B and IR when compared with OR showcasing it's limitation for HI development. This led to the development of AVCF based HI, which uses AVCF for classifying different bearing conditions. AVCF value is different for four bearing conditions and it overcomes the limitations of SV based HI. The limitation of the AVCF based HI is that it requires additional work which consumes more time i.e. in converting ordinary feature into its cumulative form. SV and AVCF based HI, results in individual values but fail to showcase any range of values which assists in classifying different conditions of the bearing. In addition to this, it doesn't have a threshold value. These shortcomings are addressed in MD based HI. MD presents a simple and effective approach for bearing fault diagnosis,

133

Figure 7. Variation of Mahalanobis Distance for Weibull Negative Log Likelihood feature at 1.7 kN and shaft speed 922 rpm

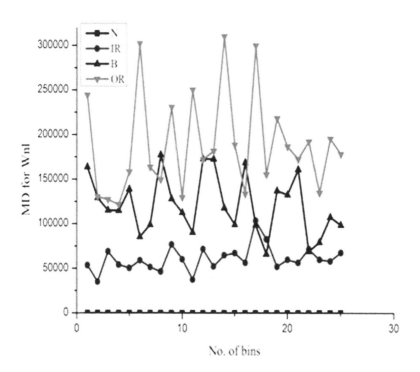

as it provides a range of values from zero to infinity. The higher MD values are of significance for defective conditions which is missing in SV based HI and AVCF based HI (Jin et. al., 2012, Kumar et. al., 2017).

MD consumes less time for computation when compared to ANN. The deviation of MD values from the MS separates the normal and defective conditions, providing a clear distinction. This concept is not found in SV based HI and AVCF based HI. The limitation of MD is that the selection of normal observations is very significant to build the MS, which in turn is used to obtain MD values for defective conditions. MD performs dual function i.e. it can be used as an index as well as a classifier which is the unique advantage, which is not found in SV and AVCF based HI. Thus MD based HI is considered as the best HI for REB fault diagnosis (Kumar et. al., 2018).The final aim of this work is to select the best approach from among the proposed approaches.

Validation

The validation of the MD based HI developed has been done using vibration signals collected at a load of 1.7 kN and the highest possible shaft speed of 922 rpm obtained by modifying the shaft pulley system of the test rig. Fig. 7 shows MD values for four bearing conditions. MD differentiates different conditions of the REB with MD values satisfying the threshold condition. Also the values are closer for both OR and B. The MD values are very high when compared to the results shown in figure 6, as the signal is acquired at a higher shaft speed of 922 rpm, which significantly enhances the feature values (Kumar et. al., 2017).

CONCLUSION

Though several techniques have been presented in the literature for bearing fault diagnosis, it is still a tough task to implement a reliable CM and fault diagnosis system for REB based on vibration signals due to complexity and operating conditions in the real world scenario. The overall objective of this work is to develop a reliable fault diagnosis system for REB using vibration signals by studying various aspects of WT and integrating them suitably to develop a HI using three different approaches and select the best possible approach for effective fault diagnosis of REB. The important conclusions drawn from this research work are as given below:

1. A comparison of the performance of the proposed approaches has been made to select the best approach i.e. MD based HI, for REB fault diagnosis.
2. The primary goal of this research work is to use different aspects of WT in developing HI using different approaches based on the work carried out by different researchers for REB fault diagnosis. The result obtained from studying different aspects of WT in this work is as follows - 'dmey' is the best MW, 'Interval-dependent' denoising scheme is the best scheme with higher kurtosis value, 'Five' statistical features are selected from seventeen features, and these findings are used in developing and investigating these HI approaches.

Thus, this research work has developed a scheme for the integration of the different aspects of WT i.e. study of different MWs, signal denoising schemes, WT, extraction of statistical features and DRTs, leading to the development of an effective HIs using various approaches and finally, the selection of the best approach which is effective in REB fault diagnosis.

ACKNOWLEDGMENT

The authors would like to thank Condition Monitoring Research Lab for providing the customized Bearing test rig and Dr. Vijay G.S, Dept. of Mechanical and Manufacturing Engg., MIT, MAHE, Manipal, INDIA for helping in acquisition of the vibration signals from Rolling Element Bearings, fabrication of bearing test rig and in the coding required for implementing algorithms required for this research work. Also, I would like thank Mrs. Jayanti, Rao, English lecturer Govt. P. U. College Mulki, India, for her help to carry out the language related editing of the chapter.

REFERENCES

Abboud, D., Elbadaoui, M., Smith, W. A., & Randall, R. B. (2019). Advanced bearing diagnostics: A comparative study of two powerful approaches. *Mechanical Systems and Signal Processing*, *114*, 604–627. doi:10.1016/j.ymssp.2018.05.011

Abdusslam, S. A. (2012). *Detection and diagnosis of rolling element bearing faults using time encoded signal processing and recognition*. University of Huddersfield.

Akhbardeh, A., Junnila, S., Koivuluoma, M., Koivistoinen, T., & Värri, A. (2006). Applying novel time-frequency moments singular value decomposition method and artificial neural networks for ballistocardiography. *EURASIP Journal on Advances in Signal Processing*, *2007*(1), 1–9. doi:10.1155/2007/60576

Al-Badour, F., Sunar, M., & Cheded, L. (2011). Vibration analysis of rotating machinery using time–frequency analysis and wavelet techniques. *Mechanical Systems and Signal Processing*, *25*(6), 2083–2101. doi:10.1016/j.ymssp.2011.01.017

Alguindigue, I. E., Loskiewicz-Buczak, A., & Uhrig, R. E. (1993). Monitoring and diagnosis of rolling element bearings using artificial neural networks. *IEEE Transactions on Industrial Electronics*, *40*(2), 209–217. doi:10.1109/41.222642

Brusa, E., Bruzzone, F., Delprete, C., Di Maggio, L. G., & Rosso, C. (2020). Health Indicators Construction for Damage Level Assessment in Bearing Diagnostics: A Proposal of an Energetic Approach Based on Envelope Analysis. *Applied Sciences (Basel, Switzerland)*, *10*(22), 8131. doi:10.3390/app10228131

Caesarendra, W., Kosasih, B., Tieu, K., & Moodie, C. A. (2013). An application of nonlinear feature extraction-A case study for low speed slewing bearing condition monitoring and prognosis. In *IEEE International Conference on Advanced Intelligent Mechatronics*, (pp. 1713-1718). 10.1109/AIM.2013.6584344

Castro, O. J. L., Sisamón, C. C., & Prada, J. C. G. (2006, October). Bearing fault diagnosis based on neural network classification and wavelet transform. In *Proceedings of the 6th WSEAS international conference on Wavelet analysis & multirate systems, 2,* (pp. 16-18). WSEAS.

Chakroborty, S., & Saha, G. (2010). Feature selection using singular value decomposition and QR factorization with column pivoting for text-independent speaker identification. *Speech Communication, 52*(9), 693–709. doi:10.1016/j.specom.2010.04.002

Chen, J., Cheng, L., Yu, H., & Hu, S. (2018). Rolling bearing fault diagnosis and health assessment using ensemble empirical mode decomposition and the adjustment Mahalanobis–Taguchi system. *International Journal of Systems Science, 49*(1), 147–159. doi:10.1080/00207721.2017.1397804

Donoho, D. L. (1995). De-noising by soft-thresholding. *IEEE Transactions on Information Theory, 41*(3), 613–627. doi:10.1109/18.382009

Dron, J. P., Rasolofondraibe, L., Chiementin, X., & Bolaers, F. (2010). A comparative experimental study on the use of three denoising methods for bearing defect detection. *Meccanica, 45*(2), 265–277. doi:10.100711012-009-9243-x

Duong, B. P., Khan, S. A., Shon, D., Im, K., Park, J., Lim, D. S., & Kim, J. M. (2018). A reliable health indicator for fault prognosis of bearings. *Sensors (Basel), 18*(11), 3740. doi:10.339018113740 PMID:30400203

Gao, R. X., & Yan, R. (2010). *Wavelets: Theory and applications for manufacturing.* Springer.

GS, V., Pai, S. P., Sriram, N. S., & Rao, R. B. (2013). Radial basis function neural network based comparison of dimensionality reduction techniques for effective bearing diagnostics. *Proceedings of the Institution of Mechanical Engineers, Part J: Journal of Engineering Tribology, 227*(6), 640-653.

GS, V., HS, K., Pai P, S., NS, S., & Rao, R. B. (2012). Evaluation of effectiveness of wavelet based denoising schemes using artificial neural network and support vector machine for bearing condition classification. *Computational Intelligence and Neuroscience,* 1–12.

Guo, J., Liu, X., Li, S., & Wang, Z. (2020). Bearing Intelligent Fault Diagnosis Based on Wavelet Transform and Convolution Neural Network. *Shock and Vibration, 2020,* 1–14.

Hao, R., & Chu, F. (2009). Morphological undecimated wavelet decomposition for fault diagnostics of rolling element bearings. *Journal of Sound and Vibration, 320*(4-5), 1164–1177. doi:10.1016/j.jsv.2008.09.014

Huang, M. L., & Chen, H. Y. (2005). Development and comparison of automated classifiers for glaucoma diagnosis using Stratus optical coherence tomography. *Investigative Ophthalmology & Visual Science, 46*(11), 4121–4129. doi:10.1167/iovs.05-0069 PMID:16249489

Jardine, A. K., Lin, D., & Banjevic, D. (2006). A review on machinery diagnostics and prognostics implementing condition-based maintenance. *Mechanical Systems and Signal Processing, 20*(7), 1483–1510. doi:10.1016/j.ymssp.2005.09.012

Javed, K., Gouriveau, R., Zerhouni, N., & Nectoux, P. (2013). A feature extraction procedure based on trigonometric functions and cumulative descriptors to enhance prognostics modelling. In *IEEE Conference on Prognostics and Health Management (PHM)* (pp. 1-7). IEEE.

Javed, K., Gouriveau, R., Zerhouni, N., & Nectoux, P. (2015). Enabling health monitoring approach based on vibration data for accurate prognostics. *IEEE Transactions on Industrial Electronics, 62*(1), 647–656. doi:10.1109/TIE.2014.2327917

Jin, X., Ma, E. W., Cheng, L. L., & Pecht, M. (2012). Health monitoring of cooling fans based on Mahalanobis distance with mRMR feature selection. *IEEE Transactions on Instrumentation and Measurement, 61*(8), 2222–2229. doi:10.1109/TIM.2012.2187240

Kankar, P. K., Sharma, S. C., & Harsha, S. P. (2011). Fault diagnosis of ball bearings using continuous wavelet transform. *Applied Soft Computing, 11*(2), 2300–2312. doi:10.1016/j.asoc.2010.08.011

Khanam, S., Tandon, N., & Dutt, J. K. (2014). Fault size estimation in the outer race of ball bearing using discrete wavelet transform of the vibration signal. *Procedia Technology, 14*, 12–19. doi:10.1016/j.protcy.2014.08.003

Kumar, H. S., Pai, P. S., Sriram, N. S., & Vijay, G. S. (2013). Artificial neural network based evaluation of performance of wavelet transform for condition monitoring of rolling element bearing. *Procedia Engineering, 64*, 805–814. doi:10.1016/j.proeng.2013.09.156

Kumar, H. S., Pai, P. S., Sriram, N. S., Vijay, G. S., & Patil, M. V. (2016). Comparison of denoising schemes and dimensionality reduction techniques for fault diagnosis of rolling element bearing using wavelet transform. *International Journal of Manufacturing Research*, *11*(3), 238–258. doi:10.1504/IJMR.2016.079461

Kumar, H. S., Pai, S. P., Sriram, N. S., & Vijay, G. S. (2017). Rolling element bearing fault diagnostics: Development of health index. *Proceedings of the Institution of Mechanical Engineers. Part C, Journal of Mechanical Engineering Science*, *231*(21), 3923–3939. doi:10.1177/0954406216656214

Lin, T. R., Yu, K., & Tan, J. (2017). *Condition monitoring and fault diagnosis of roller element bearing*. Intech Open. doi:10.5772/67143

Mallat, S. G. (1989). A theory for multiresolution signal decomposition: The wavelet representation. *IEEE Transactions on Pattern Analysis and Machine Intelligence*, *11*(7), 674–693. doi:10.1109/34.192463

Mamun, M., Al-Kadi, M., & Marufuzzaman, M. (2013). Effectiveness of wavelet denoising on electroencephalogram signals. *Journal of Applied Research and Technology*, *11*(1), 156–160. doi:10.1016/S1665-6423(13)71524-4

Miao, Q., Huang, H. Z., & Fan, X. (2007). Singularity detection in machinery health monitoring using Lipschitz exponent function. *Journal of Mechanical Science and Technology*, *21*(5), 737–744. doi:10.1007/BF02916351

Michell, M. (2012). *Yves, Misti., Georges, Oppenheim., Jean-Michel, Poggi*. Wavelet Toolbox TM, User's Guide, The Mathworks, Inc.

Mojsilovic, A., Popovic, M. V., & Rackov, D. M. (2000). On the selection of an optimal wavelet basis for texture characterization. *IEEE Transactions on Image Processing*, *9*(12), 2043–2050. doi:10.1109/83.887972 PMID:18262942

Patil, M. S., Mathew, J., & RajendraKumar, P. K. (2008). Bearing signature analysis as a medium for fault detection: A review. *Journal of Tribology, 130*(1), 014001-1014001-7.

Peng, Z. K., & Chu, F. L. (2004). Application of the wavelet transform in machine condition monitoring and fault diagnostics: A review with bibliography. *Mechanical Systems and Signal Processing*, *18*(2), 199–221. doi:10.1016/S0888-3270(03)00075-X

Pinheiro, A. A., Brandao, I. M., & Da Costa, C. (2019). Vibration Analysis in Turbomachines using Machine Learning Techniques. *European Journal of Engineering and Technology Research*, *4*(2), 12–16. doi:10.24018/ejers.2019.4.2.1128

Pirra, M. (2012). *Advanced techniques for aircraft bearing diagnostics.* Polytechnic University of Milan.

Raficc, J., Rafiee, M. A., & Tse, P. W. (2010). Application of mother wavelet functions for automatic gear and bearing fault diagnosis. *Expert Systems with Applications, 37*(6), 4568–4579. doi:10.1016/j.eswa.2009.12.051

Ramani, A. (2008). *Diagnosis And Prognosis of Electrical And Mechanical Faults Using Wireless Sensor Networks And a Two-stage Neural Network Classifier, College of Engineering, ProQuest Dissertations and Theses (electronic resource collection).* University of Texas at Arlington.

Randall, R. B., & Antoni, J. (2011). Rolling element bearing diagnostics—A tutorial. *Mechanical Systems and Signal Processing, 25*(2), 485–520. doi:10.1016/j.ymssp.2010.07.017

Rao, B. K. N., Pai, P. S., & Nagabhushana, T. N. (2012). Failure diagnosis and prognosis of rolling-element bearings using Artificial Neural Networks: A critical overview. *Journal of Physics: Conference Series, 364*(1), 012023. doi:10.1088/1742-6596/364/1/012023

Saravanan, N., & Ramachandran, K. I. (2009). Fault diagnosis of spur bevel gear box using discrete wavelet features and Decision Tree classification. *Expert Systems with Applications, 36*(5), 9564–9573. doi:10.1016/j.eswa.2008.07.089

Shinde, V. D., Patil, C. G., & Ruikar, M. S. D. (2012). Wavelet based multi-scale principal component analysis for speech enhancement. *International Journal of Engineering Trends and Technology, 3*(3), 397–400.

Smith, W. A., & Randall, R. B. (2015). Rolling element bearing diagnostics using the Case Western Reserve University data: A benchmark study. *Mechanical Systems and Signal Processing, 64*, 100–131. doi:10.1016/j.ymssp.2015.04.021

Soylemezoglu, A., Jagannathan, S., & Saygin, C. (2010). Mahalanobis Taguchi system as a prognostics tool for rolling element bearing failures. *Journal of Manufacturing Science and Engineering, 132*(5), 051014. doi:10.1115/1.4002545

Sreejith, B., Verma, A. K., & Srividya, A. (2008, December). Fault diagnosis of rolling element bearing using time-domain features and neural networks. In *2008 IEEE region 10 and the third international conference on industrial and information systems* (pp. 1-6). IEEE. 10.1109/ICIINFS.2008.4798444

Sreejith, B., Verma, A. K., & Srividya, A. (2010). Comparison of Morlet wavelet filter for defect diagnosis of bearings. In *2nd International Conference on Reliability, Safety and Hazard-Risk-Based Technologies and Physics-of-Failure Methods (ICRESH)* (pp. 406-411). IEEE. 10.1109/ICRESH.2010.5779584

Sumithra, M. G., & Thanuskodi, K. (2009, June). Wavelet based speech signal de-noising using hybrid thresholding. In *International Conference on Control, Automation, Communication and Energy Conservation* (pp. 1-7). IEEE.

Tandon, N., & Choudhury, A. (1999). A review of vibration and acoustic measurement methods for the detection of defects in rolling element bearings. *Tribology International, 32*(8), 469–480. doi:10.1016/S0301-679X(99)00077-8

Tandon, N., & Nakra, B. C. (1992). Vibration and acoustic monitoring techniques for the detection of defects in rolling element bearings—a review. *The Shock and Vibration Digest, 24*(3), 3-11.

Tao, X., Lu, C., Lu, C., & Wang, Z. (2013). An approach to performance assessment and fault diagnosis for rotating machinery equipment. *EURASIP Journal on Advances in Signal Processing, 2013*(1), 1–16. doi:10.1186/1687-6180-2013-5

Tarighat, M. A. (2016). Orthogonal projection approach and continuous wavelet transform-feed forward neural networks for simultaneous spectrophotometric determination of some heavy metals in diet samples. *Food Chemistry, 192*, 548–556. doi:10.1016/j.foodchem.2015.07.034 PMID:26304383

Tyagi, C. S. (2008). A comparative study of SVM classifiers and artificial neural networks application for rolling element bearing fault diagnosis using wavelet transform preprocessing. Proceedings of World Academy of Science. *Engineering and Technology, 2*(7), 904–912.

Üstündağ, M., Şengür, A., Gökbulut, M., & Ata, F. (2013). Performance comparison of wavelet thresholding techniques on weak ECG signal denoising. *Przegląd Elektrotechniczny, 89*(5), 63–66.

Večeř, P., Kreidl, M., & Šmíd, R. (2005). Condition indicators for gearbox condition monitoring systems. *Acta Polytechnica, 45*(6), 35–43. doi:10.14311/782

Vijay, G. S. (2013). *Vibration signal analysis for defect characterization of rolling element bearing using some soft computing techniques*. VTU.

Vishwash, B., Pai, P. S., Sriram, N. S., Ahmed, R., Kumar, H. S., & Vijay, G. S. (2014). Multiscale slope feature extraction for gear and bearing fault diagnosis using wavelet transform. *Procedia Materials Science, 5*, 1650–1659. doi:10.1016/j.mspro.2014.07.353

Wang, D., Miao, Q., & Kang, R. (2009). Robust health evaluation of gearbox subject to tooth failure with wavelet decomposition. *Journal of Sound and Vibration, 324*(3-5), 1141–1157. doi:10.1016/j.jsv.2009.02.013

Wang, D., Tsui, K. L., & Miao, Q. (2017). Prognostics and health management: A review of vibration based bearing and gear health indicators. *IEEE Access: Practical Innovations, Open Solutions, 6*, 665–676. doi:10.1109/ACCESS.2017.2774261

Wang, H., & Chen, P. (2008). Fault diagnosis for a rolling bearing used in a reciprocating machine by adaptive filtering technique and fuzzy neural network. *WSEAS Transactions on Systems, 7*(1), 1–6.

Wang, Y. (2013). Wavelet transform based feature extraction for fault diagnosis of rolling-element bearing. *Journal of Information and Computational Science, 2*, 469–475.

Yan, R. (2007). *Base wavelet selection criteria for non-stationary vibration analysis in bearing health diagnosis*. University of Massachusetts Amherst.

Yan, R., Gao, R. X., & Chen, X. (2014). Wavelets for fault diagnosis of rotary machines: A review with applications. *Signal Processing, 96*, 1–15. doi:10.1016/j.sigpro.2013.04.015

Zaeri, R., Ghanbarzadeh, A., Attaran, B., & Moradi, S. (2011). Artificial neural network based fault diagnostics of rolling element bearings using continuous wavelet transform. In *2nd International Conference on Control, Instrumentation and Automation* (pp. 753-758). IEEE. 10.1109/ICCIAutom.2011.6356754

Zhang, J. F., & Huang, Z. C. (2005). Kernel Fisher discriminant analysis for bearing fault diagnosis. In *International Conference on Machine Learning and Cybernetics* (Vol. 5, pp. 3216-3220). IEEE.

Zhang, L., Bao, P., & Wu, X. (2005). Multiscale linear minimum mean square-error estimation based image denoising with optimal wavelet selection. *IEEE Transactions on Circuits and Systems for Video Technology, 15*(4), 469–481. doi:10.1109/TCSVT.2005.844456

Zhen, L., Zhengjia, H., Yanyang, Z., & Yanxue, W. (2008). Customized wavelet denoising using intra-and inter-scale dependency for bearing fault detection. *Journal of Sound and Vibration, 313*(1-2), 342–359. doi:10.1016/j.jsv.2007.11.039

Zheng, Z., Petrone, R., Péra, M. C., Hissel, D., Becherif, M., Pianese, C., & Sorrentino, M. (2013). A review on non-model based diagnosis methodologies for proton exchange membrane fuel cell stacks and systems. *International Journal of Hydrogen Energy, 38*(21), 8914–8926. doi:10.1016/j.ijhydene.2013.04.007

Zhu, J., Nostrand, T., Spiegel, C., & Morton, B. (2014). Survey of condition indicators for condition monitoring systems. In *Annu. Conf. Progn. Heal. Manag. Soc (Vol. 5*, pp. 1-13). Academic Press.

Chapter 7

Integration of Cutting-Edge Interoperability Approaches in Cyber-Physical Production Systems and Industry 4.0

Luis Alberto Estrada-Jimenez
CTS UNINOVA, Faculdade de Ciências e Tecnologia, Universidade Nova de Lisboa, Portugal

Terrin Pulikottil
CTS UNINOVA, Faculdade de Ciências e Tecnologia, Universidade Nova de Lisboa, Portugal

Nguyen Ngoc Hien
iD https://orcid.org/0000-0003-4618-9462
Mondragon Unibertsitatea, Spain

Agajan Torayev
Institute for Advanced Manufacturing, University of Nottingham, UK

Hamood Ur Rehman
University of Nottingham, UK & TQC Ltd., UK

Fan Mo
Institute for Advanced Manufacturing, University of Nottingham, UK

Sanaz Nikghadam Hojjati
iD https://orcid.org/0000-0002-0839-9250
CTS UNINOVA, Faculdade de Ciências e Tecnologia, Universidade Nova de Lisboa, Portugal

José Barata
CTS UNINOVA, Faculdade de Ciências e Tecnologia, Universidade Nova de Lisboa, Portugal

ABSTRACT

Interoperability in smart manufacturing refers to how interconnected cyber-physical components exchange information and interact. This is still an exploratory topic, and despite the increasing number of applications, many challenges remain open. This chapter presents an integrative framework to understand common practices,

DOI: 10.4018/978-1-7998-6721-0.ch007

concepts, and technologies used in trending research to achieve interoperability in production systems. The chapter starts with the question of what interoperability is and provides an alternative answer based on influential works in the field, followed by the presentation of important reference models and their relation to smart manufacturing. It continues by discussing different types of interoperability, data formats, and common ontologies necessary for the integration of heterogeneous systems and the contribution of emerging technologies in achieving interoperability. This chapter ends with a discussion of a recent use case and final remarks.

INTRODUCTION

In recent years, manufacturing has experienced several changes because of the intensive development and research in sciences and technology and the provision of necessary equipment and systems to optimize industrial processes. The fourth industrial revolution precisely describes a new manufacturing paradigm engaging emerging technologies like machine learning, big data, internet of things, etc., and offering benefits like increased efficiency, fault tolerance, cognition and autonomy. In this regard, Cyber-Physical Production Systems (CPPS) emerge as one of the main enablers of Industry 4.0. Components of CPPS are smart and autonomous, connected in all levels in the production life cycle and provide fundamentally "intelligence, connectedness and responsiveness" (Monostori et al., 2016). Usually, a smart manufacturing environment is composed of various CPPS, which are continuously exchanging information and interacting. Currently, this is a focus of continuous research considering the high degree of heterogeneity in production systems (Y. Lu, 2017) also known as manufacturing interoperability. In this work, we refer to interoperability as a set of methodologies, tools and strategies needed to achieve information exchange. This also includes strategies and technologies utilized for the digitalization of machines, products, and internet platforms for data storage and data analysis.

The development of interoperability among CPPS has been tackled by industries as a standardization issue. Many authors consider that the creation of standardized interfaces and protocols may decrease the skepticism for the introduction of CPPS in industry (Leitão, Colombo, & Karnouskos, 2016). On the other hand, various researchers have implemented approaches using emerging technologies to show the benefits of principles of CPPS (Monostori et al., 2016a; Chaplin et al., 2015; Colombo,

AW; Karnouskos, S; Mendes, 2015). Some examples are agent technologies, service based frameworks and cloud platforms. These technologies, standards and protocols are showing promising results but also new challenges that need to be overcome to reach a seamless integration. This chapter presents an integrative framework to explore common definitions, concepts, architectures, standards, technologies and a real case scenario considering interoperability approaches in smart manufacturing. The main objective of this study is to be a supportive conceptual text for researchers and practitioners in future implementations.

BACKGROUND

The fourth industrial revolution and the increasing research in information and communication technologies (ICT) results in a continuous evolution in the level of industrialization and technological development of factories. This new level of interaction and heterogeneity has brought the need of standardization and modelling of production systems as reference architectures. Those are used to describe high-level models and their internal relation.

Standard development organizations of countries such as USA, Germany and China have developed roadmaps and standardized solutions for smart manufacturing to integrate emerging ICT into the manufacturing domain. For instance, the Reference Architectural Model Industrie 4.0 (RAMI 4.0) provides a tridimensional description of the production life cycle, hierarchies and different layers of a smart production system. Similar characteristics are shared by the Smart manufacturing ecosystem (SME) developed by the National Institute of Standards and Technology (NIST - USA) and by the Intelligent Manufacturing System Architecture (IMSA) developed by the Ministry of Industry and Information technology of China.

Certainly, those standardization efforts show the high level of commitment of governments and the high interest of industrial stakeholders for the integration of cyber-physical components creating a smart and highly interconnected environment. This level of integration goes from an inter-organizational (horizontal integration) to a local or intra-organizational point of view (vertical integration), being the latest essential for a seamless collaboration in an enterprise hierarchy (Alcácer & Cruz-Machado, 2019).

A CPPS is a set of computational systems with high interconnection with physical resources, which precisely describes the necessity of interconnection and interoperability in industry 4.0. CPPS represent very heterogeneous units with the capacity of abstraction physical resources, products, legacy systems and even people's behaviors. Therefore, the communication and intercommunication of these entities are considered a challenging effort because of its heterogeneous nature. This high level of integration and collaboration requires very high levels of interoperability that is the main topic of discussion in this chapter.

To understand this issue we should understand what the definition of interoperability is. The IEEE standard computer dictionary defines interoperability as "the ability of two or more systems or components to exchange information and to use the information that has been exchanged"(Geraci, 1991). This emphasizes the capacity of communication between different systems despite their technological nature. This definition can be, however, abstract when referring to manufacturing systems. In this regard, a collection of specific definitions from selected works of the literature is presented and discussed below.

- In their work (Rojas & Rauch, 2019), describe interoperability as the continuous data and information accessibility with the production elements. Additionally, this work mentions that the challenge of interoperability is based on the data formalization, networking and connectivity. Finally, it is concluded that high levels of integration are strongly linked with high levels of interoperability.
- For (Zeid et al., 2019), the process of interoperability is highly related to the interaction of machines and the way how they are controlled. In this sense, real time interaction and communication is imperative to prevent failures and to ensure a high availability of the information. This can improve not just the safety but also the efficiency of the production process. Interoperability requires a high availability and collaboration from services inside and outside the shop floor and the utilization of cloud base technologies. For this purpose, a common understanding and data representation is required.
- For (Napoleone et al., 2020), a high degree of interoperability refers to a high degree of standardization. A well-structured representation as well as a proper integration of legacy systems is essential to implement CPPS and to ensure an easier integration of its components.
- In (Van Der Veer & Wiles, 2008), the concept of interoperability is referred as "the ability of equipment from different manufacturers (or different systems) to communicate together on the same infrastructure (same system), or on another while roaming".

Indeed, the challenge of interoperability is born with the need of a seamless and high integration and cooperation of all levels in a factory: people, machines, business, organizational aspects, etc., and in this in turn with the value chain. Previous definitions suggest that the challenge of interoperability in smart manufacturing is not a single issue and several aspects should be consider. For example, compatibility of data types, abstraction levels, proper technological enablers, etc. Additionally, in smart manufacturing, interoperability should be addressed in a robust manner. Aspects like real time communication and high availability of services and resources are imperative to achieve the expectations of industry 4.0 optimizing processes and making them autonomous with little or non-human intervention. The common understanding, standardization and continuous evolution of technologies are paving the way to fulfill current expectations and even though there are many challenges that need to be overcome; there is currently a strong baseline of concepts, research and applications.

The following sections of this document are dedicated to address common approaches, emerging technologies and applications with regard to interoperability in smart manufacturing.

Types and Levels of Interoperability in the Integration of Cyber-Physical Production Systems

The IEEE Guide to the Enterprise Information Technology Body of Knowledge (EITBOK) has categorized the interoperability approaches mainly into two types: Syntactic and Semantic (Mosley, M., 2009), but in recent years we have seen the emergence of different categories or perspectives of interoperability like technical, organizational, device, networking, platform interoperability, etc. This section explains along with the main two types also device, factory (vertical integration) and cloud manufacturing (horizontal integration) which are very relevant to the smart manufacturing applications.

Device Interoperability

The term device is mainly used in the Internet of things to refer to "smart objects" with capabilities of integration and communication. Devices are highly heterogeneous and can be exemplified as sensors, actuators, parts to be assembled, and several low-level control hardware. The literature classifies the different types of devices in low level devices like Radio Frequency Identification (RFID) tags or barcodes and high-level devices like Programmable Logic Controller (PLCs) and computational boards (e.g. Raspberry) considering their embedded computational power and communication capabilities. Additionally, for a seamless communication these devices (low level and high level) need to manage necessary standards and protocols. Thus, it can be referred to device interoperability as the way how these heterogeneous devices are integrated, including standards, protocols and different technologies.

The literature in device interoperability in smart manufacturing is by far extensive. In (Chaplin et al., 2015), the utilization of a Raspberry pi allows the integration of agent technology, which in turn allows the communication among all entities in the shop floor. This development board is later interfaced with a PLC, which acts as main controller of the process. Additionally, this work shows the utilization of RFID technology as a method to integrate and identify products in different production stages. In (Leitao & Barbosa, 2019), with the purpose of demonstrating self-organization in a modularized conveyor system, agents are implemented through the utilization of a raspberry pi which also receives signals from different sensors and communicates with other boards via WIFI technology. In (Garcia et al., 2016), a CPPS system has been developed based on the virtualization of several stations via two platforms: Arduino and Raspberry pi. Those are in charge of receiving and handling input/output signals from the connected stations and of interfacing them in the network using MODBUS TCP and OPC Unified Architecture (OPC-UA) technologies.

Syntactic Interoperability

In general, if various systems are capable of exchanging information, they have syntactic interoperability. While exchanging information or service from one system to another, the content of the message needs to be serialized. The sender encodes the data in the message and the receiver decodes the received message. The sender and receiver use rules specified in some grammar to encrypt or decrypt the messages. The need for syntactic interoperability arises when these rules are incompatible with the receiver's decoding rules, which leads to mismatching message parse trees. The European Telecommunications Standards Institute (ETSI) defines syntactic interoperability as follows (Van Der Veer & Wiles, 2008): "Syntactical Interoperability is usually associated with data formats. Certainly, the messages transferred by communication protocols need to have a well-defined syntax and encoding, even if it is only in the form of bit-tables. However, many protocols carry data or content, and this can be represented using high-level transfer syntaxes such as Hypertext Markup Language (HTML), Extensible Markup Language (XML) or Abstract Syntax Notation One (ASN.1)".

Syntactic interoperability is achieved with standardized data formats and communication protocols. This includes standards like HTML, XML or JSON. XML is widely considered in the internet community for markup in documents of arbitrary structure. XML is designed for markup in documents of arbitrary structure.

A major limitation of this type of interoperability is that it just considers the data format and gets the information from one place to another intact. It does consider the meaning of the transferred information nor applies logic to the fact being transferred and used.

Semantic Interoperability

Semantic interoperability ensures that the exchanges between requesters and providers of data make sense, and have a mutual understanding of the "meanings" of the demanded data.

Ontologies are necessary to prevent semantic issues. Therefore, numerous amounts of work are done using ontologies. Context modelling facilitates interoperability of manufacturing systems. To this end, (Bettini et al., 2010) compares different context modeling and reasoning techniques by describing requirements like heterogeneity, mobility, relationship and dependencies and efficient context provisioning for the context models and context management systems. Considering these requirements, the authors discussed and compared object-role based, spatial and ontology-based modeling techniques. Contextual ontological models provide clear advantages both in terms of heterogeneity and in terms of interoperability and is obtained only by implementing communicative languages. Consequently, a substantial number of authors employed ontologies in their works to achieve interoperability in the industrial domain. (Kumar et al., 2019) presents a survey of the ontologies for Industry 4.0, including different domains such as aerospace, construction, steel production, etc., and manufacturing processes such as packaging, process engineering, resource configuration, etc. This work gives a broad overview of the current state of the art ontologies for industry 4.0 and the standardization efforts. Authors discuss different ontologies such as Core Ontology for Robotics and Automation (CORA), Ontology for Autonomous Robotics (ROA), Ontology for Robotic Architecture (ORArch), Ontology for Industry 4.0 (O4I4) and their benefits in the representation of vocabulary to describe the key concepts in Industry 4.0. Although there are a variety of ontologies, there is a need for standardization of ontologies currently lacking in the literatures.

Interoperability in the manufacturing domain is challenged with different terms that people working within a particular group develop their vocabulary for particular elements or activities with which they often work. Ontologies provide a solution for this problem by using a common understanding of manufacturing-related terms and affecting manufacturing knowledge sharing.

Factory Interoperability

Factory interoperability is factories' ability to exchange information within and between each other in a logical and consistent manner. The latest advances in ICT have shifted the factory environment from data-drive to cooperative and knowledge driven. Factory integration and interoperability are key in tackling challenges in this environment. Some enablers to achieve integrated factories include knowledge sharing, web-based developments, use of common best practices and open-source applications. These enablers also help in achieving interoperability among factories.

Supply Chain – A network from suppliers to customers – is the most dominant structure for exchange of information in factories today (both business & technical). These information (passed using paper and telephone conversations before) has to be passed now electronically in a coherent manner throughout the supply chain considering international and regional standards. These standards along with corporate & national cultures and use of different products along the supply chain adds more challenge in sharing of coherent information. These challenges arise the need for a standard interoperability infrastructure. A slightly outdated study (Brunnermeier & Martin, 1999) on a $1 billion economic loss due to improper interoperability among the supply chain in U.S. automobile industry shows the impact of factory interoperability on manufacturing cost.

There are three principal approaches used in achieving interoperability, namely machine-to-machine solution, industry-wide standardization and Open Standards or Platforms. In machine-to-machine solution, each pair of partners has customized solution for exchanging information. The idea behind this approach is to make each machine interoperable with all its linked machine. This requires translation of syntax for each machine and clear understanding of its semantics. In Industry-wide standardization, the Original Equipment Manufacturer (OEM) commands its supply partners to have a common solution, usually an expensive proprietary one. In Open Standards, the infrastructure is built on a neutral and open standard form. This is the most effective approach in achieve interoperability as it tackles both the scalability issues in machine-to-machine solution and does not force an expensive solution as in Industry-wide standardization. This solution also provides long term stability for data storage which is especially useful for products with long life cycles like aerospace.

The reference models developed to address factory interoperability issues can be categorized into physical, functional and allocated architectures. One of the most widely discussed architecture model for manufacturing is RAMI 4.0. This model incorporates existing approaches (OPC-UA, IEC, AutomationML, ProSTEP, Field Device Integration) into the interoperability stack. Industrial Internet Reference Architecture (IIRA), another important reference model designed for Industrial Internet of Things was proposed by Industrial Internet Consortium (Lin et al., 2017). Even though IIRA was not designed for factories, IIRA shares lot of similarities with RAMI 4.0: similar layers, same tasks distribution and applies OPC-UA for network communications. Other reference architecture for achieving factory interoperability include IBM 4.0 Reference Architecture for Industry 4.0 and NIST service-oriented architecture.

Cloud Manufacturing Interoperability

Cloud computing - providing resources and services over internet - is a key enabler of smart manufacturing. Cloud computing can be adopted in manufacturing in two ways: as direct adoption of cloud computing services or as cloud manufacturing. Cloud manufacturing is an extension of cloud computing where physical assets are managed in a centralized manner by encapsulating them as cloud services. There is a need to introduce additional types of interoperability for cloud manufacturing like transport, behavioural and policy interoperability.

A typical cloud-based manufacturing architecture consists of five layers: application, interface, core service, virtualization, and physical resource. Interoperable Cloud-based Manufacturing System (ICMS) proposed by (X. V. Wang & Xu, 2013) could be taken as an example for explaining interoperability in a service-oriented system. ICMS comprises three cloud layers: user, smart and manufacturing. Common data models supported by control rules are fundamental requirement for incorporating such architectures for a wide product scheme. The data models in this case should support a common data standard like STEP/STEP NC for interoperability purpose. A detailed explanation of cloud-based services, platforms, different layers, and interoperability of cloud manufacturing is explained in next section.

Interoperability of Cyber-Physical Production Systems Through Emerging Technologies

Interoperability in CPPS could be explained by considering the various emerging technologies and its impact on the interoperability. This section explains interoperability based on agent technologies, service-oriented technologies and computing technologies like Cloud, Fog and Edge.

Agent Based Interoperability

Multi-Agent Systems (MAS) have been extensively applied in distributed artificial intelligence and software engineering to implement software units with intelligent capabilities. Michael Wooldridge (Wooldridge, 2009) defines agent as "a computer system capable of autonomous action in order to meet its design objectives". Agents have cognitive capabilities i.e. they can acquire external information, reason and perform defined preprogramed tasks.

MAS as part of a society, do not have global contextual knowledge of the operation environment; instead, they present a partial local understanding and the global reasoning is the result of the social ability, communicating needs and objectives among all the entities in the group.

Agent Communication

JADE supports the development of agents under the FIPA-ACL protocol. It is implemented in the JAVA language that facilitates the implementation of agents as objects. Furthermore, JADE can distribute agents over the networks. JADE also offers the deployment and testing of the agent communication using a graphical user interface. These properties have made JADE to be used in countless industrial applications and uses cases.

Multi-Agent Systems in Manufacturing

Traditional centralized industrial control approaches are not prepared for dealing with novel business paradigms i.e. mass customization. Furthermore, the development of ICT technologies, industry 4.0 and the globalized economy have brought the need of industries to have lower production costs, higher flexibility, higher quality of production and the need for a rapid response in case of disruptions. For this purpose, the future of manufacturing systems should be highly automated, flexible, modular, interoperable, and easily changeable (Mourtzis & Doukas, 2012). MAS appear as a powerful technological enabler for having not just modularity and autonomy but also interoperability among the resources in the workshop (Leitão, 2009). This general conception takes the definition of resource virtualization, which means the encapsulation of the digital behavior, properties and functionalities of physical resources as intelligent entities, in this case agents. These smart units can interact, have social abilities and communicate their necessities. In manufacturing this is translated to machines that can communicate with mobile elements, resources, products, humans, etc. For these reasons, agents are considered as very powerful enablers of integration and interoperability for CPPS.

Multi-Agent Systems for Achieving Interoperability and Integration in CPS

The general conception of CPS requires the confluence of physical devices with communication and computation aspects, which as stated before can be achieved using agent technologies. Agent based-CPS also provide several characteristics that improve integration and interoperability in smart manufacturing, some of these are summarized below (Cruz Salazar et al., 2019; Leitão, Colombo, & Karnouskos, 2016; Ribeiro, 2017):

- The vertical and horizontal integration is possible through the resource agentification and its communication over the network.

- The resulting integration can be improved by the intelligence capacity of agents optimizing energy, time and resource utilization.
- Human resources can be also represented by agents, which makes feasible its integration.
- The integration of CPS becomes very robust since it can handle unexpected situations and even behave autonomy.

The CPS standardization is a key aspect for the design and development of industrial CPS. However, there are currently not many standards available for its implementation and it is a topic of continues research. Present works rely to a large extend in reusing and combining IT technologies e.g. service-oriented approaches. Agents and web services can be integrated to provide the best of both worlds, considering the autonomy of agent technology and the interoperability provided by service-oriented architectures. Generally, the components at the lowest level e.g. controllers or PLCs provide their functionalities as services using the DPWS (Device Profile for Web Services) protocol (Colombo, AW; Karnouskos, S; Mendes, 2015). This creates virtual resources which highest control and interoperability can be implemented using a multi-agent approach.

The integration of low-level controllers with MAS normally relies on legacy PLC programming standards like IEC-61131 or IEC-61149. These standards are based on a control logic and in service-based function blocks respectively. In higher levels this control logic is managed by a multi-agent based approach (Leitão, Colombo, & Karnouskos, 2016). This execution is generally designed in a higher level that can adapt its behavior to different scenarios. To complete the orchestration, this process is normally governed by business or higher functions that manage the whole enterprise integration (Colombo, AW; Karnouskos, S; Mendes, 2015).

The application of agent technologies in smart manufacturing is wide in terms of the type of functionalities or level of integration. As resources are abstracted by single mechatronic agents those in turn can also be abstracted by different alliances according to the needed collaboration and skills (Onori et al., 2012). This resource virtualization includes management functionalities and customer operations allowing a broader integration i.e. in cloud platforms (Vogel-Heuser et al., 2014). This also influences the interoperability of various entities in the value chain. This evidence suggests that MAS have been implemented using different patterns depending on the type of applications. A complete discussion and classification of these patterns is made in (Cruz Salazar et al., 2019) and it is summarized below.

- **Resource access:** this type of agents generally includes the abstraction of field devices, resources and their operational control. Besides, they promote modularization and integration with higher layers.

- **Communication agent:** This pattern includes agents that manage and unify the communication of resources through upper layers. For example, resource agents normally are integrated using OPC-UA, FIPA, broker agents, ontologies, etc.
- **Process agent:** This type of pattern usually orchestrates and manages resource agents (locally). They normally do not interact with field devices but with digital entities. They are in charge of the coordination, diagnosis and supervision of processes and of their proper execution.
- **Agent management system:** It usually has a global supervisory role. Unlike, the process agent that refers to local supervision, this pattern can have a broader vision of the process.

Indeed, multi-agent technology through its inherent capabilities of autonomy and communication has brought opportunities to face with many of the current industrial integration and interoperability requirements that has been also enhanced with various technological enablers and standards.

Service Based Interoperability

An increasing complexity in manufacturing systems is often composed as a set of numerous multi-disciplinary and heterogeneous systems, such as maintenance, engineering, warehouse and management. Those systems are considered as active components offering their capabilities as services representing mechatronic functions of equipment. It leads to the requirements of communication, data processing and interconnections among these services to fully utilize the benefits of flexibility, adaptability, scalability, seamless and effective integration. The requirements are also well-recognized limitations of traditional manufacturing systems whose architectures have encountered the following main issues (Cândido et al., 2009; Ye et al., 2018):

- Complex and time-consuming reconfiguration to adapt the market changes.
- Highly centralized resource utilization, unidirectional information flow and discrete decision-making.
- Exponential complexity in scalability.
- Incompatibility between different manufacturing equipment and standalone specialized engineering tools in both internal and external business systems.
- Machines and other operating units in shop-floor systems are still commonly isolated from higher-level business environments, although manufacturing execution systems (MES) or similar enterprise management systems are becoming increasingly available in the industry.

At the same time, manufacturing today requires a dynamic environment to meet the turbulent market demand for highly customized products with high quality at low cost, fastest possible time-to-market via a complex supply chain from product level to connected business world. These limitations could be overcome by leveraging the information technology (IT) infrastructure of web services with the concept of service-oriented architecture (SOA) emerged at multiple organizational levels in business, and applied into the factory automation domain.

Generally, a SOA is composed by consumers and services that are participated and coordinated, meaning that they interact with one another to request services and resolve these requests via interactions determined by the service interface.

Main SOA Principles

To have an effective and sustainable implementation of SOA, there are more than technical capabilities. As other business systems, a successful SOA needs to integrate and embrace critical design principles related to development and management. In the context of SOA, a set of design principles is to define the framework of guidance in which service provides and business customers will plan for collaboration during the design and development of the system. Even though, the essential design principles have still been under discussion(Legner & Heutschi, 2007), below some of these critical designed principals are summarized:

- **Business values:** a SOA service is defined by focusing on how the service may fit in a larger business process context by following an outside-in approach and adapting a business process centric instead of technology centric approach where the service often represents a business task (Jammes et al., 2005).
- **Discoverability:** as the SOA service is designed, discovering a service is the first step to service consumption and reuse (Uddin et al., 2012).
- **Reusability:** a SOA service should be developed in the right extent of generalization so that the original users as well as new users can exploit its functionality (Legner & Heutschi, 2007).
- **Loose coupling:** when this principle is applied to the SOA design, the purpose is to protect the individual independency of each SOA user and SOA service to mitigate the impact of changes in underlying technology and behavior.
- **Stateless:** this principle is also represented by the granularity of services where a service interface is mostly coarse-grained and based on the exchange document and messages.

A successful building architecture of SOA and services deployment will incorporate services and artifacts that take business values, discoverability, reusability, loose coupling, stateless, interloper-ability into account. The designers also need to have a framework with a set of rules from which compliance to these principles can be measured, monitored and even the contingency plan for appropriate remediation of noncompliance can be made.

Main SOA Applications and Supporting Standards

It is very clear that SOA paradigm is currently expanding its impact in many fields of technologies, not only in the ICT sector where it originated, but also in other domains of applications in which industrial applications have been adopted with several business collaborative initiatives (Jammes et al., 2005). Many service-oriented solutions have been proposed by European research projects, such as the Internet of Things at Work, Production Logistics and Sustainability Cockpit, Architecture for Service-Oriented Process - Monitoring and Control(IMC-AESOP)(Ismail & Kastner, 2017). Those SOA solutions are not specific to any technology, vendor, or product, but there is a combination of different technology capabilities enabling SOA functionality, such as Enterprise Service Business, Service Registry and Repository, Business Process Management, Business Activities Monitoring, and Web Services Management (WSM) that is considered as one of the most common SOA service types.

Cloud Based Interoperability

The manufacturing sector is undergoing a change in which the demand of customized product is increasing and the supply chains are taking a globalized perspective. This globalization of manufacturing and supply chains has brought with itself the need and use of globally distributed, scalable, sustainable and service-oriented manufacturing platforms. A platform that takes this into account and builds on computing technologies, cloud computing, semantic web and associated service-oriented architecture is Cloud Manufacturing that caters to resource sharing, distribution and management of manufacturing services across the network. However, the system in the manufacturing environment in itself needs to be setup for combination and interoperability to cater the requirements for cloud manufacturing. The effective utilization of these modelled resources is carried out in manufacturing cloud to establish a framework for manufacturing process. For such kind of integration, it is essential that a neutral API (Application Programming Interface) is utilized to establish a direct connection to manufacturing environment without changing enterprise wide structure.

Cloud Manufacturing Architecture

Several architectures have been proposed for cloud manufacturing environments with principles catered to integration at all manufacturing levels. (Tai & Xu, 2012) developed a five-tier cloud manufacturing system that dealt with co-operation between manufacturing resources, resource management, portal for cloud manufacturing, a unified cooperation platform and cooperation support application layer. A cloud manufacturing solution for automotive sector was explored by (Jin, 2013) in which it was treated as a Software as a Service (SaaS) based on four-layer architecture (core service, business service, cloud sub-system service and related business service). A detailed architecture for cloud computed manufacturing environment was established by (Tao et al., 2011) comprising of resource, perception, resource virtualization, cloud service, application, portal, knowledge, cooperation layer, security and internet layer. (Ai et al., 2013) based their six-tiered architecture on product information sharing and integration of cloud security modules on cloud platforms. (Zhang et al., 2014) expanded the standard cloud manufacturing architecture by introducing internet of things, service-oriented technologies and high-performance computing into the mix. The research built up a prototype system for cloud manufacturing for targeting TQCSEK (Faster time to market, higher quality, lower cost, better service, cleaner environment and high knowledge). However, the prime issue with such kind of manufacturing environments is the lack of fluidity in centralized management, lack of proper service distribution mechanism, efficiency, quality and timeliness. The realization of resources is usually carried out by a perception layer that is comprised of perception, connection, information technology and processing. Service layer builds on the perception layer to establish service pool of resources and capabilities. The working layer is responsible for interaction protocols, extensive transactions and management of tasks. The application layer is primarily concerned with interacting with users through APIs and cloud-end interface.

Cloud Manufacturing Frameworks

Cloud manufacturing frameworks provide support to developed architectures. This define the principle how the layers of the architecture communicate. An idea for cloud manufacturing task scheduling for resources was developed by (Li et al., 2012) wherein tasks were decomposed and matched with resource requirement by matching static properties. A framework for sensor-driven process planning environment for distributed setups was established by (L. Wang, 2008) name Wise-Shop Floor dealing with scheduling, monitoring, control and planning of resources. A service and web-oriented architecture framework with SaaS offering collaboration of internal operation with customers and supply chain network was established by

(Y. K. Lu et al., 2012). The majority of literature builds the cloud environment in manufacturing on grounds of manufacturing resources, manufacturing capability and cloud manufacturing services. The containerization here is of vital importance as the concept can be considered as a container wherein the resource is contained inside capability and the capability deployed in the manufacturing cloud as a cloud service. Design capability, production capability, experimentation, management and communication capability set up the baseline for manufacturing capability concept. On the other hand, the resources could be broken down into hard and soft resources with combination of them and capabilities yielding into a capability description model. Manufacturing cloud can be further extended to public and private cloud. Private cloud is organizational whereas the public cloud is society oriented. In both cases, the cloud services comprise of service layer, transmission network layer, resource layer, perception layer, virtual access layer and terminal application layer.

Cloud Manufacturing Platforms

Research into Cloud manufacturing platforms involves integration of data and resources across environment. (Valilai & Houshmand, 2013) presented a cloud-manufacturing platform XMLAYMOD that supported manufacturing collaboration and data integration on ISO 10303 (step standard). Distributed Integrated Manufacturing Platform (DIMP) by (Xu, 2012) provided basis for integrative CAx environment in production. The interaction happens on requests and task from the user. Cloud Agent for integrating services in platform was developed by (Jiang et al., 2012). For cloud-based manufacturing environment a cloud service for resource sharing was discussed by (Ding et al., 2012). Functionality of cloud manufacturing services and control was explored by (Xin-yu & Wei-jia, 2011). A communicational ability embedded cloud platform was presented by (Ferreira et al., 2014) to enhance interoperability. The work proposed a cloud-based web platform to support dashboard integrating communicational services and described an experimentation to prove that efficient interoperability in dynamic environment could be achieved only with human intervention.

Fog and Edge Based Interoperability

The increase in IoT device usages in complex scenarios like monitoring manufacturing devices, controlling production applications, energy optimization and other applications has brought about new opportunities and challenges. Cloud computing follows a centralized structure wherein the resources are centralized to a region or distributed on a remote Cloud server. A major drawback in cloud computing is presented towards reduced latency and real-time response. This is going to further increase only as more and more devices are connected to IoT networks.

Edge computing may be referenced as the accompanied tasks performed at the very Edge of the in house platform that is in direct communication with the cloud environment. The major advantages of Edge computing are to minimize latency, reduce cost and reduce bandwidth industry 4.0 applications. Edge computing application caters the problems of Cloud computing by optimizing storage and computing process before processing them to cloud services. So majorly processing then plays out at a prior stage before being sent to remote servers. Also, these processing tasks utilize essential parts of storage and computing near to the 'Edge' of device locally and no longer require Cloud services for these. This benefits in reducing the associated cloud costs, network traffic overloads, computational requirements for IoT applications.

Just like challenges served by edge computing i.e. high latency, low capacity and network failure, the fog computing brings devices closer to cloud. Locally available data processing and data storage at the device is offered by fog computing hence faster response and better quality. This makes fog computing an enabler for efficient and secure services for IoT device. Fog computing is considered to be an extension of cloud computing having nodes closer to end devices themselves. Fog devices act as an intermediary between cloud and end devices bringing processing, storage and networking closer to end devices deployed anywhere in a network.

Edge Computing Architecture

The reference architectures of Edge Computing consist of recommended structures, products and services that form industry specific standards, suggestions, best practices and optimal technologies that act as an enabler for edge computing. These architectures provide a means of collaboration and communication in an organization around an implementation project.

An architecture based on Edge Computing and Distributed Ledge Technologies (DLT) was developed to aid the adoption of decentralized automation as a part of H2020 FAR-Edge project. The architecture in itself presents a framework for implementing FAREdge project platform. On a general level, the architecture could be divided on scopes and tiers. The scope consists of elements that form the industrial environment such as machines, field devices, SCADA, MES and ERP system among others. Tiers on the other hand detail the system components and their association with each other. The architecture consists of three fundamental layers, namely field layer, edge layer and cloud layer. Edge Computing Consortium (ECC) jointly working with Industrial Internet Alliance (IIA) presented by Edge Computing Reference Architecture (EC-RA) 2.0 based on international standards like ISO/IEC/IEEE 42010:2011. Edge Computing Reference Architecture 2.0

(Edge Computing Consortium & Alliance of Industrial Internet, 2017) follows vertical and horizontal services and layer model. The vertical services involved are management, data life-cycle and security offering intelligence-based service for complete life cycle. Horizontally EC-RA 2.0 open interface layer model is projected with smart layer, service fabric and connectivity and computing fabric. Industrial Internet Consortium (IIC) like ECC also developed its own reference architecture using ISO/IEC/IEEE 42010:2011 standard. This standard assists in identification of convention, principle and practices for coherent architectures and frameworks. This architecture majorly consists of three layers mainly edge, platform and enterprise layer. Edge layer is responsible for data acquisition from edge nodes through its nearest proximity devices. The constituents feature of the layer is depth of distribution, nature of proximity network, the location of nodes and devices and governance policy. The intermittent platform layer is mainly responsible for sending command from Enterprise to Edge layer. It groups the processes for analysis of data flows and manages the active devices by consultation and analysis through domain servers. Enterprise layer houses support platforms responsible for generating control commands to Platform and Edge layer and receiving data flow.

The architectures provide a means of complimenting Cloud services as the last level of architecture rather than replace them. This presents a beneficial case whenever significant population of IoT data exists. Edge nodes in such cases could be the initiating point for accumulation, controlling and reducing the data before passing it forwards to cloud services.

Fog Computing Architecture

Traditional fog computing architectures consists of six layers, namely physical and virtualization, monitoring, pre-processing, temporary storage, security and transport layer. The physical and virtualization layer involves physical nodes, virtual nodes and sensor networks. The management of nodes in this case is dynamic depending on their types and service demand. Sensor network deployed over geographical locations sense the surroundings and send data to higher layers via gateways for analysis and processing. Monitoring layer on the other hand keeps check on availability and usage of resources, sensors, fog nodes and network infrastructure. This layer also deals with the type of tasks that need to be performed by this and consecutive nodes. Energy consumption may also serve as a driver for this layer as fog nodes uses many devices with varying energy requirement conditions. Data management is primarily deal in at pre-processing layer. Data collected, analyzed, filtered, and trimmed to drive useful information. The data stream from this layer is then housed in temporary storage layer. The data transferred to cloud is redacted from the local temporary storage layer. The transmission of data is affected by security layer where the encryption and decryption of data comes into play. Moreover, privacy and integrity features extend the security of data making it prone from tampering. This data, which is now hosted in transport layer, uploads the data in cloud for further usage. Fog computing enables segments of data to be uploaded in cloud through a smart gateway that manages data distribution to cloud. This emphasizes on proper communication protocols for fog computing with efficient, lightweight and customization of data stream to be major concerns. Therefore, fog computing communication protocols depend on application scenario of fog.

USE CASE ANALYSIS

Several state of the art industrial use cases show the continuous research effort to achieve integration and interoperability in the context of industry 4.0. In this section, the European project PERFoRM (Production harmonized Reconfiguration of Flexible Robots and Machinery) will be discussed as it covers a wide variety of interoperability and integration features that fit within the context of this chapter. Additional reading about this project can be found in (Angione et al., 2017; Leitão, Barbosa, Pereira, et al., 2016).

Context of PERFoRM and General Requirements

The H2020 PERFoRM is based on various European projects and has envisioned a set of best practices to develop an innovative distributed control architecture. PERFoRM highlights industry 4.0 compliant requirements based on three fundamental aspects **high interconnectivity** of components, a **dynamic reconfiguration** to prevent unexpected situations and the integration of **novel functionalities** like simulations and data analytics to promote industry 4.0 autonomy. The implementation of cyber-physical components rely on service-oriented approaches and a centralized middleware that provides the needed **infrastructure** to integrate, encapsulate and dynamically distribute services. This flexibility allows the integration of various manufacturing components e.g. people, legacy systems, software tools, etc. Additionally, enabling technologies and standards enhance the applicability of PERFoRM. An extract of this architecture is presented in Figure 1 and more details about its configuration are described in the following subsections.

The Role of Interoperability and Integration in PERFoRM

The service-oriented design of PERFoRM facilitates the exposure of atomic functionalities of the components as services. These services can be thereafter

Figure 1. PERFoRM architecture
Source: (Leitão, Barbosa, Pereira, et al., 2016)

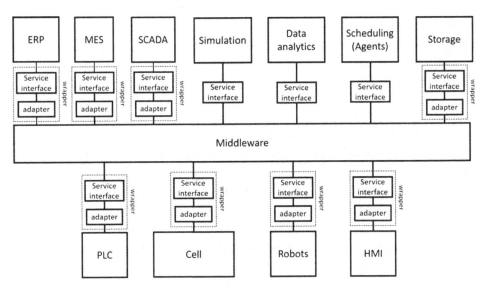

easily integrated. Examples of this process servitization are found at single manufacturing machines (e.g. robots), industrial cells, human machine interfaces (**human integration**), servitization of ERP, MES, etc. This whole integration breaks the traditional pyramidal and hierarchical control schema. As a result, all elements in the factory are interconnected making manufacturing systems more efficient, robust and ready to business changes. The servitization promotes **factory interoperability** creating an integrated enterprise concept. Additionally, the use of **cloud architectures** make possible the integration of resource planning and data analytics tools. In PERFoRM, the integration of cloud technologies paves the way towards the introduction of external services for instance to implement supervisory or remote control. Furthermore, those services can be interconnected with the value chain creating a well stablished inter-enterprise model (**horizontal integration**).

The integration and events in PERFoRM rely to a large extend in multi-agent technology. This autonomy provides an intelligent environment for dynamic task scheduling in which the operational activities are virtualized utilizing agent technology and subsequently autonomously allocated. Such a way of task representation makes the process **robust** and **self-sufficient**. Another point of consideration in PERFoRM is the utilization of **technological adapters.** Adapters allow the integration of **legacy systems.** The utilization of adapters is based on the creation of **data models** compliant with the PERFoRM architecture but primarily with the ability to abstract functionalities of legacy systems in a detailed way so that they can be integrated.

We should to note the role of **standardization** in PERFoRM. On the one hand it is worth mentioning the capability of resources to be abstracted as part of the **RAMI 4.0 administration shell** and on the other hand the application of **AutomationML** and **OPC-UA** vendor independent standards. In the first case, the compliance with the RAMI 4.0 suggests a promising applicability of the architecture for practitioners and an adequate level of formalization to integrate heterogeneous resources into this formalized model. In the second case, the use of AutomationML and OPC-UA ensure standard interfaces and enables vendor independent integration of resources, assuring a **syntactic interoperability**.

The overall results achieved through the discussion of the PERFoRM architecture and its fundamental characteristics suggest different levels of manufacturing integration and interoperability, in which the servitization of all functional resources plays a fundamental role. Additionally, the use of enabling technologies increases the potentiality of PERFoRM, applying cloud platforms, agent technologies and adding a certain degree of autonomy and supplementary capabilities.

Particular Applications of PERFORM Aligned With Recent Interoperability Approaches

The PERFoRM architecture has been applied in several use cases e.g. large compressor, micro-electric vehicle and microwave ovens producer (Leitão, Barbosa, Foehr, et al., 2016). This has generated a technological assessment of methodologies to validate the applicability of the framework. In this sense, we have collected some of these results to validate them against the presented cutting-edge interoperability approaches.

The compressor producer use case consists of complex structural systems with heterogeneous components and which machines that have limited production, normally developed for specific applications. It also includes heavy equipment that cannot be set up multiple times. This cause maintenance tasks to be purely reactive and thus cannot be scheduled accordingly. Therefore, the objective of the application to stablish a proactive maintenance system reducing also possible delays. Specific blocks of this architecture include legacy hardware devices and software tools. Some examples are Maintenance task list, Data analytics and Simulation Reconfiguration for Maintenance services. Additionally, we should highly the presence of databases for maintenances tools and machines and for order equipment efficiency (OEE) services with specific interfaces (legacy systems). The whole architecture is integrated by the industrial middleware.

The micro-electrical vehicles producer use case aims to automate a manual factory that makes electrical vehicles. With the application of PERFoRM, it is envisaged to support efficiency, re-configurability and the integration of PLCs of various robotic cells. Resources of this architecture are integrated to the central middleware via web services. Some examples include welding robotic cells, testing stations and MES. Additionally, an agent based simulation, as well as scheduling tools are considered to increase efficiency and flexibility of the approach. A human machine interface (HMI) and related efficiency measures are also integrated to increase the traceability of the system.

While previous examples introduce general ideas of the description and implementation of PERFoRM, it is necessary to describe some of the specific requirements aligned with this architecture, as shown below.

Syntactic Interoperability

The selection of the adopted data exchange format is imperative considering standard interfaces for the applicability and interconnection of legacy hardware e.g. PLCs, SCADAs, MES and databases. Additionally, the compatibility with various automation layers (considering ISA 95) e.g. L1 (automation control), L2 (supervisory control), L3 (manufacturing operations management) and L4 (business planning and logistics) was considered. After an assessment with various associated criteria e.g. domain specific concepts, performance analysis, quality monitoring, material resource management, maintenance, etc., it was determined that a joint solution of B2MML (Business To Manufacturing Markup Language) and AutomationML (Peres et al., 2016) was successfully at fulfilling PERFoRM requirements. Particularly AutimationML highlights the lower level data integration and B2MML emphasizes standards for the integration of Enterprise control systems.

Human Integration

Under the umbrella of the PERFoRM architecture, two human integration types were considered: Human-in-the-Loop (HitL) and Human in the Mesh (HitM) (Fantini et al., 2016). HitL includes overseen and adjustment of set points, direct commands with the system and the capability of humans as a data source. Such activities refer to direct interaction with the CPS network and interaction with other humans. In general, specific requirements of HitL covers collaboration between humans and CPS, integrating the physical world sensing and controlling devices and digitizing resources.

HitL can be utilized for different application domains e.g. for planning (Fantini et al., 2016). They are more related to organizational methods that can influence human behaviour and its performance. Some of its requirements include simulation and continuous extraction of decision making with the aim of empowering human skills and CPS production scenarios.

Middleware

A middleware is a software application, responsible for the connectivity of the actors involved in the industrial communication. It can receive, translate and forward data from and to various components. (Gosewehr et al., 2016). A general assessment of requirements and functionalities for PERFoRM resulted in three candidates to be used depending on the use case scenario (Gosewehr et al., 2016). Those are WinCC OA (Siemens), mBS (Prosyst) and FuseESB (Red Hat). *Siemens WinCC OA* has a very flexible architecture and provides direct PLCs interfaces (device interoperability). Additionally, it has various components compatible with SCADA interfaces and even with Raspberry pi' hardware. *Prosyst mBS is* also an alternative for PERFoRM. Several advantages can be considered from the low processing RAM required. In addition, the solution seems very promising considering the compatibility with OPC-UA/DA support. Finally, *Red Hat Fuse ESB* highlights the utilization of technologies like *Apache Camel*, which can be used over almost any operative system that has a java virtual machine.

System Integration

The integration of the adapters utilized in PERFoRM consider REST services (Angione et al., 2017). Those are instantiated in Java and are linked to MySQL databases. Data models are described using for instance JSON objects (syntactic interoperability). These models harmonize the communication of various actors e.g. machines, adapters, middleware, etc. The messages are consumed using **REST services** and are routed using the middleware. Additionally, the PERFoRM **service provider** includes **WADL** (Web application Description Language) as an integrated description into each service and can be used to expose and discover available services via the common API. XML and JSON are used to interface the various services and as a parsing mechanism decreasing the necessary integration.

This discussion does not claim to be a complete analysis of the PERFoRM architecture, but intends to show how new research effort is managing new challenges in the interoperability and integration of CPPS and how these results can bring new possibilities in the future of manufacturing.

CONCLUSION

Emerging technologies and paradigms in manufacturing like CPPS, cloud manufacturing, smart manufacturing, Internet of Things etc., follow a highly interoperable and decentralized structure. This arises a need for integration among shop-floor devices, services and between enterprises and cloud service platforms. This chapter gives a brief overview of different interoperability approaches in smart manufacturing. The chapter also explains in detail the emerging technologies like MAS, SOA, Cloud and Edge/Fog for achieving interoperability. Future work in this direction will consider developing communication protocols built upon industrial standards e.g. OPC-UA and focusing on individual level of the network in smart manufacturing.

ACKNOWLEDGMENT

This project has received funding from the European Union's Horizon 2020 research and innovation programme under the Marie Skłodowska-Curie [grant No. 814078].

REFERENCES

Ai, Q., Mo, K., Wang, Y., & Zhao, L. (2013). Research of product information sharing system based on cloud manufacturing. *Applied Mechanics and Materials*, *248*, 533–538. doi:10.4028/www.scientific.net/AMM.248.533

Alcácer, V., & Cruz-Machado, V. (2019). Scanning the Industry 4.0: A Literature Review on Technologies for Manufacturing Systems. *Engineering Science and Technology, an International Journal, 22*(3), 899–919.

Angione, G., Barbosa, J., Gosewehr, F., Leitão, P., Massa, D., Matos, J., Peres, R. S., Rocha, A. D., & Wermann, J. (2017). Integration and Deployment of a Distributed and Pluggable Industrial Architecture for the PERFoRM Project. *Procedia Manufacturing*, *11*(June), 896–904. doi:10.1016/j.promfg.2017.07.193

Bettini, C., Brdiczka, O., Henricksen, K., Indulska, J., Nicklas, D., Ranganathan, A., & Riboni, D. (2010). A survey of context modelling and reasoning techniques. *Pervasive and Mobile Computing, 6*(2), 161–180. doi:10.1016/j.pmcj.2009.06.002

Brunnermeier, S. B., & Martin, S. A. (1999). *99-1 Planning Report: Interoperability Cost Analysis of the U.S. Automotive Supply Chain*. Academic Press.

Cândido, G., Barata, J., Colombo, A. W., & Jammes, F. (2009). SOA in reconfigurable supply chains: A research roadmap. *Engineering Applications of Artificial Intelligence*, *22*(6), 939–949. doi:10.1016/j.engappai.2008.10.020

Chaplin, J. C., Bakker, O. J., De Silva, L., Sanderson, D., Kelly, E., Logan, B., & Ratchev, S. M. (2015). Evolvable assembly systems: A distributed architecture for intelligent manufacturing. *IFAC-PapersOnLine*, *48*(3), 2065–2070. doi:10.1016/j.ifacol.2015.06.393

Colombo, A. W., Karnouskos, S., & Mendes, J. L. P. (2015). Industrial Agents in the Era of Service-Oriented Architectures and Cloud-Based Industrial Infrastructures. In *Industrial Agents* (pp. 67–87). Morgan Kaufmann. doi:10.1016/B978-0-12-800341-1.00004-8

Cruz Salazar, L. A., Ryashentseva, D., Lüder, A., & Vogel-Heuser, B. (2019). Cyber-physical production systems architecture based on multi-agent's design pattern—Comparison of selected approaches mapping four agent patterns. *International Journal of Advanced Manufacturing Technology*, *105*(9), 4005–4034. doi:10.100700170-019-03800-4

Ding, B., Yu, X. Y., & Sun, L. J. (2012). A cloud-based collaborative manufacturing resource sharing services. *Information Technology Journal*, *11*(9), 1258–1264. doi:10.3923/itj.2012.1258.1264

Edge Computing Consortium & Alliance of Industrial Internet. (2017). *Edge Computing Reference Architecture 2.0.* http://en.ecconsortium.net/Uploads/file/20180328/1522232376480704.pdf

Fantini, P., Tavola, G., Taisch, M., Barbosa, J., Leitao, P., Liu, Y., Sayed, M. S., & Lohse, N. (2016). Exploring the integration of the human as a flexibility factor in CPS enabled manufacturing environments: Methodology and results. In *IECON 2016-42nd Annual Conference of the IEEE Industrial Electronics Society* (pp. 5711-5716). IEEE.

Ferreira, L., Putnik, G., Cruz-Cunha, M. M., Putnik, Z., Castro, H., Alves, C., & Shah, V. (2014). Dashboard services for pragmatics-based interoperability in cloud and ubiquitous manufacturing. *International Journal of Web Portals*, *6*(1), 35–49. doi:10.4018/ijwp.2014010103

Garcia, M. V., Irisarri, E., Perez, F., Estevez, E., Orive, D., & Marcos, M. (2016). Plant floor communications integration using a low cost CPPS architecture. In *2016 IEEE 21st International Conference on Emerging Technologies and Factory Automation (ETFA)* (pp. 1-4). IEEE. 10.1109/ETFA.2016.7733631

Geraci, A. (1991). *IEEE standard computer dictionary: Compilation of IEEE standard computer glossaries*. IEEE Press.

Gosewehr, F., Wermann, J., & Colombo, A. W. (2016). Assessment of industrial middleware technologies for the PERFoRM project. In *IECON 2016-42nd Annual Conference of the IEEE Industrial Electronics Society* (pp. 5699-5704). IEEE. 10.1109/IECON.2016.7793611

Ismail, A., & Kastner, W. (2017). Surveying the Features of Industrial SOAs. In *2017 IEEE International Conference on Industrial Technology (ICIT)* (pp. 1199-1204). IEEE. 10.1109/ICIT.2017.7915533

Jammes, F., Smit, H., Martinez Lastra, J. L., & Delamer, I. M. (2005). *Orchestration of service-oriented manufacturing processes. In 2005 IEEE conference on emerging technologies and factory automation* (Vol. 1). IEEE.

Jiang, W., Ma, J., Zhang, X., & Xie, H. (2012). Research on cloud manufacturing resource integrating service modeling based on cloud-agent. In *2012 IEEE International Conference on Computer Science and Automation Engineering* (pp. 395-398). IEEE. 10.1109/ICSESS.2012.6269488

Jin, Z. (2013). Research on solutions of cloud manufacturing in automotive industry. In *Proceedings of the FISITA 2012 World Automotive Congress* (pp. 225-234). Springer Berlin Heidelberg. 10.1007/978-3-642-33747-5_21

Kumar, V. R., Khamis, A., Fiorini, S., Carbonera, J., Alarcos, A. O., Habib, M., Goncalves, P., Li, H., & Olszewska, J. I. (2019). Ontologies for industry 4.0. *The Knowledge Engineering Review, 34*, 1–14.

Legner, C., & Heutschi, R. (2007). *SOA Adoption in Practice - Findings from Early SOA Implementations*. Academic Press.

Leitão, P. (2009). Agent-based distributed manufacturing control: A state-of-the-art survey. *Engineering Applications of Artificial Intelligence, 22*(7), 979–991. doi:10.1016/j.engappai.2008.09.005

Leitao, P., & Barbosa, J. (2019). Modular and Self-organized Conveyor System Using Multi-agent Systems. In *International Conference on Practical Applications of Agents and Multi-Agent Systems* (pp. 259-263). Springer. 10.1007/978-3-030-24209-1_26

Leitão, P., Barbosa, J., Foehr, M., Calà, A., Perlo, P., Iuzzolino, G., Petrali, P., Vallhagen, J., & Colombo, A. W. (2016). Instantiating the PERFORM system architecture for industrial case studies. In *International Workshop on Service Orientation in Holonic and Multi-Agent Manufacturing* (pp. 359-372). Springer.

Leitão, P., Barbosa, J., Pereira, A., Barata, J., & Colombo, A. W. (2016). Specification of the PERFoRM architecture for the seamless production system reconfiguration. In *IECON 2016-42nd Annual Conference of the IEEE Industrial Electronics Society* (pp. 5729-5734). 10.1109/IECON.2016.7793007

Leitão, P., Colombo, A. W., & Karnouskos, S. (2016). Industrial automation based on cyber-physical systems technologies: Prototype implementations and challenges. *Computers in Industry*, *81*, 11–25. doi:10.1016/j.compind.2015.08.004

Li, C., Yang, P., Shang, Y., Hu, C., & Zhu, P. (2012). Research on cloud manufacturing resource scheduling and performance analysis. *Advanced Science Letters*, *12*(1), 240–243. doi:10.1166/asl.2012.2780

Lin, S.-W., Murphy, B., Clauser, E., Loewen, U., Neubert, R., Bachmann, G., Pai, M., & Hankel, M. (2017). Architecture Alignment and Interoperability: An Industrial Internet Consortium and Plattform Industrie 4.0 Joint Whitepaper. *Plattform Industrie 4.0*, 19.

Lu, Y. (2017). Industry 4.0: A survey on technologies, applications and open research issues. *Journal of Industrial Information Integration*, *6*, 1–10. doi:10.1016/j.jii.2017.04.005

Lu, Y. K., Liu, C. Y., & Ju, B. C. (2012). Cloud manufacturing collaboration: An initial exploration. In *2012 Third World Congress on Software Engineering* (pp. 163-166). IEEE. 10.1109/WCSE.2012.39

Monostori, L., Kádár, B., Bauernhansl, T., Kondoh, S., Kumara, S., Reinhart, G., Sauer, O., Schuh, G., Sihn, W., & Ueda, K. (2016). Cyber-physical systems in manufacturing. *CIRP Annals*, *65*(2), 621–641. doi:10.1016/j.cirp.2016.06.005

Mourtzis, D., & Doukas, M. (2012). Decentralized manufacturing systems review: Challenges and outlook. *Logistics Research*, *5*(3-4), 113–121. doi:10.100712159-012-0085-x

Napoleone, A., Macchi, M., & Pozzetti, A. (2020). A review on the characteristics of cyber-physical systems for the future smart factories. *Journal of Manufacturing Systems*, *54*, 305–335. doi:10.1016/j.jmsy.2020.01.007

Onori, M., Lohse, N., Barata, J., & Hanisch, C. (2012). The IDEAS project: Plug & produce at shop-floor level. *Assembly Automation*, *32*(2), 124–134. doi:10.1108/01445151211212280

Peres, R. S., Parreira-Rocha, M., Rocha, A. D., Barbosa, J., Leitao, P., & Barata, J. (2016). Selection of a data exchange format for industry 4.0 manufacturing systems. In *IECON 2016-42nd Annual Conference of the IEEE Industrial Electronics Society* (pp. 5723-5728). IEEE.

Ribeiro, L. (2017). Cyber-physical production systems' design challenges. In *2017 IEEE 26th International Symposium on Industrial Electronics (ISIE)* (pp. 1189-1194). IEEE.

Rojas, R. A., & Rauch, E. (2019). From a literature review to a conceptual framework of enablers for smart manufacturing control. *International Journal of Advanced Manufacturing Technology*, *104*(1–4), 517–533. doi:10.100700170-019-03854-4

Tai, D., & Xu, F. (2012). Cloud manufacturing based on cooperative concept of SDN. *Advanced Materials Research*, *482*, 2424–2429. doi:10.4028/www.scientific.net/AMR.482-484.2424

Tao, F., Cheng, Y., Zhang, L., Luo, Y. L., & Ren, L. (2011). Cloud manufacturing. *Advanced Materials Research*, *201*, 672–676. doi:10.4028/www.scientific.net/AMR.201-203.672

Uddin, M. K., Puttonen, J., Scholze, S., Dvoryanchikova, A., & Martinez Lastra, J. L. (2012). Ontology-Based context-Sensitive computing for FMS optimization. *Assembly Automation*, *32*(2), 163–174. doi:10.1108/01445151211212316

Valilai, O. F., & Houshmand, M. (2013). A collaborative and integrated platform to support distributed manufacturing system using a service-oriented approach based on cloud computing paradigm. *Robotics and Computer-integrated Manufacturing*, *29*(1), 110–127. doi:10.1016/j.rcim.2012.07.009

Van Der Veer, H., & Wiles, A. (2008). *Achieving Technical Interoperability: the ETSI Approach*. European Telecommunications Standards Institute.

Vogel-Heuser, B., Diedrich, C., Pantförder, D., & Göhner, P. (2014). Coupling heterogeneous production systems by a multi-agent based cyber-physical production system. In *2014 12th IEEE International Conference on Industrial Informatics (INDIN)* (pp. 713-719). IEEE. 10.1109/INDIN.2014.6945601

Wang, L. (2008). Wise-ShopFloor: An integrated approach for web-based collaborative manufacturing. *IEEE Transactions on Systems, Man and Cybernetics. Part C, Applications and Reviews*, *38*(4), 562–573. doi:10.1109/TSMCC.2008.923868

Wang, X. V., & Xu, W. W. (2013). ICMS: a cloud-based manufacturing system. In *Cloud manufacturing* (pp. 1–22). Springer. doi:10.1007/978-1-4471-4935-4_1

Wooldridge, M. (2009). *An introduction to multiagent systems*. John Wiley & Sons.

Xin-yu, Y., & Wei-jia, L. (2011). Research and application of the management and control platform oriented the cloud manufacturing services. In *2011 International Conference on System science, Engineering design and Manufacturing informatization* (Vol. 1, pp. 286-289). IEEE. 10.1109/ICSSEM.2011.6081208

Xu, X. (2012). From cloud computing to cloud manufacturing. *Robotics and Computer-integrated Manufacturing*, *28*(1), 75–86. doi:10.1016/j.rcim.2011.07.002

Ye, X., Park, T. Y., Hong, S. H., Ding, Y., & Xu, A. (2018). Implementation of a Production-Control System Using Integrated Automation ML and OPC UA. In *2018 Workshop on Metrology for Industry 4.0 and IoT* (pp. 1-6). IEEE. 10.1109/METROI4.2018.8428310

Zeid, A., Sundaram, S., Moghaddam, M., Kamarthi, S., & Marion, T. (2019). Interoperability in smart manufacturing: Research challenges. *Machines*, *7*(21), 1–17.

Zhang, L., Luo, Y., Tao, F., Li, B. H., Ren, L., Zhang, X., Guo, H., Cheng, Y., Hu, A., & Liu, Y. (2014). Cloud manufacturing: A new manufacturing paradigm. *Enterprise Information Systems*, *8*(2), 167–187. doi:10.1080/17517575.2012.683812

Chapter 8

Intelligent Traffic Signal Monitoring System Using Image Processing

SureshKumar M.

https://orcid.org/0000-0002-9805-9670
Sri SaiRam Engineering College, India

Anu Valliammai R.
Sri SaiRam Engineering College, India

ABSTRACT

This project aims at making an intelligent traffic signal monitoring system that makes decisions based on real-time traffic situations. The choices will be such that the traditional red, green, or amber lighting scheme is focused on the actual number of cars on the road and the arrival of emergency services rather than using pure timing circuits to control car traffic by using what the traffic appears like via smart cameras to capture real-time traffic movement pictures of each direction. The control system will modify the traffic light control parameters dynamically in various directions due to changes in traffic flow, thus increasing the traffic intersection efficiency and ensuring improved traffic management. This work involves performing a traffic management study of the city.

DOI: 10.4018/978-1-7998-6721-0.ch008

1. INTRODUCTION

City traffic congestion is a major problem particularly in developed countries, several researchers have suggested multiple traffic network models to fix that. Proposals have been developed on several means of making the traffic network smarter, more efficient and more secure. This paper discusses the numerous approaches for enhancing the worldwide transportation networks. A quantitative analysis on various future operations was conducted, in which the Intelligent Traffic System (ITS) emerges as an important area of application. Important key points of each procedure are illustrated and analyzed in developing countries such as India, based on their implementation. It also indicates a model using infrared proximity sensors and a centrally positioned microcontroller, and using vehicle length to incorporate Integrated Traffic Monitoring Program.

Computer vision is an interdisciplinary discipline that deals with how artificial images or videos can be used to create applications for a broad degree of comprehension. From a technological point of view it makes it possible for the human visual system to simplify functions that can be done. Training requires converting mental input into tangible objects that then communicate with other cognitive processes and contribute to practical behavior during this process. This image interpretation can be seen as disengaging abstract information from image data using models generated with the aid of geometry, physics, statistics and learning theory. Computer vision sub-domains include scene analysis, simulation of events, camera detection, perception of objects, and estimate of object orientation, observation, indexing, image processing and study of motion.

Traffic signals are the most powerful method for handling traffic at a busy intersection. Yet where a single lane has more traffic than the other lanes, we can see that these signals fail to efficiently control the traffic. The condition makes the crowded lane worse than the other lanes. Traffic congestion in developing nations is rising at an unprecedented pace, requiring increasing Advance Intelligent Traffic Signals to replace the existing manual and time-based traffic signal network. Traffic officers also find it impossible to monitor the whole situation around the clock. When traffic signals are wise enough to assign automatic scheduling to specific lanes, depending on the number of cars in a given lane, this problem can be largely solved. The key goal of developing Intelligent Traffic Controllers is to allow traffic controllers to respond to real-time data from detectors (or sensors) with a view to constantly improving the signal timing strategy for intersections in a network to reduce traffic congestion at intersections, which is currently the major problem of traffic flow management.

The 8051 Controller receives data from IR Sensors located on each path. The timing of green light for a particular lane depends on the number of vehicles currently occupying that lane. It is counters numerated. The lane with more congestion gave more time to green light, and vice versa. In addition to solving the traffic control problem particularly during peak hours, this proposed system also has provision to penalize those who try to cross the red signal. It can be done by installing Traffic Enforcement Cameras (or Red Light Camera) on each traffic post. It takes still pictures of high quality when activated. The trigger will be provided by an IR sensor that sends a signal to the Microcontroller when any vehicle crosses the stop zone for a red light for that path.

The key aim of the Intelligent Traffic Signal Simulator software and implementation is to reduce the waiting time on each vehicle's lane. The three main components of the Unified Traffic Signal Control System are the Microcontroller hardware and the second portion. These typically include red, orange, green signals, counters and traffic control units. The sensors are monitoring the motions of the vehicles. We plan to use the IR Sensor to identify obstacles in front of it. The main priorities of the project are as follows:

- Exploring the possibility of developing a fully automated real-time traffic control network with low-cost electronic components which can be quickly adjusted to the current traffic situation.
- Investigate the possibility of prompt clearing and making way for emergency services for car and foot traffic;
- Evaluating the operability and performance of computer components
- Reducing traffic warder heat.
- To determine the degree and nature of the project's usefulness.

This paper is further categorized into different sections. Section II discuss about the Background of the Invention, then moves to Section III with the Literature survey, Section-IV The Development History of the Existing Traffic Self-Adaptive Control System, Section-V with the problem solution with different methodologies discussed in various research papers, Section VI discussed about experimental analysis for traffic monitoring, Section VII gives a conclusion and finally give some idea about future works.

2. BACKGROUND OF THE INVENTION

2.1 Field of the Invention

This breakthrough includes traffic control systems and, more precisely, traffic management systems that provide instantaneous, continuous and reliable data.

2.2 Description of the Related Art

Most cities are using video cameras placed on top of elevated poles to track traffic congestion, positioned along roadways at different locations. Individuals in a central control room observe the video cameras, and watch a series of monitors displaying traffic pictures from the video cameras. Trained individuals will determine traffic congestion by looking at these images and provide some accurate estimates (i.e. slow, slow, below or at speed limits; and mild, moderate, heavy, grid-locked). Local TV and radio stations also relay this detail about the current traffic situation to drivers who turn about their televisions and radios. This method of monitoring and recording traffic congestion is commonly called the view-and-relay process.

One concern with the view-and-relay system is that information is not immediately changed, and is visible to drivers instantly. For hundreds of video cameras mounted around a town, it sometimes takes several minutes to identify and communicate to the public about an incident or a slow down on a highway. The precise location or source of the traffic congestion and the traffic lanes affected will be difficult to determine before a study is actually written. The statistical jargon used to explain the traffic-causing chaos may be too complex to be useful.

Another issue with the view-and-relay approach is that it does not have approximate travel time between points on a road. This details may be given with estimated arrival times (ETA) from the point of departure to a destination on a chosen route or alternative routes, taking into account current or possible traffic conditions along the routes used.

Another problem with the view-and-relay approach is that it does not have comparative statistics on road traffic conditions which will allow drivers to select alternate, less congested routes. Alternate roads are typically accessible in a large metropolitan area to get to a preferred destination. Understanding the existing and expected traffic patterns on the preferred road and alternate routes would allow drivers to adjust their plans on which routes to minimize their travel time and more fairly spread traffic through all the roads of the region.

Another problem with the view-and-relay approach is that the view-and-relay system doesn't include traffic flow information in individual lanes. The flow of traffic in single lanes on a multi-lane highway is well known to vary considerably. Although collisions and mixing traffic are often the cause of variation, drivers with different driving styles in some cases cause the differences. A lot of drivers would think that what lane travels quicker would be helpful.

Another issue with the view-and-relay approach is that it lacks predictive or planned traffic congestion information. For instance, when a lane closes for construction at 10:00 p.m., how is traffic congestion impacted on a freeway? Or is traffic congestion affected in the area when a major sporting event ends on various roadways? In order to address these questions, information needs to be identified on selected roadways on both real and expected traffic congestion. Sadly the view-and-relay mechanism does not provide this detail.

2.3 Summary of the Invention

The purpose of the present innovation is to provide tracking and reporting for an enhanced method of traffic congestion. The aim of the current innovation is to provide such a system which provides more accurate and comprehensive traffic information. The objective of the present innovation is to provide such a device that can be used to provide alternate routes for vehicles. The objective of the present technology is to provide such a method that can be used either by using the preferred road or by using alternate roads to provide approximate arrival times for a route. Another purpose of the present invention is to provide such a tool that can provide comparative road and route information to drivers, thereby allowing them to choose less congested roads and faster routes. Predictive or planned information on traffic congestion is just another topic of the invention.

The revealed improved traffic control system, which uses a plurality of electronic monitoring systems mounted in various motor vehicles operating through a selected area on different roadways, satisfies these and other things. Each electronic surveillance system which can be a mobile device, a laptop, a PDA (Personal Digital Assistant), or an on-board computer is fitted with a means that can immediately determine the physical location, heading and velocity of the electronic tracking unit (collectively referred to as movement information) at any time while driving. A central computer links to the wide area network, designed for collecting activity information from a variety of monitoring electronic devices.

During operation, the central computer continuously transmits and stores the information about the flow to create a comprehensive traffic condition database for that area. The database on traffic congestion is continuously managed and used in tandem with other databases to provide the local road users with traffic and other traffic related statistics. More specifically, the information in the databases can be used to alert users on roadways along their current routes and on roads along alternate routes about real or planned traffic conditions. Additionally, computer information can be used to alert users about traffic movement on a multi-lane path along separate traffic lines, such as the HOV lanes.

In addition to providing current information on traffic delays, the program can also be used to provide approximate arrival times (ETAs) for established or alternate routes, depending on the anticipated real traffic conditions. Users submit a message for ETA information for a particular route to the central computer during operation. The form must be sent with the launch date, the destination information and the road description. The central computer can use an optional road-specific database to include an ETA providing detailed information on the different routes along the route, the approximate distance to be travelled along the route, the number of stoplights along each lane, and the anticipated speed of the motor vehicle of the user based on the speed limit shown, historical details of the route and the speed predicted. However, the central computer can also use an alternative roadway event database that offers information about actual, current and future activities that impact road traffic along the route, such as construction, sports events, a parade, etc . The central computer can generate fairly accurate ETAs 24 hours a day, 7 days a week, by using all the above-mentioned repositories.

The central machine may suggest taking less congested roads when measuring ETAs for both an actual route and alternate routes. Nonetheless, once a user has chosen a direction and made their choice clear to the machine, the central computer can monitor the progress and traffic conditions of the user on roads ahead of the user and suggest alternate paths or separate traffic lanes that travel quicker. The program is adaptable for gathering manually generated traffic data from users or other sources, such as businesses and municipalities located and state. This manually generated data is often used in the ETA calculation, which is distributed as traffic information to users.

2.4 Advantages

1. Traffic signals help regulate the passage of cars, cyclists, and bi-cycles through in an orderly manner providing "right-of - way" to the various movements.
2. Signals properly arranged, planned, and preserved may:
   ○ Provide for organized traffic flow.
   ○ Greater intersection efficiency.
   ○ Include uninterrupted traffic flow at a definite pace along a specific road.
   ○ Interrupt heavy traffic at intervals to encourage other vehicles or pedestrians to cycle.
   ○ Perform traffic management effectively.
   ○ Typically, traffic signals help us navigate to where we're going in a secure and timely way.

3. LITERATURE SURVEY

Smart Traffic Optimization Utilizing Image Processing (Pranav Maheshwari et. al 2015) proposed the Smart Traffic Network analyzes and monitors traffic on the basis of organizational management. It makes use of devices placed on red lights and intersections to continuously track traffic at the same time. Otsu and the ORB

Algorithm are the methodologies used in this operation. It is a versatile and cost-effective device.

Still image processing techniques for intelligent traffic monitoring (Dinkar Sitaram et.al 2015) proposed the techniques for image processing could be applied in situations where the surveillance camera is not fast enough to send the live video within a fraction of a second or in cases where the server of the website that displays the live feed from these surveillance cameras is slow.

Video-Based Distance Traffic Analysis: Application to Vehicle Tracking and Counting (Angel Sanchez et.al 2011) proposed the video-based traffic network is intended to detect and record cars that travel into a monitored environment, thereby detecting irregular incidents such as traffic congestion breaches and even injuries. The traffic dimensions of the vehicles involved, including their speeds, types or total numbers, can be calculated using images in the analyzed road zone.

Detecting and positioning of traffic incidents via video-based analysis of traffic states in a road segment (Jianqiang Ren et.al 2016) proposes strategies for video-based identification and positioning by analyzing the connectivity features of road traffic networks. Traffic incident detection and monitoring shall receive traffic indicators such as flow rate, average vehicle speed and average room occupancy. The methodologies used are Fuzzy Recognition and Context Sensitive Subtraction. The benefits of this method are: it can more accurately identify traffic incidents, properly find accident points and prevent mistakes during the extraction of traffic parameters.

Smart Traffic Control System using PLC and SCADA (Mohit Dev Srivastava 2012) proposed the initial steps in the implementation of a smart traffic light control system based on Programmable Logic Controller (PLC) technology. Also it measure the traffic density by counting the number of vehicles in each lane and their weight, then park in automated parking or diverge them accordingly. It is also difficult for a traffic police to monitor the whole scenario round the clock.

WSN Applications: Automated Intelligent Traffic Control System using Sensors (Rashid Hussian 2013) proposed the use of Wireless sensor network technology to sense presence of Traffic near any circle or junction and then able to route the Traffic based on Traffic availability or based on density in desire direction. This system does not require any system in vehicles so can be implemented in any Traffic system quite easily with less time and less expensive also.

PLC Based Intelligent Traffic Control System (Muhammad Arshad Khattak 2011) proposed the intelligent traffic control systems that sense the presence or absence of vehicles within certain range by setting the appropriate duration for the traffic signals to react accordingly. Hardware simulation tests were successfully performed on the algorithm implemented into a PLC (programmable logic controller). The new timing scheme that was implemented promises an improvement in the current traffic light system.

Wireless Sensor Networks for Intelligent Transportation Systems (Wenjie Chen et.al 2006) proposed the traffic monitoring system implemented through Wireless Sensor Network (WSN) technology within SAFESPOT. It provide a flexible, robust, low-cost and low-maintenance wireless solution for obtaining traffic-related data that can be used for automatically generating safety warnings at black spots along the road network. The system has been tested and performance evaluated under a number of real use-case scenarios.

Digital Twins in the Intelligent Transport Systems (**Andrey Rudskoy** et.al 2021) proposed the traffic management problems with accuracy. The introduction of Intelligent Transport Systems allows solving the main problems of the transport network and effectively developing it. Intelligent Transport Systems implementation are analysed, a reference model of the services of such a system is developed.

A Survey on Intelligent Transportation System Using Internet of Things (**P Patel** et.al 2019) proposed An Intelligent Transportation System (ITS) can reduce traffic congestion on roads through reduced use of private vehicles. This paper surveys a set of solutions available in the literature to design of an ITS system using IoT along with challenges and future scope for the improvement of the existing solutions.

3.1 Study Overview

The research has two main elements. First is microcontroller research and second component is smart traffic control systems. The smart traffic control network is now broken into two major components: programming and hardware. The 89cxx family series of Atmel programs represented in Fig 1 is used for scripting. The positioning of the vehicles in prototype is sensed in hardware IR sensors represented in the Fig 2.

3.2 What is a Microcontroller?

A microcontroller is a small computer (SoC) that contains a central processor, memory, and programmable input / output peripherals on a single integrated circuit. As well as a usually small amount of RAM, the computer memory in the form of a Ferroelectric RAM, NOR flash, or OTP ROM is also installed on the processor.

An Infrared (IR) sensor is used to detect objects in front of it, or to detect colors according to the type of sensor. The picture shown is a black box device with very simple IR Sensor. The sensor emits IR light, which generates a warning upon observation of the reflected light.

The IR system consists of the emitter, the detector and the related circuitry. Both the circuit emitter and the circuit receiver are two components of the system used to

Figure 1. IC 89s51 Block Diagram IR Sensor

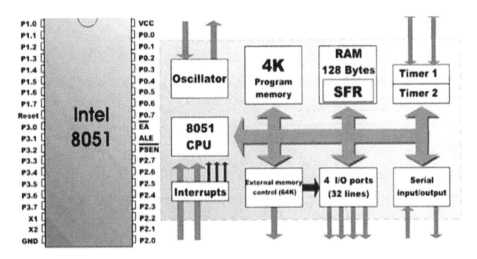

Figure 2. IR Sensor

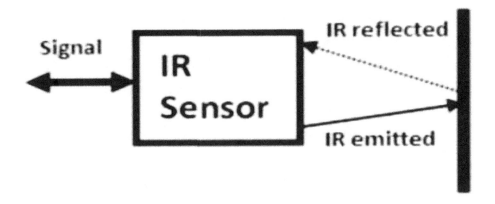

generate an IR sensor. The emitter is indeed an IR LED, and the detector is simply a sensitive IR photodiode of the same wavelength as the IR LED

As the IR light falls on the photodiode, the resistance and the output voltage vary depending on the magnitude of the IR light emitted. It is the basic concept of the application of an IR sensor. The circuit diagram of Emitter Circuit and Receiver circuit is shown in the Fig 3 and Fig 4 respectively.

Figure 3. Emitter Circuit

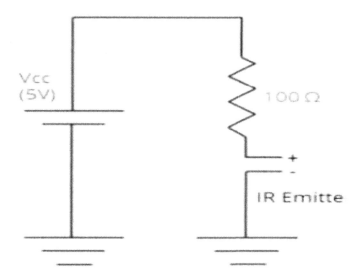

Figure 4. Receiver Circuit

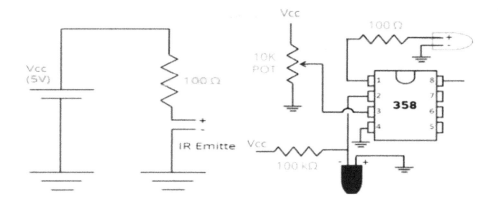

3.3 Light Emitting Diode (LED)

The transmitting light diode (LED) is a double-leading, semiconductor light source. This is a p-n junction diode that emits light when triggered. Electrons recombine with electron holes within the system when adequate voltage is added to the conductors, releasing photon-formed electricity. This phenomenon is called electroluminescence, because the colour of light (which refers to the frequency of the photon) is defined by the variation in the energy band of the semiconductor. They use red, yellow and green LEDs to serve as traffic signals at the base of the network.

3.4 Counter

Counter is a solid state tool which is used to count the number of occurrences of a case. It operates on discrete pulses. The counter sends the pulses of the trigger to the PLC and sends the output to the LEDs.

Figure 5. Traffic Enforcement Camera

A camera for traffic protection (also Red Light Camera, Road Safety Camera, Road Safety Code Camera, Video Sensor, Image Detector, Traffic Monitor, Gatso, Security Camera, Bus Lane Camera, Stable- T-Cam, depending on use) is a device that may be placed on or off the road or fitted in a safety vehicle to detect traffic offenses such as pace, light vehicles, illegal use of bus lines or cars. After activation it can be used to take high quality pictures of cars. The Traffic Enforcement camera is represented in the Fig 5.

4. THE DEVELOPMENT HISTORY OF THE EXISTING TRAFFIC SELF-ADAPTIVE CONTROL SYSTEM

According to NCHRP, more than 20 self-adaptive traffic management systems have been built worldwide by transportation science institutes and organizations but less than half of the systems have been used.

Figure 6. Level of Intelligent Decision Making

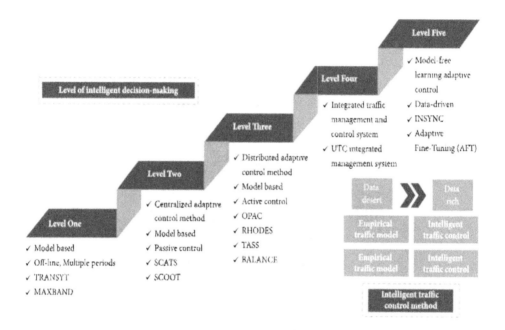

The Fig 6 shows the various generation level of Intelligent Decision Making. First generation self-adaptive control system adopts multi-time timing regulation of the loop's fine division, or fully autonomous self-adaptive regulation, in order to understand basic traffic flow management. Consider as an example the multi-period timing control mechanism, which divides traffic flows arriving at different times within one day (such as peak, nonpeak) taking into account daily traffic demand adjustments to optimize the signal timing scheme over several time spans per day; use the detailed performance matrix structure or Green Wave band timing method to refine and create a signal timing scheme. The traffic controller must pick precisely the correct offline scheme from the scheme register, depending on the number of weeks and the length of the evaluation. Second-generation traffic signal management network dynamically modifies the signal timing mechanism parameters (signal frequency, green signal ratio, and phase variation). Compared to the timing and induction synchronization control process, the second generation architecture greatly enhanced the control system accuracy and the dynamic adjustment capabilities. Typical second generation control schemes include the SCATS and SCOOT.

The third generation control system uses the same principle as the second generation to dynamically adjust the parameter of signal timing due to the fluctuation in the time-varying traffic flow at the intersections. Typical control systems for third generation include OPAC and RHODES. Kosmatopoulos et al. selected three transport networks with very different traffic and control system functions: Chania, Greece -23 junctions; Southampton, UK -53 junctions; and Munich, Germany 25 junctions, in which TASS, SCOOT and BALANCE compared with the respective resident real-time signal management approaches. The primary conclusion taken from this high-efficiency inter-European endeavor is that traffic-responsive urban regulation is an easy-to-use, interoperable, low-cost real-time signal management technique, the effects of which, with very limited fine tuning, have proven to be better or, at least, comparable to those obtained by long-standing strategies, most of which have been well configured.

The self-adaptive fourth generation traffic signal control system is an integrated traffic detection and control system capable of performing advanced network traffic management and maximizing multiple technological and reliability benefits for subsystems. This combines self-adaptive traffic signal control systems and other ITS traffic management technologies for the development of network hardware and application implementations, such as automatic traffic transfer and dynamic flow control models for various signal optimization strategies. It is committed to creating an efficient integrated system for urban traffic management to achieve incorporation into mobile network activities, so that local authorities can better facilitate decision making.

The self-adaptive fifth-generation traffic signal control network focuses on the autonomous vehicles' self-learning and high-efficiency tracking capabilities, as well as the normal road environment. The revolutionary twentieth-century traffic signal control scheme, focused on experimental studies and a real-time traffic environment, explores the principle of traffic enforcement independently and cleverly prevents numerical optimisation. As of June 2014, the InSync system had been deployed at 1350 intersections in over 100 cities across the U.S., being the fastest-growing, self-adaptive traffic control in the U.S., and also approved by the FWHA. Too much, Manolis. Above all, this modern method, known as adaptive fine tuning (AFT), has been designed to increase system performance and take into account the effect of ongoing behavioral changes that could result from internal or external developments. AFT 's findings from real-life experiments indicate that in a safe and stable way it will greatly boost device efficiency. In reality, AFT's ability to adapt and effectively compensate for adjustments in system activity was shown by the real-life experiments.

4.1 The Deficiency and Expectation of the Existing Traffic Self-Adaptive Control System

Not only has each generation system maintained the excellent characteristics of the previous generation traffic system but it also aggressively pursues the development of traffic control systems with the aid of major core developments and the new traffic management route approach.

1. The new paradigm of static traffic analysis and timing scheme loses the learning ability. So the relevant teams will only recalibrate the layout parameters if the dynamics of network traffic have changed considerably.
2. With the extension of the traffic network, the reliability of data transfer through a large national road network using centralized controls is difficult to guarantee. The current system is only suitable for regional traffic with a large corridor effect (only one-way green wave can be accomplished due to the fixed step sequence) and the control ability of the traditional network traffic flow is restricted in the vast majority of cities.
3. Local road networks lack a prompt solution to the internal traffic fluctuation, and it is impossible to obtain real-time control.
4. Present traffic control techniques for the most part simplify the control restrictions for evaluating the exact mathematical model, but these techniques differ from the actual traffic flow conditions and the control effect is minimal.
5. The system requires a lot of human contact, and professional and technical workers are needed to simplify and operate the system because of the issue of the regional migration process.

Many of the existing self-adaptive traffic control systems use the traffic model to predict the evolution of network traffic flow under the condition of minimum traffic flow data and then use the comprehensive index algorithm to optimize the signal timing parameters. But volume calculation is an integral part of this. Predictions come in two dimensions: probability and precision. Research on the relationship and trade-off between the control mechanism, prediction resolution and its associated error is important for the development of self-adaptive traffic management systems. In a phrase, it is the potential alternative for research into the theory and method of adaptive urban road regulation.

5. PROBLEM SOLUTION

The Figure 7 represents the system architecture of Intelligent Traffic Monitoring System (ITMS). It consists of 3 parts

1. Road Side Unit (RSU)
2. Cloud Centre
3. On Board Unit(OBU)

Figure 7. System Architecture of Intelligent Traffic Monitoring System (ITMS)

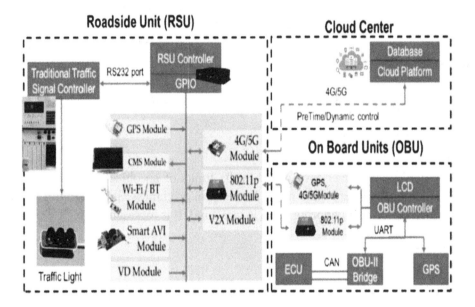

i. Pre-Processing

Preprocessing is a method used to transform the RGB light to a image of grey colour. The luminance converter seen in the equation below is shown in Eqn 1.

$$IS = 0.2896*IR + 0.5870*IG + 0.1140*IB \qquad (1)$$

IS is a gray picture of the point. IR, IG, IB are luminance in red, green light and blue light.

ii. Image Enhancement

The improvement of a contrasting image to an unenhanced image offers increased contrast and insightful insight. Any method of imagery processing involves power-law transition, linear method, and logarithmic method. The following theorem gives the correct solution for the power- law transformation process, as shown in Eqn 2.

$$V = K \, v\gamma \tag{2}$$

Where the quantity of V and v is I / O gray, a positive (K=1) constant of ÿ & K is present. Therefore, in the process of elevating the image, a pretentious technique can be rendered by agreeing on an appropriate usefulness of ÿ. To obtain a Gamma correction, the relation between the light input and the output signals has to be taken. The equation 3 below satisfies the

$$S(0)=K.(e)(E) \; S(0)=K.(e)(E) \tag{3}$$

is output gain and K is the intensity- and linear-vehicle exposure time.

iii. Object Detection

The borders of an image correspond to the limits of an object. Such edges are nothing but pixels where there might be a gap in brightness, and operation of the image element of a neighboring pixel is measured. It is represented in the Fig 8.

iv. Count

We need to know information about the number of vehicles and the situation in order to avoid the problem of traffic especially destiny. To achieve the traffic volume, a search for an algorithm needs a connecting pixel.

5.1 Automatic Signal Control System Module

The central control panel, responsible for the initial traffic control on each traffic lights section and traffic time. Intelligent cameras package, which detects the presence of the vehicle at a distance of 100 m, records the image of the vehicles and then measures the volume of the car.

Following are the steps involved

1.   Image acquisition

Figure 8. Object Detection

2.   RGB to gray conversion
3.   Image enhancement
4.   Image matching using edge detection

Image Acquisition

Image Acquisition's ultimate aim is to turn an visual image (Real World Images) into an array of numerical data that can be processed later on a computer before any video or image processing can begin, an image must be recorded by camera and transformed into a manageable object.

The Image Acquisition process consists of three steps:

1.   Optical system which focuses the energy
2.   Energy reflected from the object of interest
3.   A sensor which measure the amount of energy.

Photo Acquisition is performed with correct camera. We're using multiple cameras for different applications. If we need an x-ray image, we'll use a sensitive x-ray camera (film). If we want infra red image, we use camera sensitive to radiation from the infrarots. We use cameras that are immune to normal images (family pictures, etc.)

RGB to Gray Scale

The lightness method: (max(R, G, B)+min(R, G, B))/2 is an combination of the more common and less prominent colours.

The average form measures the quantities, is shown in Eqn 4.

$$(R + G + B) / 3. \tag{4}$$

The Luminosity method is one more modern version of the traditional solution. It also measures the meanings, allowing use of a weighted average to compensate for human interpretations. These are more color-sensitive than other colors, and thus rely more heavily on light. Formula lights is shown in Eqn 5.are

$$0.21 R + 0.72 G + 0.07 B. \tag{5}$$

The lightening approach is seeming to put down contrast. The luminosity approach works well overall, and is the main method used when GIMP is required to move an RGB image from the Image->Mode panel to a gray scale. But with one of the other methods, certain pictures do appear better. Yet in truth, the three methods yield very similar results.

Image Matching Using Edge Detection

The basis of edge detection depends on the image gradient. The gradient in a continuous space is defined by Eqn. 6.

$$\nabla(f) = grad(f) = \begin{bmatrix} g_x \\ g_y \end{bmatrix} = \begin{bmatrix} \dfrac{\partial f}{\partial x} \\ \dfrac{\partial f}{\partial y} \end{bmatrix} \tag{6}$$

The gradient of an image has two geometric properties: its magnitude and direction given between its two components by the angle between them.

$$\begin{cases} g_x = \dfrac{\partial f(x,y)}{\partial x} = f(x+1,y) - f(x,y) \\ g_y = \dfrac{\partial f(x,y)}{\partial y} = f(x,y+1) - f(x,y) \end{cases} \tag{7}$$

In a digital image the gradient is determined on a discrete structure, so we need to measure it with the following equations for each pixel: which gives us the following discrete kernel to be applied in both x and y direction:

Let's also add Sobel's edge detection filter which we will use as a reference when implementing the edge detection.

$$S_h = \begin{bmatrix} -1 & 2 & -1 \\ 0 & 0 & 0 \\ 1 & 2 & 1 \end{bmatrix} and\, S_v = \begin{bmatrix} -1 & 0 & 1 \\ -2 & 0 & 2 \\ -1 & 0 & 1 \end{bmatrix} \tag{8}$$

WORKING

Stage-1

- Image processing is initially performed with the help of a webcam
- If there is no traffic on the road, the first view of the lane is caught
- The image of this empty road is stored as reference picture at a different location defined in the software
- RGB is translated to gray on reference picture
- Now gamma correction is performed to achieve image enhancement on the reference gray image
- Edge detection of this reference image is then achieved using Prewitt edge detection operator

Stage 2

- Traffic pictures are collected.
- RGB to gray conversion happens in the image series caught
- Gamma correction is now performed to achieve color enhancement on each gray image captured
- Edge detection of these real time road pictures is now achieved using prewitt edge detection operator

Stage 3

- Comparison and real-time images are compared during the edge detection process and traffic lights can be managed depending on the percentage of matching.
- Fits between 10 and 50 percent-60seconds of green light
- Between 50 and 70 per cent match-30 seconds green light
- Between 70 and 90 per cent match-20 seconds green light
- Between 90 and 100 percent matching-60 seconds red light

Figure 9. Automatic Signal Control System Block diagram

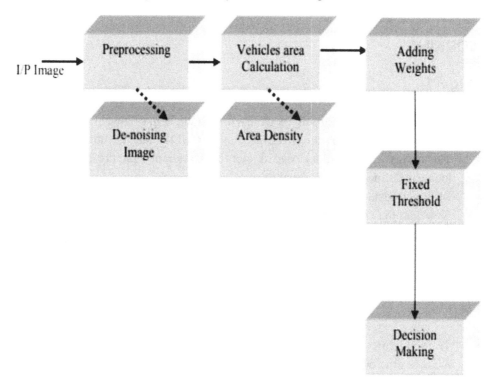

5.2 Emergency Vehicle Clearance Module

Also the emergency vehicle is equipped with the RFID tag and when the vehicle arrives the server can sense that the vehicle is in emergency and immediately turn the traffic light green. Intelligent sensor unit, which prioritizes emergency vehicles

Figure 10. Emergency Vehicle Clearance Activity Diagram

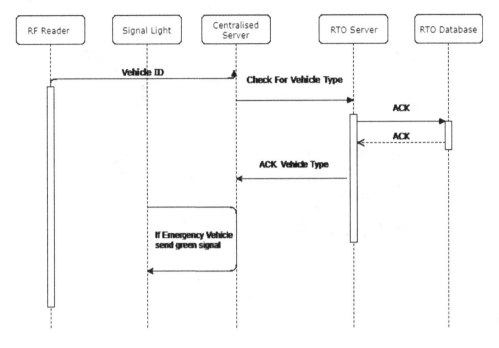

passing through the roads. The activity diagram of Emergency Vehicle Clearance is explained in the following figure 10.

6. EXPERIMENTAL ANALYSIS

In this section the design and hardware implementation details of the Intelligent Traffic Monitoring system (ITMS) are discussed and are represented in the flowing figure 11.

The following result Fig 12 shows the estimation of unknown traffic volumes to vary the time of green signal light:

7. CONCLUSION AND FUTURE ENHANCEMENT

Owing to the rise in congestion on bridges, highways and traffic, there are a large number of potential uses of vehicle identification and tracking on expressways and highways. We also developed a computer-based vision system for accurate monitoring and counting of vehicles traveling on highways. The main goal of our system is to recognise moments in cars by using pattern to process camera pictures. The way

Figure 11. Hardware components of ISTM a) OBU embedded computer b) 802.11 Module c) RSU Controller d) RSU prototype e) OBU Prototype

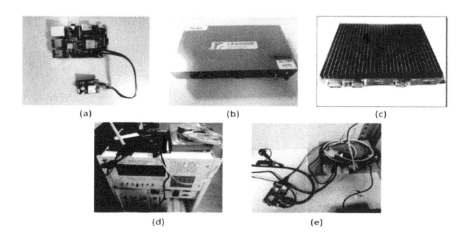

Figure 12. Waveform and density flow for flow=60vph

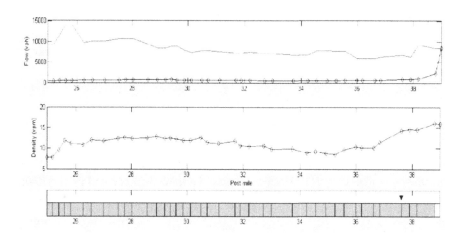

vehicles are registered takes the images from a single camera, counts and lists the vehicles. Kits for generating OpenCV picture are used to construct a framework for monitoring vehicles and counting highways. The app helps customers to quantify congestion in the relevant region through smartphones. Use high-resolution video cameras mounted on all traffic signals, this concept will be applied in the future, all traffic signals in town should provide Wi-Fi coverage, better precision will be accomplished by classifying various categories of cars and extra available parking spaces. Further changes can be made to the prototype by comparing it to longer-length RFID readers. Although the device is automated, the use of the IoT and AI concept can still improve its performance. The system which is currently being introduced by considering one road from the traffic junction. Extending multi-road junction to all roads will improve it.

REFERENCES

Chen, Chen, Chen, & Tu. (2006). WITS: A Wireless Sensor Network for Intelligent Transportation System. *IEEE, IMSCCS'06.*

Hussian. (2013). WSN Applications: Automated Intelligent Traffic Control System using Sensors. *International Journal of Soft Computing and Engineering, 3*(3).

Khattak, M. A. (2011). PLC Based Intelligent Traffic Control System. *International Journal of Electrical & Computer Sciences, 11*(6).

Maheshwari, P., Suneja, D., Singh, P., & Mutneja, Y. (2015). Smart Traffic Optimization Using Image Processing. *IEEE 3rd International Conference on MOOCs, Innovation and Technology in Education (MITE).*

Patel, P., Narmawala, Z., & Thakkar, A. (2019). *A Survey on Intelligent Transportation System Using Internet of Things. In Emerging Research in Computing, Information, Communication and Applications, Advances in Intelligent Systems and Computing book series* (Vol. 882). AISC.

Ren, J., Chen, Y., Xin, L., Shi, J., Li, B., & Liu, Y. (2016). Detecting and positioning of traffic incidents via video- based analysis of traffic states in a road segment‖. *IET Intelligent Transport Systems, 10*(6), 428–437. doi:10.1049/iet-its.2015.0022

Rudskoy, A., Ilin, I., & Prokhorov, A. (2021). Digital Twins in the Intelligent Transport Systems. *Transportation Research Procedia, 54,* 927–935. doi:10.1016/j.trpro.2021.02.152

Sanchez, A., Suarez, P. D., Conci, A., & Nunes, E. O. (2011). Video-Based Distance Traffic Analysis: Application to Vehicle Tracking and Counting. *IEEE CS and the AIP, 13*(3), 38–45. doi:10.1109/MCSE.2010.143

Sitaram, Padmanabha, & Shibani. (2015). Still Image Processing Techniques for Intelligent Traffic Monitoring. *IEEE 3rd International Conference on Image Information Processing.*

Srivastava, M. D. (2012, December). Smart traffic control system using PLC and SCADA. *International Journal of Innovative Research in Science, Engineering and Technology, 1*(2).

Chapter 9
A General Overview of E–Maintenance and Possible Applications

Pierluigi Rea
University of Cagliari, Italy

Erika Ottaviano
(iD) https://orcid.org/0000-0002-7903-155X
University of Cassino and Southern Lazio, Italy

José Machado
(iD) https://orcid.org/0000-0002-4917-2474
University of Minho, Portugal

Katarzyna Antosz
Rzeszow University of Technology, Poland

ABSTRACT

I4.0 concepts allow a very important approach concerning improving competitiveness of modern industry and services in several domains of economic activity. Maintenance of cyber-physical systems is an important issue that can be crucial for the availability of those systems for developing their activities in a standard way, with respective desired behavior. With the most recent evolution of methodologies and available tools, e-maintenance is a concept that has been evolved in last years, and the use of this approach is of the utmost importance for the competitiveness of companies at several levels. In this chapter, the authors highlight the benefits of using an e-maintenance approach for the success of maintenance of cyber-physical systems, mainly when, on those systems, it is critical to keep and assure the reliability of respective behavior. For this purpose, a robot, as an illustration example, is used, and some conclusions are obtained concerning this global overview and proposed approach.

DOI: 10.4018/978-1-7998-6721-0.ch009

INTRODUCTION

Maintenance is a key issue for guaranteeing the accurate and reliable behavior of cyber-physical systems (CPS). In fact, new developments on the domain of industry 4.0 (I4.0), maintenance 4.0 (M4.0), and industrial internet of things (IIoT) are deeply influencing the way that we face maintenance tasks (Civerchia et al., 2017).

Maintenance is supported by internet of things (IoT) in order to get the information that is needed to the right place. Consequently, e-maintenance can be seen as a sub-category of IoT concentrated in to support maintenance activities. Following from the above mentioned concept, e-maintenance is the technology that in practice can enable the everyday use of Condition Based Maintenance (CBM) (Jantunen at al, 2017).

In order to facilitate e-Maintenance tasks, some technologies can be used, as virtual reality (VR), augmented reality (AR) and others. This aspect is very important, mainly when technicians are not physically near to the CPS to be maintained and for training of future technicians, for being specialists in maintenance tasks. Another important aspect of AR and VR is that maintenance tasks can be more efficient and damages of CPS systems can be avoided. This issue is particularly important on the maintenance tasks of critical systems.

In this chapter authors intend to highlight the benefits of using an e-Maintenance approach for the success tasks of maintenance of cyber-physical systems, mainly when, on those systems, it is critical keeping and assuring reliability of respective behavior. In order to achieve this purpose, this chapter presents, in section 2 an overview about CPS, e-Maintenance and IIoT. In section 3, a robotic system is presented and, additionally, the main reliability issues that must be assured, as well as physical parameters that must be monitored. In section 4, some sensors to be considered in e-Maintenance are presented. In section 5, a simple overview about failure models is discussed and in section 6 some conclusions and future main directions are indicated as key issues in this domain.

BACKGROUND

In the context of I4.0 the complete fusion of virtual and physical worlds is performed through the concept of Cyber-Physical Systems. Those systems are the key and the core of the new developments in this context, considering several technologies such as, among others, computing, big data, Internet of Things and artificial intelligence (Zheng et al., 2018).

Several points of view and approaches can be considered for studying and developing CPS. In the context of this chapter, authors are focused on assuring the correct and reliable behavior of those systems by using e-Maintenance for those purposes. In this context - despite a correct understanding about physical part, as well as control part of CPS – it is necessary to understand and make clear some aspects related with e-Maintenance and IIoT in the larger context of I4.0.

I4.0 (Yin et al., 2018) can be understood as a set of concepts, together, mainly leading to digitalization of processes and technologies (Amaral et al., 2021) in order to facilitate the storage and sharing the information when different stakeholders need to access it (Tang et al., 2020).

Cyber-Physical Systems

The term CPS was appeared in 2006, referred by Helen Gill at the National Science Foundation in the United States. This concept is based on the connection between physical and virtual worlds that is, sometimes, neglected in a world in which many applications run in personal computers (PCs). CPS are the "integrations of computational and physical processes" (Lee & Seshia, 2011) as integration of physical and virtual worlds.

In recent past industrial reality was directly connected with using of PLC controllers for automation tasks and controlling equipment and machines; it was the context of industry 3.0. Nowadays, on the context of industry 4.0 control tasks are more based on non-PLC subsystems (Zhu et al., 2000), integrating CPS (Cheng *et al.*, 2018).

Nowadays, more than 98% of processors are embedded and connected with sensors and actuators (each one with each other) and all of them with internet. The upmost importance of networked systems is an evidence, however CPS are more than just only networked systems; it is supposed that information from the physical world is integrated and used within the cyber world, while creating sustainable feed-back loops, where computed decisions within the cyber world affect the physical world and vice versa (Sanislav & Miclea, 2012).

CPS include a huge variety of systems and this kind of systems appear in a wide range of possible applications and domains, since medical, military, transportation, manufacturing and others. For the correct design and handling the CPS, there are some theories, approaches and tools that can be used (Iarovyi et al., 2016).

In (Huang, 2008) CPS are described as systems accomplishing some characteristics:

- Full integration between processes, man and machines, with perfect match between physical entities and cyberspace;
- High level of automation with closed loops between physical and virtual worlds;
- Networked complexity with reliable and dynamic behavior;

Conceptually, CPS can be seen as systems with high degree of automation, involving physical and cyber worlds, involving, sometimes, large scale systems or critical systems with complex and integrated control, relying on their virtual representation (i.e. the modelled behavior of cyber entities; conversely).

Internet of Things

IoT is a set of interconnected intelligent, or non-intelligent, devices capable for exchanging information across internet without direct human intervention. A device (interconnected) can be an automobile, a chip implanted in a human, a manufacturing machine or any other device capable for sensing and/or actuating and sharing information with other devices trough an Internet Protocol (IP) address over a network.

Not so complex as CPS, IoT solutions can provide and enable seamless integration between the physical and virtual worlds, i.e. to enable the easy and rapid access to the physical world contents and events (e.g. information) by means of computers and networked devices according to the paradigm "anytime, anywhere" (Uckelmann et al. 2011), not involving real-time control (as CPS do). IoT is characterized by introducing concepts as operational intelligence, remote monitoring and servicing and, mainly, predictive and corrective maintenance. Several developed works and approaches intended, and are implementing, adoption of IoT worldwide (Li et al., 2018).

The most sensible issue related with IoT is related with service providers and better solutions for each application. According last developments, Low Power Wide Area Networks (LPWAN) are becoming the most popular radio communication technologies in this context (Asghari et al., 2019).

IoT concepts are used across industry and services such as manufacturing hi-tech, media, telecommunications, travel and aerospace, logistics, hospitality, financial services, insurance, healthcare, energy and utilities, public sector, consumer and transport systems. Several case studies are more related with smart cities, connected industry, smart automotive, smart energy and utilities, smart retail, smart health, smart supply chain and smart agriculture.

Several issues are related with use and application of IoT concepts. Nowadays, the main concern of companies is related with cybersecurity of applications.

The increasing of using IoT technology, has, as consequence, the increase of the number of end-points users; this issue that can be a threat for systems' security. In this context, service providers must study very well each system configurations and choose the correct solution, adapted to each application, in order to increase security of systems. In this context, it must be avoided security breaches in device levels, connectivity layers and application systems.

At industrial level, industrial and SCADA (Supervisory Control And Data Acquisition) systems use proprietary communication protocols and fail to fulfill interoperability. In this context, solutions as, for instance, MODBUS TCP must be preferred, as it is an open standard used for automation and control systems.

Main used IoT protocols, offered by different service providers are Wifi (standard IEEE 802.11n, frequency 2.4 GHz and 5 GHz bands, range 50meter that can go up to 100 meters); Bluetooth (standard Bluetooth 4.2 core specification, frequency 2.4 GHz (ISM), range 50-150meter(Smart/BLE)); Zigbee (standard Zigbee 3.0 based on IEEE802.15.4, frequency 2.4 Ghz, range 10-100m); MQTT, Message Queuing Telemetry Transport (standard ISO/IEC 20922, up to 256 Mb in size); OPC- UA, Open Platform Communications - Unified Architecture (one of the most important communication protocols for Industry 4.0 and IoT; in the context of machine-to-machine (M2M) communication protocol); Cellular (standard GSM/GPRS/EDGE (2G) UMTS/HSPA(3G) LTE(4G), frequency 900/1800/1900/2100MHz, range 35 km max for GSM, 200 km max for HSPA); Z wave (standard Z-wave Alliance, several frequencies, range 30m); NFC - Near Field Communication (standard ISO/IEC 18000-3, frequency 13.56MHz (ISM), range 10cm); LoRaWAN, Long Range Wide Area Network (standard LoRaWAN, several frequencies, range 2.5 km at urban, 15 km at suburban); and SigFox (standard SigFox, frequency 900Mhz, range 30-50 km rural and 3-10 km urban)

e-Maintenance

In a global point of view, corrective and preventive maintenance approaches are complementary and both are interesting, depending of the situation and the system to be maintained. However, it is on the domain of preventive maintenance that the main attention is usually focused because of keeping reliability of systems behavior. In the current development of technologies and demands from a very competitive market, E-Maintenance is a key issue and a challenge.

e-Maintenance is a concept that combines two very important trends in the modern economy. One of them is the growing importance of maintenance as a key technology to ensure the correct, effective and safe operation of machines in industry and transport. The second is the very rapid development of communication and information technologies. In the literature, the following definitions are used (Holmberg et al., 2010):

- "e-Maintenance is the ability to monitor production hall resources, connect with production systems and maintenance systems, collect feedback from remote customer sites and integrate the listed elements in the enterprise within high-level applications."

- "e-Maintenance is a processing system that enables near-zero downtime performance manufacturing operations and enables them to be synchronized with business systems using a wide spectrum of network technologies. ".

The main concept of e-Maintenance refers a system that allows (Crespo-Marquez at al., 2007):

- monitoring of production resources,
- connection with production systems and maintenance systems,
- collecting data about machines and devices,
- integration of the listed elements within the high-level application.

In addition, e-maintenance is a developing concept of maintenance in which resources can be monitored and managed via the Internet (IoT). Main maintenance strategy used in e- Maintenance is Condition Based Maintenance (CBM). This approach consists in controlling the technical conditions of an object and developing diagnostic information on this basis, enabling rational decisions to be made in the operation system and its surroundings.

There are two ways of assessing the technical condition: continuous (condition monitoring) or periodic at selected moments of time - different time distances between subsequent assessments. Thanks to this approach, it is possible to operate almost until the failure occurs. This solution is also the most advantageous from the economic point of view. This approach does not set fixed dates and scopes of maintenance and repairs, all decisions are made on the basis of diagnostic information containing data: about the technical conditions of machines, operators, the environment and forecasts of changes in these states during the implementation of specific production tasks by machines (Friedrich et al.,2014).

Diagnosing is a multi-stage operation, expanding the knowledge of a diagnostician about the subject of diagnosis (e.g. a machine or device). Due to the scope of the diagnosis, the diagnosis can be distinguished (Fumagalli et al., 2009, Feng et al, 2014):

- classification, the result of which is the classification of the diagnosed object to a specific list of classes, e.g. functional (fit) objects,
- genetic, i.e. explaining the reason for classifying an object to the class of objects, e.g. unfit (explaining the object's unfitness)
- significance, i.e. determining the scale of possible effects of the impact of the identified cause of the assessment,
- prognostic, i.e. determining the future courses of the system functioning (condition of facilities) and the probabilities of these courses.

Proper development of a diagnosis of the exploitation system is the result of a compromise of meeting certain requirements, such as: usefulness, accuracy, timeliness, non-interference, and a specific cost. One of the ways to meet these requirements is to indicate a minimal or optimal ordered set of observed symptoms, i.e. a diagnostic test. All data are collected by a properly designed diagnostic system, then processed and prepared by an appropriate IT system.

The main advantages of this strategy include:

- extension of inter-repair periods (increased efficiency and reduced repair costs),
- real increased elimination of unexpected failures (increased reliability and, as a result, efficiency),
- elimination of subsequent damages (e.g. simple bearing damage ends with the destruction of the gear),
- elimination of component losses (no replacement of unrepairable parts),
- reduction of spare parts inventory (the method indicates the required spare parts),
- reduction of repair time (planning of necessary operations).

The disadvantages are:

- high costs of designing and building diagnostic systems,
- high costs of installing IT programs,
- costs of training engineers and employees in collecting and analyzing data from the diagnostic system.

In practice, as emphasized in (Keizer at al., 2017), it is very often based on a partially rigid action plan, and partially on diagnostics carried out continuously or periodically (mixed approach). The practical implementation of such an approach consists in equipping operation systems in which the strategy according to the resource is implemented with diagnostic subsystems, supporting rational activities in the field of machine operation. The use of such an approach allows for a partial reduction of costs incurred for repairs of machines in good technical condition by partially diagnosing them with the use of an appropriately selected diagnostic system. Often, due to the high costs of diagnostic systems, it applies to selected elements of the technical infrastructure, and not to its entirety.

The success of CBM depends on the ability to develop accurate diagnostic / prognostic models. These models must be cognitive user-friendly to gain user acceptance, especially in safety-critical applications. Emphasis is placed on the understandability of the model so that it can effectively serve as a decision aid for experts (Feng *et al.*, 2017; Feng *et al.*, 2014).

CASE STUDY

In order to better present and highlight the above-mentioned concepts, in this section a case study consisting of a mechatronic system is presented and related issues are discussed.

Description of the Mechatronic System

According to the considerations reported in previous sections, a robotic system that can be used in environments that could be hazardous and / or dangerous or inaccessible to operators for a number of reasons is illustrated as a case of study. Inspection robotic devices can be based on automatic or tele-operated solutions, and a mechanical structure, a control system, and sensors and actuators for the task compose them. In particular, a hybrid mobile robot is the mechanical part, as it assures the best compromise for flexibility, mobility, energy consumption and cost for moving on the terrain. The high payload capacity makes it suitable for carrying suitable sensors and allows inspection of sites difficult to access by operators. The prototype described here as an example of the robotic platform, was proposed in (Ottaviano et al., 2014, Rea & Ottaviano, 2018), it has been used for inspection applications, such as in industrial sites, due to its good adaptability in overpassing obstacles and move in cluttered environment. The design philosophy on which THROO (Tracked Hybrid Rover to Overpass Obstacles) is based relies on low-cost functionality and ease of use. The use of tracks and legs assure efficient locomotion and ability to overpass obstacles. Other issues for its mechatronic design are compactness, lightweight, reduced number of degrees of freedom to simplify control and decrease the overall cost, and robust mechanical structure. The load capacity is another important issue, because the mechatronic system is designed to carry instrumentation. Since the overall concept in the project (low-cost and ease of use), THROO is designed to have a single DOF robotic legs composed by a 4-bar mechanism having only one actuator. The reduced number of degrees of freedom allows reducing the complexity of both construction and control.

The mechanical part of the THROO robot in given in Figure 1, it has three DOFs, two of which are used for the tracks, giving the robot the ability of omnidirectional motion in the plane. Two pairs of legs, namely front and rear legs, are driven by and share an additional actuator for providing a symmetrical trajectory of the end point of the leg. This innovative design and rather simple solution has been adopted to get the contemporary action of the front and rear pairs of legs to facilitate climbing and overcoming possible obstacles. The leg has been synthesized according to (Ottaviano et al., 2014; Ottaviano & Rea, 2013). Since the pairs act at the same time, the front ones are used to climb obstacles, the rear ones can be seen as additional propulsion system because the push the terrain behind the robot. This function will be clarified illustrating the simulation results.

If we focus the attention on industrial environment, the operating condition usually consists in regular floors with steps and ramps mainly typical of buildings and structures, although the prototype has been tested on uneven terrain, demonstrating a good ability in overpassing obstacles and good stability to overturning, as it was reported in (Rea *et al.*, 2017).

The main characteristics of the THROO robot are reported in Table I. Dimensions of the chassis are 550 x 400 x 200 mm, components are made of aluminum, actuation and transmission systems are of commercial type. The total mass of the prototype is 4.5 kg (batteries not included).

Figure 1. Mechanical design of the THROO prototype: a) 3D view, b) trajectory of the leg endpoint

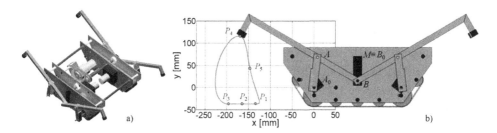

Sensors and Actuators (According Needs for e-Maintenance Issues)

The mechatronic design for the THROO inspection robot can be ideally composed two main parts; one is needed to the robot mobility and operation modes, and the other one is used to manage the external sensor suite. The first one is the internal sensor suite in Fig. 2 and it is devoted to control and manage the robot that interacts with the environment. According to the task and overall costs, three navigation modes are possible, pure tele-operation, safeguarded tele-operation, and autonomous navigation. The choice depends by the application and the environment.

The sensorization is strictly related to the navigation type and the level of sophistication of the inspection (Rea & Ottaviano, 2019). The internal sensors' suite gives the robot mobility control and navigation capabilities. They are proximity sensors, encoders, GPS, accelerometers, gyroscopes, magnetic compasses, tilt and shock sensors. The THROO is intended to be used in teleoperation mode; indeed, it moves with the direct and continuative action of the pilot. This operation mode is useful when it is not known a priori what is searched, or in an unstructured, or cluttered environment.

The THROO standard configuration for the internal sensor suit is composed by a camera, inclinometer, triaxial accelerometer and a proximity sensor that can allow the activation of the additional motor for legs.

The low-resolution camera is used for guiding the robotic in a tele-operated navigation mode, while the inclinometer and tri-axial accelerometer are useful to control the asset of the robot and avoid overthrowing of the system during the interaction with the environment. In outdoor application, the latter are aiding sensors for the evaluation of system arrangement and its stability during operations on uneven terrain.

In Figure 2 it is possible to recognize the tablet in (8), which is able to connect to the CAM in order to see the direction, two soft sliders in (7), which are able to control the movement of the robot; (2) represents the USB Router WiFi of type TP-Link, Model TL-WR841N ; Labeled with (3) there is the USB CAM model Logitech C270. (4) is the Dension Wirc Hardware, provided by 4 digital Input, 4 Digital Out and 8 channels to control Servo Motors. (5) is the Arduino Electronic Board, controlled by the Wirc and used to control (by means of relay) the DC motors of the robot; (6) is the relay; (7) is the touch soft control pad, for controlling (Go Forward/Backard, Turn Left/Right); (8) is the target of the robot; finally (9) is the overall view of the robot and the control system. The motor used to actuate the legs has a power supply of 24V, maximum torque 12 Nm, a nominal power of 24W. The two actuators used for the tracks are DC motors of 24 V, maximum torque of 5 Nm, a nominal power of 3.9 W x2.

Figures 2 shows a scheme with the main sensors, they are used for the two tasks, the tele-operated control of the robot during its operation, and sensors needed for the survey or any other specific application of a robot. According to the inspection and surveillance task, the so-called external sensors' suit can be composed by a large and variegated list of devices, such as cameras, thermal cameras, laser, light, temperature, gas, smoke, oxygen, humidity, listening and ultrasound, the choice depends of course by the specific agent we want to control.

For the case of study presented here, the external sensors suite of the THROO robot is composed by instrumentation used for indoor/outdoor inspection. The overall external sensors constituting the onboard equipment for the hybrid rover suite is composed by a thermal imaging camera, a 3D scanning system based on two micro cameras with infrared sensor, a GPS sensor, and a tri-axial accelerometer,

Figure 2. A scheme for the internal sensors' suite for the THROO robot

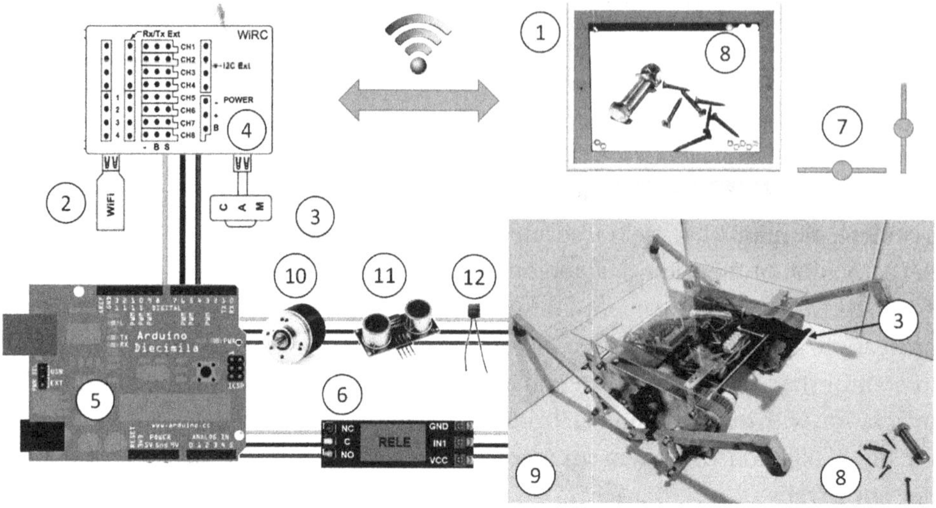

as it shown in Figure 3. As mentioned previously, a number of internal sensors is used to check, control and aid the operation/maneuver of the pilot during the survey. In addition to the front camera used for navigation, proximity sensors P_i are used to detect obstacles, encoders E_i are used for the 3 motors M_1, M_2 and M_3 and on transmission shafts. Finally, temperature sensors T_i are mounted on the actuation system to prevent anomalies and failures during the survey.

e - Maintenance Issues – Problem Statement

Changes in the technical condition of the robot may affect the duration of the task assigned to it. Therefore, changes in the robot's work should be monitored so that symptoms of incorrect work can be identified. In fact, it is possible to use sensors to monitor the robot's operation in real time, and the collected information will be used to build and optimize the maintenance of the technical condition of the robot, i.e. the implementation of maintenance and repair activities for the robot.

The technical condition of the analysed object (robot) is caused by various factors. During its operation, the following factors affect it: working factor $F_w(t)$, external factor $F_e(t)$ and anthropotechnical factor $F_{an}(t)$. These factors cause changes in the $S(t)$ state of an object, which can be written as (1):

$$\frac{dw}{dt} = f[S(t_0), F_w(t), F_e(t), F_{an}(t)] \tag{1}$$

Figure 3. An overview of the proposed mechatronic system based on THROO robot for inspection

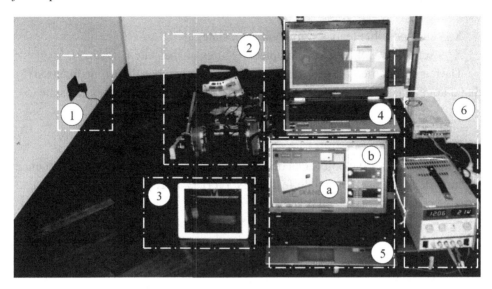

Solving equation (1) we obtain (2):

$$S(t) = f[t_0, S(t_0), F_w(t), F_e(t), F_{an}(t), t]$$ (2)

where:

$S(t)$ - the state of the object at time t

$S(t_0)$ - the state of the object at time t_0 (initial state)

Equation (2) determines the state of the object S(t) at time t, depending on this moment t, the initial moment $t_0 < t$ the state - $S(t_0)$ at the initial moment t_0 and the variability of the inputs $F_w(t)$, $F_e(t)$ and $F_{an}(t)$.

At the time of data collection, the object $t \in T$ will be in one of the possible technical states $S_i(t)$. Its technical condition $S_i(t)$ will be the set X_{zm} of states of independent values and complete features of the state $x_1(t)$, $x_2(t)$,..., $x_m(t)$ at a given moment t (3), (4):

$$w_i(t) = \{x_m \in X_{zn} \subset X\}$$ (3)

$$X = \{x_m(t)\};\ m = 1,M \tag{4}$$

where:

X - set of possible features of an object's state

X_{zn} - set of independent and complete features of the state.

The features of the state of an object are independent when there is no function (5) that uniquely describes the features of x_i by means of other features of the state (5):

$$x_i = f(x_1, x_2,..., x_m) \tag{5}$$

Then the state of the object can be presented in the form of an ordered sequence of numerical values of the state features x_i (t) (i = 1, 2, ..., m), also called state variables or coordinates, and treated as a vector (6):

$$S(s) = \begin{bmatrix} x_1(t) \\ ... \\ x_m(t) \end{bmatrix} \tag{6}$$

In the analysed period of operation $(0,\ t_k)$ of the object, individual states S_i (t) will form a set of states (7):

$$S = \{S_i(t); i = 1,..,n\} \tag{7}$$

From a physical point of view, the state space will be limited and continuous. In the analysed case, the set of S states of the object can be divided into two classes (8):

$$S = \{S_1, S_0\} \tag{8}$$

Where:

S_0 - is defined as normal work

S_1 – is defined as incorrect work

In the analyzed case, the object will be in the S_1 state if the value of all state features is present within acceptable limits, i.e. it met certain requirements. It can be written as follows (10):

$$\underset{m=1,M}{\wedge} \left(xm\text{min}\left(t \right) < xm\left(t \right) < xm\text{max}\left(t \right) \right) \tag{10}$$

If the value of just one state feature exceeds the permissible limits, then the object does not meet the requirements, i.e. it is in a state of incorrect work.

In the analysed case during the experiment, the data values obtained from individual sensors, as well as the observation of the robot's work, will allow for the collection of data, which will permit the identification of parameters that affect the normal work and incorrect work of the robot and thus identify the proper maintenance tasks.

SENSORS TO BE CONSIDERED IN e-MAINTENANCE

Proper implementation of e-Maintenance tasks requires the monitoring of essential operating parameters of the technical device (robot) in all conditions of working environment (Lass, 2020). This operation requires the installation of additional sensors that will allow monitoring of work at every stage of the implementation of tasks, thus taking maintenance and repair actions (Ghobakhloo,2018). During the robot is working, data from available sensors mounted on the robot will be collected (Fig.2). Additionally to monitor working conditions, the measurements may also include measurement related to gas analysis in ATEX zones; dust-air cleanliness measurement; zone radiation measurement; flame sensor (control of inflammatory zones exposed to fire) and UV environmental sensor. The data from sensors will allow determining the parameters of robot work and analysing the correlation among them. In the analyses should be considered: e.g., load on driving axles (torque), system vibrations (speed and acceleration of vibrations), temperature, gyro position, orientation from space and identification of dangerous conditions for the robot's operation.

The methodology of e-maintenance tasks will consist of four stages, as follows.

Stage I: Development of a Robot Monitoring System

This stage covers the identification and installation of sensors on the robot, and method of collecting data from sensors. Analysis and integration of traditional and modern data collection methods (smart sensors that allow, among others, digital signal processing and wireless data streaming, IoT, Cloud computing).

Stage II: Development of a Data Processing and Analysis System

This stage consists of the identification of states of correct and incorrect robot operation and identification of factors influencing the technical condition of the robot's working conditions. Determining the relationship among parameters. Determining the future runs of the system (robot state) and the probabilities of these runs. To provide guidance on practical recommendations for making decisions and improving and/or optimizing future maintenance processes. In order to effectively apply the analysis of sensors data it is necessary to integrate skills and knowledge in the field of information and communication technologies with engineering and expert knowledge.

Stage III: Defining Recommendations for Maintenance Activities for the Robot

This stage includes making decisions and improving and / or optimizing future maintenance processes (defining the scope of autonomous and preventive maintenance). Determining the type and scope of maintenance and repair activities for the identified dependencies. Identification of a minimal or optimally structured set of symptoms observed.

Stage IV. Remote Monitoring and Servicing of the Robots Work

Periodic monitoring is the basis of knowledge about the technical condition of the robot. Applying models and methods of data analysing from monitored resources in real time to ensure optimal service interventions. Enabling the ongoing analysis of the technical condition will allow to plan the service in advance during the expected downtime and to plan the purchase of the necessary consumables. Constant monitoring of the robot also allows extending the time between failures. Maintenance activities will be performed when the technical condition of the robot indicates it.

DEVELOPMENT OF FAILURE PREDICTION MODELS

The analysis of data from different sensors will enable a response to the factors indicating a potential risk of deterioration of the robot's condition. Another aim is to support decision making in the process of failure mechanism identification, which could be achieved due to the developed models and created knowledge base. The knowledge base contains a set of knowledge and principles learned through appropriate machine learning methods. Knowledge base rules narrow down the maintenance history data and are made available for inference. By analysing and making decisions based on a machine-learning algorithm, it is possible define the optimal scope, range and plan for maintenance activities. One of the most important stage this task is proper data processing.

During the experiment, data from available sensors mounted on the robot will be collected. Obviously, these data, in accordance with the methodology of knowledge discovery from the database, will be appropriately transformed and analysed. Discovery of knowledge in databases is a process whose main role is a comprehensive data analysis, starting from the proper definition of the problem under study, through the appropriate preparation of data, development of appropriate models and finally evaluation of the developed models. The developed models and the information obtained from them are transformed into knowledge that will be used to build a decision support system (Rogalewicz and Sika, 2016). For the presented object (robot), the knowledge discovery process will be divided into the following stages: data pre-processing, data mining (processing), analysis of results and evaluation of the developed models (post-processing) (Figure 4).

The first stage of data analysis will be data pre - processing. Actual datasets may be inconsistent or, for example, have errors in data recording equipment. In order to counteract these negative phenomena, the phase of proper data analysis will be preceded by the initial processing, in which such activities as: data selection, cleaning and transformation are carried out. Selection consists in selecting appropriate data for further stages of research. The data discovery process will result in finding previously undiscovered knowledge, so it is important to understand the data beforehand and identify the relevant data. The second basic task of data pre-processing will be to clean the data set i.e. to remove observations containing erroneous data. There may also be "gaps" in the data, e.g. because of improper operation of the measuring apparatus recording data.

The most common technique for processing missing data is to remove the missing case, which reduces the size of the data set (Wang 2008; Cheng *et al.*, 2018; Hsu and Chien, 2007). Moreover, if possible, missing observations can be replaced by using other observations from the data set (Amiri & Jensen, 2016).

The second step of the knowledge discovery process will be the data processing According to the authors of work (Lepenioti *et al.*, 2020), which gives an overview of the methods used at this stage, primarily methods related to statistical data analysis, artificial intelligence and machine learning can be applied.

Mostly, these approaches can be divided into three groups. First one are the classical statistical methods, second methods based on the use of artificial intelligence, machine learning and deep learning and the last one probabilistic models (Figure 5).

Figure 4. Methodology of data processing

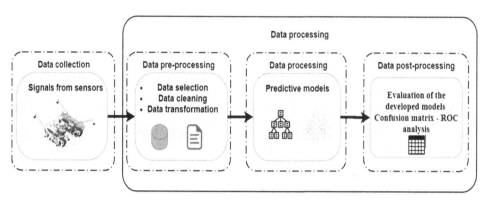

The authors of work (Lepenioti *et al.*, 2020) after analysing the results obtained in many publications, point out that in the case of large data sets, the methods from the second group are the most effective and most often used for data processing. For the analysed object (robot), the different data mining methods will be chose to develop the predictive models.

The last stage of knowledge discovery from data set will be the interpretation and evaluation of the developed models. To analyse the performance of predictive models the Receiver Operating Characteristics (ROC) will be used. This method is mainly suggested for assessing the quality of models (Fawcett, 2001; Provost, *et al.*, 1998). This analysis uses the confusion matrix (TP – True positive, TN – true negative, FP - false positive, FN – false negative) assessing the accuracy of the developed classifier. The errors of the developed classifier are defined as FP and FN. The classifier quality assessment is carried out by assessing whether the objects have been properly classified from positive to negative class and vice versa (Fawcett, 2001; Provost, *et al.*, 1998). For the evaluation of the developed models, performance the indicators will be used (Table I.).

In order to calculate the indicators for all developed models the confusion matrices will be generate.

The following assumptions will be made: the normal state of work as a negative case (N) and incorrect state of robot work a positive case (P). The values specified in the confusion matrix are as follows: TP (True Positive), which means a number of cases for which the state of robot work will be properly recognized (as incorrect state), TN (True Negative) - a number of cases for which the robot state will be properly recognized (as normal work), FP (False Positive) - a number of cases for which the robot state will be not properly recognized (as incorrect instead of normal

Figure 5. Probabilistic models

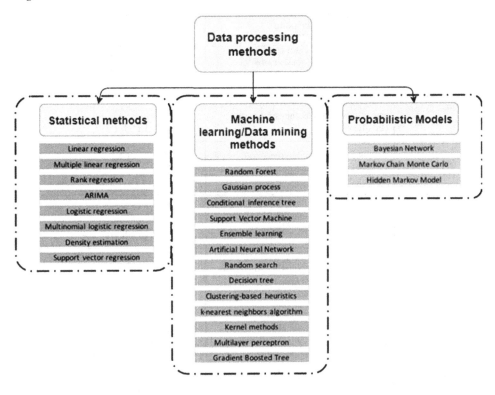

work), FN (False Negative) - a number of cases for which the robot condition will be not properly recognized (normal instead of incorrect work).

The obtained values of the above indicators will allow for the selection of an appropriate prediction model with the lowest prediction error. This model will be used to build a decision support system that can be used for the appropriate planning of the type and frequency of maintenance and repair work carried out on the analysed object (robot THROO).

CONCLUSIONS AND FUTURE WORK

In this chapter, an overview was presented about e-maintenance and possible applications. A case of study has been presented and discussed. The considerations and analyses can be extrapolated and extended to other similar systems and it is important to consider e-maintenance as a concept to be adopted in the modern industry. In addition, concepts of I4.0 were presented and authors intended to highlight e-maintenance, mainly because of the huge importance of this concept in

Table 1. Indicators of the developed models performance assessment

Indicator	Description	Equation
Acc - Accuracy	Properly classified cases (positive and negative) to the total number of predictions (ability of prediction model).	$Acc = \dfrac{TP + TN}{TP + TN + FP + FN}$
TPR - True Positives Rate	True positive cases classified to all true positive and false negative cases classified.	$TPR = \dfrac{TP}{TP + FN}$
TNR - True Negatives Rate	True negative cases classified to all true negative and false positive cases classified.	$TNR = \dfrac{TN}{TN + FP}$
PPV - Positive Predictive Value	True positive cases classified to all true and false positive cases classified.	$PPV = \dfrac{TP}{TP + FP}$
NPV - Negative Predictive Value	True negative cases classified to all cases classified as true and false negative.	$NPV = \dfrac{TN}{TN + FN}$
PV - Prevalence	True positive and false negative cases classified to the total number of predictions.	$PV = \dfrac{TP + FN}{TP + TN + FP + FN}$
DR – Detection Rate	True positive cases classified to the total number of predictions.	$DR = \dfrac{TP}{TP + TN + FP + FN}$
DPV – Detection Prevalence	All positive classified (true and false) cases to the total number of predictions.	$DPV = \dfrac{TP + FP}{TP + TN + FP + FN}$

the today industry, related with competitive issues to be solved, concerning the use of advanced tools and concepts that support the true development of companies. Future work will be devoted to the development and implementation of the presented ideas, collecting and analyzing data, storing it and taking decisions, supported by the developed analysis, concerning e-maintenance tasks on the presented robot. Main achievements will be extended to other similar systems.

ACKNOWLEDGMENT

This work has been supported by FCT – Fundação para a Ciência e Tecnologia within the R&D Units Project Scope: UIDP/04077/2020 and UIDB/04077/2020.

REFERENCES

Amaral, A., & Peças, P. (2021). SMEs and Industry 4.0: Two case studies of digitalization for a smoother integration. *Computers in Industry*, *125*, 103333. Advance online publication. doi:10.1016/j.compind.2020.103333

Amiri, M., & Jensen, R. (2016). Missing data *imputation* using fuzzy-rough methods. *Neurocomputing*, *205*, 152–164. doi:10.1016/j.neucom.2016.04.015

Asghari, M., Yousefi, S., & Niyato, D. (2019). Pricing strategies of IoT wide area network service providers with complementary services included. *Journal of Network and Computer Applications*, *147*, 102426. Advance online publication. doi:10.1016/j.jnca.2019.102426

Cheng, B., Zhang, J., Hancke, G.P., Karnouskos, S., & Colombo, A.W. (2018). Industrial cyberphysical systems: realizing cloud-based big data infrastructures. *IEEE Ind. Electron.*, 25–35. . doi:10.1109/MIE.2017.2788850

Chien, C.-F., Wang, W.-C., & Cheng, J.-C. (2007). Data mining for yield enhancement in semiconductor manufacturing and an empirical study. *Expert Systems with Applications*, *33*(1), 192–198. doi:10.1016/j.eswa.2006.04.014

Civerchia, F., Bocchino, S., Salvadori, C., Rossi, E., Maggiani, L., & Petracca, M. (2017). Industrial Internet of Things monitoring solution for advanced predictive maintenance applications. *Journal of Industrial Information Integration*, *7*, 4–12. doi:10.1016/j.jii.2017.02.003

Civerchia, F., Bocchino, S., Salvadori, C., Rossi, E., Maggiani, L., & Petracca, M. (2017). Industrial Internet of Things monitoring solution for advanced predictive maintenance applications. *Journal of Industrial Information Integration*, *7*, 4–12. doi:10.1016/j.jii.2017.02.003

Crespo-Marquez, A., Iung, B., & Levrat, E. (2007). *On the Concept of e-Maintenance. Information and Communication Technologies Applied to Maintenance*. Review and Current Research. Proceedings.

Fawcett, T. (2001). Using rule sets to maximize ROC performance. Proc. IEEE Internat. Conf. on Data Mining (ICDM-2001), 131–138. doi:10.1109/ICDM.2001.989510

Fawcett, T. (2006). An introduction to ROC analysis. *Pattern Recognition Letters*, *27*(8), 861–874. doi:10.1016/j.patrec.2005.10.010

Feng, Q., Chen, Y., Sun, B., & Li, S. (2014). An optimization method for condition based maintenance of aircraft fleet considering prognostics uncertainty. *TheScientificWorldJournal*, *2014*(1), 430190. doi:10.1155/2014/430190 PMID:24892046

Feng, Q., Zhao, X., & Chen, Y. (2017). Heuristic hybrid game approach for fleet condition-based maintenance planning. *Reliability Engineering & System Safety*, *157*, 166–176. doi:10.1016/j.ress.2016.09.005

Friedrich, Ch., Lechler, A., & Verl, A. (2014). Autonomous systems for maintenance tasks. Requirements and design of a control architecture. *Procedia Technology*, *15*, 595–604. doi:10.1016/j.protcy.2014.09.020

Fumagalli, L., Marco Macchi, M., & Rapaccini, M. (2009). Computerized maintenance management systems in SMEs. A survey in Italy and some remarks for the implementation of condition based maintenance. *IFAC Proceedings*, *42*(4), 1615–1619.

Ghobakhloo, M. (2018). The future of manufacturing industry: A strategic roadmap toward Industry 4.0. *Journal of Manufacturing Technology Management*, *2018*(29), 910–936. doi:10.1108/JMTM-02-2018-0057

Holmberg, K., Adgar, A., Arnaiz, A., Jantunen, E., Mascolo, J., & Mekid, S. (2010). *E-maintenance*. Springer Verlag. doi:10.1007/978-1-84996-205-6

Hsu, S.-C., & Chien, C.-F. (2007). Hybrid data mining approach for pattern extraction from wafer bin map to improve yield in semiconductor manufacturing. *International Journal of Production Economics*, *107*(1), 88–103. doi:10.1016/j.ijpe.2006.05.015

Huang, B.X. (2008). *Cyber physical systems: a survey*. Presentation Report.

Iarovyi, S., Mohammed, W. M., Lobov, A., Ferrer, B. R., & Lastra, J. L. M. (2016). Cyber-Physical Systems for Open-Knowledge-Driven Manufacturing Execution Systems. *Proceedings of the IEEE*, *104*(5), 1142–1154. doi:10.1109/JPROC.2015.2509498

Jantunen, E., Junnola, J., & Gorostegui, U. (2017). Maintenance supported by cyber-Physical systems and cloud technology. *2017 4th International Conference on Control, Decision and Information Technologies, CoDIT*, 708-713. 10.1109/CoDIT.2017.8102678

Keizer, M. C. A. O., Flapper, S. D. P., & Teunter, R, H. (2017). Conditionbased maintenance policies for systems with multiple dependent components: A review. *European Journal of Operational Research*, *261*(2).

Lass, S., & Gronau, N. (2020). A factory operating system for extending existing factories to Industry 4.0. *Computers in Industry*, *2020*(115), 103128. doi:10.1016/j.compind.2019.103128

Lee, E. A., & Seshia, S. A. (2011). *Introduction to Embedded Systems: A Cyber-physical Systems Approach*. http://LeeSeshia.org

Lepenioti, K., Bousdekis, A., Apostolou, D., & Mentzas, G. (2020). Prescriptive analytics: Literature review and research challenges. *International Journal of Information Management*, *50*, 57–70. doi:10.1016/j.ijinfomgt.2019.04.003

Li, W., Wang, B., Sheng, J., Dong, K., Li, Z., & Hu, Y. (2018). A resource service model in the industrial IoT system based on transparent computing. *Sensors*, *18*. . doi:10.339018040981

Ottaviano, E., & Rea, P. (2013). Design and operation of a 2DOF leg–wheel hybrid robot. *ROBOTICA*, *31*, 1319-1325. doi:10.1017/S0263574713000556

Ottaviano, E., Rea, P., & Castelli, G. (2014). THROO: A Tracked Hybrid Rover to Overpass Obstacles. *Advanced Robotics*, *28*(10), 683–694. doi:10.1080/0169186 4.2014.891949

Powers, D. (2011). Evaluation: From precision, recall and F-score to ROC, unforcedness, nakedness & correlation. *Journal of Machine Learning Technologies*, *2*, 37–63.

Provost, F., Fawcett, T., & Kohavi, R. (1998). The case against accuracy estimation for comparing classifiers. *Proceedings of the ICML*-98, 445 - 453.

Rea, P., & Ottaviano, E. (2018). Design and Development of an Inspection Robotic System for Indoor Applications. *Robotics and Computer-integrated Manufacturing*, *49*, 143–151. doi:10.1016/j.rcim.2017.06.005

Rea, P., & Ottaviano, E. (2019). Mechatronic Design and Control of a Robotic System for Inspection Tasks. In J. Machado, F. Soares, & G. Veiga (Eds.), *Innovation*. Engineering.

Rea, P., Pelliccio, A., Ottaviano, E., & Saccucci, M. (2017). The Heritage Management and Preservation Using the Mechatronic Survey. *International Journal of Architectural Heritage*, *11*(8), 1121–1132. doi:10.1080/15583058.2017.1338790

Rogalewicz, M., & Sika, R. (2016). Methodologies of knowledge discovery from data and data mining methods in mechanical engineering. *Management and Production Engineering Review*, *7*(4), 97–108. Advance online publication. doi:10.1515/mper-2016-0040

Sanislav, T., & Miclea, L. (2012). Cyber-Physical Systems - Concept, Challenges and Research Areas. *J. Control Eng. Appl. Inform.*, *14*(2), 28–33.

Tang, H., Li, D., Wan, J., Imran, M., & Shoaib, M. (2020). A Reconfigurable Method for Intelligent Manufacturing Based on Industrial Cloud and Edge Intelligence. *IEEE Internet of Things Journal*, *7*(5), 4248-4259. doi:10.1109/JIOT.2019.2950048

Uckelmann, D., Harrison, M., & Michahelles, F. (2011). An Architectural Approach Towards the Future Internet of Things. In *Architecting the Internet of Things* (pp. 1–24). Springer Berlin Heidelberg. doi:10.1007/978-3-642-19157-2_1

Yin, Y., Stecke, K. E., & Li, D. (2018). The evolution of production systems from Industry 2.0 through Industry 4.0. *International Journal of Production Research*, *56*(1-2), 848–861. doi:10.1080/00207543.2017.1403664

Zheng, P., Wang, H., Sang, Z., Zhong, R. Y., Liu, Y., Liu, C., Mubarok, K., Yu, S., & Xu, X. (2018). Smart manufacturing systems for Industry 4.0: Conceptual framework, scenarios, and future perspectives. *Frontiers of Mechanical Engineering*, *13*(2), 137–150. doi:10.100711465-018-0499-5

Zhu, W., Wang, Z., & Zhang, Z. (2020). Renovation of automation system based on industrial internet of things: A case study of a sewage treatment plant. *Sensors (Basel)*, *20*(8), 2175. doi:10.339020082175 PMID:32290552

Chapter 10
Network Intrusion Detection System in Latest DFA Compression Methods for Deep Packet Scruting

Vinoth Kumar K

iD https://orcid.org/0000-0002-3009-1658
New Horizon College of Engineering, India

ABSTRACT

The vast majority of the system security applications in today's systems depend on deep packet inspection. In recent years, regular expression matching was used as an important operator. It examines whether or not the packet's payload can be matched with a group of predefined regular expressions. Regular expressions are parsed using the deterministic finite automata representations. Conversely, to represent regular expression sets as DFA, the system needs a large amount of memory, an excessive amount of time, and an excessive amount of per flow state, limiting their practical applications. This chapter explores network intrusion detection systems.

INTRODUCTION

Today, a computer network has become an essential part of our day by day life. Internet has a fast growth from the most recent decade with increasing requirement of society on it. Internet provides a wide range of benefits to society however it is infected by many security attacks that disrupt the functionality of networking and computing infrastructure. To enhance the security of the network a large number of

DOI: 10.4018/978-1-7998-6721-0.ch010

devices are introduced. Network Intrusion Detection Systems (NIDS) are amongst the foremost broadly used for this purpose (Kumar, Turner, Crowley et al, 2007). Snort (Liu & Wu, 2013) and Bro (Roesch, 1999) are two open source NIDS examples that have been broadly used to safeguard the network.

Network Intrusion Detection Systems use Deep Packet Inspection (DPI) for a variety of applications that enhances security like spam, monitoring and detecting viruses, malevolent traffic, unauthorized access and attacks. The main role of deep packet inspection is to permit Network Intrusion Detection System to effectively match the details of the network packets with respect to signature attacks and thereby be aware of malicious traffic. Formerly, string matching algorithms were used to match the signature attacks. There is an increasing obstacle in network attacks that has possessed the society of research to investigate a best string matching or signature representation. In spite of this a large research community suggests the regular expression as a dominant signature representation. Regular expression consists of a character sets that identify a search pattern. Regular expressions are grammars that denote the regular language. Regular expression matching is a traditional problem of computer science and technology. The authors in (Becchi & Crowley, 2007; Thompson, 2006; Myers, 1992) have made productive developments to promote the research of regular expression in algorithms and theories. There are mainly two primary requirements that must be satisfied for any regular expression representations. They are time efficiency and space efficiency. Space efficiency specifies the size of the system representation and it must be less so that it guarantees that it fits inside the main memory of NIDS. Time efficiency specifies the amount of time that is required by the NIDS to process every byte of network traffic and it must be little so as to permit a large degree of traffic to match rapidly.

When compared with the simple string patterns regular expressions are considered to be very expressive and hence they are capable to represent an ample collection of payload signatures (Hopcroft, 1971). However to implement regular expressions need greater memory space and bandwidth. On the other hand the crucial task with these extremely fast regular expressions is to trim down the usage of memory and its bandwidth.

Regular expressions are usually evaluated by finite automaton which is a mathematical framework of a system that comprises of inputs and outputs. The system initially begins at the start state and it can be in any one of the finite states. Based on the previous input characters read the state of the system understands the systems behavior for the subsequent input string. The finite automata can be categorized into Non Deterministic Finite Automata (NFA) and Deterministic Finite Automata (DFA) depending on the prime technology and current resources. The foremost dissimilarity among NFA and DFA is that for each character that is read in packet payload NFA can have multiple state transitions while DFA can have only one state transition. Owing to this NFA has a time complexity of O(m) where m is the number of states while DFA requires a large amount of memory for the same packet payload.

A significant team of research work has been concentrated on compression strategies which aim towards decreasing the memory space that are required to represent DFAs. The set of regular expression when compiled to a single DFA frequently leads to state blowup problem with an enormous or even to impractical memory consumption. One way to alleviate this difficulty is to share out the collection of regular expression into many groups and to build independent DFAs for each group. Intelligent Optimization Grouping Algorithms (IOGA) (Fu et al., 2014) can be utilized effectively to overcome the issue of state blow up problem by obtaining the comprehensive deal among the number of groups and utilization of memory. One such way to solve the state blow – up problem and to provide an efficient finite automaton is to diminish the number of DFA states. In the rest of the paper the various existing compression techniques that are used to reduce the DFA states are analyzed and the ways through which Intelligent Optimization Grouping Algorithms can be efficiently used to solve the state explosion problem are discussed.

The remainder of the manuscript is structured as follows. Section II deliberates about the regular expression model and types of regular expressions. Section III discusses and evaluates the various state compression techniques that are used to reduce the DFA states and section IV discusses about grouping the regular expression using Intelligent Optimization Grouping Algorithms and section V delivers the concluding remarks.

THE REGULAR EXPRESSION MODEL

Pattern Matching is a technique of finding a string in a text based on a specific search pattern. The search pattern can be effectively described using regular expression. Thus regular expression matching plays a vital role in pattern matching. To better understand the regular expression matching in network intrusion detection system the different types of regular expression representation and its characteristics has to be studied. The most widely used NIDS open source tool is Snort rule set thus in this paper some of the important types of regular expression that are used frequently in Snort (Liu & Wu, 2013) rule sets are discussed. In the following section, the various types of regular expression and its characteristics are discussed in the way their complexities are mounted.

EXACT-MATCH STRINGS

Exact-match strings are the simplest patterns that are mostly found in the rule set. The size of patterns in an exact match string is fixed and it occurs in the input text exactly as it is appeared. The rule set which contains exact match strings exposes two vital properties. The first vital property is that DFA based solutions using Aho-Corasick algorithm (Aho & Corasick, 1975) or the Boyer-Moore algorithm (Dharmapurikar & Lockwood, 2005) can be efficiently utilized given that their size depends on the number of characters that are present in the pattern set. Secondly, optimization that depends on the hashing schemes (Wang et al., 2009; Anantathanavit & Munlin, 2016) can be used for a maximum length pattern size and it does not measure for arbitrarily long strings. When analyzing the properties the exact match string algorithm is not so expressive and if an assaulter appends padding in the regular expression then it can't identify malicious packets. However, the advantage of the exact match string regular expression is that it is easy to implement and can accomplish a high matching speed when compared with other types of regular expressions.

CHARACTER SETS AND SIMPLE WILDCARDS

Character sets and simple wildcard regular expression are basically found in two structures either as [s1-sjsksl] expressions, or as \s, \d, \a, \S, \D, \A. In the first structure the set incorporates all characters between s1 and sj, sk and s1 and in the second structure the set comprises of all space characters (\s), all digits (\d), all alphanumerical characters (\a), and their complements (\S, \D, \A). A wildcard is represented through a non-escaped dot and these sub-patterns represent a set of exact-match strings. As a rule, character sets and wildcards do not permit for immediate utilization of the Aho-Corasick algorithm (Aho & Corasick, 1975) or the Boyer-Moore algorithm (Dharmapurikar & Lockwood, 2005) and of hashing schemes (Wang et al., 2009; Anantathanavit & Munlin, 2016). Regardless, in spending the time and cost for mounting the pattern set size it is better to perform a thorough enumeration of the exact match strings and to produce a less complicated case that do not disrupt the properties of exact match strings.

SIMPLE CHARACTER REPETITIONS.

The next type of regular expression is the simple character repetition which looks like the ch+ and ch* structure, where ch is any character of the alphabet. It does not surpass the number of characters in the pattern set and maintains the same size of the DFA. However, it is impractical to permit in-depth details of exact string match to reduce the regular expression because there are an unlimited number of such strings. Therefore, hashing techniques such as (Anantathanavit & Munlin, 2016) and (Wang et al., 2009) are not applicable. However, in a finite automaton hashing schemes are employed as a loop transition.

CHARACTER SETS AND WILDCARD REPETITIONS

In character sets and wildcard repetitions the various regular expression are compiled into a single DFA providing a memory blast in the size of DFA (Becchi & Crowley, 2007). Thus it provides an additional complexity. Subsequently, hashing techniques cannot be applied to this problem and also a single DFA cannot be a possible solution. An obtainable solution is to group rules into multiple rules and form parallel DFAs (Yu et al., 2001). This technique might reduce the consumption of memory but result in increased memory bandwidth. Precisely N number of DFAs depends on an N-fold growth in the memory bandwidth. NFA can be used as an alternative by exchanging off the utilization of memory with the requirements of memory bandwidth.

COUNTING CONSTRAINTS

Counting constraints implies the combination of simple character repetition and character sets and wildcards repetitions. The upper bound of counting constraints might or might not be constrained. As seen in the above implications a simple character repetitions having a constrained upper bound has a potential to do an in-depth enumeration of the exact match strings. As mentioned in (Yu et al., 2001; Becchi & Crowley, 2007) a single regular expression when converted into NFA and then to DFA can prompt to exponential state blow up. DFA techniques are impractical to design with counting constraints. Thus the counting constraints with bounded repetition are desirable to replace with unbounded repetition.

LITERATURE SURVEY

Deep packet inspection processes the complete packet payload and identifies a set of predefined patterns. In recent years, contemporary systems replace set of strings with regular expressions, because of their higher flexibility and expressive power. To make a pattern matching process fast and memory competent, many DFA compression techniques are carried out. In this section the merits and demerits of the various deterministic finite automata compression techniques and their performances are discussed.

DETERMINISTIC FINITE AUTOMATA (DFA)

A DFA consists of five tuples (Q, Σ, δ, q_0, F) where Q represents the set of finite states, Σ denotes the finite set of input alphabets, δ the transition function which takes a state and an input character as parameters and returns a state, q_0 denotes the start state and F represents the set of accepting states. In case of networking applications Σ contains 2^8 symbols from an extensive ASCII code. A primary characteristic of DFA is that only one state can be active at a time. It does not have multiple state transitions. However it is infeasible to build a regular expression for the most repeatedly used rule set. Especially when the regular expression contains repeated wildcards it becomes difficult to build a DFA which contains a minimum number of states (Paxson, 1998). It takes only one main memory accesses per byte. A hypothetical study was done and the worst case scenario (Hopcroft et al., 2001) illustrated on the study shows that a single regular expression of size m is represented as a NFA with a complexity of O(m) states. The same expression when transformed into a DFA generates $O(\sum^m)$ states. In a DFA the processing complexity for every input character is O(1) however when all the m states are active at the same time the complexity of NFA is $O(m^2)$.

Fang Yu et al, 2006 (Yu et al., 2001) proposed a DFA - based implementation called multiple DFAs (MDFA). It is an alternative DFA representing a set of regular expressions. The input string is compared against an MDFA by simulating every constituent DFA to determine whether there is a match or not. When compared with DFA, MDFAs are more compact because there is over a multiplicative raise in the number of states. Since all the elements of DFAs are matched against the input string the matching speed of MDFAs are slower than that of the DFAs. The regular expression matching speed of MDFA is about 50 to 700 instances higher than that of the NFA - based implementation (Sidhu & Prasanna, 2001) and they are mainly used in the Linux L7-filter (Levandoski et al., n.d.), Bro (Roesch, 1999) and Snort system (Liu & Wu, 2013). On a DFA-based parser it achieves 12- 42 times speedup. The speed of pattern matching is almost at a gigabit rates for certain pattern sets.

Todd J. Green et al, 2004 (Green et al., 2004) constructed lazy DFA in which the finite states, finite inputs and state transitions are equivalent to NFA at runtime, but they cannot be considered the same at compile time. In the lazy DFA the states and transitions form a subset of the standard DFA and they are much smaller than that of the standard DFA. The drawbacks of this technique are it leads to a high warm-up cost and large memory consumption.

NON DETERMINISTIC FINITE AUTOMATA (NFA)

The working principle of NFA is same as DFA except that the transition function δ works by transiting to a new state from a state on an input alphabet. In a NFA multiple states can be simultaneously active at a time. The number of states in NFA that are essential to express a regular expression is equal to the number of alphabets that are required in the generation of regular expression. Therefore, Sidhu et al, 2004 (Sidhu & Prasanna, 2001) proposed a NFA based approach which improved the usage of memory. In NFA several states are active in parallel and it has multiple transitions thus it required multiple parallel operations in memory. At the same time all the states in NFA can be active which needs an excessive amount of memory bandwidth.

In (Sidhu & Prasanna, 2001), Sidhu et al, 2004 were the first to use the NFA to construct regular expressions for the given input string using FPGAs. To match a regular expression of size m, a serial machine requires $O(2^m)$ memory and requires the time complexity of $O(1)$ per input character. However, the authors proposed a method that requires $O(m^2)$ space but process a character of text in $O(1)$ time. Additionally, they presented a simple and fast algorithm that rapidly constructs the NFA for the given regular expression. To construct an NFA rapidly is crucial because the NFA structure depends upon the regular expression, which is known only at runtime. Liu Yang et al, (2011) developed a novel technique that employed Ordered Binary Decision Diagrams (OBDDs) in order to improve the time-efficiency of NFAs. An OBDD is represented using arbitrary Boolean formulae. In order to increase the competence of state - space exploration algorithms (Yang et al., 2011) model checkers used OBDDs. NFA-OBDDs were evaluated with three sets of regular expression. The first set comprises of 1503 regular expressions which were obtained from the Snort HTTP signature rule set (Smith, Estan, & Jha, 2008). The next set contains 2612 regular expressions and the third set contains 98 regular expressions, which were found from the Snort HTTP and FTP signature rule sets. NFA-OBDDs are between 570x–1645x faster when compared with NFAs and uses almost the same amount of memory as that of NFA. NFA-OBDDs improved the efficiency of time of NFAs without conceding their efficiency of memory.

DELAYED INPUT DFA (D²FA)

Sailesh Kumar et al, 2006 (Beng et al., 2014) constructed D²FA by converting a DFA by means of incrementally substituting many state transitions with a single default transition. The D²FA is represented by a directed graph, whose nodes are termed as states and whose edges are termed as transitions. Transitions perform a move to a new state based on the present state and the character that is read from a finite set of input alphabet Σ. Each state has not more than one unlabeled active transition known as default transition. There is one start state and for each and every state, a set of matching patterns is defined.

The authors conducted test on the regular expression obtained from Cisco Systems, Snort rule sets (Liu & Wu, 2013), Bro NIDS rule sets (Roesch, 1999), and in the Linux layer-7 filter (Levandoski et al., n.d.) application protocol classifier. From these regular expression sets, DFAs were constructed with a small number of states and the set splitting techniques proposed by Yu et al, 2005 in (Kolias et al., 2011) were applied. The regular expressions were divided into different sets so that every set created a small DFA. Then from the Cisco regular expressions 10 sets of rules were created and the footprints of total memory were reduced to 92 MB, with an aggregate of 180138 states, and lesser than 64K states were obtained from every individual DFA. Then the Linux layer-7 expressions were split into three sets, and it obtained a total of 28889 states. Further the Snort set consisted of 22 complex expressions ware split further into four sets and the state was unpredictable. The regular expressions found from Bro rule set were simple and efficient therefore they compiled all of them into a single automaton.

This approach drastically decreased the number of distinct transitions among states. For a set of regular expressions drawn from current business and academic systems, a D^2FA representation reduced state transitions by more than 95%. For instance, using D^2FA, the space requirements used in deep packet inspection appliances of Cisco Systems were reduced to less than 2 MB. Unluckily the use of default transition decreased throughput as there was no use of input in default transition and memory has to be accessed to retrieve the next state.

CONTENT ADDRESSED DELAYED INPUT DFA (CD²FA)

S Kumar et al, 2006 (Kumar, Turner, & Williams, 2006) designed the Content Addressed Delayed Input DFA (CD²FA), that matches the throughput of the conventional uncompressed DFAs. In a conventional uncompressed DFA implementation the numbers are represented as states and the characteristic information of the given state are found out using the number specified in the table entry. The main function of CD²FA is that the state identifiers are replaced with content labels which specify the small portion of data that are stored in the table entry. The default transition that matches the present input characters are skipped using content labels. The table entry for the next state are found out using content label by means of hashing techniques.

A CD²FA deals with the consecutive states of a D²FA utilizing the content labels. This process provides the chosen information that is available in the state traversal approach and avoids unnecessary memory accesses. The number of main memory accesses required by CD²FA is equal to those required by an uncompressed DFA. Because of the lower memory footprint and high cache hit rate the throughput of uncompressed DFAs is improved. With an unassuming 1 KB data cache, CD²FA attains two times higher throughput than that of an uncompressed DFA and in the meantime only 10% of the memory is needed by table compressed DFA. Subsequently, the regular expressions are implemented by CD²FA very economically and the throughput and scalability of the system is enhanced.

The effectiveness of a CD²FA is evaluated experimentally on the regular expression sets from Cisco Systems, which contains more than 750 reasonably complex regular expressions in the Snort rule sets (Liu & Wu, 2013) and Bro NIDS rules sets (Roesch, 1999), and in the Linux layer-7 (Levandoski et al., n.d.) application protocol classifier. The authors created Cisco rules of ten sets with a total of 180138 states, and the number of states of each DFA is less than 64000 states. Then the Linux expressions were split into three sets with a total of 28889 states. Snort rules were divided into four sets which contains 22 regular expressions. Bro NIDS regular expressions were not divided because they are very simple. CD²FA constructed from the Creation Reduction Optimization (CRO) algorithm (Kumar, Turner, & Williams, 2006) achieved a memory reduction of around 2.5 to 20 times higher. The memory utilization reductions of CD²FA are 5 to 60 times higher than that of an uncompressed DFA

HYBRID FINITE AUTOMATA (HFA)

M. Becchi and P. Crowley, 2007 (Becchi & Crowley, 2007) have introduced hybrid DFA-NFA state reduction solution. A hybrid DFA-NFA solution combines the strengths of NFA and DFA. When the automaton is constructed, NFA encoding is done on any node that contributes toward state blowup, while the rest of the states are converted into DFA nodes. The end result incorporates the memory utilization of NFA, and integrates the memory bandwidth requirements of a DFA. The size of the automaton is maintained by intruding the subset construction operation of NFA states that takes place when converting NFA to DFA and the growth causes state explosion. The critical states are easily determined by doing the above case. The subset construction operation is intruded with an intermediate state that results in a hybrid automaton which contains DFA-like states, NFA-like states which are not expanded and the border state. The border states are considered to be a part of both a DFA and an NFA. Some of the useful properties of Hybrid FA are that the DFA - state is the start state; the NFA part of the automaton remains inactive till a border state is reached; and there is no backward activation of the DFA coming from the NFA.

The key factor is that the hybrid finite automaton is the first automaton that evaluates all the types of regular expression found in Snort NIDS rule set (Liu & Wu, 2013) and is implemented efficiently in real-world rapid systems. The hybrid finite automata uses default transitions (Kolias et al., 2011; Boyer & Moore, 2001) and content addressing (Kumar, Turner, & Williams, 2006) to encode the system and this leads to a variation in the storage requirements from 21KB up to 3MB. In reality, the default transition technique used in hybrid automaton eliminates approximately 98-99% of the DFA transitions, while the content addressing method implies the usage of state identifiers wide by 64 bit.

The main uniqueness of a hybrid finite automata are that it provides an unassuming memory storage requirement that is equivalent to a NFA solution, the memory bandwidth requirement of HFA in average case is also same as that of a single DFA solution, and in worst case it is linear containing dot-star condition and counting constraints. To balance memory and throughput, a new method Deep Classification – DFA (DC-DFA) was proposed by Wei et al, 2013 (He et al., 2013). DC-DFA is a compact representation that is based on hybrid finite automata which combines the advantages of NFA and DFA. It is supported mainly for large scale regular expression matching. Grade One classification approach is used to reduce the memory usage of DC-DFA and uses deep classification approach to improve the throughput of DC-DFA. The experiments evaluated on DC-DFA shows that in case of very large state explosion, DC-DFA reduces DFA states by 75% and improves the utilization of memory more efficiently and maintains high system throughput.

HISTORY BASED FINITE AUTOMATA (H-FA)

When multiple partially matching signatures are present in the DFA, the system becomes inefficient and yields to the state blow-up problem. To overcome this scenario the authors S Kumar et al, 2007 (Kumar, Chandrasekaran, Turner et al, 2007) proposed an improved Finite State Machine. The approach builds a machine which retains a lot of information, and stores the data in a small and high-speed cache memory known as history buffer (Kumar, Chandrasekaran, Turner et al, 2007). This type of system is named as History-based Finite Automaton (H-FA) which reduces space up to 95%.

Every transition is associated with a condition that depends upon the associated action and state of the history which decides whether to insert or delete the state from the history set, or both. H-FA is thus represented as a 6-tuple $H = (S, s_0, \Sigma, A, \delta, H)$, where S represents the finite set of states, s_0 denotes the start state, Σ specifies the input alphabet, A represents the set of accept states, the transition function δ, and H represents the history. The transition function δ functions by taking in an input alphabet, a state, and a history state as its arguments and returns a new state and a new history state.

$$\delta: S \times \Sigma \times H \rightarrow S \times H$$

The history buffer enhances the implementation of the H-FA and its automaton is similar to that of a DFA and contains set of states and transitions. For a single character there can be multiple transitions and leaves from a state but during execution only one of these transitions is taken, and that is resolved after investigating the details of the history buffer.

The performance was evaluated and experiments were conducted on the regular expressions used in the Cisco Systems. The rule sets from Cisco Systems contains over 750 reasonably complex regular expressions. The regular-expression signatures used in the open source Snort NIDS rule set (Liu & Wu, 2013), Bro NIDS rule set (Roesch, 1999), and in the Linux layer-7 (Levandoski et al., n.d.) application protocol classifier were also considered. Linux layer-7 protocol classifier contains seventy rules and a Snort rule set contains more than 1500 regular-expressions. The Bro NIDS contains 648 regular-expressions and the results for the HTTP signatures were present.

The number of conditional transitions is very small and causes state blow-up. The outgoing transitions of a DFA are around 256 and in most of the H-FAs there are less than 500. Hence the number of transitions increases nearly by double and there is a decrease in the number of states and conversely there is a significant reduction in memory. The size of H-FA that is registered in history buffer depends upon the partial matches. But limitation of this approach is that it has a restricted number of transitions for each input character with a huge size of transition table and a slow inspection speed.

HISTORY BASED COUNTING FINITE AUTOMATA (H-cFA)

When there is a length restriction of l on a sub expression of a given regular expression, the number of states that is needed by the sub expression gets multiplied by l. S Kumar et al, 2007 (Kumar, Chandrasekaran, Turner et al, 2007) designed a machine called as H-cFA which can count such events thereby avoiding state explosion.

In H-cFA the length restriction is replaced with a closure and the closure is represented by a flag that is present in the history buffer. A counter is added for every flag in the history buffer. The flag is set by setting the counter to the length restriction rate by the conditional transitions while the flag is reset by resetting these transitions. Besides, the flag which is set are attached with the counter value

0 which denotes an additional condition. During the execution of the machine, for every input character the value of every single positive counter is decremented.

This basic change is to a great degree compelling in reducing the number of states, particularly when long length restrictions strings are present. H-cFA is exceptionally effective in implementation of the Snort signatures because it contains many long length restriction strings. It is very effective in reducing the memory consumption. If there is no use in the counting capability of H-cFA there is a massive memory blowup in the composite automaton for Snort prefixes.

EXTENDED FINITE AUTOMATA (XFA)

Randy Smith et al, 2008 (Smith, Estan, Jha et al, 2008) designed a state based Extended Finite Automata (XFAs) which is augmented with a finite set of auxiliary variables in the standard DFA which is used to recollect different sorts of information that is relevant to the signature matching and to collect the explicit instructions that are attached to states in order to update these auxiliary variables. A state based extended finite automaton (Smith, Estan, Jha et al, 2008) is a 7-tuple (S, V, Σ, δ, U, (s_0, v_0), A), where

- S represents the finite set of states,
- Σ represents the set of input alphabets,
- $\delta: S \times \Sigma \rightarrow S$ is the transition function,
- V represents the finite set of variables,
- U: $S \times V \rightarrow V$ is the update function which describes how the data value is updated on states,
- (s_0, v_0) is the initial configuration which represents a start state s_0 and an initial variable value v_0,
- A $\rightarrow S \times V$ is the set of accepting configurations.

XFAs is a simplified version of standard DFAs which includes a finite set of possible variable values and are attached to states that operates with the variable during matching. Variable values along with a state are generalized to each of the initial states, transient state and accept state. In particular, individual XFAs are constructed and they are combined by means of standard techniques.

Randy Smith et al, 2008 (Smith, Estan, & Jha, 2008) have also proposed an edge based XFA. This work gives an informal categorization to the state blow up problem and is focused on algorithms to build XFAs from regular expressions. Semantically, edge based XFAs are equal to state-based XFAs, but a lot of states are required for state-based XFAs. Conversely, state based XFAs provide an efficient result for matching, combination and optimization algorithms.

For the test set Snort signature set were used which were obtained in March 2007. Randy Smith et al, 2008 (Smith, Estan, & Jha, 2008) collected at different time interval live traffic traces at the edge of the network, and each trace contained HTTP packets between 17,000 and 86,000. The performances were measured with the count of CPU cycles for each payload that are leveled to seconds per gigabyte (s/GB). The performance was evaluated by carrying the experiments on a standard Pentium 4 Linux workstation that runs at three GHz with three gigabyte of memory. The time complexity of Edge based XFAs is similar to DFAs and the space complexity is just like NFAs. When compared to DFA based system XFAs use 10 instances less memory and accomplish 20 instances higher matching speeds.

Michela Becchi et al, 2008 (Burch et al., 1990) proficiently handled counting constraints and back-references and proposed an advanced automation. This type of automaton covers all the patterns from the most expressive and popular Snort NIDS rule-set (Liu & Wu, 2013). When the regular expressions are represented with counting constraints in DFA form there is a huge rise in memory space. When there is an increase in the number of repetitions it is infeasible to design DFA. To solve the issues in (Burch et al., 1990) the authors have introduced the idea of the counting automaton. The automaton designed with counting constraints aims to minimize the consumption of memory and bandwidth requirements. In particular, XFA size does not depend on the number of repetitions, the main memory access count that is required for each counter and does not depend on the number of active counter instances. The value of the induced alphabet becomes larger and secondly, there is an excessive increase in the size of the DFA. To solve this in (Burch et al., 1990) the authors have proposed Extended Hybrid FA which compiles several regular expressions into a single automaton.

The experimental results were evaluated on the Bro v0.9 rule set (Roesch, 1999) and Snort () rule sets. First, they were able to compile a large number of complex regular expressions which contains simple regular expression with repeated character values, disjunctions of sub patterns, dot-star terms, and counting constraints and back references. Second, there was a decrease in the size of the NFA. Third, there was a reduction in the memory bandwidth in converted hybrid-FA representation and there was a need of an extra 156KB-16MB to hold the head- DFAs. The limited memory utilization makes a way to deploy the automata with static Random Access Memory (SRAM) in an Application Specific Integrated Circuit (ASIC) implementation that allows an excess memory access rate of 500MHz. A XFA has used number of automata alterations to eliminate restricted transitions which is limitation of HFA. XFA is confined to single supplementary state for each regular expression and it is unsuitable for tricky regular expressions.

DELTA FINITE AUTOMATA (δFA)

D Ficara et al, 2008 (Ficara et al., 2008) proposed a compressed DFA called as Delta Finite Automata. The interpretations that were obtained from the above techniques are that most default transitions stay close to the start state and a state that is defined by its transition set represents the accepted rule and for a given input character most of the transitions are directed to the same state. Based on these interpretations the δFA was designed.

The last interpretations state that most states that are adjacent contribute a considerable portion of the same transitions and hence it is sufficient to store the difference between these adjacent states. Therefore a transition set of the current state is been preserved and stored in a table which represents the supplementary structure. The number of states and transitions used by the algorithm is reduced and the study shows that nearly all adjacent states share a few common transitions and it is sufficient to store only differences between them. Essential characteristic of the delta finite automata is that it required only a single state transition for each character, thus allowed a fast string matching.

In a δFA, an arbitrary number of transitions are obtainable and therefore each state does not have a stable size and consequently there is a necessity in state pointers, which are normally standard memory addresses. Char - State compression technique (Ficara et al., 2008) based on input characters was proposed which exploited the relationship of few input characters with many states which reduced the number of bits required for each state pointer. This compression scheme has been included into the delta finite automata algorithm which provided a reduction in memory with an insignificant rise in the state lookup time.

Domenico Ficara et al, 2011 (Becchi & Crowley, 2008) proposed a compact representation that was an extension of the work (Ficara et al., 2008) which deletes most of the neighboring states that share the common transitions and keeps only the different ones. Instead of specifying the transition set of a state concerning its direct parents, this requirement can be relaxed to obtain the adoption of 1-step ancestors which increases the chances of compression. The finest method to exploit the Nth-order dependence is to describe the state transitions among child and ancestors as impermanent. This, during the construction problem leads to NP-Complete problem. Therefore, to make it simpler a direct and negligent approach is chosen. The real rule-sets result shows that the there is no much difference between the simple approach and from the optimal construction. This technique shares the same property of many other existing approaches and they are orthogonal to the various discussed existing algorithms such as XFAs (Smith, Estan, Jha et al, 2008) and H-cFA (Kumar, Chandrasekaran, Turner et al, 2007) and allows for higher compression rates.

Second Order Delta Finite Automata (δ^2FA)

δ^2FA is an extended version of δFA. An as alternative of specifying the state transition set relating to its direct parents, there is an increased probability of compression with the acceptance of 2-step ancestor's. Before proceeding with the construction process of δ^2FA (Antichi et al., 2009) δFA has to be constructed and that value should be used as input. The subsets of nodes are considered in which a transition for a given character are defined temporarily.

In a δ^2FA the table lookup is not similar to that of δFA. The main difference between δ^2FA and δFA is that there is an anxiety about the temporary transitions and the temporary transitions are not stored in the local transition set. Therefore, the lookup time complexity of δ^2FA is almost same as that of a δFA and memory consumption is better than δFA. δ^2FA takes advantage of the 2nd order precedence among states and by implementing the concept of temporary transition it reduces the number of transitions. Only a single state transition per character is required by δ^2FA thus it allows for fast string matching and higher compression rates.

DUAL FINITE AUTOMATA

Cong Liu et al, 2013 (Ficara et al., 2011) proposed a new approach called as dual finite automata (dual FA). The dual FA consists of an Extended Deterministic Finite Automaton (EDFA) and a Linear Finite Automaton (LFA). Dual FA consumes only a smaller memory when compared to DFA and the number of main memory access is very low when compared against the various discussed existing compressed DFAs. For instance it needs one or two main memory access for every byte in the payload. This is because by using linear finite automata the dual FA efficiently controls unbounded repetitions of wildcards and character sets.

This technique mitigates the state blow up problem. First, the NFA states that are not dependent to a large number of other states and those states that cause state exploitation are identified. Then, these NFA states are implemented using linear automaton. Subsequently the rest of the NFA states are compiled into a single extended DFA, which reduces the NFA states. Finally, by considering the fact that these two mechanisms cannot work separately, an interaction mechanism is implemented. EDFA has an additional feature compared with DFA to support the interaction mechanism.

The experimental results evaluated on dual finite automata demonstrate that LFA is very efficient in dropping the number of states and transitions. The number of states is reduced for up to four orders of magnitude when compared with that of DFA and the number of transitions is reduced for two orders of magnitude in contrast with MDFA (Yu et al., 2001). In dual FA there is only a rare increase in the number of main memory accesses, but in a MDFA there is a rapid increase in the number of main memory accesses as the number of DFAs increases.

Lastly one of the limitations of dual FA is that the number of LFA states cannot be large. When the dual finite automaton is implemented in personal computer, the effects in large number of LFA states considerably have lot of computational overhead. When large number of LFA states is existed in dual FA a larger per-flow state occurs, the storage size of the transition table becomes large and memory bandwidth also becomes large. The dual FA offers an effective solution among memory storage and memory bandwidth, and the implementation becomes very easy. When compared with DFA and MDFA the simulation results shows that in dual FA there is a drastic decrease in the storage demand and the memory bandwidth is almost close to that of DFA.

DETERMINISTIC FINITE AUTOMATA WITH EXTENDED CHARACTER SETS (DFA/EC)

Cong Liu et al, 2014 (Liu et al., 2014) have proposed a novel approach called Deterministic Finite Automata with Extended Character Sets(DFA/EC) which doubles the size of the character set (Liu et al., 2014; Yu et al., 2006) and considerably reduces the number of states. The DFA/EC can be efficiently implemented by dividing the design into two parts. The first part comprises of a compact DFA with a size m, which requires only one main memory access in its transition table for every byte in the packet payload. The second part consists of an efficient complementary program does not require any main memory access because it runs in the main memory without using the table lookup.

When compared with the above discussed existing compression techniques, the inspection speed of DFA/ EC is increased significantly by assigning the minimum value of one to the number of main memory accesses. The size of the inspection programs that are stored completely in the cache memory is kept small. Cong Liu et al, 2014 (Liu et al., 2014) conducted experimental results and the inspection program's speed was deliberated with C++ and JAVA implementations in a Unix machine with 16 Gigabyte of 1333 MHz DDR3 memory and with a 2.66 GHz Intel Core i5 CPU. In both C++ and JAVA implementations DFA/EC showed the fastest results, and when compared with DFA, DFA/EC were over ten times faster and were two times faster than MDFA in Java implementation. Thus DFA/EC is efficiently implemented on ASIC hardware or GPUs with less cache memory and more computation resources.

The memory bandwidth requirement of DFA/EC is much lesser than MDFAs and is very close to DFA. When considering the rule-sets exploit-19 and web-misc-28, DFA/EC can dramatically reduce the number of main memory accesses of DFA. When compared to DFA the number of states in a DFA/EC is about four orders of magnitude smaller and when compared to 2DFA it is around two orders of magnitude smaller than a 2DFA, and it is an order of magnitude smaller than a 4DFA, and is almost similar to that of an 8DFA. When compared to DFA the number of transitions of DFA/EC is almost four orders of magnitude smaller, when compared to 2DFA is it around two orders of magnitude smaller, with that of 4DFA it is 3 times smaller and 8DFA is comparable to DFA/EC.

The experiments are evaluated with the Snort rule-sets and the results shows that DFA/ECs are very compact and achieve high inspection speed. Particularly, in best case the DFA/ECs are more than four orders of magnitude lesser than DFAs. When compared with DFA, DFA/ECs require significantly lesser memory bandwidth. A DFA/EC is theoretically modest, implementation and upgrading is made easy due to faster construction speed.

DISCUSSIONS AND PROPOSED APPROACH

The various existing DFA compression techniques discussed in section 3 was analyzed to improve the memory consumption and to provide an efficient finite automata. The main reason that was analyzed from these existing DFA compression techniques for the number of states to get increased is due to the state explosion problem. The problem with exponential state explosion can be efficiently alleviated by grouping the regular expression. Grouping the regular expression falls into two cases. The first one is when the number of groups is known, the number of states in DFA can be minimized and second is when the maximum number of DFA states is known, the number of groups can be minimized (Fu et al., 2014). Though total number of groups and total number of DFA states plays major criteria in minimizing the memory, only either of these two cases cannot be concentrated in minimization process. Minimizing the number of groups will lead to state explosion and minimizing only the number of states will end up with large number of subdivided group count. Therefore to analyze the performance of the regular expression grouping method both these cases should be equally focused in correspondent with the various practical demands.

Grouping the regular expression can be done by Intelligent Optimization Grouping Algorithms. To provide memory efficient deterministic finite automata, DFA compression techniques can be used along with the Intelligent Optimization Grouping Algorithms. Intelligent Optimization Grouping Algorithms such as Tabu Search (TS) (Nino Ruiz et al., 2013), Simulated Annealing (SA) (Janakiriman

& Vasudevan, 2009), Ant Colony Optimization (ACO) (Fu et al., 2014; Navarro & Raffinot, 2001), Swarm Intelligence (SI) (Kumar, Dharmapurikar, Yu et al, 2006) and Particle Swarm Optimization (PSO) (Sommer & Paxson, 2003; Kumar, Dharmapurikar, Yu et al, 2006; Liu et al., 2011) can be used effectively to solve the state blow-up problem by obtaining the overall most favorable distribution between the consumption of memory and number of groups. By recursively analyzing each feasible optimization outcome an exact optimum solution can be effortlessly acquired.

In Fig.1 the overall structure of the proposed approach which reduces DFA states by grouping the regular expression using the Intelligent Optimization Grouping Algorithms is shown. The payload files extracted from the rule sets such as Snort (Liu & Wu, 2013), Bro NIDS (Roesch, 1999), and Linux L-7 filter (Levandoski et al., n.d.) are used as input. The set of regular expressions are determined using packet payload files. Initially the parameters for the algorithms are assigned and the initial population is generated by randomly distributing the regular expression on the search space. The performance is evaluated according to the Intelligent Optimization Grouping Algorithms such as Simulated Annealing (SA) (Janakiriman & Vasudevan, 2009), Swarm Intelligence (SI) (Kumar, Dharmapurikar, Yu et al, 2006), Ant Colony Optimization (ACO) (Fu et al., 2014; Navarro & Raffinot, 2001), Particle Swarm Optimization (PSO) (Sommer & Paxson, 2003; Kumar, Dharmapurikar, Yu et al, 2006; Liu et al., 2011), Tabu Search (Nino Ruiz et al., 2013), etc. Based on the performance the parameters such as search space, population, position, velocity

Figure 1. Overall Structure of proposed approach

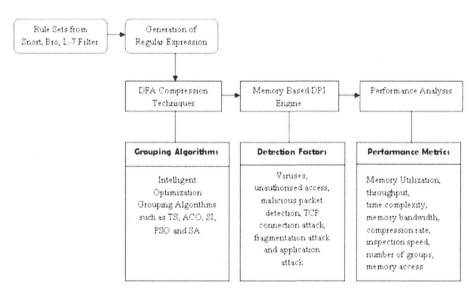

etc are adjusted and the process is continued until the optimal groups are formed or until the maximum iteration is obtained.

Once the optimal solution is obtained and the regular expressions are grouped, the finite state automata is designed based on the discussed existing DFA compression technique and is integrated with the DPI search engine to identify the packets that hold the viruses, unauthorized access and attacks such as TCP connection attacks, fragmentation attacks and application attacks. Intelligent Optimization Grouping Algorithms applied on the discussed existing DFA compression techniques for deep packet inspection will provide memory efficient automata with an improved network intrusion detection throughput through the use of DPI techniques and improved malicious packet detection.

Figure 2. Memory Consumption, Memory Bandwidth, Throughput and Compression Rate for different DFA compression techniques

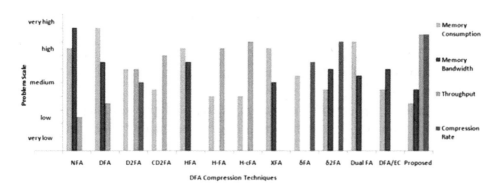

The experiments are evaluated in future on the proposed approach for the various performance metrics, and the expected outcome is compared with the various discussed existing DFA Compression techniques. Fig.2 shows the memory consumption, memory bandwidth, throughput and compression rate for the different DFA compression techniques. It depicts that the proposed approach will produce reduced memory consumption, better memory bandwidth, high throughput and better compression rate.

Fig.3 illustrates the performance measures of the main memory access time and the time complexity for the various DFA compression techniques and shows that the proposed approach will produce increased number of memory access time per input byte and will improve the time complexity.

Fig. 4 shows the inspection speed of intrusion detection and the regular expression matching speed for the various DFA compression techniques. It illustrates that the

Figure 3. Time Complexity and Main memory access time for different DFA compression techniques

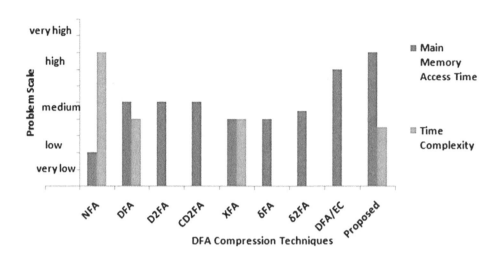

proposed approach will produce fast matching speed and high inspection speed of intrusion detection.

Thus the future experiments evaluated on the proposed approach using Intelligent Optimization Grouping Algorithms will provide an optimally efficient automaton when compared with the discussed existing DFA compression techniques and will

Figure 4. Inspection Speed and Matching Speed for different DFA compression techniques

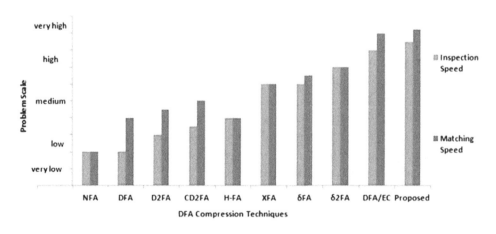

also improve the throughput of network intrusion detection through the use of DPI techniques and will enhance the malicious packet detection.

CONCLUSION

In this chapter, the different compression representations for Deterministic Finite Automata such as NFA, DFA, MDFA, Lazy DFA, NFA-OBDD, HFA, H-FA, H-cFA, XFA, D^2FA, CD^2FA, δFA, $\delta^2 FA$, Dual Finite Automata and DFA/EC are presented. MDFA increases the matching speed of the regular expression approximately to 50 to 700 times above the NFA-based implementation and achieves the speedup of up to 12-42 times over a DFA-based parser. For all practical applications the size of the lazy DFA remains little but the limitation is that it leads to a high warm-up cost and large memory consumption. NFA-OBDDs improve the time efficiency of NFA. The memory storage requirement of HFA is comparable to those of an NFA; its memory bandwidth is similar to that of a DFA, but the regular expressions that contains counting and dot-star conditions consumes high memory. H-FA reduces space close to 95% but has a vast size of transition table and a slow inspection speed. On the other hand H-cFA is extremely efficient in implementing long length restriction signature patterns. XFAs matching speed is around 20 times higher than a DFA and consumes 10 times lesser memory than DFA. The δFA substantially diminishes the number of transitions and number of states and needs only a single state transition for each character thus providing fast string matching. When compared to δFA, $\delta^2 FA$ provides an effective improvement in memory utilization and lookup speed. D^2FA representation reduces the transitions between states by more than 95% and decreases the space requirements to less than 2 MB but the usage of default transitions decreases throughput. Memory reduction achieved by CD^2FA is between 2.5 to 20 times better when compared to a compressed DFA and 5 to 60 times higher when compared with uncompressed DFA. The number of main memory access of Dual FA is much quicker than the other existing techniques. When compared to other existing techniques DFA/EC tremendously increases the data packet inspection speed and provides only one main memory access. Each of the state compression techniques that were studied has certain strengths and limitations. Thus any one of these compact representation DFAs can be used along with Intelligent Optimization Grouping Algorithms to provide memory efficient deterministic finite automata that can be used for deep packet inspection.

REFERENCES

Aho, A. V., & Corasick, M. (1975). Efficient String Matching: An aid to Bibliographic Search. *Communications of the ACM, 18*(6), 333–340.

Anantathanavit, M., & Munlin, M. (2016). Using K-Means Radius Particle Swarm Optimization for the Travelling Salesman Problem. *IETE Technical Review, 33*(2), 172–180.

Antichi, G., Di Pietro, A., Ficara, D., Giordano, S., Procissi, G., & Vitucci, F. (2009). Second-Order Differential Encoding of Deterministic Finite Automata. *Proceedings of the 28th IEEE Conference on Global Telecommunications*, 2838-2843.

Becchi, M., & Crowley, P. (2007). A Hybrid Finite Automaton for Practical Deep Packet Inspection. *Proceedings of the ACM Conference on Emerging Networking Experiments and Technologies.*

Becchi, M., & Crowley, P. (2007). An Improved Algorithm to Accelerate Regular Expression Evaluation. *Proceedings of the 3rd ACM/IEEE Symposium on Architecture for Networking and Communications Systems*, 145-154.

Becchi, M., & Crowley, P. (2008). Extending Finite Automata to Efficiently Match Perl-Compatible Regular Expressions. *Proceedings of the ACM International Conference on Emerging Networking Experiments and Technologies.*

Beng, Ramadass, & Selvakumar. (2014). A Survey of Intrusion Alert Correlation and its Design Considerations. *IETE Technical Review, 31*(3), 233–240.

Boyer, R. S., & Moore, J. S. (2001). A Fast String Searching Algorithm. *Communications of the ACM, 20*(10), 762–772.

Burch, J. R., Clarke, E. M., McMillan, K. L., Dill, D. L., & Hwang, J. (1990). Symbolic Model Checking: 1020 states and beyond. *Proceedings of the 5th Annual IEEE Symposium on Logic in Computer Science*, 428-439.

Dharmapurikar, S., & Lockwood, J. (2005). Fast and Scalable Pattern Matching for Content Filtering. *Proceedings of the ACM Symposium on Architecture for Networking and Communications Systems*, 183-192.

Ficara, D., Di Pietro, A., Giordano, S., Member, S., Procissi, G., Vitucci, F., & Antichi, G. (2011). Differential Encoding of DFAs for Fast Regular Expression Matching. *IEEE/ACM Transactions on Networking, 19*(3), 683–694.

Ficara, D., Giordano, S., Procissi, G., Vitucci, F., Antichi, G., & Pietro, A. D. (2008). An Improved DFA for Fast Regular Expression Matching. *Proceedings of the ACM SIGCOMM Computer Communication Review, 38*(5) 29-40.

Fu, Z., Wang, K., Cai, L., & Li, J. (2014). Intelligent Grouping Algorithms for Regular Expressions in Deep Inspection. *Proceedings of the International Conference on Computer Communications and Networks.*

Green, T. J., Gupta, A., Miklau, G., Onizuka, M., & Suciu, D. (2004). Processing XML Streams with Deterministic Automata and Stream Indexes. *ACM Transactions on Database Systems, 29*(4), 752–788.

He, W., Guo, Y. F., & Hu, H. C. (2013). Hybrid Finite Automata – Based Algorithm for Large Scale Regular Expression Matching. *Applied Mechanics and Materials, 263*, 3108–3113.

Hopcroft, J. (1971). *An algorithm for Minimizing States in a Finite Automaton.* Stanford University Stanford.

Hopcroft, J. E., Motwani, R., & Ullman, J. D. (2001). Introduction to Automata Theory, Languages, and Computation (2nd ed.). Addison-Wesley-Longman.

Janakiriman, S., & Vasudevan, V. (2009). ACO Based Distributed Intrusion Detection System. *Proceedings of the International Journal of Digital Content Technology and its Applications, 3*(1), 66-72.

Kolias, C., Kambourakis, G., & Maragoudakis, M. (2011). Swarm Intelligence in Intrusion Detection: A Survey. *Computers & Society, 30*(8), 625–642.

Kumar, S., Chandrasekaran, B., Turner, J., & Varghese, G. (2007). Curing Regular Expressions Matching Algorithms from Insomnia, Amnesia and Acalculia. *Proceedings of the ACM/IEEE Symposium Architecture for Networking and Communication Systems*, 155-164.

Kumar, S., Dharmapurikar, S., Yu, F., Crowley, P., & Turner, J. (2006). Algorithms to Accelerate Multiple Regular Expressions Matching for Deep Packet Inspection. *Proceedings of the Conference on Applications, Technologies, Architectures, and Protocols for Computer Communications, 36*, 339-350.

Kumar, S., Turner, J., & Williams, J. (2006). Advanced Algorithms for Fast and Scalable Deep Packet Inspection. *Proceedings of the ACM/IEEE Symposium Architecture for Networking and Communication Systems*, 81-92.

Kumar, S., Turner, J. S., Crowley, P., & Mitzenmacher, M. (2007). HEXA: Compact Data Structures for Faster Packet Processing. *Proceedings of the International Conference on Network Protocols*, 246-255.

Levandoski, J., Sommer, E., & Strait, M. (n.d.). *Application Layer Packet Classifier for Linux.* Available: http://l7-filter.sourceforge.net/

Liu, Pan, Chen, & Wu. (2014). A DFA with Extended Character-Set for Fast Deep Packet Inspection. *IEEE Transactions on Computers, 63*(8), 1925-1937.

Liu, C., Chen, A., Wu, D., & Wu, J. (2011). A DFA with Extended Character Set for Fast Deep Packet Inspection. *Proceedings of the International Conference on Parallel Processing*, 1-10.

Liu, C., & Wu, J. (2013). Fast Deep Packet Inspection with a Dual Finite Automata. *IEEE Transactions on Computers, 62*(2), 310–321.

Myers, E. W. (1992). A Four Russians Algorithm for Regular Expression Pattern Matching. *Journal of the Association for Computing Machinery, 39*(2), 430–448.

Navarro, G., & Raffinot, M. (2001). Compact DFA Representation for Fast Regular Expression Search. *Proceedings of the 5th International Workshop on Algorithm Engineering*, 1-12.

Nino Ruiz, E. D., Nieto Parra, H., & Isabel Chinchilla Camarg, A. (2013). Evolutionary Algorithm Based on Simulated Annealing for the Multi-Objective Optimization of Combinatorial Problems. *Proceedings of the International Journal of Combinatorial Optimization Problems and Informatics, 4*(2), 53–63.

Paxson, V. (1998). A System for Detecting Network Intruders in Realtime. Computer Networks. *The International Journal of Computer and Telecommunications Networking, 31*, 2435–2463.

Roesch, M. (1999). Snort: Light Weight Intrusion Detection for Networks. *Proceedings of the 13th USENIX Conference on System Administration*, 229-238.

Sidhu, R., & Prasanna, V. K. (2001). Fast Regular Expression Matching using FPGAs. *Proceedings of the 9th Annual IEEE Symposium on Field-Programmable Custom Computing Machines*, 227-238.

Smith, R., Estan, C., & Jha, S. (2008). Faster Signature Matching with Extended Automata. *IEEE Symposium on Security and Privacy*, 187-201.

Smith, R., Estan, C., Jha, S., & Kong, S. (2008). Deflating the Big Bang: Fast and Scalable Deep Packet Inspection with Extended Finite Automata. *Proceedings of the ACM SIGCOMM 2008 Conference on Applications, Technologies, Architectures, and Protocols for Computer Communications*, 207-218.

Sommer, R., & Paxson, V. (2003). Enhancing Byte- Level Network Intrusion Detection Signatures with Context. *Proceedings of the 10th ACM Conference on Computer and Communications Security*, 262-271.

Thompson, K. (2006). Programming Techniques: Regular Expression Search Algorithm. *Communications of the ACM, 11*(6), 419–422.

Wang, J., Hong, X., Ren, R., & Li, T. (2009). A Real-time Intrusion Detection System Based on PSO-SVM. *Proceedings of the International Workshop on Information Security and Application.*

Wu, J., Ran, T., & Li, Z.-Y. (2011). An improving Tabu Search Algorithm for Intrusion Detection. *Proceedings of the 3rd International Conference on Measuring Technology and Mechatronics Automation, 1*, 435-439.

Yang, L., Karim, R., Ganapathy, V., & Smith, R. (2011). Fast Memory-Efficient Regular Expression Matching with NFA-OBDDs. *Computer Networks: The International Journal of Computer and Telecommunications Networking, 55*(15), 3376–3393.

Yu, F., Chen, Z., Diao, Y., & Lakshman, T. (2006). Fast and Memory- Efficient Regular Expression Matching for Deep Packet Inspection. *Proceedings of the ACM/IEEE Symposium on Architecture for Networking and Communications Systems*, 93-102.

Yu, F., Chen, Z., Diao, Y., Lakshman, T. V., & Katz, R. H. (2001). Fast and Memory-Efficient Regular Expression Matching for Deep Packet Inspection. *Proceedings of the ACM/IEEE Symposium Architecture for Networking and Communication Systems*, 93-102.

Chapter 11
The Contribution of Obeya for Business Intelligence

Gonçalo Sousa
School of Engineering, Polytechnic of Porto, Portugal

José Carlos Sá
https://orcid.org/0000-0002-2228-5348
School of Engineering, Polytechnic of Porto, Portugal

Gilberto Santos
https://orcid.org/0000-0001-9268-3272
Design School, Polytechnic Institute of Cavado and Ave, Portugal

Francisco J. G. Silva
School of Engineering, Polytechnic of Porto, Portugal

Luís Pinto Ferreira
School of Engineering, Polytechnic of Porto, Portugal

ABSTRACT

The main objective of the study is to minimize interdepartmental communication, potentiation of fast and efficient decision making, and computerization of data. Using software such as MS Excel® and MS Power BI®, a Power BI® tool was conceived to be capable of incorporating, for the entire company, the dashboards that collect the main KPIs of each department. After the tool was implemented, the company's paradigm shift was noticeable. Quickly, the weekly meeting of the planning team began to take place using the MS Power BI® dashboard. In this way, processes were automated and the important data for the normal functioning of the company became accessible to all departments, thus minimizing interdepartmental communication. The chapter shows an Obeya Digital that was implemented in a company in which all the performance indicators of each department are incorporated. In this way, information becomes accessible to all employees and manual data update processes are minimized.

DOI: 10.4018/978-1-7998-6721-0.ch011

INTRODUCTION

A great market competitiveness exists currently. Hence, the companies increasingly invest in teams dedicated to optimizing processes and implementing Lean Manufacturing techniques, intending to increase productivity (Oliveira et al., 2017; Ribeiro et al., 2019; Correia et al., 2018; Rosa et al., 2017a). The ability to control the market and monitor the development of competing companies forces organizations to evolve their efficiency level and reduce the processes costs (Katayama & Bennett, 1996). However, it is only possible to raise the company's productivity indexes with a well-defined strategy and in accordance with pre-established objectives (Katayama & Bennett, 1996; Neves et al., 2018). Thus, companies must develop methods of data tracking related to the implementation of their strategy. The performance indicators is one of the methods used, which facilitate the control of the performance of the departments that integrate the organization (Rodrigues et al., 2019). Regularly, most companies use Key Performance Indicators (KPI) and Key Behaviour Indicators (KBI) to support daily or weekly meeting, which promote a skilful and thoughtful decision. In this sense, through KPIs and KBIs, companies are able to quickly identify problems and find the best way to solve them (Rakar et al., 2004).

The use of performance indicators helps substantially in meeting the pre-established objectives (Jiménez-Delgado et al., 2020; Santos et al., 2019b). However, it is important to enhance their use, that is, KPIs must be easily accessible to all employees (Rakar et al., 2004), so that the information is transversal to all departments, instead of being posted on a board or wall of a company room (Machado et al., 2019; Ferreira et al., 2019). An example of this is the Obeya room, which has origin in the 90s at Toyota through Takeshi Uchiyamada. He realized that he did not have the necessary authority to make the ideal decisions and that he needed the support of the leaders of the other departments to find the best solution and to apply it in a quicker way (Aasland & Blankenburg, 2012b). Obeya is a visual space, usually located in the *Gemba*, where meetings are held to discuss problems and, therefore, reach a solution to them (Sá et al., 2020). It is important for decision making that the data is up to date and truthful with the present landscape of the organization (Aasland & Blankenburg, 2012a).

In addition to this, the existence of an alternative to face-to-face meetings where KPIs are discussed represents a great advantage, as employees do not need to go to the meeting room (Aasland & Blankenburg, 2012b). Bearing this in mind and given the current scenario, namely the global pandemic COVID-19, it becomes even more crucial to find solutions that prevent these displacements and avoid large number of people gathered in the same room. Thus, digital tools have been built to rereacted the same workflow and impact, making easier the initial effect of the Obeya at the Gemba. These tools allow to create information sharing systems and meetings, where it is possible to easily analyse a resume of the main information and discuss the work progress, priorities and actions to be done, pursuing the main goals of the company at each moment. The implementation of these tools is easy and just requires a short training to allow a plain use of the tools made available. The information needs to be standardized and organized, letting all the people involved to be aware of the information and becoming them able to participate in the meetings knowing the main facts, and proficient to make decisions. Indeed, the Obeya team should work as a cross function tean, where there is an ongoing session, instead of periodic meetings. The group must be multifaceted, including members from engineering, to operators and commercial collaborators. The easy access to communication between teams and a much more visual management of processes, induces productivity that can reach double that previously achieved (Adler et al., 2011).

The group would typically include engineers, design stylists, suppliers, assembly workers and members of our marketing team. Teams in these war-rooms showed a doubling of productivity. Why? Among other things, teams had easy access to each other for both coordination of their work and for learning, and the work artifacts they posted on the walls remained visible to all. The result is fewer changes, saved time and reduced cost.

Thus, the main objectives of this article are:

- Digitalization of information, specifically, of performance indicators;
- Automation of processes associated with updating KPIs;
- Transformation of Traditional Obeya into Digital Obeya;
- Maintenance of the good performance of organizations in an adverse scenario, such as the pandemic.

The article shows the example of an Obeya Digital that was implemented in a company, in which all the performance indicators of each department are incorporated. In this way, information becomes accessible to all employees and manual data update processes are minimized. Also, with the help of this tool, it was possible to solve several previously identified problems.

Background

Since the end of the 18th century, there have been major transformations in terms of processes and even three major industrial revolutions that have led not only to the constant development of the industrial sector but also to a major change in the way products are manufactured. The First Industrial Revolution took place in England in 1784, with the appearance of the steam engine and the mechanical loom. In 1870, the use of electricity and combustion arose with the Second Industrial Revolution and, also, the appearance of the first mass productions. A century later there were advances in electronics and information technologies, in what was defined as the Third Industrial Revolution. Currently, we are experiencing the Fourth Industrial or Technological Revolution, or Industry 4.0 (Ferreira et al., 2019; Santos et al., 2018).

Falcão (2019) points out that "one of the main focuses of Industry 4.0 is mass production with the minimum cost of production", which is only possible with the evolution of technologies and the reduction of costs associated with processes. Also, it contributes to "the transformation of a centralized production system into a decentralized one", therefore increasing the company's flexibility, which translates into an improvement in the capacity to respond to customers' needs.

Concerning the present, Santos et al. (2018) states that most organizations have already applied automation and implemented information systems such as Enterprise Resource Planning (ERP) and Manufacturing Execution System (MES), denoting a considerable increase in productivity and financial results. However, the author stresses that there are still opportunities for improvement that must be explored. For example, the lengthy communication between the ERP and the factory floor, which detriments skilful decision-making. For the processes to reach the expected levels of efficiency, it is imperative to be able to access real-time production information.

According to Coelho (2016), the term Industry 4.0 is similar to a smart factory (or intelligent factory), in the sense that these terms characterize factories of the future. Thus, factories will be much more automated, intelligent, flexible, dynamic and easier to control. It is then expected that companies will be able to increase their productivity (Pinto et al., 2019; Barbosa et al., 2018).

The main pillars of Industry 4.0 are associated with the most relevant technologies for their implementation and operation, and can thus be defined by:

- **Internet of Things (IoT):** it is characterized by connectivity and interaction between physical and virtual objects and people, through connected platforms and technologies. It is present in several day-to-day situations, such as the control of the equipment that is part of the house through a personal cell phone (Coelho, 2016; Sakurai & Zuchi, 2018; Marques et al., 2018).
- **Cyber-Physical Systems (CPS):** are systems designed to manage the data stored through technologies, which enable your cooperation in a system and enhance the efficiency, safety and quality of the product (Umachandran et al., 2019; Santos et al., 2019d; Araújo et al., 2019; Bravi et al., 2019; Sá et al., 2019). The main asset that companies look for in these systems is safety, since poor data conservation can compromise all the work developed (Coelho, 2016; Sakurai & Zuchi, 2018).
- **Big Data Analytics:** given the large number of data to be generated continuously, powerful analysis tools are needed. In this sense, it is crucial

that the data considered relevant is filtered, to process it and in turn, transform it into knowledge and wisdom. Thus, companies will evolve and fit in with the path to the industry of the future (Coelho, 2016; Santos et al., 2019c; Bravi et al., 2017; Bravi et al., 2018; Félix et al., 2019b; Santos et al., 2019a; Zgodavovaet al., 2020; Marinho et al., 2020; Doiro et al., 2019).

With this in mind, Industry 4.0 can boost organizations by making them more flexible, improving relations with their customers and their requirements, optimizing decision making, increasing productivity and resource efficiency. This will allow companies to be able to respond to demographic changes in the work environment, balancing the work and life of their employees, while also allowing them to maintain a high wage economy and a highly competitive position in the market (Kagermann et al., 2013).

Industry 4.0 can complement itself with Lean Manufacturing since, despite being different models of production management, they present complementarities, and both share the same objectives of increasing productivity and flexibility. This complementarity between Industry 4.0 technologies and Lean Manufacturing methods is called Lean Automation, which aims to integrate the best practices of the two models (Cordeiro et al., 2020; Silva et al., 2020; Vieira et al., 2019). Therefore, both support each other (Ikeziri et al., 2020; Carvalho et al., 2020).

Lean is the basis for the implementation of Industry 4.0 in companies and the processes that already comply with this methodology are easily modelled and controlled, which in turn simplify the fulfilment of Industry 4.0 objectives (Buer et al., 2018; Ikeziri et al., 2020).

On the other hand, Industry 4.0 complements Lean Manufacturing management. The information provided in real-time by 4.0 technologies is useful in preparing an accurate Value Stream Mapping (VSM), a fundamental tool and considered the starting point for the implementation of Lean processes. VSM is used to map the current process and identify opportunities for improvement in the value stream. Traditionally, it is a picture of the company's process idealized through data collection. This tool makes it possible to identify waste in the process (Sousa et al., 2018). However, with the support of Industry 4.0, it is possible to implement VSM systems in real-time. In this way, a dynamic picture of the *Gemba* is created, which increases the visibility of information and enhances decision-making with accurate and current information. Consequently, processes increase efficiency and waste is minimized (Santos et al., 2011; Buer et al., 2018; Kamble, Gunasekaran, & Dhone, 2020; Bravi et al., 2020; Talapatra et al., 2019).

Examples of this combination of models are the CPS-based smart Jidoka, which increases the flexibility of processes and increases reliability. Later, with modular workstations and flexible production lines in conjunction with SMED (Single

Minute Exchange of Die), it is possible to reduce the set-up time (Rosa et al., 2017b). Besides, another example of this good combination is the implementation of autonomous *Kanbans* that detect the stock level and are able to order parts automatically, reducing stock levels. Therefore, combining Industry 4.0 and Lean Manufacturing, it is possible to increase productivity, reduce waste and thus reduce process costs (Santos et al., 2014; Buer et al., 2018; Azevedo et al., 2019; Barbosa et al., 2018; Silva & Ferreira, 2019).

The implementation of Industry 4.0 is simpler in companies that already have resources dedicated to data analysis, for example through operational applications of Business Intelligence (BI) (Bordeleau et al., 2018). According to Cunha & Paula (2019), the Business Intelligence concept emerged in 1958 through IBM (International Business Machines) researcher Hans Peter Luhn, who portrayed BI as the ability to learn the interrelationships of the facts presented, to guide direct action towards the desired goals. Business Intelligence aims to help the company to extract useful information from all internal and external data sources effectively and efficiently, consequently accumulating greater knowledge of the company and facilitating in making decisions. In general, decisions are aimed at improving the production process, promoting the company and acquiring strengths concerning the market (Cunha & Paula, 2019; Lu, 2014; Costa et al., 2019; Félix et al., 2019a; Jimenez et al., 2019b).

However, in the business management landscape, BI allows users to analyse the processes that have already been completed. On the other hand, it allows the creation of forecasting models, in order to verify the possibility of completing the projects (Negash, 2004). Additionally, it is possible to monitor all the company's processes for easier identification of undesirable situations. Finally, it also promotes the existence of control over the company's processes, insofar as the system can interact with the process based on monitoring and forecasting. In short, in BI systems it is possible to incorporate data from the past, present and future, which will allow a quick and effective decision making, given the perception of the entire panorama of the company. Moreover, this is perfectly compatible with digital Obeya features, which is a powerful source of information for all teams, allowing quick and supported decisions (Lopes et al., 2020). Consequently, coupled with this benefit, given the variability and abundance of data, some decisions can be automated, by their analogy with other similar processes (Lima, 2019).

At the structural level, BI can be subdivided into five areas (Lima, 2019; Lu, 2014):

- **Data Source:** there are two types of data sources for BI applications, internal and external. The internal ones consist of data that is obtained and maintained in the organization's system using systems such as Customer Relationship Management (CRM) and ERP. Data designated by external sources is acquired, for example, from partner companies, suppliers, the government, among others. It is critical that companies identify all their data sources, with a view to better organization and increased data reliability.

- **Extract-Transform-Load** (**ETL**): ensures that all data extracted is properly treated and in the correct format to be loaded into the database. In this case, extraction is used to read data from different sources, whether internal or external. The transformation process is associated with converting data to the ideal format in order to facilitate its analysis later. Thus, this process aims to make data operational. Finally, loading is defined as the storage of data matured in previous processes in a database.
- **Database:** all data stored in the warehouse is ready to be analysed and worked on. It consists of an Operational Data Source (ODS), which consists of a short-term memory which makes it possible to update it frequently, used to integrate the data and load it in the respective database. The main objective of this element is to retain the data in the desired and reliable format to enhance its use when necessary.
- **Cubes & Indicators:** provides several techniques as a resource, such as Online Analytical Processing (OLAP) and Data Mining. OLAP's goal is to find the answers to the company's requirements and provides users with a tool to view and analyse data relating to different areas. Regarding Data Mining, its functionality has an optimization role in relation to OLAP, as it allows the quick identification of useful information. That is, they are two tools that complement each other, and to enhance their use it is necessary to combine OLAP with Data Mining.
- **WEB Analysis:** this element is applied to all areas previously described, though it is possible to track and monitor the data flow of a single BI system/ area. It helps to normalize information, to avoid ambiguities in interpretation and also makes data access more user-friendly for all users. An example of its application is the control of business performance by managers, sometimes through a dashboard.

According to the areas analysed, it is understood that the BI process presents great complexity and, therefore, its elaboration takes longer. The existence of a dedicated team is crucial, which prevents the execution by an employee without knowledge in the area, who can show some difficulties in deal with the complexity previously referred. In the market there are plenty of solutions for BI systems, however, most of them are complex, dependant on specialized IT (Information Technology) personnel and constitute a high financial burden for their implementation (Cunha & Paula, 2019; Lima & Costa, 2017; Lima, 2019).

On the other hand, alternatives of less complexity and without dependence on technical and specific knowledge of the area are elaborated. The concept of BI Self-Service is associated with the democratization of data, which allows any employee, without technical expertise, to be able to prepare reports and dashboards in a very intuitive and instantaneous way. Currently, you can find several BI Self-Service tools on the market, including Microsoft Power BI, Tableau, Qlik and Microstrategy (Cunha & Paula, 2019; Floriano et al., 2016; Lima & Costa, 2017; Lima, 2019).

Allied to BI is the term Obeya, which is of Japanese origin and means large room, it can also be called war room, program room, control room or the pulsing room (Javadi et al., 2013). The concept was created by a Toyota employee whose main objective was to improve the coordination of departments in the execution of a complex engineering project. For its implementation, several A3 sheets were affixed to the walls of a large room, thus facilitating the perception of the different opinions of employees (Nascimento et al., 2018; Nascimento et al., 2017; Pereira et al., 2019).

Like other Lean methodologies, Obeya also optimizes business processes, as it helps in efficient and skilful decision-making, minimizes waste and eliminates organizational "barriers" that do not favour their proper functioning at all (Nascimento et al., 2018, 2017). In this way, employees have access to the opinions and concerns of other workers in the organization, which will facilitate a quick agreement between all (Javadi et al., 2013; Nascimento et al., 2018).

Although it is an important tool, there are aspects to be improved in the traditional Obeya. At a virtual level, if Obeya is computerized, it will be possible to attend the meetings without having to be physically present, allowing employees in different locations, to be able to gather and analyse the company's data. Besides, Obeya's look became more flexible, allowing employees to improve the way data is displayed, and consequently facilitate its interpretation and reaction (Aasland & Blankenburg, 2012a).

CASE STUDY: BRIEF PRESENTATION OF THE CONPANY

The study was based on the implementation of Digital Obeya in an electric chargers company, in the electric mobility sector, with around 500-750 employees. There is little product variability, differentiated mainly by their electrical capacities, and they comprise two major product groups: the slow charge and the fast charge.

The company has about five production lines, manufacturing cells dedicated to the production of parts that supply the production lines and other manufacturing cells for customized/unique products. Mostly associated with large series, it has storage in the operating range that is identical throughout the process, therefore the flexibility of the production system is low and also presents a flow close to the continuous, with a unique sequence of operations and stable demand. The level of relationship with the customer is characterized by manufacturing to order, and following the order the company supplies, manufactures, assembles and delivers.

The main sample was the Production Planning department, made up of four elements, one of whom was responsible for its management. Parameters such as workload and stress level were analysed; the number of manual processes and their duration was counted. In addition, another important variable for the study was the meetings and the way they were managed and planned.

PROBLEMS AND SOLUTIONS

How the Company Works

The Planning team has a central role in the company's good performance since they are responsible for defining the planning of their entire production. For planning the production lines, there are two Excel documents, one for each type of company equipment, with two members of the team responsible for managing them. Correspondingly, it is also expected that the elements responsible for planning the lines have full knowledge of the state of their planned equipment, that is, whenever any equipment has a problem in its production, they must know the reason for its occurrence. Consequently, these employees are endowed with great technical knowledge of the company's product range. The equipment, after being unlocked in the ERP, is placed in the respective files, considering the load of the lines, allowing to fix the production. Moreover, as production only takes place when the processes that supply the lines are completed, the files are also used by those responsible for the adjacent processes to update the data related to the material they produce. Thus, MS Excel® sheets are updated daily with the status of the equipment, in order to maintain the greatest possible control of the equipment within the factory. In addition, the test and shipping buffers are also in control of Planning, therefore being the only department with the most up-to-date status of all equipment. This information is essential for Project Managers since they need to know the status of the equipment integrated into their project portfolio and keep the client as up to date as possible regarding their delivery date.

The team is also responsible for sharing a summary table with the daily equipment entries for the current week with the Production department, which, in turn, will assist the Logistics department to carry out the kits for the respective week.

In addition, the Planning area is also responsible for guiding weekly meetings, where an analysis of all the KPIs defined by the team is carried out. Given their importance, regularly all departments are present and there is a discussion of the most critical issues in terms of production, bearing in mind the continuous improvement of the results presented.

Problems

The company has identified several problems associated with the lack of process automation. One of the examples is related to the preparation of meetings, in which the person responsible for the Planning team had to dedicate a period of their working hours to update the data and define the indicators that would be discussed. In this way, the little automation of this process is associated with the dispersion of the key performance indicators of Planning across the different MS Excel® sheets and the way of updating the KPIs individually, that is, almost manually. Thus, the meetings' flow and the information sharing is seriously compromised due to the key role of the files, creating additional difficulties in understanding and assililating all information.

Besides to the improvement opportunities mentioned above, the company also had a large flow of e-mails between departments, since there is crucial information for the normal functioning of the company that is not computerized and available to everyone. Project Managers, responsible for the project and interfacing between the company and customers, have to keep their customers updated on the production status of orders. In this way, they contact the Planning team to consult the status of the equipment, since it is the department that possesses the production data. Another case of high flow of e-mails is with the team of Commercials who are responsible for negotiating orders with customers. Thus, to assign a delivery date for a project/order, they also contact the Planning team, as it is the area that has the greatest knowledge about the overload of the lines. Planning is the only department capable of providing information about the project's expected completion date, in order to avoid overloading the lines. Therefore, due to the highlighted problems, the lack of data computerization is notorious, making it difficult to control equipment within the factory and the ability to respond with delivery dates for salespeople to inform customers.

Improvements and Implementation

After identifying the main problems with the normal functioning of the Planning Department, objectives were defined, in order to eliminate or minimize them. Table 1 shows the improvement proposals applied to each problem encountered.

For the implementation of the proposals described, applications such as MS Excel® and MS Power BI® were used. Initially, data computerization was improved through MS Excel®, thus minimizing the difficulty in controlling equipment within

Table 1. Improvement proposals for the process under analysis

Problems	Improvements
• Manual Processes	• Automation of Processes
• High E-mail Flow • Difficulty in Control of Equipment's	• Computerization of Data
• Scattering of Planning KPIs	• Development of a tool in Power BI with Planning KPIs
• Lack of a tool to bring together the KPIs of different departments	• Modelling of a tool capable of aggregating all the dashboards of the different departments

the factory. Then, a tool was created for Planning KPIs and subsequently, directories were prepared for the evolution of other departments of the company in terms of data computerization. In this way, it was expected that the company would minimize the flow of interdepartmental e-mails, the difficulty of controlling equipment, the dispersion of KPIs and, also, eliminate the problem identified regarding the lack of a tool that would agglomerate the KPIs of the different departments. Thus, it was essential to have MS Excel® files to supply MS Power BI® constantly and in an automated way.

MS Power BI's Excel® Supply Files

After the initial improvements correctly established, it is time to the Digital Obeya Room implementation. This should be supported in previous works (Nascimento et al., 2018), but is also supported in some empirical ideas. Thus, a procedure can be drawn, following some guidelines:

- The information should be prepared and improved as a physical Obeya room was going to be implemented;
- However, the network needs to be verified or updated, in order to support the new Obeya tool;
- The Obeya tool will use a commercial software, which needs to be prepared for the action:
- Collaborators need to be trained, becoming familiar with the software and all its potentialities;
- Documentation should be prepared to be used in an integrated way within the new software;
- The interrelations between documents need to be deeply explored, allowing to get the best results of this implementation;

- A transitory period of time needs to be selected, allowing the fine-tunning of documents and interrelations, providing by this way the best results. Moreover, collaborators need to ajust their behaviour to the new tool, learning how to take advantage of its implementation;
- The implementation needs to follow a PDCA (Plan-Do-Check-Act) methodology, allowing the continuous improvement of the implementation, always seeking better results.

Some od these important steps are going to be dissecated below, allowing a better perception of the relation between the documents preparation. At first, the MS Excel® files that supply MS Power BI® were developed, in order to prepare new KPIs and prepare the data. In this sense, two files emerged based on the variety of equipment, each of which is associated with the plan of production lines specialized in this type of equipment. Therefore, to facilitate data analysis, an MS Excel® file that aggregates the productions of the company's two types of equipment is used. The file is divided into several sheets:

- the production plan with detailed data for all equipment;
- outputs from production and quality checking;
- equipment in delays, where a calculation was devised to predicts the evolution of the backlog in the coming weeks;
- the future backlog in which the overdue equipment is detailed, which sheet helps in setting priorities;
- the current backlog in which the equipment that may become overdue according to the delivery date is detailed, and this sheet also aims to define priorities in the production lines.

Additionally, there is a file with important data for the MS Power BI® tool. Data updates in this file occur on Monday as they relate to the previous week. This file is important for obtaining good weekly reports and is also divided into several sheets:

- the weekly data in a macro way, that is, only numerical and not at all detailed;
- the load/capacity of the lines, which is divided into a table according to the types of equipment, with each table calculating the best distribution for planning the production lines, taking into account the capacity restrictions and equipment priorities.

Through this file, and especially the load/capacity sheet, it is expected that the members of the Planning team, responsible for planning the lines, consult the tables mentioned above for better optimization of the lines' load.

Besides, new MS Excel® files were developed for the computerization of the KPIs of each department, which is analysed in the weekly meeting, designated by Obeya, with the superiors of each department connected to the production and the Director of Operations. The MS Excel®files of all departments follow the same structure, that is, they are standardized, which facilitates the insertion of data in MS Power BI®. On the other hand, as they are held in a meeting format and, normally, tasks were created for the people present, a file was created to replace the manual action plan, making it digital and easily accessible to everyone.

Finally, to make data easily accessible to all elements present in the addressed meetings, information SharePoint's were created, enhancing the data updates in the MS Power BI® tool.

Implementation of MS Power BI

Through MS Power BI®, a tool was developed for all departments of the company that considerably improves the communication between them. The main feature of this tool, which improves its use, is the publication via a website, which can be saved in the browser's favourites, thus allowing to reduce the great complexity and increase the speed of data consultation. Initially, it was only proposed to devise a dashboard for Planning, however, given its success, a tool was developed for the entire company, capable of integrating the dashboards of each department. This means that, it is expected that the main data will be computerized so that all the important information for the normal functioning of the company is available in a robust, user-friendly and objective way.

The MS Power BI® tool is divided into five levels and the lower levels are opened if the pre-defined buttons are activated. In order to facilitate interaction with the user, menus at the upper levels have been designed to direct and filter the information the user wants to access. Therefore, the company must computerize its KPIs, so there are already departments idealizing their dashboards, such as Logistics, Processes, and Production, which will later integrate this tool and thus enhance its use within the company.

For the study carried out, the Planning and Operational Piloting Meetings (OPM) directories were developed. It should be noted that for the two areas, two MS Power BI® files are associated, and there is also a third file that has various tool menus. This file is connected with the others through hyperlinks present in the buttons, that is, pressing a certain button will open a new tab associated with another MS Power BI® file. In this way, if there is an error regarding data update, it does not interfere with the normal operation of the tool, and with its separation into separate files, it is possible to personalize the collaborators who have read and edit access to each file. In this sense, not all directories of the tool may be available to all company employees. The dashboards that make up the tool automatically update, thus using one of the potentialities of MS Power BI® that allows the data to be updated as scheduled. However, for this automatic update, it was necessary that there was a connection from the Gateway or that all the respective data sources are in the cloud. If there were connections from the Gateway, it was necessary for the computer, which has the files, to be connected when the data was updated. However, as previously mentioned, all files are in SharePoint's, which allow all updates to proceed automatically without the need for an active computer.

The idealized tool, once activated, directs the user to a home menu with three buttons associated with the main areas of the company, Technology, Commercial and Operations. Only the Operations area has been developed, which includes Planning and OPM. Thus, when clicking on the Operations button, the website page is updated with the new directory shown in Figure 1.

Figure 1. Operations Cockpit's Menu

In this directory associated with the "Operations" button, a menu is presented where the buttons for the different departments associated with the operations and a button for the OPM are highlighted. A key point to make the tool more user-friendly was the normalization of the look of all directories that resemble of Figure 1. Additionally, as it is possible to notice through the observation of Figure 1, there is also a free button (down right corner), which is prepared for any department that wants to insert its dashboard with the main KPIs in the tool.

As a result of activating the Planning button, a new tab is opened on the internet, since it is a new MS Power BI®file, called Planning Cockpit. The open directory is

Figure 2. Planning Cockpit Menu

also characterized as a menu, since it only presents buttons for the user, albeit more specific than the buttons of the overlying menus.

Afterwards, the "Planning Cockpit Menu", if the user presses any button, the data related to them are highlighted. In this study, the visual elements that integrate each page associated with the highlighted buttons will not be presented, with a view to maintain the confidentiality of company data. Briefly, the visual elements used to create these directories were bar graphs, Gantt diagrams, pie charts, performance indicators, tables, among others.

As previously mentioned, the "Planning Cockpit Menu" is associated with a file in which data is processed. In this case, updates are already scheduled through the files in Planning's SharePoint. Specifically, for the planning data, three daily updates are scheduled, one at 6:30 am, before the company starts its activity, one at 12:00 pm, around lunchtime for employees, and one at 5:00 pm hours, at the end of the working day. There is a meeting organized by the Planning team with the other departments, in order to analyse the data integrated into the tool and the consequent justification and definition of actions to be taken to improve the results. As a result of the meeting, emails are sent to other employees who need to know, with screenshots and notes of the data and KPIs analysed at the meeting. Therefore, it is a tool with a high preponderance in the company's paradigm and, consequently, training meetings have already been held with the departments of Quality, Sales and Project Management, to extract objectively and efficiently the data required for each function.

Then, in addition to the Planning Department, OPMs were also developed, specifically the Obeya meeting. To open the data integrated into the Obeya file, the user has to activate the OPM button in Figure 1, through which a new tab will be opened with a two-button menu, shown in Figure 3.

As in the "Planning Cockpit" file, the various KPIs of the company's departments are integrated and as all files are in a SharePoint, it also allows the scheduling of updates. Every week there is a meeting where this file is analysed in detail, therefore making the various daily updates that occur in Planning unnecessary. In this way, the data is updated on Monday, Tuesday and Wednesday, at three different times, at 11:00 am, at 1:30 pm and 2:30 pm, as the meeting could be held on any of those days of the week.

Figure 3. OPM Menu

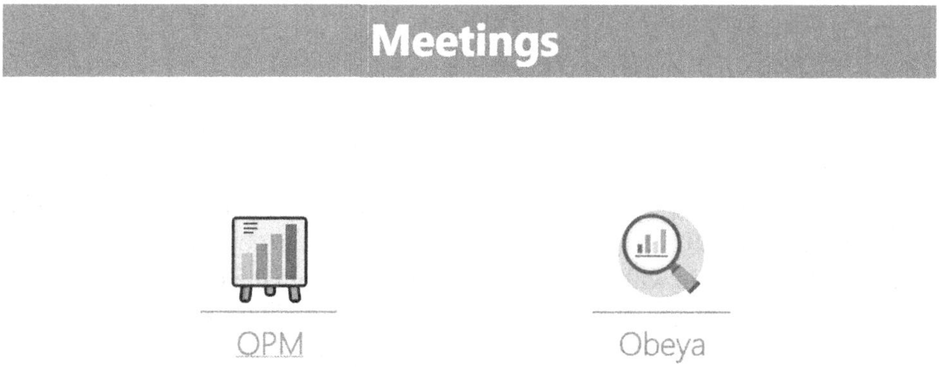

Meetings

OPM

Obeya

In Figure 3, two options are available to the user, however, only the directory associated with the Obeya button is developed. If the user places the computer mouse over the OPM button, the message "To be defined" is displayed. The user can only press the Obeya button and, as soon as user activates it, the page is updated to the Obeya menu, according Figure 4, shown below.

In this menu, buttons are defined for the various areas associated with the company's operations and, also, two buttons related to the meeting, the "Rules and Participants" and the "Action Plan", are available. Therefore, taking into account that the data are confidential to the company, an analysis of the visual elements that integrate the pages associated with the buttons will not be made.

As previously mentioned, two directories have been developed for the "Rules and Participants" and the "Action Plan". In the first directory are presented the

Figure 4. Obeya Menu

main rules that must be respected during the respective meeting, the agenda with the topics to be addressed and the respective durations and the participants who must be present at all meetings, in order to achieve their objectives. The second directory shows a table with the action plan resulting from the meeting, in which it is possible to see the task definition date, the task definition, the person responsible for its completion, the deadline and the status of the task, with constant control of its development in mind. To update the action plan, consult the MS Excel® file, which also includes Obeya's SharePoint.

OUTCOMES AND FUTURE RESEARCH DIRECTIONS

In short, MS Power BI® has gained a lot of preponderance in the current paradigm of the company and the respective control of KPIs. Initially, the objective was to computerize the planning data. However, after the company became aware of the potential of this tool, it was proposed to prepare an application to receive the dashboards of the different departments. At this point, the main limitations of the tool are:

- Need for mastery of the tool for quick detection of errors that prevent its operation;
- Automatic update of data, for which the files must be in a MS SharePoint®, which is a tool that has many limitations for teamwork;

- Minor changes in the files that supply the MS Power BI® files can block data updates, for example, if the column name of an MS Excel® file is changed.

Moreover, the implementation of this tool opens a wide range of possibilities to expand the its implementation to the other two areas not developed in this work, namely the "Technology" and "Commercial" areas. The "Technology" area can be expanded in terms of the development of new products, and can be related to the ideas brought by Commercial Team, following the market trends and allowing a faster and more productive way of developing new products. Regarding the "Commercial" are, the implementation of this tool can help in developing the more accurate strategies to search new markets and customers, congregating knowledge about the market needs and trends, helping by this way the company to define and develop new products. However, the toll can be also useful to better menage the customers distribution by the Commercial Team, getting a faster response to the customers needs, as well as a better exchange of strategies and ideas on how to achieve the company's goals in commercial terms.

In the future, the OPM button will be also developed, allowing meeting regarding the mastering of the operations management, becoming more peaceful the relation between departements into the company and allowing a better flow of the operations.

CONCLUSION

This project has become quite ambitious given the little knowledge of the MS Power BI® software, having been necessary to carry out exhaustive research and study about its potential. Something worth noting is the ease of working with MS Power BI® since it is a very intuitive and user-friendly software. After several meetings with the Planning Department in order to optimize the KPIs and visual elements that make up the tool, the Planning meetings, in which the other departments were present, started to be held using the tool. In this way, employees perceived the potential and advantages of its use.

Consequently, it was determined to develop a tool in MS Power BI® capable of aggregating all the dashboards of the different departments. This resulted in a drastic change in the mentality of employees, who now intend to computerize all company data, in order to enhance its smooth functioning and minimize the excess of interdepartmental communication, more specifically, via email. Due to the preponderance of the tool, training sessions were held for the Quality department, Project and Commercial Managers, demonstrating the utility of the application for the execution of the daily work of each employee. In this way, the company can enhance the skilful decision making without resorting to the implementation of an

ERP, which is associated with greater financial costs. However, at this moment, cooperation between all departments is necessary to computerize their associated data, intending to increase the value of the company and, consequently, increase business performance.

The Obeya that existed in the company before the computerization of the company was very old-fashioned. Those responsible for the departments associated with the production had to update the graphics and, as they were posted on the walls of the meeting room, they were updated in a very manual way, using a pen and set square. In this way, Obeya meetings have become easier to prepare, since the data only needs to be updated in the MS Excel®files that each person in charge of the departments uses.

Additionally, the application of this new tool was fundamental for adaptation to the current world pandemic scenario COVID-19, in which face-to-face meetings had to be avoided as much as possible and data needed to be computerized, maintaining the rigour of meetings through Microsoft Teams®.

In short, the preparation time for meetings and travel time to meeting rooms has been reduced. Previously, all of these processes were associated with approximately 2 hours of the workday and, at this moment, the only task performed by those responsible is to confirm that the data is up to date.

REFERENCES

Aasland, K., & Blankenburg, D. (2012a). *An analysis of the uses and properties of the Obeya*. doi:10.1109/ICE.2012.6297660

Aasland, K., & Blankenburg, D. (2012b). Virtualizing the obeya. *NordDesign 2012 - Proceedings of the 9th NordDesign Conference.*

Adler, B.-M., Baets, W., & König, R. (2011). A complexity perspective on collaborative decision making in organizations: The ecology of group-performance. *Information & Management*, *48*(4-5), 157–165. doi:10.1016/j.im.2011.04.002

Araújo, R., Santos, G., Costa, J. B., & Sá, J. C. (2019). The quality management system as a driver of organizational culture: An empirical study in the Portuguese textile industry. *Quality Innovation Prosperity*, *23*(1), 1–24. doi:10.12776/qip. v23i1.1132

Azevedo, J., Sá, J. C., Ferreira, L. P., Santos, G., Cruz, F. M., Jimenez, G., & Silva, F. J. G. (2019). Improvement of production line in the automotive industry through lean philosophy. *Procedia Manufacturing*, *41*, 1023–1030. doi:10.1016/j. promfg.2019.10.029

Barbosa, L. C. F. M., de Oliveira, O. J., & Santos, G. (2018). Proposition for the alignment of the integrated management system (quality, environmental and safety) with the business strategy. *International Journal of Qualitative Research*, *12*(4), 925–940.

Barbosa, M., Silva, F. J. G., Pimentel, C., & Gouveia, R. M. (2018). A Novel Concept of CNC Machining Center Automatic Feeder. *Procedia Manufacturing*, *17*, 952–959. doi:10.1016/j.promfg.2018.10.111

Bordeleau, F.-E., Mosconi, E., & De Santa-Eulalia, L. A. (2018). Business Intelligence in Industry 4.0: State of the art and research opportunities. *Proceedings of the 51st Hawaii International Conference on System Sciences*. Retrieved from http://hdl.handle.net/10125/50383

Bravi, L., Murmura, F., & Santos, G. (2017). Attitudes and behaviours of Italian 3D prosumer in the Era of Additive Manufacturing. *Procedia Manufacturing*, *13*, 980–986. doi:10.1016/j.promfg.2017.09.095

Bravi, L., Murmura, F., & Santos, G. (2018). Manufacturing labs: Where new digital technologies help improve life quality. *International Journal of Qualitative Research*, *12*(4), 957–974.

Bravi, L., Murmura, F., & Santos, G. (2019). The ISO 9001:2015 Quality Management System Standard: Companies' Drivers, Benefits and Barriers to Its Implementation. *Quality Innovation Prosperity Journal*, *23*(2), 64–82. doi:10.12776/qip.v23i2.1277

Bravi, L., Santos, G., Pagano, A., & Murmura, F. (2020). Environmental management system according to ISO 14001:2015 as a driver to sustainable development. *Corporate Social Responsibility and Environmental Management*, *27*(6), 1–16. doi:10.1002/csr.1985

Buer, S. V., Strandhagen, J. O., & Chan, F. T. S. (2018). The link between industry 4.0 and lean manufacturing: Mapping current research and establishing a research agenda. *International Journal of Production Research*, *56*(8), 2924–2940. doi:10.1080/00207543.2018.1442945

Carvalho, F., Santos, G., & Gonçalves, J. (2020). Critical analysis of information about integrated management systems and environmental policy on the Portuguese firms' website, towards sustainable development. *Corporate Social Responsibility and Environmental Management*, *27*(2), 1069–1088. doi:10.1002/csr.1866

Coelho, P. M. N. (2016). *Towards Industry 4.0*. Faculdade de Ciências e Tecnologia Universidade de Coimbra.

Cordeiro, P., Sá, J. C., Pata, A., Gonçalves, M., Santos, G., & Silva, F. J. G. (2020). The Impact of Lean Tools on Safety—Case Study. *Occupational and Environmental Safety and Health II, 277*, 151–159. doi:10.1007/978-3-030-41486-3_17

Correia, D., Silva, F. J. G., Gouveia, R. M., Pereira, T., & Ferreira, L. P. (2018). Improving manual assembly lines devoted to complex electronic devices by applying Lean tools. *Procedia Manufacturing, 17*, 663–671. doi:10.1016/j.promfg.2018.10.115

Costa, A. R., Barbosa, C., Santos, G., & Alves, M. R. (2019). Six Sigma: Main Metrics and R Based Software for Training Purposes and Practical Industrial Quality Control. *Quality Innovation Prosperity Journal, 23*(2), 83–99. doi:10.12776/qip. v23i2.1278

Cunha, C., & de Paula, L. B. (2019). Análise do uso de uma ferramenta de Business Intelligence em tomadas de decisão a partir de dados de mídia social (In Portuguese). *Revista Científica Da FAEX*. Retrieved from http://periodicos.faex.edu.br/index. php/e-Locucao/article/view/212/164

de Lima, R. P. (2019). *Estruturação de um Ambiente de Business Intelligence para Gestão da Informação da Secretaria Municipal de Trânsito e Transportes de Uberlândia*. Retrieved from http://repositorio.ufu.br/bitstream/123456789/27629/4/ EstruturaçãoAmbienteBusiness.pdf

Doiro, M., Santos, G., & Felix, M. J. (2019). Machining operations for components in kitchen furniture: A comparison between two management systems. *Procedia Manufacturing, 41*, 10–17. doi:10.1016/j.promfg.2019.07.023

Falcão, A. C. R. de A. (2019). *Sistematização dos Pilares da Indústria 4.0: Uma Análise Utilizando Revisão*. Universidade De São Paulo Escola De Engenharia De São Carlos.

Félix, M. J., Gonçalves, S., Jimenez, G., & Santos, G. (2019b). The contribution of design to the development of products and manufacturing processes in the Portuguese industry. *Procedia Manufacturing, 41*, 1055–1062. doi:10.1016/j. promfg.2019.10.033

Félix, M. J., Silva, S., Santos, G., Doiro, M., & Sá, J. C. (2019a). Integrated product and processes development in design: A case study. *Procedia Manufacturing, 41*, 296–303. doi:10.1016/j.promfg.2019.09.012

Ferreira, M. J., Moreira, F., & Seruca, I. (2019). *Digital Transformation Towards a New Context of Labour: Enterprise 4.0*. Advances in Logistics, Operations, and Management Science. ALOMS. doi:10.4018/978-1-5225-4936-9.ch002

Ferreira, S., Silva, F. J. G., Casais, R. B., Pereira, M. T., & Ferreira, L. P. (2019). KPI development and obsolescence management in industrial maintenance. *Procedia Manufacturing, 38*, 1427–1435. doi:10.1016/j.promfg.2020.01.145

Floriano, A. C., Lemes, E. F., & Heofacker, V. H. G. (2016). *Análise De Ferramentas De Business Intelligence*. Academic Press.

Ikeziri, L. M., Melo, J. C., Campos, R. T., Okimura, L. I., & Gobbo, J. A. Junior. (2020). A perspectiva da indústria 4.0 sobre a filosofia de gestão Lean Manufacturing. *Brazilian Journal of Development, 6*(1), 1274–1289. doi:10.34117/bjdv6n1-089

Javadi, S., Shahbazi, S., & Jackson, M. (2013). Supporting production system development through the Obeya concept. *IFIP Advances in Information and Communication Technology, 397*(PART 1), 653–660. doi:10.1007/978-3-642-40352-1_82

Jimenez, G., Santos, G., Félix, M., Hernández, H., & Rondón, C. (2019b). Good Practices and Trends in Reverse Logistics in the plastic products manufacturing industry. *Procedia Manufacturing, 41*, 367–374. doi:10.1016/j.promfg.2019.09.021

Jiménez-Delgado, G., Santos, G., Félix, M. J., Teixeira, P., & Sá, J. C. (2020). A combined ahp-topsis approach for evaluating the process of innovation and integration of management systems in the logistic sector. Lecture Notes in Computer Science (Including Subseries Lecture Notes in Artificial Intelligence and Lecture Notes in Bioinformatics), 12427 LNCS, 535–559. doi:10.1007/978-3-030-60152-2_40

Kagermann, H., Wahlster, W., & Helbig, J. (2013). *Recommendations for implementing the strategic initiative INDUSTRIE 4.0*. Academic Press.

Kamble, S., Gunasekaran, A., & Dhone, N. C. (2020). Industry 4.0 and lean manufacturing practices for sustainable organisational performance in Indian manufacturing companies. *International Journal of Production Research, 58*(5), 1319–1337. doi:10.1080/00207543.2019.1630772

Katayama, H., & Bennett, D. (1996). Lean production in a changing competitive world: A Japanese perspective. *International Journal of Operations & Production Management, 16*(2), 8–23. doi:10.1108/01443579610109811

Lima, D. R., & Costa, H. R. da C. (2017). *Uma Visão Teórica Sobre Ferramentas de Self-Service B.I. Através de Dados Públicos Sobre os Casos de Acidentes do Trabalho A Theoretical View About Self-Service Tools B.I. Through Public Data on the Cases of Work Accidents* (Vol. 7). Revista Pensar Tecnologia.

Lopes, J., Guimarães, T., & Santos, M. F. (2020). Adaptive Business Intelligence: A New Architectural Approach. *Procedia Computer Science, 177,* 540–545. doi:10.1016/j.procs.2020.10.075

Lu, M. (2014). *Discovering Microsoft Self-service BI solution: Power BI.* Academic Press.

Machado, C. G., Winroth, M., Carlsson, D., Almstrom, P., Centerholt, V., & Hallin, M. (2019). Industry 4.0 readiness in manufacturing companies: challenges and enablers towards increased digitalization. *52nd CIRP Conference on Manufacturing Systems.* 10.1016/j.procir.2019.03.262

Marinho, A., Silva, R. G., & Santos, G. (2020). Why most university-industry partnerships fail to endure and how to create value and gain competitive advantage through collaboration – a systematic review. *Quality Innovation Prosperity, 24*(2), 34–50. doi:10.12776/qip.v24i2.1389

Marques, C., Lopes, N., Santos, G., Delgado, I., & Delgado, P. (2018). Improving operator evaluation skills for defect classification using training strategy supported by attribute agreement analysis. *Measurement, 119,* 129–141. doi:10.1016/j.measurement.2018.01.034

Nascimento, D. L. de M., Quelhas, O. L. G., Meiriño, M. J., Caiado, R. G. G., Barbosa, S. D. J., & Ivson, P. (2018). Facility management using digital obeya room by integrating BIM-lean approaches – An empirical study. *Journal of Civil Engineering and Management, 24*(8), 581–591. doi:10.3846/jcem.2018.5609

Nascimento, D. L. de M., Sotelino, E. D., Lara, T. P. S., Caiado, R. G. G., & Ivson, P. (2017). Constructability in industrial plants construction: A BIM-Lean approach using the Digital Obeya Room framework. *Journal of Civil Engineering and Management, 23*(8), 1100–1108. doi:10.3846/13923730.2017.1385521

Negash, S. (2004). Business intelligence. *Communications of the Association for Information Systems,* 177–195. https://www.researchgate.net/publication/228765967

Neves, P., Silva, F. J. G., Ferreira, L. P., Pereira, T., Gouveia, A., & Pimentel, C. (2018). Implementing Lean Tools in the Manufacturing Process of Trimmings Products. *Procedia Manufacturing, 17,* 696–704. doi:10.1016/j.promfg.2018.10.119

Oliveira, J., Sá, J. C., & Fernandes, A. (2017). Continuous improvement through "Lean Tools": An application in a mechanical company. *Procedia Manufacturing, 13,* 1082–1089. doi:10.1016/j.promfg.2017.09.139

Pereira, J., Silva, F. J. G., Bastos, J. A., Ferreira, L. P., & Matias, J. C. O. (2019). Application of the A3 Methodology for the Improvement of an Assembly Line. *Procedia Manufacturing, 38*, 745–754. doi:10.1016/j.promfg.2020.01.101

Pinto, B., Silva, F. J. G., Costa, T., Campilho, R. D. S. G., & Pereira, M. T. (2019). A Strategic Model to take the First Step Towards Industry 4.0 in SMEs. *Procedia Manufacturing, 38*, 637–645. doi:10.1016/j.promfg.2020.01.082

Rakar, A., Zorzut, S., & Jovan, V. (2004). *Assesment of Production Performance by means of KPI*. Retrieved from http://eprints.uanl.mx/5481/1/1020149995.PDF

Ribeiro, P., Sá, J. C., Ferreira, L. P., Silva, F. J. G., Pereira, M. T., & Santos, G. (2019). The impact of the application of lean tools for improvement of process in a plastic company: A case study. *Procedia Manufacturing, 38*, 765–775. doi:10.1016/j.promfg.2020.01.104

Rodrigues, J., de Sá, J. C. V., Ferreira, L. P., Silva, F. J. G., & Santos, G. (2019). Lean management "quick-wins": Results of implementation. A case study. *Quality Innovation Prosperity, 23*(3), 3–21. doi:10.12776/qip.v23i3.1291

Rosa, C., Silva, F. J. G., & Ferreira, L. P. (2017a). Improving the quality and productivity of steel wire-rope assembly lines for the automotive industry. *Procedia Manufacturing, 11*, 1035–1042. doi:10.1016/j.promfg.2017.07.214

Rosa, C., Silva, F. J. G., Ferreira, L. P., & Campilho, R. (2017b). SMED methodology: The reduction of setup times for Steel Wire-Rope assembly lines in the automotive industry. *Procedia Manufacturing, 13*, 1034–1042. doi:10.1016/j.promfg.2017.09.110

Sá, J. C., Barreto, L., Amaral, A., Carvalho, F., & Santos, G. (2019). Perception of the importance to implement ISO 9001 in organizations related to people linked to quality – an empirical study. *International Journal of Qualitative Research, 13*(4), 1055–1070.

Sá, J. C., Vaz, S., Carvalho, O., Lima, V., Morgado, L., Fonseca, L., Doiro, M., & Santos, G. (2020). A model of integration ISO 9001 with Lean six sigma and main benefits achieved. *Total Quality Management & Business Excellence, 0*(0), 1–25. doi:10.1080/14783363.2020.1829969

Sakurai, R., & Zuchi, J. D. (2018). The Industrial Revolutions up to Industry 4.0. *Interface Tecnológica*, 480–491. doi:10.31510/infa.v15i2.386

Santos, B. P., Alberto, A., Lima, T. D. F. M., & Santos, F. M. (2018). *Indústria 4.0: Desafios e Oportunidades*. Revista Produção e Desenvolvimento.

Santos, G., Doiro, M., Mandado, E., & Silva, R. (2019a). Engineering learning objectives and computer assisted tools. *European Journal of Engineering Education*, *44*(4), 616–628. doi:10.1080/03043797.2018.1563585

Santos, G., Gomes, S., Braga, V., Braga, A., Lima, V., Teixeira, P., & Sá, J. C. (2019c). Value creation through quality and innovation - a case study on Portugal. *The TQM Journal*, *31*(6), 928–947. doi:10.1108/TQM-12-2018-0223

Santos, G., Mendes, F., & Barbosa, J. (2011). Certification and integration of management systems: The experience of Portuguese small and medium enterprises. *Journal of Cleaner Production*, *19*(17-18), 1965–1974. doi:10.1016/j.jclepro.2011.06.017

Santos, G., Murmura, F., & Bravi, L. (2019d). Developing a model of vendor rating to manage quality in the supply chain. *International Journal of Quality and Service Sciences*, *11*(1), 34–52. doi:10.1108/IJQSS-06-2017-0058

Santos, G., Rebelo, M., Ramos, S., Silva, R., Pereira, M., & Ramos, G. N. L. (2014). Developments regarding the integration of the occupational safety and health with quality and environment management systems. In I. G. Kavouras & M.-C. G. Chalbot (Eds.), *Occupational safety and health* (pp. 113–146). Nova Publishers.

Santos, G., Sá, J. C., Oliveira, J., Ramos, D., & Ferreira, C. (2019b). Quality and Safety Continuous Improvement Through Lean Tools. In Lean Manufacturing – Implementation, opportunities and Challenges. Nova Science Publishers.

Silva, F. J. G., & Ferreira, L. P. (2019). *Lean Manufacturing - Implementation, opportunities and challenges*. Nova Science Publishers.

Silva, S., Sá, J. C., Silva, F. J. G., Ferreira, L. P., & Santos, G. (2020). Lean Green— The Importance of Integrating Environment into Lean Philosophy - A Case Study. *Lecture Notes in Networks and Systems*, *122*, 211–219. doi:10.1007/978-3-030-41429-0_21

Sousa, E., Silva, F. J. G., Ferreira, L. P., Pereira, M. T., Gouveia, R., & Silva, R. P. (2018). Applying SMED methodology in cork stoppers production. *Procedia Manufacturing*, *17*, 611–622. doi:10.1016/j.promfg.2018.10.103

Talapatra, S., Santos, G., Uddin, K., & Carvalho, F. (2019). Main benefits of integrated management systems through literature review. *International Journal of Qualitative Research*, *13*(4), 1037–1054. doi:10.24874/IJQR13.04-19

Umachandran, K., Jurčić, I., Della Corte, V., & Sharon Ferdinand-James, D. (2019). *Industry 4.0: The New Industrial Revolution*. doi:10.4018/978-1-5225-6207-8.ch006

Vieira, T., Sá, J. C., Lopes, M. P., Santos, G., Félix, M. J., Ferreira, L. P., Silva, F. J. G., & Pereira, M. T. (2019). Optimization of the cold profiling process through Lean Tools. *Procedia Manufacturing*, *38*, 892–899. doi:10.1016/j.promfg.2020.01.171

Zgodavova, K., Bober, P., Majstorovic, V., Monkova, K., Santos, G., & Juhaszova, D. (2020). Innovative Methods for Small Mixed Batches Production System Improvement: The Case of a Bakery Machine Manufacturer. *Sustainability*, *12*(6266), 12–31. doi:10.3390u12156266

Compilation of References

Saeed, S., & SaroshUmar, M. (2015). A Hybrid Graphical User Authentication Scheme. In *International conference on Communication, Control and Intelligent Systems*. IEEE.

Smith, R., Estan, C., & Jha, S. (2008). Faster Signature Matching with Extended Automata. *IEEE Symposium on Security and Privacy*, 187-201.

Andrea, B., Ian, O., & Hyoungshick, K. (2016). PassBYOP: Bring Your Own Picture for Securing Graphical Passwords. *IEEE Transactions on Human-Machine Systems*, *46*(3).

Liu, Pan, Chen, & Wu. (2014). A DFA with Extended Character-Set for Fast Deep Packet Inspection. *IEEE Transactions on Computers, 63*(8), 1925-1937.

Bellam, A. (2013). An Effective User Authentication Method Using Persuasive Cued Click Points. *International Journal of Computational Engineering Science*.

Fu, Z., Wang, K., Cai, L., & Li, J. (2014). Intelligent Grouping Algorithms for Regular Expressions in Deep Inspection. *Proceedings of the International Conference on Computer Communications and Networks*.

Khalifa, H., & Siong, L. (2013). Graphical Password: Pass-Images Edge Detection. IEEE.

Levandoski, J., Sommer, E., & Strait, M. (n.d.). *Application Layer Packet Classifier for Linux*. Available: http://l7-filter.sourceforge.net/

He, W., Guo, Y. F., & Hu, H. C. (2013). Hybrid Finite Automata – Based Algorithm for Large Scale Regular Expression Matching. *Applied Mechanics and Materials*, *263*, 3108–3113.

Radha, A. (2013). *A Persuasive Cued Click-point based Authentication Mechanism with Dynamic User Blocks*. International Journal of Research in Engineering & Advanced Technology.

Aho, A. V., & Corasick, M. (1975). Efficient String Matching: An aid to Bibliographic Search. *Communications of the ACM*, *18*(6), 333–340.

KumarSarohi, H., & UllahKhan, F. (2013). Graphical Password Authentication Schemes: Current Status and Key issues. *IJCSI, 10*(2).

Ansari, S., Rokade, J., Khan, I., & Shaikh, A. (2018). Graphical Password Scheme Using Cued Click Point and Persuasion with Multiple Images. *International Journal on Recent and Innovation Trends in Computing and Communication*, *6*(4), 2321–8169.

Green, T. J., Gupta, A., Miklau, G., Onizuka, M., & Suciu, D. (2004). Processing XML Streams with Deterministic Automata and Stream Indexes. *ACM Transactions on Database Systems*, *29*(4), 752–788.

Zhi, L., & Qubin, L. (2005). *An Association Based Graphical Password Design Resistant to Shoulder Surfing Attack*. IEEE. doi:10.1109/ICME.2005.1521406

Towhidi, F., & Manaf, F. (2011). *The Knowledge Based Authentication Attacks*. Academic Press.

Yang, L., Karim, R., Ganapathy, V., & Smith, R. (2011). Fast Memory-Efficient Regular Expression Matching with NFA-OBDDs. *Computer Networks: The International Journal of Computer and Telecommunications Networking*, *55*(15), 3376–3393.

Alhakami, H., & Alhrbi, S. (2020). Knowledge based Authentication Techniques and Challenges. *International Journal of Advanced Computer Science and Applications*, *11*(2). doi:10.14569/IJACSA.2020.0110291

Burch, J. R., Clarke, E. M., McMillan, K. L., Dill, D. L., & Hwang, J. (1990). Symbolic Model Checking: 1020 states and beyond. *Proceedings of the 5th Annual IEEE Symposium on Logic in Computer Science*, 428-439.

Patra, K., Nemade, B., Mishra, P., & Satapathy, P. P. (2016). Cued-Click Point Graphical Password Using Circular Tolerance to Increase Password Space and Persuasive Features. *Procedia Computer Science*, *79*, 877–0509. doi:10.1016/j.procs.2016.03.071

Yu, F., Chen, Z., Diao, Y., Lakshman, T. V., & Katz, R. H. (2001). Fast and Memory-Efficient Regular Expression Matching for Deep Packet Inspection. *Proceedings of the ACM/IEEE Symposium Architecture for Networking and Communication Systems*, 93-102.

Agrawal, G., & Singh, S. (2018). Analysis of knowledge based graphical password authentication. *Computer Science & Education (ICCSE 2011)*.

Becchi, M., & Crowley, P. (2008). Extending Finite Automata to Efficiently Match Perl-Compatible Regular Expressions. *Proceedings of the ACM International Conference on Emerging Networking Experiments and Technologies*.

Ficara, D., Di Pietro, A., Giordano, S., Member, S., Procissi, G., Vitucci, F., & Antichi, G. (2011). Differential Encoding of DFAs for Fast Regular Expression Matching. *IEEE/ACM Transactions on Networking*, *19*(3), 683–694.

Golar, P., & Adane, D. (2016). Critical Analysis of 2-Dimensional Graphical Authentication Systems. In *International Conference on Computing, Analytics and Security Trends (CAST)*. IEEE. 10.1109/CAST.2016.7914957

Liu, C., & Wu, J. (2013). Fast Deep Packet Inspection with a Dual Finite Automata. *IEEE Transactions on Computers*, *62*(2), 310–321.

Roesch, M. (1999). Snort: Light Weight Intrusion Detection for Networks. *Proceedings of the 13th USENIX Conference on System Administration*, 229-238.

Paxson, V. (1998). A System for Detecting Network Intruders in Realtime. Computer Networks. *The International Journal of Computer and Telecommunications Networking*, *31*, 2435–2463.

Hopcroft, J. (1971). *An algorithm for Minimizing States in a Finite Automaton*. Stanford University Stanford.

Sommer, R., & Paxson, V. (2003). Enhancing Byte-Level Network Intrusion Detection Signatures with Context. *Proceedings of the 10th ACM Conference on Computer and Communications Security*, 262-271.

Wang, J., Hong, X., Ren, R., & Li, T. (2009). A Real-time Intrusion Detection System Based on PSO-SVM. *Proceedings of the International Workshop on Information Security and Application*.

Kumar, S., Turner, J. S., Crowley, P., & Mitzenmacher, M. (2007). HEXA: Compact Data Structures for Faster Packet Processing. *Proceedings of the International Conference on Network Protocols*, 246-255.

Beng, Ramadass, & Selvakumar. (2014). A Survey of Intrusion Alert Correlation and its Design Considerations. *IETE Technical Review*, *31*(3), 233–240.

Boonkrong, S. (2019). *An Analysis of Numerical Grid-Based Authentication*. School of Information Technology Suranaree University of Technology Thailand ACM Association for Computing Machinery. doi:10.1145/3357419.3357434

Sidhu, R., & Prasanna, V. K. (2001). Fast Regular Expression Matching using FPGAs. *Proceedings of the 9th Annual IEEE Symposium on Field-Programmable Custom Computing Machines*, 227-238.

Kumar, S., Dharmapurikar, S., Yu, F., Crowley, P., & Turner, J. (2006). Algorithms to Accelerate Multiple Regular Expressions Matching for Deep Packet Inspection. *Proceedings of the Conference on Applications, Technologies, Architectures, and Protocols for Computer Communications*, *36*, 339-350.

Kolias, C., Kambourakis, G., & Maragoudakis, M. (2011). Swarm Intelligence in Intrusion Detection: A Survey. *Computers & Society*, *30*(8), 625–642.

Yu, F., Chen, Z., Diao, Y., & Lakshman, T. (2006). Fast and Memory-Efficient Regular Expression Matching for Deep Packet Inspection. *Proceedings of the ACM/IEEE Symposium on Architecture for Networking and Communications Systems*, 93-102.

Liu, C., Chen, A., Wu, D., & Wu, J. (2011). A DFA with Extended Character Set for Fast Deep Packet Inspection. *Proceedings of the International Conference on Parallel Processing*, 1-10.

Anantathanavit, M., & Munlin, M. (2016). Using K-Means Radius Particle Swarm Optimization for the Travelling Salesman Problem. *IETE Technical Review*, *33*(2), 172–180.

Dharmapurikar, S., & Lockwood, J. (2005). Fast and Scalable Pattern Matching for Content Filtering. *Proceedings of the ACM Symposium on Architecture for Networking and Communications Systems*, 183-192.

Boyer, R. S., & Moore, J. S. (2001). A Fast String Searching Algorithm. *Communications of the ACM*, *20*(10), 762–772.

Becchi, M., & Crowley, P. (2007). An Improved Algorithm to Accelerate Regular Expression Evaluation. *Proceedings of the 3rd ACM/IEEE Symposium on Architecture for Networking and Communications Systems*, 145-154.

Thompson, K. (2006). Programming Techniques: Regular Expression Search Algorithm. *Communications of the ACM*, *11*(6), 419–422.

Myers, E. W. (1992). A Four Russians Algorithm for Regular Expression Pattern Matching. *Journal of the Association for Computing Machinery*, *39*(2), 430–448.

Hopcroft, J. E., Motwani, R., & Ullman, J. D. (2001). Introduction to Automata Theory, Languages, and Computation (2nd ed.). Addison-Wesley-Longman.

Jerome, P., & Ariel, M. (2019). *Jumbled PassSteps: A Hotspot Guessing Attack Resistant Graphical Password Authentication Scheme Basedon the Modified Pass Matrix Method ICCSP*. Malaysia ACM Association for Computing Machinery.

Navarro, G., & Raffinot, M. (2001). Compact DFA Representation for Fast Regular Expression Search. *Proceedings of the 5th International Workshop on Algorithm Engineering*, 1-12.

Janakiriman, S., & Vasudevan, V. (2009). ACO Based Distributed Intrusion Detection System. *Proceedings of the International Journal of Digital Content Technology and its Applications*, *3*(1), 66-72.

Nino Ruiz, E. D., Nieto Parra, H., & Isabel Chinchilla Camarg, A. (2013). Evolutionary Algorithm Based on Simulated Annealing for the Multi-Objective Optimization of Combinatorial Problems. *Proceedings of the International Journal of Combinatorial Optimization Problems and Informatics*, *4*(2), 53–63.

Wu, J., Ran, T., & Li, Z.-Y. (2011). An improving Tabu Search Algorithm for Intrusion Detection. *Proceedings of the 3rd International Conference on Measuring Technology and Mechatronics Automation*, *1*, 435-439.

Kumar, S., Turner, J., & Williams, J. (2006). Advanced Algorithms for Fast and Scalable Deep Packet Inspection. *Proceedings of the ACM/IEEE Symposium Architecture for Networking and Communication Systems*, 81-92.

Zujevs, N. (2019). *Authentication by Graphical Passwords Method 'Hope'*. IEEE.

Becchi, M., & Crowley, P. (2007). A Hybrid Finite Automaton for Practical Deep Packet Inspection. *Proceedings of the ACM Conference on Emerging Networking Experiments and Technologies.*

Nida, A., & Quasim, A. (2019). Conundrum-Pass: A New Graphical Password Approach. *IEEE, International Conference on Communication, Computing and Digital Systems.*

Kumar, S., Chandrasekaran, B., Turner, J., & Varghese, G. (2007). Curing Regular Expressions Matching Algorithms from Insomnia, Amnesia and Acalculia. *Proceedings of the ACM/IEEE Symposium Architecture for Networking and Communication Systems*, 155-164.

Zhen, Y., & Hesanmi, O. (2016). Usable Authentication Mechanisms for Mobile Devices: An, Exploration of 3D Graphical Passwords. Xi'an Jiaotong-Liverpool University.

Smith, R., Estan, C., Jha, S., & Kong, S. (2008). Deflating the Big Bang: Fast and Scalable Deep Packet Inspection with Extended Finite Automata. *Proceedings of the ACM SIGCOMM 2008 Conference on Applications, Technologies, Architectures, and Protocols for Computer Communications*, 207-218.

Thorpe, J., & MacRae, B. (2014). The Presentation Effect on Graphical Passwords. ACM.

Chiasson, S., Stobert, E., Paul, C., Oorschot, V., & Forget, A. (2012). Persuasive Cued Click-Points: Design, Implementation and Evaluation of a Knowledge-Based Authentication Mechanism. *IEEE Transactions on Dependable and Secure Computing, 9*(2).

Ficara, D., Giordano, S., Procissi, G., Vitucci, F., Antichi, G., & Pietro, A. D. (2008). An Improved DFA for Fast Regular Expression Matching. *Proceedings of the ACM SIGCOMM Computer Communication Review, 38*(5) 29-40.

Antichi, G., Di Pietro, A., Ficara, D., Giordano, S., Procissi, G., & Vitucci, F. (2009). Second-Order Differential Encoding of Deterministic Finite Automata. *Proceedings of the 28th IEEE Conference on Global Telecommunications*, 2838-2843.

Biddle, R., Chiasson, S., Stobert, E., Paul, C., Oorschot, V., & Forget, A. (2012). Graphical Passwords: Learning from the First Twelve Years. *ACM Computing Surveys, 44*(4), 1–41. doi:10.1145/2333112.2333114

Aasland, K., & Blankenburg, D. (2012a). *An analysis of the uses and properties of the Obeya.* doi:10.1109/ICE.2012.6297660

Aasland, K., & Blankenburg, D. (2012b). Virtualizing the obeya. *NordDesign 2012 - Proceedings of the 9th NordDesign Conference.*

Abboud, D., Elbadaoui, M., Smith, W. A., & Randall, R. B. (2019). Advanced bearing diagnostics: A comparative study of two powerful approaches. *Mechanical Systems and Signal Processing, 114*, 604–627. doi:10.1016/j.ymssp.2018.05.011

Abdul-Kadir, A., Xu, X., & Hämmerle, E. (2011). Virtual machine tools and virtual machining—A technological review. *Robotics and Computer-integrated Manufacturing, 27*(3), 494–508. doi:10.1016/j.rcim.2010.10.003

Abdusslam, S. A. (2012). *Detection and diagnosis of rolling element bearing faults using time encoded signal processing and recognition.* University of Huddersfield.

Adler, B.-M., Baets, W., & König, R. (2011). A complexity perspective on collaborative decision making in organizations: The ecology of group-performance. *Information & Management, 48*(4-5), 157–165. doi:10.1016/j.im.2011.04.002

Ai, Q., Mo, K., Wang, Y., & Zhao, L. (2013). Research of product information sharing system based on cloud manufacturing. *Applied Mechanics and Materials, 248*, 533–538. doi:10.4028/www.scientific.net/AMM.248.533

Akhbardeh, A., Junnila, S., Koivuluoma, M., Koivistoinen, T., & Värri, A. (2006). Applying novel time-frequency moments singular value decomposition method and artificial neural networks for ballistocardiography. *EURASIP Journal on Advances in Signal Processing, 2007*(1), 1–9. doi:10.1155/2007/60576

Akyildiz, I. F., & Wang, X. (2005). A survey on wireless mesh networks. *IEEE Communications Magazine, 43*(9), 23–30. doi:10.1109/MCOM.2005.1509968

Akyildiz, I. F., Wang, X., & Wang, W. (2005). Wireless mesh networks: A survey. *Computer Networks, 47*(4), 445–487. doi:10.1016/j.comnet.2004.12.001

Alappatt, V., & Prathap, P. J. (2020). Hybrid cryptographic algorithm based key management scheme in MANET. *Materials Today: Proceedings.*

Al-Badour, F., Sunar, M., & Cheded, L. (2011). Vibration analysis of rotating machinery using time–frequency analysis and wavelet techniques. *Mechanical Systems and Signal Processing, 25*(6), 2083–2101. doi:10.1016/j.ymssp.2011.01.017

Alcácer, V., & Cruz-Machado, V. (2019). Scanning the Industry 4.0: A Literature Review on Technologies for Manufacturing Systems. *Engineering Science and Technology, an International Journal, 22*(3), 899–919.

Alguindigue, I. E., Loskiewicz-Buczak, A., & Uhrig, R. E. (1993). Monitoring and diagnosis of rolling element bearings using artificial neural networks. *IEEE Transactions on Industrial Electronics, 40*(2), 209–217. doi:10.1109/41.222642

Alguliyev, R., Imamverdiyev, Y., & Sukhostat, L. (2018). Cyber-physical systems and their security issues. *Computers in Industry, 100*, 212–223.

Altini, M., Brunelli, D., Farella, E., & Benini, L. (2010). Bluetooth indoor localization with multiple neural networks. *Wireless Pervasive Computing (ISWPC), 2010 5th IEEE International Symposium on*, 295–300. 10.1109/ISWPC.2010.5483748

Amaral, A., & Peças, P. (2021). SMEs and Industry 4.0: Two case studies of digitalization for a smoother integration. *Computers in Industry, 125*, 103333. Advance online publication. doi:10.1016/j.compind.2020.103333

American Public Power Association. (2018). *Creating a smart city roadmap for public power utilities.* https://www.publicpower.org/system/files/documents/APPA-Smart-City-Roadmap-FINAL.pdf

Amiri, M., & Jensen, R. (2016). Missing data *imputation* using fuzzy-rough methods. *Neurocomputing, 205,* 152–164. doi:10.1016/j.neucom.2016.04.015

Anastasi, G., Bandelloni, R., Conti, M., Delmastro, F., Gregori, E., & Mainetto, G. (2003). Experimenting an indoor Bluetooth-based positioning service. *Proceedings of the 23rd International Conference on Distributed Computing Systems Workshops,* 480–483.

Angione, G., Barbosa, J., Gosewehr, F., Leitão, P., Massa, D., Matos, J., Peres, R. S., Rocha, A. D., & Wermann, J. (2017). Integration and Deployment of a Distributed and Pluggable Industrial Architecture for the PERFoRM Project. *Procedia Manufacturing, 11*(June), 896–904. doi:10.1016/j.promfg.2017.07.193

An, L., & Yang, G. H. (2019). Opacity enforcement for confidential robust control in linear cyber-physical systems. *IEEE Transactions on Automatic Control, 65*(3), 1234–1241.

Araújo, R., Santos, G., Costa, J. B., & Sá, J. C. (2019). The quality management system as a driver of organizational culture: An empirical study in the Portuguese textile industry. *Quality Innovation Prosperity, 23*(1), 1–24. doi:10.12776/qip.v23i1.1132

Armendia, M., Alzaga, A., Peysson, F., Fuertjes, T., Cugnon, F., Ozturk, E., & Flumm, D. (2019) Machine Tool: From the Digital Twin to the Cyber-Physical Systems. In Twin-Control. Springer.

Asghari, M., Yousefi, S., & Niyato, D. (2019). Pricing strategies of IoT wide area network service providers with complementary services included. *Journal of Network and Computer Applications, 147,* 102426. Advance online publication. doi:10.1016/j.jnca.2019.102426

Ashibani, Y., & Mahmoud, Q. H. (2017). Cyber physical systems security: Analysis, challenges and solutions. *Computers & Security, 68,* 81–97. doi:10.1016/j.cose.2017.04.005

Ashok, S. N. (2012). ZigBee: A low power wireless technology for industrial applications. *International Journal of Control Theory & Computer Modeling, 2*(3), 27–33. doi:10.5121/ijctcm.2012.2303

Azevedo, J., Sá, J. C., Ferreira, L. P., Santos, G., Cruz, F. M., Jimenez, G., & Silva, F. J. G. (2019). Improvement of production line in the automotive industry through lean philosophy. *Procedia Manufacturing, 41,* 1023–1030. doi:10.1016/j.promfg.2019.10.029

Babun, L., Aksu, H., & Uluagac, A. S. (2021). CPS Device-Class Identification via Behavioral Fingerprinting: From Theory to Practice. *IEEE Transactions on Information Forensics and Security, 16,* 2413–2428.

Baheti, R., & Gill, H. (2011). Cyber-physical systems. *The Impact of Control Technology, 12*(1), 161-166.

Bahl, P., & Padmanabhan, V. N. (2000). RADAR: An In-Building RF-Based User Location and Tracking System. Proceedings of IEEE Infocom 2000, 775–784.

Barbosa, L. C. F. M., de Oliveira, O. J., & Santos, G. (2018). Proposition for the alignment of the integrated management system (quality, environmental and safety) with the business strategy. *International Journal of Qualitative Research*, *12*(4), 925–940.

Barbosa, M., Silva, F. J. G., Pimentel, C., & Gouveia, R. M. (2018). A Novel Concept of CNC Machining Center Automatic Feeder. *Procedia Manufacturing*, *17*, 952–959. doi:10.1016/j.promfg.2018.10.111

Barfurth, M. A. (1995). Understanding the Collaborative learning process in a technology rich environment: The case of children's disagreements. *Proc CSCL 1995*. 10.3115/222020.222042

Bargh, M., & Groote, R. (2008). Indoor localization based on response rate of bluetooth inquiries. *Proceedings of the first ACM international workshop on Mobile entity localization and tracking in GPS-less environments*.

Bari, A., Jiang, J., Saad, W., & Jaekel, A. (2014). Challenges in the smart grid applications: An overview. *International Journal of Distributed Sensor Networks*, *4*(2), 1–11. doi:10.1155/2014/974682

Basagni, S., Conti, M., Giordano, S., & Stojmenovic, I. (2004). *Mobile Ad Hoc networking with a view of 4G wireless: imperatives and challenges*. Wiley-IEEE Press.

Benveniste, A., Bourke, T., Caillaud, B., & Pouzet, M. (2012). *Hybrid Systems Modeling Challenges Caused by Cyber-Physical Systems?* Available at: http://people.rennes.inria.fr/Albert.Benveniste/pub/NIST2012.pdf

Bettini, C., Brdiczka, O., Henricksen, K., Indulska, J., Nicklas, D., Ranganathan, A., & Riboni, D. (2010). A survey of context modelling and reasoning techniques. *Pervasive and Mobile Computing*, *6*(2), 161–180. doi:10.1016/j.pmcj.2009.06.002

Bhasin, S., & Mukhopadhyay, D. (2016, December). Fault injection attacks: Attack methodologies, injection techniques and protection mechanisms. In *International Conference on Security, Privacy, and Applied Cryptography Engineering* (pp. 415-418). Springer.

Bhattacharya, R. (2013). A comparative study of physical attacks on wireless sensor networks. *International Journal of Research in Engineering and Technology*, *2*(1), 72–74. doi:10.15623/ijret.2013.0201014

Bluetooth® SIG. (2019). *Bluetooth® 5 Core Specification*. https://www.bluetooth.com/specifications/bluetooth-core-specification

Bordeleau, F.-E., Mosconi, E., & De Santa-Eulalia, L. A. (2018). Business Intelligence in Industry 4.0: State of the art and research opportunities. *Proceedings of the 51st Hawaii International Conference on System Sciences*. Retrieved from http://hdl.handle.net/10125/50383

Bouchiba, K., Kayvantash, K., & Hanna, K. (2020). *The Emergence of Artificial Intelligence & Machine Learning in CAE Simulation Executive summary*. White paper. https://www.researchgate.net/publication/346420781_The_Emergence_of_Artificial_Intelligence_Machine_Learning_in_CAE_Simulation_Executive_summary

Boyle, T., Giurco, D., Mukheibir, P., Liu, A., Moy, C., White, S., & Stewart, R. (2013). Intelligent metering for urban water: A review. *Water (Basel)*, *5*(3), 1052–1081.

Bravi, L., Murmura, F., & Santos, G. (2017). Attitudes and behaviours of Italian 3D prosumer in the Era of Additive Manufacturing. *Procedia Manufacturing*, *13*, 980–986. doi:10.1016/j.promfg.2017.09.095

Bravi, L., Murmura, F., & Santos, G. (2018). Manufacturing labs: Where new digital technologies help improve life quality. *International Journal of Qualitative Research*, *12*(4), 957–974.

Bravi, L., Murmura, F., & Santos, G. (2019). The ISO 9001:2015 Quality Management System Standard: Companies' Drivers, Benefits and Barriers to Its Implementation. *Quality Innovation Prosperity Journal*, *23*(2), 64–82. doi:10.12776/qip.v23i2.1277

Bravi, L., Santos, G., Pagano, A., & Murmura, F. (2020). Environmental management system according to ISO 14001:2015 as a driver to sustainable development. *Corporate Social Responsibility and Environmental Management*, *27*(6), 1–16. doi:10.1002/csr.1985

Brecher, C., & Witt, S. (2006). Simulation of machine process interaction with flexible mulit-body simulation. *Proceedings of the 9th CIRP International Workshop on Modeling of Machining Operations*.

Brunnermeier, S. B., & Martin, S. A. (1999). *99-1 Planning Report: Interoperability Cost Analysis of the U.S. Automotive Supply Chain*. Academic Press.

Bruno, R., & Delmastro, F. (2003). *Design and analysis of a Bluetooth-based indoor localization system*. Personal Wireless Communications. doi:10.1007/978-3-540-39867-7_66

Brusa, E., Bruzzone, F., Delprete, C., Di Maggio, L. G., & Rosso, C. (2020). Health Indicators Construction for Damage Level Assessment in Bearing Diagnostics: A Proposal of an Energetic Approach Based on Envelope Analysis. *Applied Sciences (Basel, Switzerland)*, *10*(22), 8131. doi:10.3390/app10228131

Buer, S. V., Strandhagen, J. O., & Chan, F. T. S. (2018). The link between industry 4.0 and lean manufacturing: Mapping current research and establishing a research agenda. *International Journal of Production Research*, *56*(8), 2924–2940. doi:10.1080/00207543.2018.1442945

Caesarendra, W., Kosasih, B., Tieu, K., & Moodie, C. A. (2013). An application of nonlinear feature extraction-A case study for low speed slewing bearing condition monitoring and prognosis. In *IEEE International Conference on Advanced Intelligent Mechatronics*, (pp. 1713-1718). 10.1109/AIM.2013.6584344

Calvaresi, D., & Calbimonte, J. P. (2020). Real-time compliant stream processing agents for physical rehabilitation. *Sensors (Basel)*, *20*(3), 746.

Cândido, G., Barata, J., Colombo, A. W., & Jammes, F. (2009). SOA in reconfigurable supply chains: A research roadmap. *Engineering Applications of Artificial Intelligence, 22*(6), 939–949. doi:10.1016/j.engappai.2008.10.020

Cannavò, A., Cermelli, F., Chiaramida, V., Ciccone, G., Lamberti, F., Montuschi, P., & Paravati, G. (2017). T4T: Tangible interface for tuning 3D object manipulation tools. *2017 IEEE Symposium on 3D User Interfaces, 3DUI 2017 - Proceedings*, 266–267. 10.1109/3DUI.2017.7893374

Carvalho, F., Santos, G., & Gonçalves, J. (2020). Critical analysis of information about integrated management systems and environmental policy on the Portuguese firms' website, towards sustainable development. *Corporate Social Responsibility and Environmental Management, 27*(2), 1069–1088. doi:10.1002/csr.1866

Cassell, J. (2004). Towards a model of technology and literacy development: Story listening systems. *Journal of Applied Developmental Psychology, 25*(1), 75–105. doi:10.1016/j.appdev.2003.11.003

Cassell, J., & Ryokai, K. (2001). Making space for voice: Technologies to support children's fantasy and storytelling. *Personal and Ubiquitous Computing, 5*(3), 169–190. doi:10.1007/PL00000018

Castro, O. J. L., Sisamón, C. C., & Prada, J. C. G. (2006, October). Bearing fault diagnosis based on neural network classification and wavelet transform. In *Proceedings of the 6th WSEAS international conference on Wavelet analysis & multirate systems, 2*, (pp. 16-18). WSEAS.

Chakroborty, S., & Saha, G. (2010). Feature selection using singular value decomposition and QR factorization with column pivoting for text-independent speaker identification. *Speech Communication, 52*(9), 693–709. doi:10.1016/j.specom.2010.04.002

Chaplin, J. C., Bakker, O. J., De Silva, L., Sanderson, D., Kelly, E., Logan, B., & Ratchev, S. M. (2015). Evolvable assembly systems: A distributed architecture for intelligent manufacturing. *IFAC-PapersOnLine, 48*(3), 2065–2070. doi:10.1016/j.ifacol.2015.06.393

Chen, Chen, Chen, & Tu. (2006). WITS: A Wireless Sensor Network for Intelligent Transportation System. *IEEE, IMSCCS'06*.

Chen, C., Yan, J., Lu, N., Wang, Y., Yang, X., & Guan, X. (2015). Ubiquitous monitoring for industrial cyber-physical systems over relay-assisted wireless sensor networks. *IEEE Transactions on Emerging Topics in Computing, 3*(3), 352–362. doi:10.1109/TETC.2014.2386615

Cheng, B., Zhang, J., Hancke, G.P., Karnouskos, S., & Colombo, A.W. (2018). Industrial cyberphysical systems: realizing cloud-based big data infrastructures. *IEEE Ind. Electron.*, 25–35. . doi:10.1109/MIE.2017.2788850

Chen, J., Cheng, L., Yu, H., & Hu, S. (2018). Rolling bearing fault diagnosis and health assessment using ensemble empirical mode decomposition and the adjustment Mahalanobis–Taguchi system. *International Journal of Systems Science, 49*(1), 147–159. doi:10.1080/00207721.2017.1397804

Chen, S., Ma, M., & Luo, Z. (2016). An authentication scheme with identity-based cryptography for M2M security in cyber-physical systems. *Security and Communication Networks, 9*(10), 1146–1157.

Chien, C.-F., Wang, W.-C., & Cheng, J.-C. (2007). Data mining for yield enhancement in semiconductor manufacturing and an empirical study. *Expert Systems with Applications, 33*(1), 192–198. doi:10.1016/j.eswa.2006.04.014

Choley, J. Y., Mhenni, F., Nguyen, N., & Baklouti, A. (2016). Topology-based safety analysis for safety critical CPS. *Procedia Computer Science, 95*, 32–39.

Christie, J., & Johnson, E. (1983). The role of play in social-intellectual development. *Review of Educational Research, 53*, 93-115.

Civerchia, F., Bocchino, S., Salvadori, C., Rossi, E., Maggiani, L., & Petracca, M. (2017). Industrial Internet of Things monitoring solution for advanced predictive maintenance applications. *Journal of Industrial Information Integration, 7*, 4–12. doi:10.1016/j.jii.2017.02.003

Coelho, P. M. N. (2016). *Towards Industry 4.0*. Faculdade de Ciências e Tecnologia Universidade de Coimbra.

Coelho, V. N., Cohen, M. W., Coelho, I. M., Liu, N. A., & Guimaraes, F. G. (2017). Multi-agent systems applied for energy systems integration: State-of-the-art applications and trends in microgrids. *Applied Energy, 187*, 820–832. doi:10.1016/j.apenergy.2016.10.056

Colombo, A. W., Karnouskos, S., & Mendes, J. L. P. (2015). Industrial Agents in the Era of Service-Oriented Architectures and Cloud-Based Industrial Infrastructures. In *Industrial Agents* (pp. 67–87). Morgan Kaufmann. doi:10.1016/B978-0-12-800341-1.00004-8

Cordeiro, P., Sá, J. C., Pata, A., Gonçalves, M., Santos, G., & Silva, F. J. G. (2020). The Impact of Lean Tools on Safety—Case Study. *Occupational and Environmental Safety and Health II, 277*, 151–159. doi:10.1007/978-3-030-41486-3_17

Correia, D., Silva, F. J. G., Gouveia, R. M., Pereira, T., & Ferreira, L. P. (2018). Improving manual assembly lines devoted to complex electronic devices by applying Lean tools. *Procedia Manufacturing, 17*, 663–671. doi:10.1016/j.promfg.2018.10.115

Costa, A. R., Barbosa, C., Santos, G., & Alves, M. R. (2019). Six Sigma: Main Metrics and R Based Software for Training Purposes and Practical Industrial Quality Control. *Quality Innovation Prosperity Journal, 23*(2), 83–99. doi:10.12776/qip.v23i2.1278

Cottam, M., & Wray, K. (2009). Sketching tangible interfaces: Creating an electronic palette for the design community. *IEEE Computer Graphics and Applications, 29*(3), 90–95. doi:10.1109/MCG.2009.51 PMID:19642619

Crespo-Marquez, A., Iung, B., & Levrat, E. (2007). *On the Concept of e-Maintenance. Information and Communication Technologies Applied to Maintenance*. Review and Current Research. Proceedings.

Cruz Salazar, L. A., Ryashentseva, D., Lüder, A., & Vogel-Heuser, B. (2019). Cyber-physical production systems architecture based on multi-agent's design pattern—Comparison of selected approaches mapping four agent patterns. *International Journal of Advanced Manufacturing Technology, 105*(9), 4005–4034. doi:10.100700170-019-03800-4

Cuadra, L., Salcedo, S. S., Ser, J. D., Fernández, S. J., & Geem, Z. W. (2015). A critical review of robustness in power grids using complex networks concepts. *Energies*, *8*(9), 9211–9265. doi:10.3390/en8099211

Cunha, C., & de Paula, L. B. (2019). Análise do uso de uma ferramenta de Business Intelligence em tomadas de decisão a partir de dados de mídia social (In Portuguese). *Revista Científica Da FAEX*. Retrieved from http://periodicos.faex.edu.br/index.php/e-Locucao/article/view/212/164

Dahlman, E., Jading, Y., Parkvall, S., & Murai, H. (2009). 3G radio access evolution— HSPA and LTE for mobile broadband. *IEICE Transactions on Communications*, *92*(5), 1432–1440. doi:10.1587/transcom.E92.B.1432

Davis, R., Vochozka, M., Vrbka, J., & Neguri, O. (2020). Industrial artificial intelligence, smart connected sensors, and big data-driven decision-making processes in Internet of Things-based real-time production logistics. *Economics. Management and Financial Markets*, *15*, 1–16.

de Lima, R. P. (2019). *Estruturação de um Ambiente de Business Intelligence para Gestão da Informação da Secretaria Municipal de Trânsito e Transportes de Uberlândia*. Retrieved from http://repositorio.ufu.br/bitstream/123456789/27629/4/EstruturaçãoAmbienteBusiness.pdf

Dervojeda, K., Rouwmaat, E., Probst, L. & Frideres, L. (2015). *Internet of Things: Smart machines and tools*. Report of the Business Innovation Observatory for the European Commission.

Ding, B., Yu, X. Y., & Sun, L. J. (2012). A cloud-based collaborative manufacturing resource sharing services. *Information Technology Journal*, *11*(9), 1258–1264. doi:10.3923/itj.2012.1258.1264

Doiro, M., Santos, G., & Felix, M. J. (2019). Machining operations for components in kitchen furniture: A comparison between two management systems. *Procedia Manufacturing*, *41*, 10–17. doi:10.1016/j.promfg.2019.07.023

Donoho, D. L. (1995). De-noising by soft-thresholding. *IEEE Transactions on Information Theory*, *41*(3), 613–627. doi:10.1109/18.382009

Dranka, G. G., & Ferreira, P. (2020). Towards a smart grid power system in Brazil: Challenges and opportunities. *Energy Policy*, *136*, 1–16. doi:10.1016/j.enpol.2019.111033

Dron, J. P., Rasolofondraibe, L., Chiementin, X., & Bolaers, F. (2010). A comparative experimental study on the use of three denoising methods for bearing defect detection. *Meccanica*, *45*(2), 265–277. doi:10.100711012-009-9243-x

Duong, B. P., Khan, S. A., Shon, D., Im, K., Park, J., Lim, D. S., & Kim, J. M. (2018). A reliable health indicator for fault prognosis of bearings. *Sensors (Basel)*, *18*(11), 3740. doi:10.339018113740 PMID:30400203

Edge Computing Consortium & Alliance of Industrial Internet. (2017). *Edge Computing Reference Architecture 2.0*. http://en.ecconsortium.net/Uploads/file/20180328/1522232376480704.pdf

Ejaz, W., Naeem, M., Shahid, A., Anpalagan, A., & Jo, M. (2017). Efficient energy management for the Internet of Things in smart cities. *IEEE Communications Magazine*, *55*(1), 84–91. doi:10.1109/MCOM.2017.1600218CM

Espe, E., Potdar, V., & Chang, E. (2018). Prosumer communities and relationships in smart grids: A literature review, evolution and future directions. *Energies*, *11*(10), 1–24. doi:10.3390/en11102528

Falcão, A. C. R. de A. (2019). *Sistematização dos Pilares da Indústria 4.0: Uma Análise Utilizando Revisão*. Universidade De São Paulo Escola De Engenharia De São Carlos.

Fan, D. M., Ren, Y., Feng, Q., Liu, Y. L., Wang, Z. L., & Lin, J. (2021). (20201). Restoration of smart grids: Current status, challenges, and opportunities. *Renewable & Sustainable Energy Reviews*, *143*, 1–17. doi:10.1016/j.rser.2021.110909

Fantini, P., Tavola, G., Taisch, M., Barbosa, J., Leitao, P., Liu, Y., Sayed, M. S., & Lohse, N. (2016). Exploring the integration of the human as a flexibility factor in CPS enabled manufacturing environments: Methodology and results. In *IECON 2016-42nd Annual Conference of the IEEE Industrial Electronics Society* (pp. 5711-5716). IEEE.

Farhangi, H. (2010). The path of the smart grid. *IEEE Power & Energy Magazine*, *8*(1), 18–28.

Fawcett, T. (2001). Using rule sets to maximize ROC performance. Proc. IEEE Internat. Conf. on Data Mining (ICDM-2001), 131–138. doi:10.1109/ICDM.2001.989510

Fawcett, T. (2006). An introduction to ROC analysis. *Pattern Recognition Letters*, *27*(8), 861–874. doi:10.1016/j.patrec.2005.10.010

Fein, G. (1987). Pretend play: Creativity and consciousness. In P. Gorlitz & J. Wohlwill (Eds.), *Curiosity, imagination, and play* (pp. 281–304). Lawrence Erlbaum Associates, Inc.

Félix, M. J., Gonçalves, S., Jimenez, G., & Santos, G. (2019b). The contribution of design to the development of products and manufacturing processes in the Portuguese industry. *Procedia Manufacturing*, *41*, 1055–1062. doi:10.1016/j.promfg.2019.10.033

Félix, M. J., Silva, S., Santos, G., Doiro, M., & Sá, J. C. (2019a). Integrated product and processes development in design: A case study. *Procedia Manufacturing*, *41*, 296–303. doi:10.1016/j.promfg.2019.09.012

Feng, Q., Chen, Y., Sun, B., & Li, S. (2014). An optimization method for condition based maintenance of aircraft fleet considering prognostics uncertainty. *TheScientificWorldJournal*, *2014*(1), 430190. doi:10.1155/2014/430190 PMID:24892046

Feng, Q., Zhao, X., & Chen, Y. (2017). Heuristic hybrid game approach for fleet condition-based maintenance planning. *Reliability Engineering & System Safety*, *157*, 166–176. doi:10.1016/j.ress.2016.09.005

Ferreira, L., Putnik, G., Cruz-Cunha, M. M., Putnik, Z., Castro, H., Alves, C., & Shah, V. (2014). Dashboard services for pragmatics-based interoperability in cloud and ubiquitous manufacturing. *International Journal of Web Portals*, *6*(1), 35–49. doi:10.4018/ijwp.2014010103

Ferreira, M. J., Moreira, F., & Seruca, I. (2019). *Digital Transformation Towards a New Context of Labour: Enterprise 4.0*. Advances in Logistics, Operations, and Management Science. ALOMS. doi:10.4018/978-1-5225-4936-9.ch002

Ferreira, S., Silva, F. J. G., Casais, R. B., Pereira, M. T., & Ferreira, L. P. (2019). KPI development and obsolescence management in industrial maintenance. *Procedia Manufacturing*, *38*, 1427–1435. doi:10.1016/j.promfg.2020.01.145

Floriano, A. C., Lemes, E. F., & Heofacker, V. H. G. (2016). *Análise De Ferramentas De Business Intelligence*. Academic Press.

Friedrich, Ch., Lechler, A., & Verl, A. (2014). Autonomous systems for maintenance tasks. Requirements and design of a control architecture. *Procedia Technology*, *15*, 595–604. doi:10.1016/j.protcy.2014.09.020

Fumagalli, L., Marco Macchi, M., & Rapaccini, M. (2009). Computerized maintenance management systems in SMEs. A survey in Italy and some remarks for the implementation of condition based maintenance. *IFAC Proceedings, 42*(4), 1615–1619.

Gao, R. X., & Yan, R. (2010). *Wavelets: Theory and applications for manufacturing*. Springer.

Garber, L. (2012). Tangible user interfaces: Technology you can touch. *Computer*, *45*(6), 15–18. doi:10.1109/MC.2012.218

Garcia, M. V., Irisarri, E., Perez, F., Estevez, E., Orive, D., & Marcos, M. (2016). Plant floor communications integration using a low cost CPPS architecture. In *2016 IEEE 21st International Conference on Emerging Technologies and Factory Automation (ETFA)* (pp. 1-4). IEEE. 10.1109/ETFA.2016.7733631

Geraci, A. (1991). *IEEE standard computer dictionary: Compilation of IEEE standard computer glossaries*. IEEE Press.

Ghobakhloo, M. (2018). The future of manufacturing industry: A strategic roadmap toward Industry 4.0. *Journal of Manufacturing Technology Management*, *2018*(29), 910–936. doi:10.1108/JMTM-02-2018-0057

Gisin, N., Ribordy, G., Tittel, W., & Zbinden, H. (2002). Quantum cryptography. *Reviews of Modern Physics*, *74*(1), 145.

Goncu, A. (1993). Development of intersubjectivity in the dyadic play of preschoolers. *Early Childhood Research Quarterly*, *8*(1), 99–116. doi:10.1016/S0885-2006(05)80100-0

Gosewehr, F., Wermann, J., & Colombo, A. W. (2016). Assessment of industrial middleware technologies for the PERFoRM project. In *IECON 2016-42nd Annual Conference of the IEEE Industrial Electronics Society* (pp. 5699-5704). IEEE. 10.1109/IECON.2016.7793611

Gray, D. (2006). *Mobile WiMAX-Part I: a technical overview and performance evaluation.* Mobile Wimax White Papers.

Grewal, M. S., & Andrews, A. P. (2010). Applications of Kalman filtering in aerospace 1960 to the present [historical perspectives]. *IEEE Control Systems Magazine, 30*(3), 69–78. doi:10.1109/MCS.2010.936465

GS, V., HS, K., Pai P, S., NS, S., & Rao, R. B. (2012). Evaluation of effectiveness of wavelet based denoising schemes using artificial neural network and support vector machine for bearing condition classification. *Computational Intelligence and Neuroscience*, 1–12.

GS, V., Pai, S. P., Sriram, N. S., & Rao, R. B. (2013). Radial basis function neural network based comparison of dimensionality reduction techniques for effective bearing diagnostics. *Proceedings of the Institution of Mechanical Engineers, Part J: Journal of Engineering Tribology, 227*(6), 640-653.

Guerrero, G., Ayala, A., Mateu, J., Casades, L., & Alamán, X. (2016). Integrating Virtual Worlds with Tangible User Interfaces for Teaching Mathematics: A Pilot Study. *Sensors (Basel), 16*(11), 1775. doi:10.339016111775 PMID:27792132

Gunes, B., Kayisoglu, G., & Bolat, P. (2021). Cyber security risk assessment for seaports: A case study of a container port. *Computers & Security, 103*, 102196.

Guo, B., Zhang, D., Wang, Z., Yu, Z., & Zhou, X. (2013). Opportunistic IoT: Exploring the harmonious interaction between human and the internet of things. *Journal of Network and Computer Applications, 36*(6), 1531–1539. doi:10.1016/j.jnca.2012.12.028

Guo, J., Liu, X., Li, S., & Wang, Z. (2020). Bearing Intelligent Fault Diagnosis Based on Wavelet Transform and Convolution Neural Network. *Shock and Vibration, 2020*, 1–14.

Guo, M. J., Liu, Y. H., Yu, H. B., Hu, B. Y., & Sang, Z. Q. (2016). An overview of smart city in China. *China Communications, 13*(5), 203–211. doi:10.1109/CC.2016.7489987

Habib, H. F., Youssef, T., Cintuglu, M. H., & Mohammed, O. A. (2017). Multi-agent-based technique for fault location, isolation, and service restoration. *IEEE Transactions on Industry Applications, 53*(3), 1841–1851. doi:10.1109/TIA.2017.2671427

Hackmann, G., Guo, W., Yan, G., Sun, Z., Lu, C., & Dyke, S. (2013). Cyber-physical codesign of distributed structural health monitoring with wireless sensor networks. *IEEE Transactions on Parallel and Distributed Systems, 25*(1), 63–72. doi:10.1109/TPDS.2013.30

Hai, F. Z., & Wei, H. S. (2020). *Design of Multiple Protection Mechanism for Smart Meter Data Transmission Communication.* Value Engineering.

Hallberg, J., Nilsson, M., & Synnes, K. (2003). Positioning with Bluetooth. *Proceedings of the 10th International Conference on Telecommunications, 2*(23), 954–958.

Hanna, K. (2019). *Co-Simulation - Breaking the Back of Multiphysics CAE Simulation, MSC Software, IDC: Artificial Intelligence Global Adoption Trends and Strategies.* IDC Report 2019. https://www.idc.com/getdoc.jsp?containerId=US45120919

Hao, R., & Chu, F. (2009). Morphological undecimated wavelet decomposition for fault diagnostics of rolling element bearings. *Journal of Sound and Vibration, 320*(4-5), 1164–1177. doi:10.1016/j.jsv.2008.09.014

He, W., Breier, J., Bhasin, S., & Chattopadhyay, A. (2016, May). Bypassing parity protected cryptography using laser fault injection in cyber-physical system. In *Proceedings of the 2nd ACM International Workshop on Cyber-Physical System Security* (pp. 15-21). ACM.

Hoffmann, P., & Maksoud, T. M. A. (2010). Virtual commissioning of manufacturing systems: a review and new approaches for simplification. *Proceedings of 24th European Conference on Modelling and Simulation.* 10.7148/2010-0175-0181

Holmberg, K., Adgar, A., Arnaiz, A., Jantunen, E., Mascolo, J., & Mekid, S. (2010). *E-maintenance.* Springer Verlag. doi:10.1007/978-1-84996-205-6

Horizon Europe. (2019). *The next EU research & innovation investment programme (2021-2027).* https://ec.europa.eu/info/sites/info/files/research_and_innovation/strategy_on_ research_and_ innovation/presentations/horizon_europe_en_investing_to_shape_our_future.pdf

Hsu, S.-C., & Chien, C.-F. (2007). Hybrid data mining approach for pattern extraction from wafer bin map to improve yield in semiconductor manufacturing. *International Journal of Production Economics, 107*(1), 88–103. doi:10.1016/j.ijpe.2006.05.015

Huang, A. (2005). *The use of Bluetooth in Linux and location aware computing.* Master of Science dissertation.

Huang, B.X. (2008). *Cyber physical systems: a survey.* Presentation Report.

Huang, X., & Dong, J. (2020). Learning-based switched reliable control of cyber-physical systems with intermittent communication faults. *IEEE/CAA Journal of Automatica Sinica, 7*(3), 711-724.

Huang, M. L., & Chen, H. Y. (2005). Development and comparison of automated classifiers for glaucoma diagnosis using Stratus optical coherence tomography. *Investigative Ophthalmology & Visual Science, 46*(11), 4121–4129. doi:10.1167/iovs.05-0069 PMID:16249489

Huang, S., Zhou, C. J., Yang, S. H., & Qin, Y.-Q. (2015). Cyber-physical system security for networked industrial processes. *Int. J. Autom. Comput., 12*(6), 567–578. doi:10.100711633-015-0923-9

Huguenin, M., Archour, G., Commun, D., Pinonand, O. J., & Mavris, D. N. (2019). *3D Cloud Modeling using Data Fusion and Machine Learning Techniques.* In AIAA Aerospace Sciences Meeting, AIAA SciTech Forum, San Diego, CA.

Hussian. (2013). WSN Applications: Automated Intelligent Traffic Control System using Sensors. *International Journal of Soft Computing and Engineering, 3*(3).

Hutton, J. S., Phelan, K., Horowitz-Kraus, T., Dudley, J., Altaye, M., DeWitt, T., & Holland, S. K. (2017). Story time turbocharger? Child engagement during shared reading and cerebellar activation and connectivity in preschool-age children listening to stories. *PLoS One*, *12*(5), 1–20. doi:10.1371/journal.pone.0177398 PMID:28562619

Iarovyi, S., Mohammed, W. M., Lobov, A., Ferrer, B. R., & Lastra, J. L. M. (2016). Cyber-Physical Systems for Open-Knowledge-Driven Manufacturing Execution Systems. *Proceedings of the IEEE*, *104*(5), 1142–1154. doi:10.1109/JPROC.2015.2509498

Ikeziri, L. M., Melo, J. C., Campos, R. T., Okimura, L. I., & Gobbo, J. A. Junior. (2020). A perspectiva da indústria 4.0 sobre a filosofia de gestão Lean Manufacturing. *Brazilian Journal of Development*, *6*(1), 1274–1289. doi:10.34117/bjdv6n1-089

Ismail, A., & Kastner, W. (2017). Surveying the Features of Industrial SOAs. In *2017 IEEE International Conference on Industrial Technology (ICIT)* (pp. 1199-1204). IEEE. 10.1109/ICIT.2017.7915533

Jammes, F., Smit, H., Martinez Lastra, J. L., & Delamer, I. M. (2005). *Orchestration of service-oriented manufacturing processes. In 2005 IEEE conference on emerging technologies and factory automation* (Vol. 1). IEEE.

Jantunen, E., Junnola, J., & Gorostegui, U. (2017). Maintenance supported by cyber-Physical systems and cloud technology. *2017 4th International Conference on Control, Decision and Information Technologies, CoDIT*, 708-713. 10.1109/CoDIT.2017.8102678

Jardine, A. K., Lin, D., & Banjevic, D. (2006). A review on machinery diagnostics and prognostics implementing condition-based maintenance. *Mechanical Systems and Signal Processing*, *20*(7), 1483–1510. doi:10.1016/j.ymssp.2005.09.012

Javadi, S., Shahbazi, S., & Jackson, M. (2013). Supporting production system development through the Obeya concept. *IFIP Advances in Information and Communication Technology*, *397*(PART 1), 653–660. doi:10.1007/978-3-642-40352-1_82

Javed, K., Gouriveau, R., Zerhouni, N., & Nectoux, P. (2013). A feature extraction procedure based on trigonometric functions and cumulative descriptors to enhance prognostics modelling. In *IEEE Conference on Prognostics and Health Management (PHM)* (pp. 1-7). IEEE.

Javed, K., Gouriveau, R., Zerhouni, N., & Nectoux, P. (2015). Enabling health monitoring approach based on vibration data for accurate prognostics. *IEEE Transactions on Industrial Electronics*, *62*(1), 647–656. doi:10.1109/TIE.2014.2327917

Jevring, M., Groote, R., & Hesselman, C. (2008). Dynamic optimization of Bluetooth networks for indoor localization. *First International Workshop on Automated and Autonomous Sensor Networks*. 10.1145/1456223.1456357

Jiang, W., Ma, J., Zhang, X., & Xie, H. (2012). Research on cloud manufacturing resource integrating service modeling based on cloud-agent. In *2012 IEEE International Conference on Computer Science and Automation Engineering* (pp. 395-398). IEEE. 10.1109/ICSESS.2012.6269488

Jiménez-Delgado, G., Santos, G., Félix, M. J., Teixeira, P., & Sá, J. C. (2020). A combined ahp-topsis approach for evaluating the process of innovation and integration of management systems in the logistic sector. Lecture Notes in Computer Science (Including Subseries Lecture Notes in Artificial Intelligence and Lecture Notes in Bioinformatics), 12427 LNCS, 535–559. doi:10.1007/978-3-030-60152-2_40

Jimenez, G., Santos, G., Félix, M., Hernández, H., & Rondón, C. (2019b). Good Practices and Trends in Reverse Logistics in the plastic products manufacturing industry. *Procedia Manufacturing*, *41*, 367–374. doi:10.1016/j.promfg.2019.09.021

Jin, Z. (2013). Research on solutions of cloud manufacturing in automotive industry. In *Proceedings of the FISITA 2012 World Automotive Congress* (pp. 225-234). Springer Berlin Heidelberg. 10.1007/978-3-642-33747-5_21

Jin, X., Ma, E. W., Cheng, L. L., & Pecht, M. (2012). Health monitoring of cooling fans based on Mahalanobis distance with mRMR feature selection. *IEEE Transactions on Instrumentation and Measurement*, *61*(8), 2222–2229. doi:10.1109/TIM.2012.2187240

Kagermann, H., Wahlster, W., & Helbig, J. (2013). *Recommendations for implementing the strategic initiative INDUSTRIE 4.0*. Academic Press.

Kagermann, H., & Wahlster, W. (2013). Recommendations for Implementing the strategic initiative INDUSTRIE 4.0. In *Final Report of the Industrie 4.0 Working Group*. Forschungsunion Press.

Kamble, S., Gunasekaran, A., & Dhone, N. C. (2020). Industry 4.0 and lean manufacturing practices for sustainable organisational performance in Indian manufacturing companies. *International Journal of Production Research*, *58*(5), 1319–1337. doi:10.1080/00207543.2019.1630772

Kankar, P. K., Sharma, S. C., & Harsha, S. P. (2011). Fault diagnosis of ball bearings using continuous wavelet transform. *Applied Soft Computing*, *11*(2), 2300–2312. doi:10.1016/j.asoc.2010.08.011

Katayama, H., & Bennett, D. (1996). Lean production in a changing competitive world: A Japanese perspective. *International Journal of Operations & Production Management*, *16*(2), 8–23. doi:10.1108/01443579610109811

Kayvantash, K., Kolera-Gokula, H., Scannavino, F., Chene, M., & Spote, R. (2019). *Enabling Accurate Design Decisions while Compressing Engineering Timelines with CADLM Technology*. Hexagon MSC Software. https://www.mscsoftware.com/sites/default/files/enabling-accurate-design-decisions-while-compressingengineering-timelines-with-cadlm-technology.pdf

Kayvantash, K., Thiam, A.-T., Ryckelynck, D., Ben Chaabane, S., Touzeau, J., & Ravie, P. (2015). *Model Reduction Techniques for LS-DYNA ALE and Crash Applications*. In 10th European LS-DYNA Conference 2015, Würzburg, Germany.

Keizer, M. C. A. O., Flapper, S. D. P., & Teunter, R, H. (2017). Conditionbased maintenance policies for systems with multiple dependent components: A review. *European Journal of Operational Research*, *261*(2).

Khanam, S., Tandon, N., & Dutt, J. K. (2014). Fault size estimation in the outer race of ball bearing using discrete wavelet transform of the vibration signal. *Procedia Technology, 14*, 12–19. doi:10.1016/j.protcy.2014.08.003

Khattak, M. A. (2011). PLC Based Intelligent Traffic Control System. *International Journal of Electrical & Computer Sciences, 11*(6).

Kirkpatrick, M., Bertino, E., & Sheldon, F. T. (2009, January). Restricted authentication and encryption for cyber-physical systems. DHS CPS Workshop Restricted Authentication and Encryption for Cyber-physical Systems.

Köhlke, J. (2019). *Relevance and boundaries of innovation cooperation in the Smart Grid and its influence on energy transition.* Academic Press.

Koopman, P., & Wagner, M. (2014). *Transportation CPS safety challenges.* Carnegie Mellon University.

Kumar, P., Reddy, L., & Varma, S. (2009). Distance measurement and error estimation scheme for RSSI based localization in Wireless Sensor Networks. *Wireless Communication and Sensor Networks (WCSN), 2009 Fifth IEEE Conference on*, 1–4. 10.1109/WCSN.2009.5434802

Kumar, H. S., Pai, P. S., Sriram, N. S., & Vijay, G. S. (2013). Artificial neural network based evaluation of performance of wavelet transform for condition monitoring of rolling element bearing. *Procedia Engineering, 64*, 805–814. doi:10.1016/j.proeng.2013.09.156

Kumar, H. S., Pai, P. S., Sriram, N. S., Vijay, G. S., & Patil, M. V. (2016). Comparison of denoising schemes and dimensionality reduction techniques for fault diagnosis of rolling element bearing using wavelet transform. *International Journal of Manufacturing Research, 11*(3), 238–258. doi:10.1504/IJMR.2016.079461

Kumar, H. S., Pai, S. P., Sriram, N. S., & Vijay, G. S. (2017). Rolling element bearing fault diagnostics: Development of health index. *Proceedings of the Institution of Mechanical Engineers. Part C, Journal of Mechanical Engineering Science, 231*(21), 3923–3939. doi:10.1177/0954406216656214

Kumar, V. R., Khamis, A., Fiorini, S., Carbonera, J., Alarcos, A. O., Habib, M., Goncalves, P., Li, H., & Olszewska, J. I. (2019). Ontologies for industry 4.0. *The Knowledge Engineering Review, 34*, 1–14.

Ladd, A. M., Bekris, K. E., Rudys, A., Kavraki, L. E., & Wallach, D. S. (2005). Robotics-based location sensing using wireless ethernet. *Wireless Networks, 11*(1-2), 189–204. doi:10.100711276-004-4755-8

Lan, T., Kang, Q., An, J., Yan, W., & Wang, L. (2011). Sitting and sizing of aggregator controlled park for plug-in hybrid electric vehicle based on particle swarm optimization. *Neural Computing & Applications, 22*(2), 249–257. doi:10.100700521-011-0687-2

Lass, S., & Gronau, N. (2020). A factory operating system for extending existing factories to Industry 4.0. *Computers in Industry, 2020*(115), 103128. doi:10.1016/j.compind.2019.103128

Lee, E. A. (2008, May). Cyber physical systems: Design challenges. In *2008 11th IEEE international symposium on object and component-oriented real-time distributed computing (ISORC)* (pp. 363-369). IEEE.

Lee, E. A., & Seshia, S. A. (2011). *Introduction to Embedded Systems: A Cyber-physical Systems Approach*. http://LeeSeshia.org

Lee, J., Bagheri, B., & Kao, H. A. (2015). A cyber-physical systems architecture for industry 4.0-based manufacturing systems. *Manufacturing Letters, 3*, 18–23.

Legner, C., & Heutschi, R. (2007). *SOA Adoption in Practice - Findings from Early SOA Implementations*. Academic Press.

Leitão, P., Barbosa, J., Pereira, A., Barata, J., & Colombo, A. W. (2016). Specification of the PERFoRM architecture for the seamless production system reconfiguration. In *IECON 2016-42nd Annual Conference of the IEEE Industrial Electronics Society* (pp. 5729-5734). 10.1109/IECON.2016.7793007

Leitão, P. (2009). Agent-based distributed manufacturing control: A state-of-the-art survey. *Engineering Applications of Artificial Intelligence, 22*(7), 979–991. doi:10.1016/j.engappai.2008.09.005

Leitao, P., & Barbosa, J. (2019). Modular and Self-organized Conveyor System Using Multi-agent Systems. In *International Conference on Practical Applications of Agents and Multi-Agent Systems* (pp. 259-263). Springer. 10.1007/978-3-030-24209-1_26

Leitão, P., Barbosa, J., Foehr, M., Calà, A., Perlo, P., Iuzzolino, G., Petrali, P., Vallhagen, J., & Colombo, A. W. (2016). Instantiating the PERFORM system architecture for industrial case studies. In *International Workshop on Service Orientation in Holonic and Multi-Agent Manufacturing* (pp. 359-372). Springer.

Leitão, P., Colombo, A. W., & Karnouskos, S. (2016). Industrial automation based on cyber-physical systems technologies: Prototype implementations and challenges. *Computers in Industry, 81*, 11–25. doi:10.1016/j.compind.2015.08.004

Lepenioti, K., Bousdekis, A., Apostolou, D., & Mentzas, G. (2020). Prescriptive analytics: Literature review and research challenges. *International Journal of Information Management, 50*, 57–70. doi:10.1016/j.ijinfomgt.2019.04.003

Li, W., Wang, B., Sheng, J., Dong, K., Li, Z., & Hu, Y. (2018). A resource service model in the industrial IoT system based on transparent computing. *Sensors, 18*. . doi:10.339018040981

Li, C., Yang, P., Shang, Y., Hu, C., & Zhu, P. (2012). Research on cloud manufacturing resource scheduling and performance analysis. *Advanced Science Letters, 12*(1), 240–243. doi:10.1166/asl.2012.2780

Liebennan, J. N. (1977). *Playfulness: Its relationship to imagination and creativity*. Academic.

Li, G. F., Bie, Z. H., Kou, Y., Jiang, J. F., & Bettinelli, M. (2015). Reliability evaluation of integrated energy systems based on smart agent communication. *Applied Energy, 167*, 397–406. doi:10.1016/j.apenergy.2015.11.033

Lima, D. R., & Costa, H. R. da C. (2017). *Uma Visão Teórica Sobre Ferramentas de Self-Service B.I. Através de Dados Públicos Sobre os Casos de Acidentes do Trabalho A Theoretical View About Self-Service Tools B.I. Through Public Data on the Cases of Work Accidents* (Vol. 7). Revista Pensar Tecnologia.

Lin, S.-W., Murphy, B., Clauser, E., Loewen, U., Neubert, R., Bachmann, G., Pai, M., & Hankel, M. (2017). Architecture Alignment and Interoperability: An Industrial Internet Consortium and Plattform Industrie 4.0 Joint Whitepaper. *Plattform Industrie 4.0*, 19.

Lin, T. R., Yu, K., & Tan, J. (2017). *Condition monitoring and fault diagnosis of roller element bearing*. Intech Open. doi:10.5772/67143

Liu, B., Zhang, Y., Lv, J., Majeed, A., Chen, C. H., & Zhang, D. (2021). A cost-effective manufacturing process recognition approach based on deep transfer learning for CPS enabled shop-floor. *Robotics and Computer-integrated Manufacturing, 70*, 102128.

Liu, C., & Xu, X. (2017). Cyber-physical machine tool—the Era of Machine Tool 4.0. In *Proceeding of The 50th CIRP Conference on Manufacturing Systems* (vol. 63, pp. 70-75). Elsevier. 10.1016/j.procir.2017.03.078

Liu, H., Darabi, H., Banerjee, P., & Liu, J. (2007). Survey of wireless indoor positioning techniques and systems. *IEEE Transactions on Systems, Man and Cybernetics. Part C, Applications and Reviews, 37*(6), 1067–1080. doi:10.1109/TSMCC.2007.905750

Liu, J., Li, X., Chen, X., Zhen, Y., & Zeng, L. (2011, February). Applications of internet of things on smart grid in China. In *13th International Conference on Advanced Communication Technology (ICACT2011)* (pp. 13-17). IEEE.

Lopes, H., Carvalho, V., & Sylla, C. (2021). Mobeybou-Tangible Interfaces for Cognitive Development. *International Conference on Innovation in Engineering*.

Lopes, J., Guimarães, T., & Santos, M. F. (2020). Adaptive Business Intelligence: A New Architectural Approach. *Procedia Computer Science, 177*, 540–545. doi:10.1016/j.procs.2020.10.075

Lu, M. (2014). *Discovering Microsoft Self-service BI solution: Power BI*. Academic Press.

Lu, T., Du, S., Li, Y., Dong, P., & Zhang, X. (2015). A framework for analyzing anonymous network topology. *International Journal of Future Generation Communication and Networking, 8*(4), 1–16. doi:10.14257/ijfgcn.2015.8.4.01

Lu, Y. (2017). Industry 4.0: A survey on technologies, applications and open research issues. *Journal of Industrial Information Integration, 6*, 1–10. doi:10.1016/j.jii.2017.04.005

Lu, Y. K., Liu, C. Y., & Ju, B. C. (2012). Cloud manufacturing collaboration: An initial exploration. In *2012 Third World Congress on Software Engineering* (pp. 163-166). IEEE. 10.1109/WCSE.2012.39

Lyn, K. G. (2015). *Classification of and resilience to cyber-attacks on cyber-physical systems* (Doctoral dissertation). Georgia Institute of Technology.

Machado, C. G., Winroth, M., Carlsson, D., Almstrom, P., Centerholt, V., & Hallin, M. (2019). Industry 4.0 readiness in manufacturing companies: challenges and enablers towards increased digitalization. *52nd CIRP Conference on Manufacturing Systems.* 10.1016/j.procir.2019.03.262

Magargle, R., Johnson, L., Mandloi, P., Davoudabadi, P., Kesarkar, O., Krishnaswamy, S., Batteh, J., & Pitchaikani, A. (2017). A simulation-based digital twin for model-driven health monitoring and predictive maintenance of an automotive braking system. In *Proceedings of the 12th International Modelica Conference* (Issue No. 132, pp. 35–46). 10.3384/ecp1713235

Maheshwari, P., Suneja, D., Singh, P., & Mutneja, Y. (2015). Smart Traffic Optimization Using Image Processing. *IEEE 3rd International Conference on MOOCs, Innovation and Technology in Education (MITE).*

Maheshwari, P. (2016). Security issues of cyber physical system: A review. *International Journal of Computers and Applications*, (1), 7–11.

Mallat, S. G. (1989). A theory for multiresolution signal decomposition: The wavelet representation. *IEEE Transactions on Pattern Analysis and Machine Intelligence*, *11*(7), 674–693. doi:10.1109/34.192463

Mamun, M., Al-Kadi, M., & Marufuzzaman, M. (2013). Effectiveness of wavelet denoising on electroencephalogram signals. *Journal of Applied Research and Technology*, *11*(1), 156–160. doi:10.1016/S1665-6423(13)71524-4

Marinho, A., Silva, R. G., & Santos, G. (2020). Why most university-industry partnerships fail to endure and how to create value and gain competitive advantage through collaboration – a systematic review. *Quality Innovation Prosperity*, *24*(2), 34–50. doi:10.12776/qip.v24i2.1389

Marques, C., Lopes, N., Santos, G., Delgado, I., & Delgado, P. (2018). Improving operator evaluation skills for defect classification using training strategy supported by attribute agreement analysis. *Measurement*, *119*, 129–141. doi:10.1016/j.measurement.2018.01.034

Marshall, P. (2007). Do tangible interfaces enhance learning? *Proceedings of TEI'07*, 163–170. 10.1145/1226969.1227004

Maskuriy, R., Selamat, A., Ali, K. N., Maresova, P., & Krejcar, O. (2019). Industry 4.0 for the construction industry—How ready is the industry? *Applied Sciences (Basel, Switzerland)*, *9*(14), 2819.

Massoud, A. (2014). A smart self-healing grid: In pursuit of a more reliable and resilient system. *IEEE Power & Energy Magazine*, *12*(1), 112–110. doi:10.1109/MPE.2013.2284646

Medawar, S., Scholle, D., & Šljivo, I. (2017, June). Cooperative safety critical CPS platooning in SafeCOP. In *2017 6th Mediterranean Conference on Embedded Computing (MECO)* (pp. 1-5). IEEE.

Meltz, B. F. (1999). Pretend play enriches development. *Boston Globe*, p. C1.

Menezes, A. J., Van Oorschot, P. C., & Vanstone, S. A. (2018). *Handbook of applied cryptography*. CRC Press.

Meskina, S. B., Doggaz, N., Khalgui, M., & Li, Z. W. (2016). Multiagent framework for smart grids recovery. *IEEE Transactions on Systems, Man, and Cybernetics. Systems*, *47*(99), 1284–1300.

Miao, Q., Huang, H. Z., & Fan, X. (2007). Singularity detection in machinery health monitoring using Lipschitz exponent function. *Journal of Mechanical Science and Technology*, *21*(5), 737–744. doi:10.1007/BF02916351

Michell, M. (2012). *Yves, Misti., Georges, Oppenheim., Jean-Michel, Poggi*. Wavelet Toolbox TM, User's Guide, The Mathworks, Inc.

Mohammadi, H. S. M., Fereidunian, A., Shahsavari, A., & Lesani, H. (2016). A healer reinforcement approach to self-healing in smart grid by PHEVs parking lot allocation. *IEEE Transactions on Industrial Informatics*, *2*(6), 2020–2030. doi:10.1109/TII.2016.2587773

Moi, T., Cibicik, A., & Rølvåg, T. (2020). Digital twin based condition monitoring of a knuckle boom crane: An experimental study. *Engineering Failure Analysis*. doi:10.1016/j.engfailanal.2020.104517

Mojsilovic, A., Popovic, M. V., & Rackov, D. M. (2000). On the selection of an optimal wavelet basis for texture characterization. *IEEE Transactions on Image Processing*, *9*(12), 2043–2050. doi:10.1109/83.887972 PMID:18262942

Monostori, L., Kádár, B., Bauernhansl, T., Kondoh, S., Kumara, S., Reinhart, G., Sauer, O., Schuh, G., Sihn, W., & Ueda, K. (2016). Cyber-physical systems in manufacturing. *CIRP Annals*, *65*(2), 621–641. doi:10.1016/j.cirp.2016.06.005

Moore, S. J., Nugent, C. D., Zhang, S., & Cleland, I. (2020). IoT reliability: A review leading to 5 key research directions. *CCF Transactions on Pervasive Computing and Interaction*, *2*(3), 147–163. doi:10.100742486-020-00037-z

Morais, J. (1994). *L'Art de Lire*. Odile Jacob.

Mourtzis, D., & Doukas, M. (2012). Decentralized manufacturing systems review: Challenges and outlook. *Logistics Research*, *5*(3-4), 113–121. doi:10.100712159-012-0085-x

Munir, S., Stankovic, J. A., Liang, C. J. M., & Lin, S. (2013). Cyber physical system challenges for human-in-the-loop control. *8th International Workshop on Feedback Computing (Feedback Computing 13)*.

Nakagawa, H., Ogata, S., Aoki, Y., & Kobayashi, K. (2020, March). A model transformation approach to constructing agent-oriented design models for CPS/IoT systems. In *Proceedings of the 35th Annual ACM Symposium on Applied Computing* (pp. 815-822). ACM.

Naor, M., & Shamir, A. (1994, May). Visual cryptography. In *Workshop on the Theory and Application of of Cryptographic Techniques* (pp. 1-12). Springer.

Napoleone, A., Macchi, M., & Pozzetti, A. (2020). A review on the characteristics of cyber-physical systems for the future smart factories. *Journal of Manufacturing Systems*, *54*, 305–335. doi:10.1016/j.jmsy.2020.01.007

Nascimento, D. L. de M., Quelhas, O. L. G., Meiriño, M. J., Caiado, R. G. G., Barbosa, S. D. J., & Ivson, P. (2018). Facility management using digital obeya room by integrating BIM-lean approaches – An empirical study. *Journal of Civil Engineering and Management*, *24*(8), 581–591. doi:10.3846/jcem.2018.5609

Nascimento, D. L. de M., Sotelino, E. D., Lara, T. P. S., Caiado, R. G. G., & Ivson, P. (2017). Constructability in industrial plants construction: A BIM-Lean approach using the Digital Obeya Room framework. *Journal of Civil Engineering and Management*, *23*(8), 1100–1108. doi:10.3 846/13923730.2017.1385521

Negash, S. (2004). Business intelligence. *Communications of the Association for Information Systems*, 177–195. https://www.researchgate.net/publication/228765967

Neves, P., Silva, F. J. G., Ferreira, L. P., Pereira, T., Gouveia, A., & Pimentel, C. (2018). Implementing Lean Tools in the Manufacturing Process of Trimmings Products. *Procedia Manufacturing*, *17*, 696–704. doi:10.1016/j.promfg.2018.10.119

Nguyen, C. P., & Flueck, A. J. (2012). Agent based restoration with distributed energy storage support in smart grids. *IEEE Transactions on Smart Grid*, *3*(2), 1029–1038. doi:10.1109/TSG.2012.2186833

O'Malley, C. (1992). Designing Computer Systems to support peer learning. *European Journal of Psychology of Education*, *7*(4), 339–352. doi:10.1007/BF03172898

Oliveira, J., Sá, J. C., & Fernandes, A. (2017). Continuous improvement through "Lean Tools": An application in a mechanical company. *Procedia Manufacturing*, *13*, 1082–1089. doi:10.1016/j. promfg.2017.09.139

Oliveira, L., Mitchell, V., & May, A. (2020). Smart home technology—Comparing householder expectations at the point of installation with experiences 1year later. *Personal and Ubiquitous Computing*, *24*(5), 613–626. doi:10.100700779-019-01302-4

Onori, M., Lohse, N., Barata, J., & Hanisch, C. (2012). The IDEAS project: Plug & produce at shop-floor level. *Assembly Automation*, *32*(2), 124–134. doi:10.1108/01445151211212280

Ottaviano, E., & Rea, P. (2013). Design and operation of a 2DOF leg–wheel hybrid robot. *ROBOTICA*, *31*, 1319-1325. doi:10.1017/S0263574713000556

Ottaviano, E., Rea, P., & Castelli, G. (2014). THROO: A Tracked Hybrid Rover to Overpass Obstacles. *Advanced Robotics*, *28*(10), 683–694. doi:10.1080/01691864.2014.891949

Palaigeorgiou, G., Karakostas, A., & Skenderidou, K. (2017). Finger Trips: Learning Geography through Tangible Finger Trips into 3D Augmented Maps. *Proceedings - IEEE 17th International Conference on Advanced Learning Technologies, ICALT 2017*, 170–172. 10.1109/ICALT.2017.118

Pandya, D., Jain, R., & Lupu, E. (2003). Indoor location estimation using multiple wireless technologies. *14th IEEE Proceedings on Personal, Indoor and Mobile Radio Communications, 3*, 2208–2212.

Patel, P., Narmawala, Z., & Thakkar, A. (2019). *A Survey on Intelligent Transportation System Using Internet of Things. In Emerging Research in Computing, Information, Communication and Applications, Advances in Intelligent Systems and Computing book series* (Vol. 882). AISC.

Patil, M. S., Mathew, J., & RajendraKumar, P. K. (2008). Bearing signature analysis as a medium for fault detection: A review. *Journal of Tribology, 130*(1), 014001-1014001-7.

Peng, H., Kan, Z., Zhao, D. D., Han, J. M., Lu, J. F., & Lu, Z. L. (2018). Reliability analysis in interdependent smart grid systems. *Physica A*, *500*, 50–59. doi:10.1016/j.physa.2018.02.028

Peng, Z. K., & Chu, F. L. (2004). Application of the wavelet transform in machine condition monitoring and fault diagnostics: A review with bibliography. *Mechanical Systems and Signal Processing*, *18*(2), 199–221. doi:10.1016/S0888-3270(03)00075-X

Peng, Z. R., Yin, H., Dong, H. T., Li, H., & Pan, A. (2015). A harmony search based low-delay and low-energy wireless sensor network. *Int. J. Future Gener. Commun. Netw*, *8*(2), 21–32. doi:10.14257/ijfgcn.2015.8.2.03

Pereira, J., Silva, F. J. G., Bastos, J. A., Ferreira, L. P., & Matias, J. C. O. (2019). Application of the A3 Methodology for the Improvement of an Assembly Line. *Procedia Manufacturing*, *38*, 745–754. doi:10.1016/j.promfg.2020.01.101

Peres, R. S., Parreira-Rocha, M., Rocha, A. D., Barbosa, J., Leitao, P., & Barata, J. (2016). Selection of a data exchange format for industry 4.0 manufacturing systems. In *IECON 2016-42nd Annual Conference of the IEEE Industrial Electronics Society* (pp. 5723-5728). IEEE.

Peterson, C., & McCabe, A. (1983). *Developmental psycholinguistics: three ways of looking at a child's narrative*. Plenum. doi:10.1007/978-1-4757-0608-6

Pinheiro, A. A., Brandao, I. M., & Da Costa, C. (2019). Vibration Analysis in Turbomachines using Machine Learning Techniques. *European Journal of Engineering and Technology Research*, *4*(2), 12–16. doi:10.24018/ejers.2019.4.2.1128

Pinto, B., Silva, F. J. G., Costa, T., Campilho, R. D. S. G., & Pereira, M. T. (2019). A Strategic Model to take the First Step Towards Industry 4.0 in SMEs. *Procedia Manufacturing*, *38*, 637–645. doi:10.1016/j.promfg.2020.01.082

Pirra, M. (2012). *Advanced techniques for aircraft bearing diagnostics*. Polytechnic University of Milan.

Powers, D. (2011). Evaluation: From precision, recall and F-score to ROC, unforcedness, nakedness & correlation. *Journal of Machine Learning Technologies*, 2, 37–63.

Provost, F., Fawcett, T., & Kohavi, R. (1998). The case against accuracy estimation for comparing classifiers. *Proceedings of the ICML*-98, 445 - 453.

Pu, C. (2011, July). A world of opportunities: CPS, IOT, and beyond. In *Proceedings of the 5th ACM international conference on Distributed event-based system* (pp. 229-230). ACM.

Qi, R., Ji, S., Shen, J., Vijayakumar, P., & Kumar, N. (2021). Security preservation in industrial medical CPS using Chebyshev map: An AI approach. *Future Generation Computer Systems*.

Rad, C. R., Hancu, O., Takacs, I. A., & Olteanu, G. (2015). Smart monitoring of potato crop: A cyber-physical system architecture model in the field of precision agriculture. *Agriculture and Agricultural Science Procedia*, 6, 73–79.

Rafiee, J., Rafiee, M. A., & Tse, P. W. (2010). Application of mother wavelet functions for automatic gear and bearing fault diagnosis. *Expert Systems with Applications*, 37(6), 4568–4579. doi:10.1016/j.eswa.2009.12.051

Raghavan, A. N., Ananthapadmanaban, H., Sivamurugan, M. S., & Ravindran, B. (2010). Accurate mobile robot localization in indoor environments using Bluetooth®. *Proceedings - IEEE International Conference on Robotics and Automation*, 4391–4396. 10.1109/ROBOT.2010.5509232

Rajkumar, R., Lee, I., Sha, L., & Stankovic, J. (2010). Cyber-physical systems: the next computing revolution. In *Proceedings of 47th ACM/IEEE, Design Automation Conference* (pp. 731-736). Association for Computing Machinery Press.

Rajkumar, R., Lee, I., Sha, L., & Stankovic, J. (2010, June). Cyber-physical systems: the next computing revolution. In *Design automation conference* (pp. 731–736). IEEE.

Rakar, A., Zorzut, S., & Jovan, V. (2004). *Assesment of Production Performance by means of KPI*. Retrieved from http://eprints.uanl.mx/5481/1/1020149995.PDF

Ramani, A. (2008). *Diagnosis And Prognosis of Electrical And Mechanical Faults Using Wireless Sensor Networks And a Two-stage Neural Network Classifier, College of Engineering, ProQuest Dissertations and Theses (electronic resource collection)*. University of Texas at Arlington.

Randall, R. B., & Antoni, J. (2011). Rolling element bearing diagnostics—A tutorial. *Mechanical Systems and Signal Processing*, 25(2), 485–520. doi:10.1016/j.ymssp.2010.07.017

Rao, B. K. N., Pai, P. S., & Nagabhushana, T. N. (2012). Failure diagnosis and prognosis of rolling-element bearings using Artificial Neural Networks: A critical overview. *Journal of Physics: Conference Series*, 364(1), 012023. doi:10.1088/1742-6596/364/1/012023

Rea, P., & Ottaviano, E. (2018). Design and Development of an Inspection Robotic System for Indoor Applications. *Robotics and Computer-integrated Manufacturing*, *49*, 143–151. doi:10.1016/j.rcim.2017.06.005

Rea, P., & Ottaviano, E. (2019). Mechatronic Design and Control of a Robotic System for Inspection Tasks. In J. Machado, F. Soares, & G. Veiga (Eds.), *Innovation*. Engineering.

Rea, P., Pelliccio, A., Ottaviano, E., & Saccucci, M. (2017). The Heritage Management and Preservation Using the Mechatronic Survey. *International Journal of Architectural Heritage*, *11*(8), 1121–1132. doi:10.1080/15583058.2017.1338790

Reed, J. L., Vo, T. D., Schilling, C. H., & Palsson, B. O. (2003). An expanded genome-scale model of Escherichia coli K-12 (iJR904 GSM/GPR). *Genome Biology*, *4*(54).

Ren, J., Chen, Y., Xin, L., Shi, J., Li, B., & Liu, Y. (2016). Detecting and positioning of traffic incidents via video- based analysis of traffic states in a road segment‖. *IET Intelligent Transport Systems*, *10*(6), 428–437. doi:10.1049/iet-its.2015.0022

Ren, Y., Fan, D. M., Feng, Q., Wang, Z. L., Sun, B., & Yang, D. Z. (2019). Agent-based restoration approach for reliability with load balancing on smart grids. *Applied Energy*, *2019*, 46–57.

Ribeiro, L. (2017). Cyber-physical production systems' design challenges. In *2017 IEEE 26th International Symposium on Industrial Electronics (ISIE)* (pp. 1189-1194). IEEE.

Ribeiro, P., Sá, J. C., Ferreira, L. P., Silva, F. J. G., Pereira, M. T., & Santos, G. (2019). The impact of the application of lean tools for improvement of process in a plastic company: A case study. *Procedia Manufacturing*, *38*, 765–775. doi:10.1016/j.promfg.2020.01.104

Rodrigues, J., de Sá, J. C. V., Ferreira, L. P., Silva, F. J. G., & Santos, G. (2019). Lean management "quick-wins": Results of implementation. A case study. *Quality Innovation Prosperity*, *23*(3), 3–21. doi:10.12776/qip.v23i3.1291

Rogalewicz, M., & Sika, R. (2016). Methodologies of knowledge discovery from data and data mining methods in mechanical engineering. *Management and Production Engineering Review*, *7*(4), 97–108. Advance online publication. doi:10.1515/mper-2016-0040

Rogoff, T. (1990). *Apprenticeship in Thinking: Cognitive development in social context*. Oxford University Press.

Rojas, R. A., & Rauch, E. (2019). From a literature review to a conceptual framework of enablers for smart manufacturing control. *International Journal of Advanced Manufacturing Technology*, *104*(1–4), 517–533. doi:10.100700170-019-03854-4

Romanosky, S., & Goldman, Z. (2016). Cyber collateral damage. *Procedia Computer Science*, *95*, 10–17.

Rosa, C., Silva, F. J. G., & Ferreira, L. P. (2017a). Improving the quality and productivity of steel wire-rope assembly lines for the automotive industry. *Procedia Manufacturing*, *11*, 1035–1042. doi:10.1016/j.promfg.2017.07.214

Rosa, C., Silva, F. J. G., Ferreira, L. P., & Campilho, R. (2017b). SMED methodology: The reduction of setup times for Steel Wire-Rope assembly lines in the automotive industry. *Procedia Manufacturing*, *13*, 1034–1042. doi:10.1016/j.promfg.2017.09.110

Rudskoy, A., Ilin, I., & Prokhorov, A. (2021). Digital Twins in the Intelligent Transport Systems. *Transportation Research Procedia*, *54*, 927–935. doi:10.1016/j.trpro.2021.02.152

Russ, S. (1996). Development of creative processes in children. In M. Runco (Ed.), Creativity from childhood through adulthood: The developmental issues (vol. 72, pp. 3 1-42). San Francisco: Jossey-Bass. doi:10.1002/cd.23219967204

Russ, S. (1993). *Affect and creativity: The role of affect and play in the creative process.* Lawrence Erlbaum Associates, Inc.

Saha, D., Mukhopadhyay, D., & Chowdhury, D. R. (2009). A Diagonal Fault Attack on the Advanced Encryption Standard. *IACR Cryptol. ePrint Arch., 2009*(581).

Sá, J. C., Barreto, L., Amaral, A., Carvalho, F., & Santos, G. (2019). Perception of the importance to implement ISO 9001 in organizations related to people linked to quality – an empirical study. *International Journal of Qualitative Research*, *13*(4), 1055–1070.

Sá, J. C., Vaz, S., Carvalho, O., Lima, V., Morgado, L., Fonseca, L., Doiro, M., & Santos, G. (2020). A model of integration ISO 9001 with Lean six sigma and main benefits achieved. *Total Quality Management & Business Excellence*, *0*(0), 1–25. doi:10.1080/14783363.2020.1829969

Sakurai, R., & Zuchi, J. D. (2018). The Industrial Revolutions up to Industry 4.0. *Interface Tecnológica*, 480–491. doi:10.31510/infa.v15i2.386

Sanchez, A., Suarez, P. D., Conci, A., & Nunes, E. O. (2011). Video-Based Distance Traffic Analysis: Application to Vehicle Tracking and Counting. *IEEE CS and the AIP*, *13*(3), 38–45. doi:10.1109/MCSE.2010.143

Sanislav, T., & Miclea, L. (2012). Cyber-Physical Systems - Concept, Challenges and Research Areas. *J. Control Eng. Appl. Inform.*, *14*(2), 28–33.

Santos, G., Sá, J. C., Oliveira, J., Ramos, D., & Ferreira, C. (2019b). Quality and Safety Continuous Improvement Through Lean Tools. In Lean Manufacturing – Implementation, opportunities and Challenges. Nova Science Publishers.

Santos, B. P., Alberto, A., Lima, T. D. F. M., & Santos, F. M. (2018). *Indústria 4.0: Desafios e Oportunidades*. Revista Produção e Desenvolvimento.

Santos, G., Doiro, M., Mandado, E., & Silva, R. (2019a). Engineering learning objectives and computer assisted tools. *European Journal of Engineering Education*, *44*(4), 616–628. doi:10.1080/03043797.2018.1563585

Santos, G., Gomes, S., Braga, V., Braga, A., Lima, V., Teixeira, P., & Sá, J. C. (2019c). Value creation through quality and innovation - a case study on Portugal. *The TQM Journal*, *31*(6), 928–947. doi:10.1108/TQM-12-2018-0223

Santos, G., Mendes, F., & Barbosa, J. (2011). Certification and integration of management systems: The experience of Portuguese small and medium enterprises. *Journal of Cleaner Production, 19*(17-18), 1965–1974. doi:10.1016/j.jclepro.2011.06.017

Santos, G., Murmura, F., & Bravi, L. (2019d). Developing a model of vendor rating to manage quality in the supply chain. *International Journal of Quality and Service Sciences, 11*(1), 34–52. doi:10.1108/IJQSS-06-2017-0058

Santos, G., Rebelo, M., Ramos, S., Silva, R., Pereira, M., & Ramos, G. N. L. (2014). Developments regarding the integration of the occupational safety and health with quality and environment management systems. In I. G. Kavouras & M.-C. G. Chalbot (Eds.), *Occupational safety and health* (pp. 113–146). Nova Publishers.

Saravanan, N., & Ramachandran, K. I. (2009). Fault diagnosis of spur bevel gear box using discrete wavelet features and Decision Tree classification. *Expert Systems with Applications, 36*(5), 9564–9573. doi:10.1016/j.eswa.2008.07.089

Sethi, P., & Sarangi, S. R. (2017). Internet of things: Architectures, protocols, and applications. *Journal of Electrical and Computer Engineering, 2017*, 2017. doi:10.1155/2017/9324035

Sha, L., Gopalakrishnan, S., Liu, X., & Wang, Q. (2008, June). Cyber-physical systems: A new frontier. In *2008 IEEE International Conference on Sensor Networks, Ubiquitous, and Trustworthy Computing (sutc 2008)* (pp. 1-9). IEEE.

Shih, C. S., Chou, J. J., Reijers, N., & Kuo, T. W. (2016). Designing CPS/IoT applications for smart buildings and cities. *IET Cyber-Physical Systems: Theory & Applications, 1*(1), 3–12.

Shinde, V. D., Patil, C. G., & Ruikar, M. S. D. (2012). Wavelet based multi-scale principal component analysis for speech enhancement. *International Journal of Engineering Trends and Technology, 3*(3), 397–400.

Silva, F. J. G., & Ferreira, L. P. (2019). *Lean Manufacturing - Implementation, opportunities and challenges*. Nova Science Publishers.

Silva, S., Sá, J. C., Silva, F. J. G., Ferreira, L. P., & Santos, G. (2020). Lean Green—The Importance of Integrating Environment into Lean Philosophy - A Case Study. *Lecture Notes in Networks and Systems, 122*, 211–219. doi:10.1007/978-3-030-41429-0_21

Simon, H., & Robert, H. (2009). Bluetooth Tracking without Discoverability. *LoCA 2009: The 4th International Symposium on Location and Context Awareness.*

Singer, D. L., & Singer, J. (1990). *The house of make-believe*. Harvard University Press.

Singer, J. L., & Singer, D. L. (1981). *Television, imagination, and aggression*. Lawrence Erlbaum Associates, Inc.

Sitaram, Padmanabha, & Shibani. (2015). Still Image Processing Techniques for Intelligent Traffic Monitoring. *IEEE 3rd International Conference on Image Information Processing.*

Skare, P. M. (2013). *Method and system for cyber security management of industrial control systems.* U.S. Patent No. 8,595,831.

Smith, W. A., & Randall, R. B. (2015). Rolling element bearing diagnostics using the Case Western Reserve University data: A benchmark study. *Mechanical Systems and Signal Processing, 64,* 100–131. doi:10.1016/j.ymssp.2015.04.021

Sousa, E., Silva, F. J. G., Ferreira, L. P., Pereira, M. T., Gouveia, R., & Silva, R. P. (2018). Applying SMED methodology in cork stoppers production. *Procedia Manufacturing, 17,* 611–622. doi:10.1016/j.promfg.2018.10.103

Soylemezoglu, A., Jagannathan, S., & Saygin, C. (2010). Mahalanobis Taguchi system as a prognostics tool for rolling element bearing failures. *Journal of Manufacturing Science and Engineering, 132*(5), 051014. doi:10.1115/1.4002545

Sreejith, B., Verma, A. K., & Srividya, A. (2008, December). Fault diagnosis of rolling element bearing using time-domain features and neural networks. In *2008 IEEE region 10 and the third international conference on industrial and information systems* (pp. 1-6). IEEE. 10.1109/ICIINFS.2008.4798444

Sreejith, B., Verma, A. K., & Srividya, A. (2010). Comparison of Morlet wavelet filter for defect diagnosis of bearings. In *2nd International Conference on Reliability, Safety and Hazard-Risk-Based Technologies and Physics-of-Failure Methods (ICRESH)* (pp. 406-411). IEEE. 10.1109/ICRESH.2010.5779584

Srivastava, M. D. (2012, December). Smart traffic control system using PLC and SCADA. *International Journal of Innovative Research in Science, Engineering and Technology, 1*(2).

Stankovic, J. A. (2014). Research directions for the internet of things. *IEEE Internet of Things Journal, 1*(1), 3–9. doi:10.1109/JIOT.2014.2312291

Su, K., Li, J., & Fu, H. (2011). Smart city and the applications. *International Conference on Electronics, Communications and Control (ICECC).*

Sumithra, M. G., & Thanuskodi, K. (2009, June). Wavelet based speech signal de-noising using hybrid thresholding. In *International Conference on Control, Automation, Communication and Energy Conservation* (pp. 1-7). IEEE.

Sun, Y., & Song, H. (Eds.). (2017). *Secure and trustworthy transportation cyber-physical systems.* Springer Singapore.

Sylla, C., Pereira, I. S. P., Coutinho, C. P., & Branco, P. (2016). Digital Manipulatives as Scaffolds for Preschoolers 2019; Language Development. *IEEE Transactions on Emerging Topics in Computing, 4*(3), 439–449. doi:10.1109/TETC.2015.2500099

Tai, D., & Xu, F. (2012). Cloud manufacturing based on cooperative concept of SDN. *Advanced Materials Research, 482,* 2424–2429. doi:10.4028/www.scientific.net/AMR.482-484.2424

Talapatra, S., Santos, G., Uddin, K., & Carvalho, F. (2019). Main benefits of integrated management systems through literature review. *International Journal of Qualitative Research*, *13*(4), 1037–1054. doi:10.24874/IJQR13.04-19

Tandon, N., & Nakra, B. C. (1992). Vibration and acoustic monitoring techniques for the detection of defects in rolling element bearings—a review. *The Shock and Vibration Digest, 24*(3), 3-11.

Tandon, N., & Choudhury, A. (1999). A review of vibration and acoustic measurement methods for the detection of defects in rolling element bearings. *Tribology International*, *32*(8), 469–480. doi:10.1016/S0301-679X(99)00077-8

Tang, H., Li, D., Wan, J., Imran, M., & Shoaib, M. (2020). A Reconfigurable Method for Intelligent Manufacturing Based on Industrial Cloud and Edge Intelligence. *IEEE Internet of Things Journal*, *7*(5), 4248-4259. doi:10.1109/JIOT.2019.2950048

Tao, F., Cheng, Y., Zhang, L., Luo, Y. L., & Ren, L. (2011). Cloud manufacturing. *Advanced Materials Research*, *201*, 672–676. doi:10.4028/www.scientific.net/AMR.201-203.672

Tao, X., Lu, C., Lu, C., & Wang, Z. (2013). An approach to performance assessment and fault diagnosis for rotating machinery equipment. *EURASIP Journal on Advances in Signal Processing*, *2013*(1), 1–16. doi:10.1186/1687-6180-2013-5

Tarighat, M. A. (2016). Orthogonal projection approach and continuous wavelet transform-feed forward neural networks for simultaneous spectrophotometric determination of some heavy metals in diet samples. *Food Chemistry*, *192*, 548–556. doi:10.1016/j.foodchem.2015.07.034 PMID:26304383

Topping, K. (1992). Cooperative learning and peer tutoring: An overview. *The Psychologist*, *5*(4), 151–157.

Tuballa, M. L., & Abundo, M. L. (2016). A review of the development of smart grid technologies. *Renewable & Sustainable Energy Reviews*, *59*(Jun), 710–725. doi:10.1016/j.rser.2016.01.011

Tyagi, C. S. (2008). A comparative study of SVM classifiers and artificial neural networks application for rolling element bearing fault diagnosis using wavelet transform preprocessing. Proceedings of World Academy of Science. *Engineering and Technology*, *2*(7), 904–912.

Uckelmann, D., Harrison, M., & Michahelles, F. (2011). An Architectural Approach Towards the Future Internet of Things. In *Architecting the Internet of Things* (pp. 1–24). Springer Berlin Heidelberg. doi:10.1007/978-3-642-19157-2_1

Uddin, M. K., Puttonen, J., Scholze, S., Dvoryanchikova, A., & Martinez Lastra, J. L. (2012). Ontology-Based context-Sensitive computing for FMS optimization. *Assembly Automation*, *32*(2), 163–174. doi:10.1108/01445151211212316

Umachandran, K., Jurčić, I., Della Corte, V., & Sharon Ferdinand-James, D. (2019). *Industry 4.0: The New Industrial Revolution*. doi:10.4018/978-1-5225-6207-8.ch006

Üstündağ, M., Şengür, A., Gökbulut, M., & Ata, F. (2013). Performance comparison of wavelet thresholding techniques on weak ECG signal denoising. *Przegląd Elektrotechniczny, 89*(5), 63–66.

Valilai, O. F., & Houshmand, M. (2013). A collaborative and integrated platform to support distributed manufacturing system using a service-oriented approach based on cloud computing paradigm. *Robotics and Computer-integrated Manufacturing, 29*(1), 110–127. doi:10.1016/j.rcim.2012.07.009

Van Der Veer, H., & Wiles, A. (2008). *Achieving Technical Interoperability: the ETSI Approach.* European Telecommunications Standards Institute.

Večeř, P., Kreidl, M., & Šmíd, R. (2005). Condition indicators for gearbox condition monitoring systems. *Acta Polytechnica, 45*(6), 35–43. doi:10.14311/782

Vegh, L., & Miclea, L. (2014, May). Enhancing security in cyber-physical systems through cryptographic and steganographic techniques. In *2014 IEEE International Conference on Automation, Quality and Testing, Robotics* (pp. 1-6). IEEE. 10.1109/AQTR.2014.6857845

Vieira, T., Sá, J. C., Lopes, M. P., Santos, G., Félix, M. J., Ferreira, L. P., Silva, F. J. G., & Pereira, M. T. (2019). Optimization of the cold profiling process through Lean Tools. *Procedia Manufacturing, 38*, 892–899. doi:10.1016/j.promfg.2020.01.171

Vijay, G. S. (2013). *Vibration signal analysis for defect characterization of rolling element bearing using some soft computing techniques.* VTU.

Vishwash, B., Pai, P. S., Sriram, N. S., Ahmed, R., Kumar, H. S., & Vijay, G. S. (2014). Multiscale slope feature extraction for gear and bearing fault diagnosis using wavelet transform. *Procedia Materials Science, 5*, 1650–1659. doi:10.1016/j.mspro.2014.07.353

Vogel-Heuser, B., Diedrich, C., Pantförder, D., & Göhner, P. (2014). Coupling heterogeneous production systems by a multi-agent based cyber-physical production system. In *2014 12th IEEE International Conference on Industrial Informatics (INDIN)* (pp. 713-719). IEEE. 10.1109/INDIN.2014.6945601

Wang, D., Miao, Q., & Kang, R. (2009). Robust health evaluation of gearbox subject to tooth failure with wavelet decomposition. *Journal of Sound and Vibration, 324*(3-5), 1141–1157. doi:10.1016/j.jsv.2009.02.013

Wang, D., Tsui, K. L., & Miao, Q. (2017). Prognostics and health management: A review of vibration based bearing and gear health indicators. *IEEE Access: Practical Innovations, Open Solutions, 6*, 665–676. doi:10.1109/ACCESS.2017.2774261

Wang, H., & Chen, P. (2008). Fault diagnosis for a rolling bearing used in a reciprocating machine by adaptive filtering technique and fuzzy neural network. *WSEAS Transactions on Systems, 7*(1), 1–6.

Wang, L. (2008). Wise-ShopFloor: An integrated approach for web-based collaborative manufacturing. *IEEE Transactions on Systems, Man and Cybernetics. Part C, Applications and Reviews, 38*(4), 562–573. doi:10.1109/TSMCC.2008.923868

Wang, X. V., & Xu, W. W. (2013). ICMS: a cloud-based manufacturing system. In *Cloud manufacturing* (pp. 1–22). Springer. doi:10.1007/978-1-4471-4935-4_1

Wang, Y. (2013). Wavelet transform based feature extraction for fault diagnosis of rolling-element bearing. *Journal of Information and Computational Science*, *2*, 469–475.

Wan, J., Yan, H., Li, D., Zhou, K., & Zeng, L. (2013). Cyber-physical systems for optimal energy management scheme of autonomous electric vehicle. *The Computer Journal*, *56*(8), 947–956. doi:10.1093/comjnl/bxt043

Wan, J., Yan, H., Liu, Q., Zhou, K., Lu, R., & Li, D. (2013). Enabling cyber–physical systems with machine–to–machine technologies. *International Journal of Ad Hoc and Ubiquitous Computing*, *13*(3-4), 187–196. doi:10.1504/IJAHUC.2013.055454

Wheeler, A. (2007). Commercial applications of wireless sensor networks using ZigBee. *IEEE Communications Magazine*, *45*(4), 70–77. doi:10.1109/MCOM.2007.343615

Wood, D., & O'Malley, C. (1996). Collaborative learning between peers: An overview. *Educational Psychology in Practice*, *11*(4), 4–9. doi:10.1080/0266736960110402

Wooldridge, M. (2009). *An introduction to multiagent systems*. John Wiley & Sons.

Xiao, J., Wu, K., Yi, Y., Wang, L., & Ni, L. M. (2013). Pilot: Passive device free indoor localization using channel state information. *Distributed computing systems (ICDCS), 2013 IEEE 33rd international conference on*, 236–245. 10.1109/ICDCS.2013.49

Xin-yu, Y., & Wei-jia, L. (2011). Research and application of the management and control platform oriented the cloud manufacturing services. In *2011 International Conference on System science, Engineering design and Manufacturing informatization* (Vol. 1, pp. 286-289). IEEE. 10.1109/ICSSEM.2011.6081208

Xu, Z., Liu, X., Zhang, G., He, W., Dai, G., & Shu, W. (2008, June). A certificateless signature scheme for mobile wireless cyber-physical systems. In *2008 The 28th International Conference on Distributed Computing Systems Workshops* (pp. 489-494). IEEE. 10.1109/ICDCS. Workshops.2008.84

Xu, X. (2012). From cloud computing to cloud manufacturing. *Robotics and Computer-integrated Manufacturing*, *28*(1), 75–86. doi:10.1016/j.rcim.2011.07.002

Yang, Z., Zhou, Z., & Liu, Y. (2013). From RSSI to CSI: Indoor localization via channel response. *ACM Computing Surveys*, *46*(2), 25. doi:10.1145/2543581.2543592

Yan, R. (2007). *Base wavelet selection criteria for non-stationary vibration analysis in bearing health diagnosis*. University of Massachusetts Amherst.

Yan, R., Gao, R. X., & Chen, X. (2014). Wavelets for fault diagnosis of rotary machines: A review with applications. *Signal Processing*, *96*, 1–15. doi:10.1016/j.sigpro.2013.04.015

Ye, X., Park, T. Y., Hong, S. H., Ding, Y., & Xu, A. (2018). Implementation of a Production-Control System Using Integrated Automation ML and OPC UA. In *2018 Workshop on Metrology for Industry 4.0 and IoT* (pp. 1-6). IEEE. 10.1109/METROI4.2018.8428310

Yilmaz, R. M., Kucuk, S., & Goktas, Y. (2017). Are augmented reality picture books magic or real for preschool children aged five to six? *British Journal of Educational Technology, 48*(3), 824–841. doi:10.1111/bjet.12452

Yin, Y., Stecke, K. E., & Li, D. (2018). The evolution of production systems from Industry 2.0 through Industry 4.0. *International Journal of Production Research, 56*(1-2), 848–861. doi:10.1080/00207543.2017.1403664

Yongfu, L., Dihua, S., Weining, L., & Xuebo, Z. (2012, July). A service-oriented architecture for the transportation cyber-physical systems. In *Proceedings of the 31st Chinese Control Conference* (pp. 7674-7678). IEEE.

Yoon, S. G., Kang, S. G., Jeong, S., & Nam, C. (2017). Priority inversion prevention scheme for PLC vehicle-to-grid communications under the hidden station problem. *IEEE Transactions on Smart Grid, 9*(6), 5887–5896.

Zaeri, R., Ghanbarzadeh, A., Attaran, B., & Moradi, S. (2011). Artificial neural network based fault diagnostics of rolling element bearings using continuous wavelet transform. In *2nd International Conference on Control, Instrumentation and Automation* (pp. 753-758). IEEE. 10.1109/ICCIAutom.2011.6356754

Zafari, F., Gkelias, A., & Leung, K. K. (2019). A Survey of Indoor Localization Systems and Technologies. *IEEE Communications Surveys and Tutorials, 21*(3), 2568–2599. doi:10.1109/COMST.2019.2911558

Zehn, M. (2021). *Benchmark-January-2021-Future-of-Simulation-Setting-a-Realistic-Agenda.* https://www.nafems.org/

Zeid, A., Sundaram, S., Moghaddam, M., Kamarthi, S., & Marion, T. (2019). Interoperability in smart manufacturing: Research challenges. *Machines, 7*(21), 1–17.

Zgodavova, K., Bober, P., Majstorovic, V., Monkova, K., Santos, G., & Juhaszova, D. (2020). Innovative Methods for Small Mixed Batches Production System Improvement: The Case of a Bakery Machine Manufacturer. *Sustainability, 12*(6266), 12–31. doi:10.3390u12156266

Zhang, J. F., & Huang, Z. C. (2005). Kernel Fisher discriminant analysis for bearing fault diagnosis. In *International Conference on Machine Learning and Cybernetics* (Vol. 5, pp. 3216-3220). IEEE.

Zhang, L., Bao, P., & Wu, X. (2005). Multiscale linear minimum mean square-error estimation based image denoising with optimal wavelet selection. *IEEE Transactions on Circuits and Systems for Video Technology, 15*(4), 469–481. doi:10.1109/TCSVT.2005.844456

Zhang, L., Luo, Y., Tao, F., Li, B. H., Ren, L., Zhang, X., Guo, H., Cheng, Y., Hu, A., & Liu, Y. (2014). Cloud manufacturing: A new manufacturing paradigm. *Enterprise Information Systems, 8*(2), 167–187. doi:10.1080/17517575.2012.683812

Zhang, Y., Qiu, M., Tsai, C. W., Hassan, M. M., & Alamri, A. (2015). Health-CPS: Healthcare cyber-physical system assisted by cloud and big data. *IEEE Systems Journal*, *11*(1), 88–95.

Zhao, T., & Ding, Z. (2018). Distributed finite-time optimal resource management for microgrids based on multi-agent framework. *IEEE Transactions on Industrial Electronics*, *65*(8), 6571–6580.

Zheng, J. S., Ma, J. Y., & Wang, L. (2018). Consensus of hybrid multi-agent systems. *IEEE Transactions on Neural Networks and Learning Systems*, *29*(4), 1359–1365.

Zheng, P., Wang, H., Sang, Z., Zhong, R. Y., Liu, Y., Liu, C., Mubarok, K., Yu, S., & Xu, X. (2018). Smart manufacturing systems for Industry 4.0: Conceptual framework, scenarios, and future perspectives. *Frontiers of Mechanical Engineering*, *13*(2), 137–150. doi:10.100711465-018-0499-5

Zheng, Z., Petrone, R., Péra, M. C., Hissel, D., Becherif, M., Pianese, C., & Sorrentino, M. (2013). A review on non-model based diagnosis methodologies for proton exchange membrane fuel cell stacks and systems. *International Journal of Hydrogen Energy*, *38*(21), 8914–8926. doi:10.1016/j.ijhydene.2013.04.007

Zhen, L., Zhengjia, H., Yanyang, Z., & Yanxue, W. (2008). Customized wavelet denoising using intra-and inter-scale dependency for bearing fault detection. *Journal of Sound and Vibration*, *313*(1-2), 342–359. doi:10.1016/j.jsv.2007.11.039

Zhu, J., Nostrand, T., Spiegel, C., & Morton, B. (2014). Survey of condition indicators for condition monitoring systems. In *Annu. Conf. Progn. Heal. Manag. Soc* (*Vol. 5*, pp. 1-13). Academic Press.

Zhu, W., Wang, Z., & Zhang, Z. (2020). Renovation of automation system based on industrial internet of things: A case study of a sewage treatment plant. *Sensors (Basel)*, *20*(8), 2175. doi:10.339020082175 PMID:32290552

Ziegler, S., Skarmeta, A., Bernal, J., Kim, E. E., & Bianchi, S. (2017, June). ANASTACIA: Advanced networked agents for security and trust assessment in CPS IoT architectures. In 2017 Global Internet of Things Summit (GIoTS) (pp. 1-6). IEEE.

About the Contributors

Pierluigi Rea is Associate Professor at the Dept. of Mechanical, Chemical and Materials Engineering (DIMCM) at the University of Cagliari, Cagliari, Italy. He got the Master Degree in Mechanical Engineering in 2002 at the University of Cassino by discussing a thesis on the Experimental Analysis of a PWM Modulated Digital Valve. In 2007 he got the Ph.D. in Civil and Mechanical Engineering by discussing a thesis on the Mechatronic Design of a Robotic Hand with Pneumatic Actuation. From 2007 to 2010 he was Assistant Researcher at the University of Cassino. His main research interests concern topics on the Fluid Automation and Mechatronics, Mechanical Design and Robotics. He is author and/or co-author of more than 85 scientific papers, which appeared on Proceedings of National and International Conferences, International Journals and Books.

Erika Ottaviano is Assistant Professor at the Dept. of Civil and Mechanical Engineering at the University of Cassino and Southern Lazio, Cassino, Italy. She got the Habilitation of Associate professor since 2014. Since 2004, she is member of the IFToMM Technical Committee for Computational Kinematics (TCCK). She served as secretary of this Committee from 2009 to 2017. Since 2014, she served as project evaluator for Int. Science Foundation programs at EU and Non EU level. Since 2011, she served as a member of the Editorial Board of the Int. Journal of Advanced Robotic Systems, INTECH Open Access Publisher. Since 2012, she has been appointed Editor for the Int. Journal of Imaging and Robotics (ISSN 2231-525X). Since 2013, she become member of the Editorial Board of the Scientific World Journal, Hindawi Pub. Corporation, Mechanical Engineering. Since 2015, she has been appointed Associate Editor for Mechatronics of the Journal of Applied Sciences, Acta Polytechnica Hungarica, from 2016, she is Editor for American Journal of Engineering and Applied Sciences, Science Publications. Research interests cover aspects of Mechanics, Robotics and Mechanical Design of Manipulators and Mobile Robots. Specific subjects of interest are workspace analysis and design of parallel manipulators, with specific emphasis to cable-based parallel manipulators. Since 2005, she started working on assisting devices as based on parallel manipulators with cables, cable-based system and mobile walking and hybrid systems designed for indoor and outdoor inspection. She is author and/or co-author of more than 170 papers published in Proceedings of Int. Conferences or in Journals. In 2018, she served as Editor of the book titled "Mechatronics for Cultural Heritage and Civil Engineering (86726336)", Intelligent Systems, Control and Automation: Science and Engineering, http://www.springer.com/series/6259. In 2019 she served as Guest Editor of the Special Issue "Advances in Inspection Robotic Systems", in the Journal Robotics (ISSN 2218-6581).

José Machado concluded Habilitation degree in February 2019 at University of Minho, Portugal. He received his PhD degree in Mechanical Engineering – Automation, from University of Minho, Portugal and, in simultaneous, from Ecole Normale Superieure de Cachan, France, in 2006. He is Deputy Director of MEtRICs Research Center and Assistant Professor at Mechanical Engineering department of University of Minho. He has authored, or co-authored, more than 220 refereed journal and conference proceedings papers. He coordinates and has coordinated - and participated as collaborator - in several Research and Technology Transfer Projects on Mechatronics and Automation domains. His main interests are related with Industry 4.0, more specifically, on the design and development of Cyber-Physical Systems; design and analysis of dependable controllers for obtaining dependable mechatronic systems; and mechatronic systems design with special focus on medical or biomedical applications, wellbeing and/or rehabilitation. He is member of IEEE and member of IFAC.

Katarzyna Antosz, Ph.D., Ds.C., Eng., Associate Professor, since 2002 has been working at Rzeszow University of Technology, Faculty of Mechanical Engineering and Aeronautics, Department of Manufacturing and Production Engineering and is a member of the Lean Learning Academy Polska. She is a specialist in the field of improving and increasing the efficiency of production in organizations, using the methods and tools of Lean Manufacturing and Six Sigma, and the reliability and operation of machines and maintenance services in enterprises. Author of many publications in this fields.

* * *

Daniele Catelani is Senior Project Manager at MSC Software. He is also technical manager for University Program in Italy. His main tasks currently consist in consulting, support, development, training and management of technical projects in Aerospace and Machinery industries. His activity is carried out in the field of multibody and multidiscipline simulation, involving integration between multibody system, finite element analysis, control systems, computational fluid dynamics. He has participated in the development of features and toolkits of the MSC.Adams package and project manager and coordinator for Simulation Data Management and Vertical products integration for Aerospace companies. He is technical coordinator of all MSC Conferences and Events in Italy. He is teacher for Adams, FEM, and many other courses in all Italian universities and he has been tutor for hundreds of students from 1994, and at the same time technical consultant for main OEM (automotive, aerospace, general machinery industries). He has been author and co-author of article and scientific papers.

Luis Alberto Estrada Jimenez is a researcher at CTS UNINOVA, Facultade de Ciencias e Tecnologia, Universidade Nova de Lisboa, Portugal. He holds a master's degree in Mechatronic Engineering at the University of Oviedo, Spain, and a BSc degree in Electronics and Control engineering from Escuela Politecnica Nacional, Quito, Ecuador. Current interests are Intelligent Manufacturing, Cyber-Physical Production Systems, Mechatronics, Control Systems, and Artificial Intelligence.

Dongming Fan received the B.S. degree in Detection guidance and control technology of Beihang University, Beijing, China. He is currently working toward a Dr. Degree in reliability and systems engineering at the School of Reliability and Systems Engineering of Beihang University, Beijing, China. His research interests include prognostics and health management, reliability modeling and evaluation.

Qiang Feng received the Ph.D. degree in reliability engineering and systems engineering from Beihang University, Beijing, China; and the B.S. degree in mechanical engineering from Beijing University, Beijing, China. He is currently an associate professor and a member of the Faculty of Systems Engineering at the School of Reliability and Systems Engineering at Beihang University in Beijing, China. He is a supervisor of MS students and teaches two courses for undergraduate and master students. His current research interests include reliability modeling of complex systems, maintenance planning, and integrated design of product reliability and performance. Dr. Feng has led over 10 projects supported by companies and industries. In the past few years, he has also participated in more than 10 projects supported by government and national commissions. He has published more than 70 papers and 3 book chapters.

Luís Pinto Ferreira is PhD in Engineering by University of Vigo (Spain), MSc in Industrial Engineering - Logistics and Distribution by School of Engineering, University of Minho (Portugal) and Bachelor Degree in Industrial Electronic Engineering by School of Engineering, University of Minho (Portugal). He taught in

Higher Education since 2000. He is currently Sub-Director of Master's Degree in Engineering and Industrial Management at School of Engineering, Polytechnic of Porto (Portugal) and he has supervised more than 40 MSc students. He has more than 60 papers and 1 international book published. ORCID: https://orcid.org/0000-0003-4225-6525.

Kumar H. S. obtained PhD in Mechanical Engineering, Visvesvarya Technological University, Belagavi, India and his B.E. in Mechanical Engg., from S.I.T., Tumkur in 2001 and M.Tech. in Production Engineering Systems Technology from University B.D.T. college of Engineering, Davanagere. Currently working as Associate Professor in the Dept. of Mechanical Engg. at NMAMIT, Nitte, Karnataka. He has 5 years industrial and 10 years of teaching experience. He has 12 papers in various National and International Journals and Conferences. His research interests are condition monitoring and wavelet analysis. He is a reviewer for Proceedings of the Institution of Mechanical Engineers, Part C: Journal of Mechanical Engineering Science SAGE publications. Journal of Quality in Maintenance Engineering, Emerald publication, International Review of Electrical Engineering (IREE), Measurement, Journal of the Brazilian Society of Mechanical Sciences and Engineering.

Vinoth Kumar K. received the B.E degree in Electrical & Electronics Engineering from Anna University, India in 2006. He has completed his Master of Technology from Vellore Institute of Technology and Ph.D Degree in Electrical & Electronics Engineering from Karunya Institute of Technology and Sciences, India in 2008 and 2017 respectively. Currently, He is working as an Associate professor in Electrical and Electronics Engineering Department at New Horizon College of Engineering, Bengaluru, India. His main research areas are intelligent control, Instrumentation, automation & process control, condition monitoring, fault analysis, Power Electronics and AC/DC Machines. He published research papers in both international and national journals as well as in conferences. He is authored the Book titled "Basic Electrical and Electronics Engineering" published by John Wiley & Sons India and Neural Networks, Soft Computing textbooks, Special Electrical Machines, Power Electronics.

Suresh Kumar M. has 19 years of experience in the field of Teaching and Research and is currently working as an Associate Professor, Information Technology Department, Sri Sai Ram Engineering College, Chennai. He received his Ph.D degree under Information and Communication Engineering, Anna University in Web Service composition. Also his research area includes Web Service, Cloud Computing, IoT, Machine Learning, Semantic Web and Cyber Security. Around thirty numbers of peer reviewed International Journal and Conference publications are there in his credit.

Sriram N. S. is working as Professor & Head in the Department of Mechanical Engineering, Vidya Vikas Institute of Engineering and Technology, Mysore. He obtained his Ph.D. in Mechanical Engg., from NITK, Surathkal in 2006. He has 15 years of Industrial experience and more than ten years of teaching and research experience. He has 20 papers in various National and International Journals and Conferences. He has won PMT-CMTI award certificate for contributing in design and development of special lathe attachment COMPANION, during IMTEX, 1992, Bangalore International Trade Centre, Bangalore.

Srinivasa Pai P. is currently working as Professor in the Dept. of Mechanical Engg. at NMAMIT, Nitte, Karnataka. He obtained his Ph.D in Mechanical Engg., from Mysore University in 2004. He has over 24 years of teaching and research experience. He has 190 papers in various National and International Journals and Conferences. He completed a VTU, Belgavi sponsored research project titled "Defect Characterization in Antifriction Bearing using Vibration Signal Analysis for Condition Monitoring" with a funding of Rs. 6.5 lakhs in 2011. In June 2013, he received a grant of Rs. 17.4 lakhs from AICTE, New Delhi, under RPS for a research project entitled "Optimization of surface roughness during machining of Ti-based alloys using Vibration". Currently he is working on a ARDB, DRDO funded project on "surface integrity studies in Al-Li alloys" with a funding of Rs. 12. 93 lakhs. He has conducted several conferences, training programs, STTPs, workshops and FDPs with funding from AICTE, ISTE, TEQIP and DRDO. He has guided 7 research scholars for their PhD and three are currently working under him.

Terrin Babu Pulikottil is a researcher at CTS UNINOVA, Faculdade de Ciências e Tecnologia, Universidade Nova de Lisboa, Portugal currently working on Computer Integrated Manufacturing. After completing his Post Graduation in Mechanical Engineering with specialization in Industrial Production from Politecnico di Milano, Italy, he worked in National Research Council of Italy in the field of Industrial Robotics and Human Robot Collaboration for three years. He has also worked in CUMI, a materials manufacturing company as Deputy Manager after his Under Graduation in Manufacturing Engineering from CEG, Anna University, India.

Yi Ren received a Ph.D. degree in reliability engineering and systems engineering from Beihang University. He is currently an associate professor, a reliability specialist, and a member on the faculty of system engineering at the Department of System Engineering of Engineering Technology at Beihang University in Beijing, China. He has over 10 years of research and teaching experience in reliability engineering and system engineering. He is the Team Leader of the KW-GARMS© reliability engineering software platform and a holder of six Chinese ministry-level professional awards and one Chinese nation-level professional award. His recent research interests include the reliability of electronics, model-based reliability system engineering (MBRSE), and computer-aided reliability maintainability and supportability design, and product life-cycle management.

José Carlos Sá in 2015 he is awarded the Title of Specialist in Quality Management, by the Polytechnic Institute of Viana do Castelo. He holds a Master's Degree in Industrial Engineering and is graduated in Production Engineering, both from Minho University. José Carlos has been a professor in higher education since 2005. He is currently a Adjunct Professor at Engineering School of Porto (ISEP), at the Polytechnic of Porto, and also in Invited Adjunct Professor at Polytechnic Institute of Viana do Castelo. He was Director of Production and Quality at several companies. He was also a consultant in several companies, in safety, quality management, lean and industrial engineering. In 2015, José Carlos became a "Senior Member" of the Portuguese Engineer Association. He has supervised more than 30 MSc. students at ISEP-IPP and has more than 40 papers (ISI+SCOPUS) on quality management, safety and lean six sigma published. Scopus Author: ID: 56029853700. ORCID: http://orcid.org/0000-0002-2228-5348.

Gilberto Santos is Professor at the Polytechnic Institute Cávado Ave (IPCA), Barcelos, Portugal, where he founded a master's course on "Integrated Management Systems QES (Quality, Environment and Safety) and was the director of it for 7th editions. He holds an Aggregation (DSc) title in Industrial Engineering from de New University of Lisbon and a PhD degree in Mechanical Engineering from the Minho University, Portugal. He participates as a Speaker in several national and international conferences and is the author of several publications, reviewer for International Journals. ORCID: https://orcid.org/0000-0001-9268-3272.

Francisco J. G. Silva is PhD, MSc, and BSc in Mechanical Engineering by FEUP and ISEP (Portugal). He is Post-Graduated in Materials and Manufacturing. He is currently Head of the Master's Degree in Mechanical Engineering at ISEP, Polytechnic of Porto. He also was Head of the Bachelor's Degree in Mechanical Engineering at ESEIG, Polytechnic of Porto (2003 to 2006). He has supervised some PhD students FEUP (Portugal), as well as more than 140 MSc. students at ISEP and co-supervised more than 40 MSc students at ISEP and FEUP. He has more than 175 papers (ISI+SCOPUS) and 3 international books published. ORCID: https://orcid.org/0000-0001-8570-4362.

Gonçalo Sousa is graduated in Industrial Management and Engineering by School of Engineering, Polytechnic of Porto. Currently is a Project Manager at Efacec Electric Mobility.

Cristina Sylla received the master's degrees in technology and digital art, and literature studies, and the Ph.D. degree in educational technology. She is a member of the Research Centre on Child Studies, CIEC, University of Minho and ITI/LAR-SyS, she currently leads the Mobeybou (http://mobeybou.com) and the Erasmus+ Gamelet projects (https://www.gamelet.eu). Her work focuses on the development of innovative materials that combine the digital and the physical component, promoting exploratory playful learning. Her work is regularly published in international journals and conferences. She is a member of the Editorial Board of the International Journal for Child-Computer Interaction (https://www.sciencedirect.com/journal/international-journal-of-child-computer-interaction/about/editorial-board), a fellow of the World Technology Network and a Fellow of the EAI Community, European Alliance for Innovation. Her work has been distinguished with several awards, such as the Golden Award for Best Demo at the International Conference on Advances in Computer Entertainment Technology in 2012 and 2015, and the World Technology Award, Category Entertainment in 2013. She has chaired several international conferences and is a member of the Steering Committee of the EAI International Conference on Technology, Innovation, Entrepreneurship and Education (TIE) http://educateinnovate.org

Hamood Ur Rehman, a mechanical engineer by profession, is a researcher at University of Nottingham working on cloud manufacturing and its associated applications with regards to self-configured production systems. He has worked as a Lecturer at Department of Industrial and Manufacturing Engineering in NED University of Engineering and Technology, Karachi, Pakistan teaching tool design, advanced manufacturing processes and finite element analysis among others. He has worked at multiple industries in positions relating to design, supply chain and automation. He currently works at TQC Ltd. as Mechanical Design Engineer on automation and IoT device applications. He is also a Marie Sklodowska Curie Early-Stage Researcher.

Index

A

actuation 204, 206

application 1, 3-5, 7-10, 15, 19, 21, 37, 44-45, 48, 51-54, 67, 75-76, 81, 88-89, 94-95, 97-99, 106, 110, 112, 119, 136, 139-141, 152, 154, 157-160, 162, 164-166, 172, 174, 179, 181, 185, 195, 199, 201, 204-205, 226-227, 229, 231, 237, 242-243, 250, 260-262, 266-267

Artificial Intelligence 5, 11, 20, 29, 37-38, 46-47, 99-100, 107, 110, 152, 167, 169, 197, 211, 265

authentication system 63, 67, 70, 75-76, 78, 88-89

automation 1, 5, 8, 11-12, 15-16, 39, 61, 96, 98, 141-142, 150, 156, 160, 165, 168-172, 198-200, 218, 231, 243, 246-248, 253

B

Business Intelligence 244, 249, 263-266

C

children 40-45, 54-62

cloud computing 1, 20, 28, 152, 157, 159-160, 171-172, 209

cognitive development 40-43, 45, 56, 60-61

communication 1-2, 5, 8, 13-14, 30, 35-36, 43, 46, 56, 60, 90-92, 94-98, 101-102, 104-106, 108, 137, 141, 146-149, 153, 155, 159-160, 162, 166-167, 195, 199-200, 210, 215, 241, 243-244, 246-247, 256, 261, 265

Cosimulation Digital Twin 18

cryptography 3, 5-7, 13-15

Cyber attacks 1

-Cyber Physical Systems 1

Cyber-Physical Production Systems 144-145, 148, 152, 168, 171

cyber-physical systems 12-17, 19-20, 28, 37-39, 43, 58, 170, 196-198, 216-218, 247

D

dashboard 159, 168, 244, 250, 256-257

Deep Packet Inspection 219-220, 223, 226, 237, 239-243

Deterministic Finite Automata 219-220, 224-225, 234-235, 239-240

digital transformation 2, 18, 20, 264

Digital Twins 20, 29, 37, 110, 180, 195

E

Edge Computing 99, 110, 160-161, 168

edge detection 71, 90, 189-192

e-Maintenance 196-198, 200-201, 204, 209, 213-216

emerging technologies 145, 148, 152, 166-169

F

feature extraction 11, 115-116, 118, 123, 127, 138, 142

feedback loop 1-2, 5-6

G

game 40-41, 44-45, 49-51, 53-58, 216

H

health index 112, 115, 120, 131, 139

I

Image Matching 189-190

image processing 46-47, 112, 114-116, 139, 173-174, 178-179, 189, 191, 195

Industrial Artificial Intelligence 99, 107, 110

Industry 4.0 1-3, 6, 10, 15, 20, 28, 34, 144-146, 148, 150-151, 153, 160, 162, 167, 169-172, 197-198, 200, 215-218, 247-249, 263, 265-268

informatization 172

integration 3, 12, 18-20, 23, 26, 36, 50, 57, 94, 97, 99, 107, 112, 115, 135, 144-148, 150-151, 153-155, 157-159, 162-168, 170, 198-199, 201, 209, 215, 265, 267-268

Intelligent Optimization Grouping Algorithms 221, 235-239

Internet of Things 1, 3, 13-14, 16-17, 20, 28, 37, 94, 107, 109-110, 145, 148, 151, 157-158, 166, 180, 195-197, 199, 215, 218, 247

interoperability 1, 97, 99, 144-155, 157, 159, 162-168, 170-172, 200

IoT-based smart grid 92, 94-95, 98, 100, 102-104, 106

K

KPI 245, 265, 267

L

Lean 245, 248-249, 251, 262-269

M

modeling 30-31, 37-38, 92, 106, 128, 150, 169

mother wavelet 112, 114, 122, 140

Multi physics 18

multi-agent system 92, 100, 104, 106, 110

Multi-Agent Systems 107, 109-110, 152-153, 169

Multibody 18-19, 23, 25-26, 31, 36

N

Network Intrusion Detection System 219-221

network layer 3, 159

O

Obeya 244-246, 249, 251, 254, 256, 258-260, 262, 265-266

Object Detection 173, 188-189

P

Pattern Matching 221, 223-224, 240, 242

physical layer 1-2, 8

Power BI 244, 251, 253-257, 260-261, 266

R

randomness and security 63

regular expression 219-229, 231, 235-237, 239-243

reliability 5-6, 27, 30, 71, 92, 94, 98-99, 101, 104, 106, 108-109, 111, 141, 185-186, 196-197, 200, 202, 216, 248, 250

Reliability Engineering 111, 216

restoration 92, 94, 98-100, 102-109

S

sensing 2, 11-12, 60, 94-95, 102, 165, 199

sensor 4, 13, 15-16, 29, 35-36, 44, 57, 60, 94-95, 98, 102, 106, 109, 140, 161, 175, 179-181, 183, 189, 192, 195, 204-205, 209

sensors 1-3, 8-10, 13, 19, 23, 29, 34-37, 44, 57, 59, 95, 98, 107, 110, 137, 148-149, 161, 174-175, 179-180, 195, 197-198,

203-206, 209-211, 217-218
Service-Oriented Architectures 154, 168
smart city 92, 106-107, 109
smart grid 3, 6, 8, 13-14, 92-98, 100-104,
   106-111
smart manufacturing 144-148, 152-154,
   166-167, 171-172, 218

T

tangible interfaces 40, 42-43, 45, 56, 59-60
Traffic Monitoring 173-175, 179-180, 187,
   193, 195

U

usability 63, 66-67, 70-73, 75-77, 79, 85,
   87-89

W

wavelet denoising 112, 124, 139, 143
wavelet transform 112-113, 115, 126, 137-
   139, 141-142

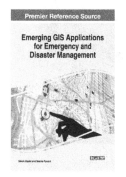
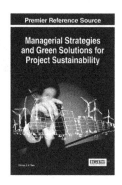

IGI Global Author Services

Providing a high-quality, affordable, and expeditious service, IGI Global's Author Services enable authors to streamline their publishing process, increase chance of acceptance, and adhere to IGI Global's publication standards.

Benefits of Author Services:

- **Professional Service:** All our editors, designers, and translators are experts in their field with years of experience and professional certifications.
- **Quality Guarantee & Certificate:** Each order is returned with a quality guarantee and certificate of professional completion.
- **Timeliness:** All editorial orders have a guaranteed return timeframe of 3-5 business days and translation orders are guaranteed in 7-10 business days.
- **Affordable Pricing:** IGI Global Author Services are competitively priced compared to other industry service providers.
- **APC Reimbursement:** IGI Global authors publishing Open Access (OA) will be able to deduct the cost of editing and other IGI Global author services from their OA APC publishing fee.

Author Services Offered:

 English Language Copy Editing
Professional, native English language copy editors improve your manuscript's grammar, spelling, punctuation, terminology, semantics, consistency, flow, formatting, and more.

 Scientific & Scholarly Editing
A Ph.D. level review for qualities such as originality and significance, interest to researchers, level of methodology and analysis, coverage of literature, organization, quality of writing, and strengths and weaknesses.

 Figure, Table, Chart & Equation Conversions
Work with IGI Global's graphic designers before submission to enhance and design all figures and charts to IGI Global's specific standards for clarity.

 Translation
Providing 70 language options, including Simplified and Traditional Chinese, Spanish, Arabic, German, French, and more.

Hear What the Experts Are Saying About IGI Global's Author Services

 "Publishing with IGI Global has been an amazing experience for me for sharing my research. The strong academic production support ensures quality and timely completion." – **Prof. Margaret Niess, Oregon State University, USA**

"The service was very fast, very thorough, and very helpful in ensuring our chapter meets the criteria and requirements of the book's editors. I was quite impressed and happy with your service." – **Prof. Tom Brinthaupt, Middle Tennessee State University, USA**

Learn More or Get Started Here: For Questions, Contact IGI Global's Customer Service Team at cust@igi-global.com or 717-533-8845

www.igi-global.com

Printed in the United States
by Baker & Taylor Publisher Services